Oeconomies in the Age of Newton

Oeconomies in the Age of Newton

Annual Supplement to Volume 35
History of Political Economy

Edited by Margaret Schabas and Neil De Marchi

Duke University Press
Durham and London 2003

Printed in the United States of America
on acid-free paper. ISBN 0-8223-6586-3
This is the 2003 supplement to
History of Political Economy, ISSN 0018-2702.

Contents

Acknowledgments

Many besides the authors here have helped to bring this book to completion. Our thanks to Paul Dudenhefer for taking care of the arrangements for the conference at which these essays were first presented, in April 2001, and for shepherding the project along since then. Thanks also to a number of scholars who refereed one or more of the submissions: Timothy Alborn, Joel Kaye, Simon Schaffer, Pamela Smith, and Paul Wood. Without their comments and criticisms, and the ongoing exchanges among the contributors themselves on each other's essays, the book might not have developed as a cross-disciplinary collaboration to the extent that it has. We, the editors, are extremely grateful for the time and effort each participant, and the outside readers, so willingly gave. Our thanks, too, to the office of the Vice-Provost for Interdisciplinary Studies, Duke University, for financial support toward the conference expenses.

—M. S. and N. D.

Introduction to *Oeconomies in the Age of Newton*

Margaret Schabas and Neil De Marchi

While the history of early modern science is well-charted terrain, far less has been recorded on economic thinking of the same period and considerably less that addresses the intersection of these two fields. Our volume is a modest stab at mapping this new land, and we can only hope that it will inspire more efforts to explore this rich set of topics. Our essays cover the ideas of a number of Europeans—from France, Italy, Sweden, Prussia, Ireland, Scotland, and England—as well as specimens from the far reaches of the world. Oeconomies will prove to encompass a cabinet of curiosities: peaches and peacocks, alchemical retorts and seltzer water, unorthodox medical cures such as the tarantella (an Italian dance) or quassia (a Surinamese plant). In short, oeconomics was as colorful a subject as one could imagine, far removed from kinked oligopoly curves or fixed-point theorems. But then, economic reflections harked back to the Greek concept of household management, and households have gardens, require medicines, and attend to the sympathies of their members. How *oe*conomics came to be more narrowly construed and defined as *e*conomics is a story that falls outside our purview, but we hope that by providing a more vivid and detailed account of the oeconomic concepts and constructs of the seventeenth and eighteenth centuries, we can at least serve those who might attempt to make sense of the transition.

The title of this volume reflects a decision to concentrate on the period that scholars of Newton would address, the seventeenth and eighteenth centuries. While we are not inclined to reinforce the great-men-of-science perspective, there is no denying Newton's preeminence. Isaac

Newton (1642–1727) first came to prominence at the age of twenty-five, with his appointment as the Lucasian professor of mathematics at Cambridge University (1669). His breakthroughs on the calculus, the inverse-square law of gravitational attraction, and the heterogeneity of white light came even earlier, in his anni mirabiles of 1664–66 (see Westfall 1980, chap. 5). These methods and ideas crystallized into his two major tomes, *Principia Mathematica* (1687) and the *Opticks* (1704). External recognition came with his election as a member of Parliament (1689), his knighthood (1701), and his appointment first as warden (1696) and then as master of the Mint (1699), and as president of the Royal Society (1703). But perhaps the greatest honor was being the first nonroyal to be buried in Westminster Abbey, with much of the pomp and circumstance befitting a king. Inspired by the occasion, Voltaire carried the torch of Newtonianism over to France. His *Éléments de la philosophie de Newton* (1738) and the translation into French of Newton's *Principia* (1747) by his partner Emilie du Chatelet, coupled with a number of empirical discoveries, did much to insure that Newtonian philosophy became the reigning doctrine by the mid-1750s, putting the Cartesian and Leibnizian alternatives a distant second.

Newton's *Principia* has traditionally marked the close of the so-called Scientific Revolution, a rubric that is remarkably enduring and robust among historians. Commencing with the work of Herbert Butterfield ([1949] 1975) and A. Rupert Hall ([1954] 1962), the Scientific Revolution has been revived recently, legitimized by several book titles (see Cohen 1994a, 1994b, Jardine 1999, Lindberg and Westman 1990, Porter and Teich 1992, and Shapin 1996). Of course, there are some skeptics, those who emphasize the continuity with the past or the lack of coherence among the leading instigators. Some of the scholars who have championed this view are John Schuster (1990), Catherine Wilson (1995), and one of the most radical historians active today, Steven Shapin (1996), notwithstanding his use of the term in the book's title. And in our own volume, there are those who downplay the influence of the Scientific Revolution on economic thinking, and others who deem it of central importance.

Following the publication of Nicholas Copernicus's *On the Revolutions* (1543), natural philosophers embraced new theories, new methods, and a new metaphysics. The heliocentric system also mandated a new physics, one that is compatible with a moving earth, hence the formulation of the principle of inertia, which became codified as Newton's first law. The new physics called for new branches of mathematics, hence the formulation of analytical geometry by René Descartes, probability theory by Blaise Pascal, Pierre de Fermat, and Christian Huygens, and the differential calculus by Gottfried Leibniz and Newton. New experimental traditions also emerged in the seventeenth century. Most notable in this respect were Galileo, Pascal, Robert Boyle, and Newton, whose findings served to confirm many of the new laws of mechanics, optics, and astronomy. Physiology also was transformed, by Andreas Vesalius, William Harvey, and Hermann Boerhaave most notably. Even natural history shed its ties to Aristotle and Pliny, culminating with the new systems of Carl Linnaeus and Georges-Louis Leclerc de Buffon. Also significant were the formation of scientific academies and journals, official state support for astronomers and cartographers, and an expansion of scientific teaching in the universities beyond the traditional subjects of mathematics and medicine. But perhaps the most sweeping change of all was the advent of Cartesian dualism, which fostered the mechanical philosophy and the belief that nature was inherently mathematical. The Scientific Revolution, as has been proclaimed so often, swept aside once and for all the commonsense and directly accessible world of Aristotle for one that forevermore would be grasped indirectly, by convoluted acts of reasoning and experimentation.

The Scientific Revolution endures, despite its fuzzy temporal and spatial borders, and despite the fact that it was a prolonged transformation, stretching over more than a hundred years. Granting its efficacy, there are even stronger historical claims to be made; for example, that the political revolutions in Britain (1688), America (1776), and France (1789) are mere progeny of the Scientific Revolution. Less tenuously, the Scientific Revolution was itself partly a product of the economic and technological transformations that Europe experienced in the sixteenth and seventeenth centuries. The rise of a merchant class and breakdown of feudalism, the advent of the printing press and assimilation of perspective in the visual arts, the development of new techniques in metallurgy and the manufacture of glass, have all found their exponents as the key that opened the way for the new science. In that respect, the ideas that were forged in the natural and moral sciences fed directly on the same cultural sources, although arguably the emergence and development of modern capitalism and global networks of trade had a more profound influence on the actual content of economic writings. To see this, one could engage the following counterfactual. It would be unthinkable for classical and neoclassical economics to have the content that they have without the advent of capitalism, whereas one might entertain the evolution of modern natural science more or less as we know it in a world as economically abundant but without the capitalist system. Nevertheless, there is ample evidence to suggest that the natural science we have owed a great deal to the rise of the European capitalist economy and that, as a result, the factors governing the development of economic thinking of the time shared a great deal with the factors governing natural science.

Not only did early modern science and economics derive from the same cultural and material setting, but there are also many indications of symbiosis: the new scientific findings and methods of the early modern period seeped over into economic discourse, and vice versa. Indeed, there was a double seepage, as much or more between political economy and physiology, or botanical oeconomy, public *benessere*, or mineral riches, as between political economy and rational mechanics. The essays contained in this volume provide much material to buttress these more general historical claims. There are some already well-established links, such as Thomas Hobbes and Adam Smith, who explicitly applied the methods of the new science to political economy. There are dozens more, however, who either implicitly or explicitly wedded economic ideas with those in natural philosophy, conceptually or methodologically. Some names that figure prominently in one or more of the following essays are Pierre de Boisguilbert, Jacob Bernoulli, Pietro Verri, George Berkeley, Carl Linnaeus, François Quesnay, Marquis de Condorcet, and Thomas Reid.

Oeconomies is a bit of an eyepopper. However, it serves as a constant reminder that economic thinking of the early modern period was significantly different from what came after. Yet it is also far more than just an account of the management of households, as found in Xenophon's *Oikonomikos* or Aristotle's *Politics* (see Booth 1993). Just as there were Aristotelian vestiges in the writings of early modern natural philosophers, so, too, economic texts reflect the Aristotelian notion of the oeconomy right up until the end of the eighteenth century. As Ann Firth (1998, 21) has observed, "central to the notion of householding is stewardship, with its connotations of fostering and increasing available resources." Even as late as 1767, we find in James Steuart's *Principles of Political Oeconomy* the depiction of the sovereign as steward of one nation-sized household. But the term *oeconomy* was in common use from at least the sixteenth century and applied to a variety of contexts. By the seventeenth century it had been extended to all of God's domain, with God as the supreme manager of nature's larder. The term *oeconomy of nature* was most likely coined by Kennelm Digby in 1658 and circulated widely, most notably in the work of Linnaeus, Charles Lyell, and Charles Darwin, until Ernst Haeckel declared in 1866 that *oecologie* would serve in its place (see Worster 1977, 37, 192; and Schabas 1990). Other assorted applications were the animal oeconomy, the body oeconomy, and even the oeconomy of love (see Spary 1996).

There is thus a deeper tension to be found in economic theories of the period, with strong allegiances to Greek notions of wealth, social hierarchy, and virtue ethics. But in other respects, economic thinking had weaned itself of its Aristotelian roots far more than had natural science at the time, and it already more closely resembled its modern guise insofar as it was predominantly secular and more or less emancipated from some of the metaphysical debates that beset Cartesian physics. Economics seems to have bypassed the debates on occasionalism, for example, or the problems of causation in general that run right through eighteenth-century natural philosophy. It was worldly philosophy in the true sense of the term, grounded in debates about currency, trade, and economic growth. If metaphysics played a part, it was in the work of John Locke, who seemed so keenly enamored with the intrinsic value and efficacy of gold (see Appleby 1978).

As Michel Foucault (1966) observed, and as Keith Tribe (1978) has argued more forcefully, the concept of an economy is a relatively new one, commencing in the early 1800s with David Ricardo most saliently. At best one can point to a rich discourse on economic phenomena—money, trade, population, prices, and so forth—that was primarily wedded to agricultural production. While these claims have been challenged—Samuel Hollander (1976), for one, sees Adam Smith's economics as an integrated account of an economy—it would not be misleading to view most contributions to economic discourse of the early modern period as piecemeal rather than synthetic. Even wealth, as readers will observe in many of the essays here, was conceived of as a natural property, coextensive with animal, mineral, and plant. It is not surprising, then, that the treatment of many economic phenomena borrowed imagery and methods from natural philosophy, as the one available discourse to make sense of such properties. In short, the economy was not a detached and self-regulating entity, at least to the degree it became, and hence economic concepts were also developed hand in hand with those in natural philosophy. Whether one takes note of Boisguilbert's appreciation for Gassendian atomism, Verri's and Antonio Genovesi's assimilation of Galilean and Newtonian methods, or Smith's respect for Joseph Black's chemistry, there are unmistakable links between the two fields. We do not wish to urge the view, however, that there was but one subject at the time. Natural philosophy and its separate branches, optics, astronomy, physics, botany, and zoology, had distinct and separate identities that reach right back to Aristotle's treatises. Political economy can also trace its roots in Aristotle's texts, notably the *Politics* and the *Nicomachean Ethics*, although the term was only coined in the early 1600s, with Antoine de Montchrétien's *Traité de l'oeconomie politique* ([1615] 1939). It had acquired a relatively distinct identity and coherence by the middle of the seventeenth century, when several schools of thought had taken form: the Salamanca school, cameralism, mercantilism, Colbertism, and political arithmetic (see Hutchison 1988). By the early Enlightenment, Locke, William Petty, and David Hume launched a more liberal doctrine that reached a fuller identity with Adam Smith and the so-called classical school of political economy. And Quesnay and his associates gave birth to the school of physiocracy, complete with periodicals. There were thus multiple traditions or discourses at the time, much as debates in natural science were beset with different and conflicting traditions: Leibnizian, Cartesian, and Newtonian. It is helpful to keep this in mind as one proceeds through the volume. Some of the articles serve to forge coherent traditions, and others seem positively centrifugal.

What is most striking is that so many of the contributors to political economy in the period were also engaged in natural philosophy. Some of the names that stand out are William Petty, John Locke, Carl Linnaeus, Adam Smith, Thomas Reid, François Quesnay, Antoine Lavoisier, and A. R. J. Turgot, but under closer scrutiny one would be hard-pressed to find a writer on political economy who did not at some point issue a paper on metaphysics or epistemology, if not address a specific branch of scientific inquiry. Indeed, an obvious instantiation is Newton himself, who issued several papers on the currency crisis of his day. Another is Jean-Jacques Rousseau, who wrote on botany as well as economic inequality. Yet another is David Hume, whose essays on political economy were complemented by his monumental *Treatise of Human Nature*.

One of the factors that have helped bring this volume into being is the growing appreciation among historians of science of the political and economic context that shaped scientific theories. The first bit of ground was dug long ago, by the Marxist historians Boris Hessen ([1931] 1971) and John Desmond Bernal ([1954] 1965). But the Cold War muffled their efforts until, in the wake of its thaw, several books of a non-Marxist persuasion appeared, notably Steven Shapin and Simon Schaffer's *Leviathan and the Air-Pump* (1985), Mario Biagoli, *Galileo, Courtier* (1993), and Steven Shapin's *A Social History of Truth* (1994). The strict internalist accounts of science, once offered by E. J. Dijksterhuis ([1950] 1986) and Alexandre Koyré (1965), are no longer in vogue. Similarly, a focus on quantification in science, and its links to evolving concepts of objectivity, has helped to bring historians of science to look at political arithmetic and economics more generally (see Rusnock 2002). From a different angle, there are also some recent studies that show the extent to which early modern science played a role in the economic and technological development of Western Europe, a view that had once been considerably soft-pedaled.[1]

The literature that looks at early modern intersections of economics and natural science is modest in size but nonetheless very good (see Schabas 2002). Probably word for word, no one has yet surpassed Joseph Schumpeter's magisterial account (1954), which, for all its distortions of the historical record, draws extensive and incisive links between economics and natural science. Some preliminary efforts at concrete studies by historians of science are Vernard Foley (1976), Peter Buck (1982), and Charles Gillispie (1980). Over the past twenty or so years, the literature has grown substantially, thanks in part to the efforts of some of the contributors of this volume. Some monographs (listed alphabetically) that marry early modern science and economics are by Lorraine Daston (1988), Richard Drayton (2000), Joel Kaye (1998), Judy Klein (1997), Lisbet Koerner (1999), Jean-Pierre Poirier (1993), Deborah Redman (1997), Jessica Riskin (2002), Andrea Rusnock (2002), and Pamela Smith (1994). Two recent edited collections that bear directly on this subject are Groenewegen 2001 and Smith and Findlen 2002. Finally, articles by Ken Alder (1995), Paul Christensen (1989, 1994), I. Bernard Cohen (1994a), Judith Grabiner (1998), Myles Jackson (1994), Margaret Schabas (2001), Simon Schaffer (1989), and E. C. Spary (1996), among others, have also deepened our understanding of this theme. In

1. D. S. L. Cardwell (1971) had argued the surprising thesis that the causal chain went from new technologies to science rather than the other way round. The more intuitive claim, that science played an instrumental role in industrialization, has been argued recently by Margaret Jacob (1997) and Lisa Jardine (1999).

sum, efforts to chronicle and account for the natural-science component of economic thinking in early modern Europe have intensified considerably.

In fact, most of the essays in this volume are directed at extending our understanding of nature and its role in economic accounts in the seventeenth and eighteenth centuries. Historians of economics are familiar with nature mainly through the intersection of two traditions: (1) the developmental tradition in which surplus appears as a precondition for escaping "stationarity," prefigured in parts of Smith, and (2) the specifically physiocratic, with its insistence that agriculture is the sole source of surplus. It is now becoming steadily clearer that concern with nature in the age of Newton extended far beyond just tax reform and freedom for the grain trade. Natural resources viewed as a component of wealth required their mapping (Cooper, this volume), although German efforts in this direction independently emulated earlier pioneering attempts by Petty. Emerging perceptions that agriculture sustained all parts of society required that attention be given to husbandry and to productivity in particular (Christensen, this volume; Lowry, this volume). Meanwhile, a growing awareness of exotic plants, some with important medicinal or other capacities, raised new questions about proprietorship, the natural boundaries of stewardship, and the relation between trade and "domestic" production; it even posed afresh the issue of necessity versus luxury (Spary, this volume). Nature could take on mystical overtones, as with Linnaeus (Rausing, this volume). It could also become a subject for abstraction-making and modeling, even system-building. Among the abstractions were balance (Riskin, this volume) and value (Müller-Wille, this volume). The process by which (temporary) stable meanings for these concepts were reached is of course part of the history of political economy, but the essays in this volume remind us that there was a veritable clamor of opinion out of which the now familiar meanings emerged. These, moreover, have been colored by that passage.

It may be helpful to spell out an example. Linnaeus's understanding of botanical exchange clearly turned on the fact that the tradables comprised "unlikes"—seeds of different sorts: differing genera and newness status. Hence values or prices here were a matter of judgment by those well qualified to assess what was novel and important, namely, "consummate botanists." Such exchanges were limited to specific items and particular pairs of individuals, and they were bound to the conditions prevailing at single moments in time. The prices generated are comparable to those in markets for new goods, rather than those applying in old trades, to use Smith's broad classification. So a place exists for Linnaean exchanges in Smith's discussion of pricing, only Smith had almost nothing to say about particular market prices, concentrating rather on generic exchange and the process whereby market prices settle at their average or ordinary level. The reasons why Smith focused on generic exchange rather than on market prices are also the reasons why Linnaean exchange finds no place in modern economic ideas about value. But within the Smithian choice is a decision to move away from talk of value in specific uses and toward cost-based talk (almost) exclusively. Linnaean exchange thus reminds us of a road not taken in political economy and economics, and to encounter it is to understand anew both the judgments implicit in the choice and their further analytical implications.

But to return to the modern recovery of nature, historians of science also remind us that natural and moral concerns in the seventeenth and eighteenth centuries were separated by very permeable boundaries. The metaphorical traffic, as well as real or supposed influences, operated in both directions. A notion of stewardship perhaps motivated the new agronomy (Christensen, this volume), whereas the physiocratic notion of wealth is best captured by the metaphor of organic balance-seeking processes (Riskin, this volume). Smith's notion of sympathy called upon William Cullen's neurology (Forget, this volume; Schabas, this volume), but for Robert Whytt and Thomas Reid it was the sentient principle that activated bodily functions via the nerves (Maas, this volume), and it was after all the imagination that led to monetary "madness" (Caffentzis, this volume). Moreover, as Edith Dudley Sylla (this volume) shows, so-called mathematical probability did not originate in mathematics as such or with the frequentist notion of probability. Instead, the thinking was that embodied in business contracts, and in particular in problems such as the terms on which a place in a game (venture) with time still to run could be fairly purchased.

Not all the subjects treated by the contributors here can be positioned in terms of direct and contemporaneous borrowings, or metaphors and abstractions passing across the boundaries separating the natural and the moral. But the natural is never far away, if at times perceived in more obscure ways than even eighteenth-century investigators typically allowed. Thus, and at the very least, alchemical dreams of solving the problems of limited gold stocks for the coinage at one fell swoop supplied the model for thinking about alternatives, among them a paper currency, in late-seventeenth-century England (Wennerlind, this volume). In the case of "sympathy," while it is true that physiological and social investigations in the eighteenth century shared a lot of understandings concerning sympathetic interactions, these also had common roots in an older, more occult tradition according to which universal sympathies (attractions) and antipathies connected all entities (Forget, this volume). On the other hand, there is in this collection an instance of natural philosophy serving as workshop for the modern reshaping of ancient and scholastic notions. The notions were those of public felicity and *economia civile*, refracted through Galilean and Newtonian prisms to form an original political economy of "moral Newtonian" caste, in eighteenth-century Milan and Naples (Porta and Bruni, this volume). All in all, many rich and detailed accounts of economic phenomena and relations await the attentive reader.

References

Alder, Ken. 1995. A Revolution to Measure: The Political Economy of the Metric System in France. In *The Values of Precision*, edited by M. Norton Wise. Princeton, N.J.: Princeton University Press.

Appleby, Joyce Oldham. 1978. *Economic Thought and Ideology in Seventeenth-Century England*. Princeton, N.J.: Princeton University Press.

Bernal, John Desmond. [1954] 1965. *The Scientific and Industrial Revolutions*. Vol. 2 of *Science in History*. 3d ed. Cambridge: MIT Press.

Biagoli, Mario. 1993. *Galileo, Courtier*. Chicago: University of Chicago Press.

Booth, William James. 1993. *Households: On the Moral Architecture of the Economy*. Ithaca, N.Y.: Cornell University Press.

Buck, Peter H. 1982. People Who Counted: Political Arithmetic in the Eighteenth Century. *Isis* 73:28–45.

Butterfield, Herbert S. [1949] 1975. *The Origins of Modern Science*. Toronto: Clarke, Irwin, and Co.

Cardwell, D. S. L. 1971. *From Watt to Clausius: The Rise of Thermodynamics in the Early Industrial Age*. London: Heinemann.

Christensen, Paul. 1989. Hobbes and the Physiological Origins of Economic Science. *HOPE* 21.4:689–709.

———. 1994. Fire, Motion, and Productivity: The Proto-Energetics of Nature and Economy in François Quesnay. In *Natural Images in Economic Thought*, edited by Philip Mirowski. Chicago: University of Chicago Press.

Cohen, H. Floris. 1994. *The Scientific Revolution: A Historiographical Inquiry*. Chicago: University of Chicago Press.

Cohen, I. Bernard. 1994a. Newton and the Social Sciences, with Special Reference to Economics, or, The Case of the Missing Paradigm. In *Natural Images in*

Economic Thought, edited by Philip Mirowski. Chicago: University of Chicago Press.

———. 1994b. The Scientific Revolution and the Social Sciences. In *The Natural Sciences and the Social Sciences*, edited by I. Bernard Cohen. Dordrecht: Kluwer.

Copernicus. [1543] 1978. *On the Revolutions*. Edited by Jerzy Dobrzycki. Translated and with commentary by Edward Rosen. Baltimore: Johns Hopkins University Press.

Daston, Lorraine. 1988. *Classical Probability in the Enlightenment*. Princeton, N.J.: Princeton University Press.

Dijksterhuis, E. J. [1950] 1986. *The Mechanization of the World Picture*. Translated by C. Dikshoorn. Princeton, N.J.: Princeton University Press.

Drayton, Richard. 2000. *Nature's Government: Science, Imperial Britain, and the "Improvement" of the World*. New Haven, Conn.: Yale University Press.

Firth, Ann. 1998. From Oeconomy to "the Economy": Population and Self-Interest in Discourses on Government. *History of the Human Sciences* 11:19–35.

Foley, Vernard. 1976. *The Social Physics of Adam Smith*. Lafayette, Ind.: Purdue University Press.

Foucault, Michel. 1966. *Les mots et les choses: Une archéologie des sciences humaines*. Paris: Gallimard.

Gillispie, Charles Coulston. 1980. *Science and Polity in France at the End of the Old Regime*. Princeton, N.J.: Princeton University Press.

Grabiner, Judith V. 1998. Some Disputes of Consequence: Maclaurin among the Molasses Barrels. *Social Studies of Science* 28:139–68.

Groenewegen, Peter, ed. 2001. *Physicians and Political Economy: Six Studies of the Work of Doctor-Economists*. London: Routledge.

Hall, A. Rupert. [1954] 1962. *The Scientific Revolution: 1500–1800*, 2d ed. Boston: Beacon Press.

Hessen, Boris. [1931] 1971. The Social and Economic Roots of Newton's *Principia*. In *Science at the Cross Roads*, edited by N. I. Bukharin et al. London: Frank Cass.

Hollander, Samuel. 1976. *The Economics of Adam Smith*. Toronto: University of Toronto Press.

Hutchison, Terence. 1988. *Before Adam Smith*. Oxford: Basil Blackwell.

Jackson, Myles. 1994. Natural and Artificial Budgets: Accounting for Goethe's Economy of Nature. *Science in Context* 7:409–31.

Jacob, Margaret. 1997. *Scientific Culture and the Making of the Industrial West*. New York: Oxford University Press.

Jardine, Lisa. 1999. *Ingenious Pursuits: Building the Scientific Revolution*. New York: Doubleday.

Kaye, Joel. 1998. *Economy and Nature in the Fourteenth Century*. Cambridge: Cambridge University Press.

Klein, Judy L. 1997. *Statistical Visions in Time: A History of Time Series Analysis: 1662–1938*. Cambridge: Cambridge University Press.

Koerner, Lisbet. 1999. *Linnaeus, Nature, and Nation*. Cambridge: Harvard University Press.

Koyré, Alexandre. 1965. *Newtonian Studies*. Chicago: University of Chicago Press.

Lindberg, David C., and Robert S. Westman, eds. 1990. *Reappraisals of the Scientific Revolution*. Cambridge: Cambridge University Press.

Montchrétien, Antoine de. [1615] 1939. *Traité de l'oeconomie politique*. Paris: Marcel Rivière.

Newton, Sir Isaac. [1687] 1759. *Principia Mathematica*. Translated by Emilie du Chatelet. Paris: Desaint and Saillant.

———. [1704] 1979. *Opticks*. Edited by I. Bernard Cohen. New York: Dover.

Poirier, Jean-Pierre. 1993. *Laviosier: Chemist, Biologist, Economist*. Translated by Rebecca Balinski. Philadelphia: University of Pennsylvania Press.

Porter, Roy, and Mikuláš Teich, eds. 1992. *The Scientific Revolution in National Context*. Cambridge: Cambridge University Press.

Redman, Deborah A. 1997. *The Rise of Political Economy as a Science*. Cambridge: MIT Press.

Riskin, Jessica. 2002. *Science in the Age of Sensibility*. Chicago: University of Chicago Press.

Rusnock, Andrea. 2002. *Vital Accounts: Quantifying Health and Population in Eighteenth-Century England and France*. New York: Cambridge University Press.

Schabas, Margaret. 1990. Ricardo Naturalized: Lyell and Darwin on the Economy of Nature. In *Perspective on the History of Economic Thought*, edited by Donald E. Moggridge. Aldershot: Edward Elgar.

———. 2001. David Hume on Experimental Natural Philosophy, Money, and Fluids. *HOPE* 33.3:411–35.

———. 2002. Coming Together: History of Economics as History of Science. In *The Future of the History of Economics*, edited by E. Roy Weintraub. Supplement to volume 34 of *HOPE*. Durham, N.C.: Duke University Press.

Schaffer, Simon. 1989. Defoe's Natural Philosophy and the Worlds of Credit. In *Nature Transfigured: Science and Literature: 1700–1900*, edited by John R. R. Christie and Sally Shuttleworth. Manchester: Manchester University Press.

Schumpeter, Joseph A. 1954. *A History of Economic Analysis*. New York: Oxford University Press.

Schuster, John. 1990. The Scientific Revolution. In *Companion to the History of Modern Science*, edited by R. C. Olby et al. London: Routledge.

Shapin, Steven. 1994. *A Social History of Truth*. Chicago: University of Chicago Press.

———. 1996. *The Scientific Revolution*. Chicago: University of Chicago Press.

Shapin, Steven, and Simon Schaffer. 1985. *Leviathan and the Air-Pump*. Princeton, N.J.: Princeton University Press.

Smith, Pamela. 1994. *The Business of Alchemy*. Princeton, N.J.: Princeton University Press.

Smith, Pamela, and Paula Findlen, eds. 2002. *Merchants and Marvels*. London: Routledge.

Spary, E. C. 1996. Political, Natural, and Bodily Economies. In *Cultures of Natural History*, edited by N. Jardine, J. A. Secord, and E. C. Spary. Cambridge: Cambridge University Press.

Steuart, James. [1767] 1966. *An Enquiry into the Principles of Political Oeconomy*. Edited by Andrew S. Skinner. Chicago: University of Chicago Press.

Tribe, Keith. 1978. *Land, Labour, and Economic Discourse*. London: Routledge and Kegan Paul.

Voltaire. 1738. *Éléments de la philosophie de Newton*. Amsterdam: E. Ledet.

Westfall, Richard S. 1980. *Never at Rest: A Biography of Isaac Newton*. Cambridge: Cambridge University Press.

Wilson, Catherine. 1995. *The Invisible World: Early Modern Philosophy and the Invention of the Microscope*. Princeton, N.J.: Princeton University Press.

Worster, Donald. 1977. *Nature's Economy*. Cambridge: Cambridge University Press.

“Peaches Which the Patriarchs Lacked”: Natural History, Natural Resources, and the Natural Economy in France

E. C. Spary

Reflecting on commerce and finance, the economist Charles Ferrère Du Tot (1738) turned his attention to the Compagnie des Indes, that enterprise part royal, part commercial. From the perspective of the French nation, he argued, the company's role was to acquire “spices, drugs, and other things not produced in our country, which we cannot do without and which we would be absolutely required to obtain from our neighbours” (quoted in Haudrère 1993, 93). Du Tot was writing after several turbulent decades of military, monarchical, and fiscal crises that ended the prosperity resulting from Jean-Baptiste Colbert's reforms of sciences, manufactures, and commerce in Louis XIV's reign. But in 1738, the volume of France's colonial trade had recently entered a period of steady increase that would persist until the Seven Years' War (Butel 1990, 155). During this first half-century, relations between the sciences and colonialism would begin a process of transformation that would render scientific activities inseparable from the colonial enterprise and would make the colonial enterprise itself a measure of national strength.

Natural history, commerce, and the condition of the nation were all closely configured in writings on exotic plants and their uses and cultivation. Elsewhere I have explored the political and social ends served by models of the natural economy deployed by French naturalists and

My particular thanks to Alix Cooper, who gave permission to refer to her unpublished work on the indigenous and the exotic as it appeared in an early version of Cooper 1998; and to the Council of Jesus College, Cambridge, and Dr. Frances Willmoth, for access to botanical works owned by Jean-Jacques Rousseau.

medical practitioners in the second half of the eighteenth century (Spary 2000, 1996). Here, my concern is with the ways in which naturalists and medical botanists at the beginning of the century began to insert themselves into networks of global and colonial trade, by portraying their enterprises of classification and cultivation as indispensable contributions to national wealth, and by explaining how nonindigenous, plant-derived luxuries could be converted into sources of profit for the state. Such views reflected the assimilation of two literary and commercial traditions of enquiry into botany: first, the resounding therapeutic successes of medical botany since the 1670s, and second, a genre of writings on rustic or rural economy that formed an important foundation for the political economy of the midcentury.

The involvement of botanists in enterprises of colonial and exotic exploitation marked the extension of forms of resource management characteristic of *économie* to the global setting. Representations by Du Tot and others of global commercial enterprises as indispensable might seem self-evident in a period when the consumption of exotic goods was generally rising throughout Europe. But such portrayals were hotly contested by some, who characterized exotic natural substances as harmful, addictive luxuries. Two very different models of nature were at stake: was it a treasury to be plundered at man's discretion, or a precious frugal resource to be used only in cases of true need? Here, botanists participated in a broader economic debate over the relative value of global and local resources that would define the nation as a natural entity and set limits to its dependency on particular natural resources. Simultaneously, they began to redefine the basis of wealth. As economic resources, plants, unlike coin, could be cultivated and replicated.

1. Medical Botany in the Sun King's Reign

In 1703, a Jesuit reviewer ([Review of *Nova plantarum*] 1703) scolded the Minim father Charles Plumier: "It is to be wished that he had worked [as much] for Public utility, as he has fulfilled his curiosity." The publication of such a criticism about a leading seventeenth-century traveling naturalist indicates that natural history was acquiring a new agenda at the beginning of the new century. For naturalists in France, the reviewer indicated that curiosity, here characterized as private, was no adequate justification for travel and collecting. The voyager needed an eye to the public good, to exploitable natural resources (Harris 1998; Daston and

Park 1998; Whitaker 1996; Licoppe 1996, chap. 3): "If Father Plumier had added the use that can be made of these plants and the aid they give to medicine to his descriptions, he would have reached the point of perfection that one looks for in these sorts of works, by joining the useful to the agreeable."[1] For another contemporary (Biron 1703, xiii), useful natural history was contrasted with the scholastic pursuit of essences and formal causes. "There are some persons full of sense, who wish that the study of Physicists would turn toward researching the virtues and properties that the Author of Nature has placed in Minerals, Plants, and Animals. Indeed, this knowledge would cost them less, and would be more useful for human society, than all those vain disputes that have occupied men for so many centuries." This was no secularization of natural history—Biron's readers were urged to study the structure of a plant "in the silence of a Religious contemplation." Still, to be a naturalist in the new century meant to concern oneself with the good of the polity, with being a useful and productive member of society (Bourguet 1997). Nevertheless, in 1700 few could make a living from the practice of botany. Naturalist experts occupied different walks of life, from religious communities, medical practice, and scientific institutions to colonial commercial enterprises. At a time when new definitions and uses of the "exotic" were being developed (Porter and Rousseau 1990), exotic natural productions could be exploited by linking the expertise of individual scientific or medical practitioners to the prosperity of national or commercial interests. Only during these decades did the Crown, commercial interests, and scientific practitioners begin to cooperate to harness the exotic, bringing the triple instruments of commercial exploitation, natural historical modes of managing nature, and foreign policies of the early modern state into alignment.

A reassessment of natural history as a science of useful knowledge that could serve the state encouraged enquiry into the medicinal qualities of plants. In France, this took the form of increased attention to simples—tinctures, tisanes, decoctions, and other preparations of medicinal herbs. The king made pharmacy a compulsory part of a medical student's training in 1707 (Brockliss and Jones 1997, 94).[2] Botany was viewed as the science by means of which licensed medical practitioners could best display expertise and discredit charlatans. As one reviewer

1. This shift seems to have taken a different form and chronology in botany than in other areas of collecting, such as those discussed by Krzysztof Pomian ([1978] 1987, 143–62).

2. For the effects of Crown support on the practice of botany, see Stroup 1990 and 1987.

put it, "The best means of undeceiving the Public, prejudiced in favor of Charlatans, . . . would be . . . to perfect oneself in materia medica, and to have to hand, besides those remedies that are the usual weapons of Medicine, several other remedies drawn from Nature's bosom" ([Review of Chomel 1712] 1713, 154–55; Lémery 1697, [1698] 1714). Pierre Pomet's (1694) much lauded history of drugs offered French readers just such a resource: a systematic survey of the animals, plants, and minerals from which medicinal substances were derived. Pomet, a grocer and druggist, was also a student of natural history who had assiduously attended lectures and demonstrations at the Paris Jardin du Roi, who dedicated his book to Guy-Crescent Fagon—the director of that garden and the king's premier physician—and who had spent twenty years composing a collection of natural historical specimens with medicinal virtues, acquired via a global network of correspondents.[3] For outlining a materia medica founded upon natural historical knowledge, Pomet was recognized by thirteen medical men, whose words of high praise appeared after the preface to his book. Commentators singled out Pomet's approach for its novelty in uniting the useful with the scientific and attaching both to issues of expertise and authenticity. This was a recipe that subsequent writers on medical botany would follow. Some emphasized that studying the botany of simples would convince polite individuals to call upon expert, licensed medical practitioners rather than relying on themselves or—worse still—turning to charlatans. Within the hotly contested medical marketplace (Brockliss and Jones 1997; Ramsey 1988; Gillispie 1980, chap. 3), such statements were polemical claims (Chomel 1712, "Discours préliminaire"). Botanical expertise affirmed the privileged status of licensed medical practitioners and legitimated their claims to possess superior knowledge concerning the identity and quality of medicaments.

Maintaining such expertise, however, depended upon access to exotic naturalia, which was vastly facilitated by recruiting powerful patrons, including the Crown. In 1700 the French medical world was still resounding with the remarkable successes of practitioners who had managed to monopolize particular exotic drugs. Materia medica had quite recently become a subject of state interest, as Louis XIV and his ministers demonstrated a willingness to buy the secrets of exotic medicaments

3. Fagon was also an important patron of institutionalized botanists (Jussieu 1718; Sturdy 1995, chap. 14).

at considerable prices. Most famous in this regard are the cases of quinquina and ipecacuanha, both added to the French pharmacopoeia in the late seventeenth century. Initially monopolized in France by the Jesuits, quinquina or cinchona bark, along with the secret of its preparation and administration, was bought by the Crown from an Irish-English physician in 1679, in exchange for a pension and two thousand louis d'or (Hobhouse 1985). Ipecacuanha began to be imported to Paris in 1672 by a physician by the name of Legras, but a large medical market for this drug developed only in the late 1680s. At this time, a Paris-based Dutch physician, Jean Adrien Helvétius, capitalized upon a large shipment of the drug by touting it as a specific remedy for dysentery. After successful trials at a large Paris hospital, the Hôtel-Dieu, Helvétius obtained a monopoly over the sale of ipecacuanha. Its nature and origin, however, remained a secret until the king's first physician, Antoine d'Acquin, was commissioned to purchase the secret from Helvétius for one thousand louis d'or (Flückiger and Hanbury 1874, 332).

The turn of the century was thus a time of considerable optimism among medical public and practitioners alike with regard to exotic plant substances (Cook 1996; Delaunay 1906, chap. 12). Prominent physician botanists such as Joseph Pitton de Tournefort (1708, 189–90) praised Louis XIV's "Royal Bounty" in purchasing and publicizing goods such as ipecacuanha, and the active interest taken by his minister, de Pontchartrain, in the Paris Royal Academy of Sciences and in plant-hunting expeditions.[4] Tournefort himself, together with the botanical artist Claude Aubriet, received Crown funding to undertake a voyage to the Levant, then an important source of exotic imports, including medicinal or alimentary plants such as cassia or coffee.[5] The cultivation of ministerial and royal support for the discovery of new exotic plants continued after Tournefort's untimely death in 1708, when his successor as the royal professor of medicine, Etienne-François Geoffroy, used his inaugural lecture to praise Crown-sponsored enquiry, exploration, and conquest as regards exotic natural productions. Geoffroy (1708) insisted that the "science of remedies" had at no time in history made such giant strides as

4. De Pontchartrain was the uncle of the abbé Jean-Paul Bignon, the perpetual secretary of the Paris Académie Royale des Sciences.

5. Tournefort's travel account was posthumously published as Tournefort 1717. Jean-Baptiste Chomel (1712) reveals that a substantial proportion of plants used in French medicine was imported from the Levant. Coffee also reached the French ports from Mocha or Cairo. See La Roque 1716, dedicated to de Pontchartrain.

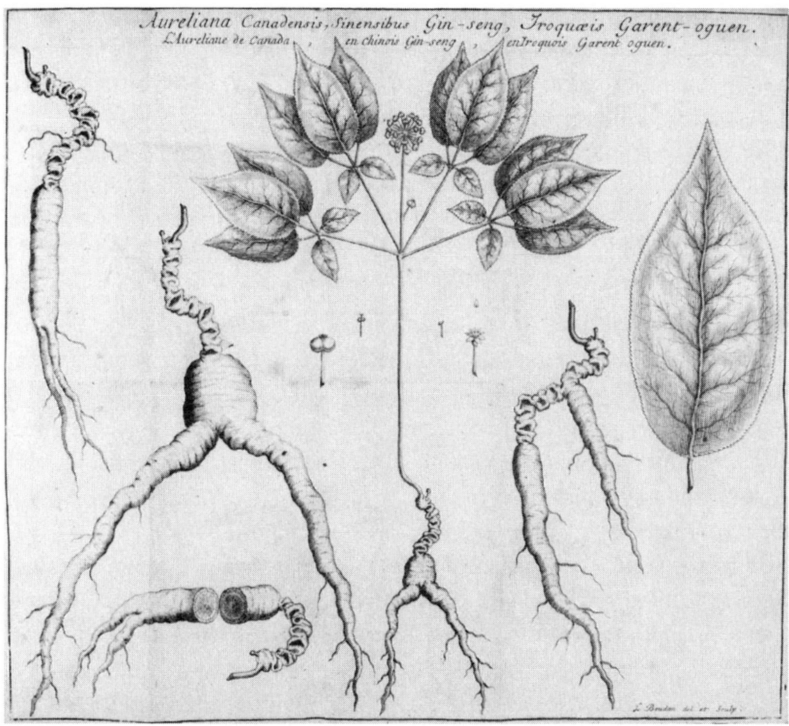

Figure 1 "Aureliana Canadensis Sinensibus, Gin-seng Iroquœis, Garent-oguen," drawn and engraved by L. Boudan (from Lafitau 1717). Reprinted by permission of the British Library, shelfmark C.113.a.20.

under the Sun King's reign, particularly in the discovery and exploitation of American natural resources. Royal patronage continued to be courted into the Regency, when the Jesuit naturalist Joseph-François Lafitau (1717) commemorated the duc d'Orléans by naming the "Canadian ginseng" in his honor. The discovery of this plant on French terrain, Lafitau claimed, would liberate France from dependency on a costly Chinese trade in the prized medicament. His plate, reproduced in figure 1, thus linked botanical novelty and the exploitation of exotic resources with royal wealth and colonial power. From the very beginning of the eighteenth century, Parisian medical botanists thus actively solicited involvement in colonization as a political program. And unlike rival iatrochemists and iatromechanists in the same medical faculty, this group would prove highly successful in attaching itself to Crown and *Compagnie* concerns. By the 1760s botanists in France managed global networks for introducing and cultivating exotic plants, both formally and informally supported by the state (Spary 2000, chap. 2).

2. Forms of the Economic, Dilemmas of the Exotic

Collectively, useful plants came to be known in France as "economic" plants. Publications from the early years of the century suggest that exotic botany entered economic writings via the literary genre of rustic or rural economy, typified by the Auxerre landowner Louis Liger's (1700, 1704, 1709) numerous publications. For Liger (1700, 1:2, 4), economy was "the Art of knowing how to prescribe an order for oneself, such that in the necessary government of things in our charge or that belong to us, there is nothing . . . that will not return us plenty of profit." Unlike the work on which his "general oeconomy of the countryside" was based, the *Maison rustique* of Charles Estienne and Jean Liebault ([1567] 1659), Liger explicitly defined *oeconomie*. This rational science, a form of husbandry of oneself and one's resources, was designed for middling readers who were literate, wealthy, and concerned to attain the twin goals of profitability and order. From the late seventeenth century onward, this group distinguished its ways of life, forms of dress and consumption, and manners from courtiers and the *peuple* (Elias 1978–82, 1983; Goodman 1994). Its members owned or frequented country estates and formed a principal market for scientific books, specimens, and experiments. It was they who participated in the new prominence of rustic or rural economy during the early to mid-eighteenth century, and who made the introduction and cultivation of exotic plants profitable through fashions for particular medicinals or ornamentals (Charlton 1984) and for a useful natural history, targeted at the discovery and exploitation of beneficial properties in natural productions.

Oeconomie in the early eighteenth century included aspects typical of the *maison rustique* genre: medicinal and culinary receipts (Estienne and Liebault were physicians), accounting, agriculture, and household management. The inclusion of exotic plants under the heading of the "economic" was closely linked with their medicinal role, as is evident from a contemporary economic dictionary written by the curé of a Lyon parish (Chomel [1709] 1740). Among many other methods for enriching oneself that were to be discovered by reading his book, the author promised in his subtitle "A Quantity of Means for rearing, nourishing, healing, and making profitable all manner of Domestic animals, as Ewes, Mutton, Oxen, Horses, Mules, Bees, and Silkworms . . . An infinity of Secrets uncovered in Gardening, Botany, Agriculture, Estates, Vineyards, Trees; as also the knowledge of Plants from Foreign Parts, and their specific qualities." As one reviewer commented, the subtitle gave an "extract in advance" of the book! But the same individual also remarked upon the novelty of Chomel's magnum opus: "Our century, so fertile in Dictionaries, has not yet seen the like of this: it is a totally new invention, of which he may be proud" ([Review of Chomel (1709) 1740] 1710).

The recruitment of botanists by the state shows that faith in natural history as a wealth-creating enterprise extended from the private activities of landowners to the public concerns of ministers. Where the household was a fundamental economic model for resource management, a resource-oriented model might serve to discuss the management of state resources—which is what we now generally understand by the expression "the economy"—but it also figured in accounts of the appropriate or inappropriate use of natural resources. The economy of nature did not feature in Jean-Jacques Rousseau's (1751–72, 337) well-known article "Economie" for Diderot and d'Alembert's *Encyclopédie*; instead, families and states formed the two poles of the "economic." But resources were still central: the family provided a model for the proper management of resources by the state, and Rousseau reminded readers that the etymology of *économie* derived from the Greek words for household and law. A resource-based account of natural productions is exemplified in the next entry, which lyrically proclaimed "Economie rustique" to be "the art of knowing all the useful and lucrative objects of the countryside, of procuring them, preserving them, and extracting the greatest possible advantage from them. This manner of enriching oneself has a prodigious extent; it is a tribute imposed on all the beings in nature; the very elements are not excepted" (Diderot 1751–72, 349). Rousseau (1972, 125) can also be shown to have practiced botany as a science of resources; while criticizing the scrutiny of nature for "our material interest," searching for remedies or for profit, he nevertheless claimed to have "often thought that the vegetable kingdom was a storehouse of foods given by nature to man and the animals."

While rural economy assumed various guises of resource management and agricultural improvement from the late seventeenth century onward, botany and particularly the "knowledge of Plants from Foreign Parts" figured increasingly within rural economy as a discipline. Throughout the eighteenth century, botanists recruited support for their plant-collecting enterprises by attaching themselves to projects of natural-resource management. The interest in exotic plants exhibited by French physicians, botanists, ministers, and entrepreneurs from the final years of the seventeenth century onward extended beyond the lucrative pharmaceutical trade to plants with uses as foods, dyestuffs, fabrics, lacquers, or for shipbuilding and carpentry (Spary 2000, chap. 2; Bourde 1967; Viel 1985; Rosenthal 1992; Regourd 1998). The successes of medical practitioners armed with new exotic medicaments lent support to a pro-global model of natural resources.[6] At stake was not whether nature was a resource for mankind, but rather how the natural world was properly to be exploited. Legitimations of this hinged on the relationship between the natural economy laid down by Providence and its variations across the globe, and the national economy of wealth and resources. Here the pursuit of botanical novelty was presented as a new form of wealth creation. Louis Feuillée (1714), a traveling natural philosopher, Minim, and correspondent of the Paris Royal Academy of Sciences, dedicated his journal of South American astronomical and natural-historical observations to the king. As he claimed on the dedication page,

> Nature having diversified animals and plants in this country, I thought it useful to the Public to describe them and discover their uses. I drew them with their natural color in the manner in which I had the honor of presenting them last year to YOUR MAJESTY. I was the more led to this work, in that I was not ignorant of the utilities they might offer for Medicine. The Savages successfully make use of many of these Plants to cure themselves of their diseases. In that way Nature has supplemented their lack of knowledge; she has given them Specifics, whose effect is marvelous, and some of which, such as *Quinquina* and *Ipecacuanha*, we know. Might one not find remedies of like certainty for the other diseases, which, by the good they procure for the Public, could be regarded as riches far more considerable than those that are taken from the mines of Peru.

By presenting himself as a public servant, this astronomer naturalist justified the scientific pursuit of useful knowledge as worthy of royal

6. On the appeal of foreign remedies for the medical public of eighteenth-century Europe, see Porter 1989, 108–10; Ramsey 1988; and Isherwood 1986, 15–18.

patronage. But at the same time, his self-presentation depended on a particular account of Nature as oeconomist, distributing natural resources around the world for human benefit, but favoring enterprising Europeans over idle savages (Hulme 1990; Pagden 1983; Duchet 1971). Crown support for Feuillée's voyage of discovery was justified by suggesting that scientific activity was actually part of nature's plan for European nations.

Contemporary French enthusiasm for the exotic is typified by the abbé Pierre Le Lorrain de Vallemont (1701, 12), one of Biron's correspondents: "Would you believe that there are skilled men, who make no great case of all the drugs of the Indies, and claim that they are only for the Orientals beneath whose sky, and in whose country nature produces them; and that we Occidentals should be content with what that wise mother [nature] does for us here?" De Vallemont resurrected a seventeenth-century argument in favor of exotic drugs. As distinct from a craving for the new and strange for its own sake, for which consumers could rightly be criticized, de Vallemont and Biron represented global commerce as part of a divine plan for the allocation, use, and distribution of natural resources among all humanity.

> God willed that there should be a social bond between all men; . . . it is for that reason that every country has gifts, and advantages proper to itself, and which commerce and navigation make common to the regions where they are lacking. . . . Would one want to leave the use of sugar, which is so agreeable and healthy, to those regions alone where the cane grows . . . ? We may boast of our garden Sage as much as we like. . . . We may publish that the Chinese, who do not possess it, give three pounds of their Tea for one pound of Sage. But it must be acknowledged in good faith, that Tea is infinitely better than Sage. This is not a prejudice in favor of foreign things. (De Vallemont 1701, 18–19)

De Vallemont went on to cite quinquina as an outstanding proof of this thesis. However, the discussion over indigenous versus exotic was an old one: disputants could find animadversions on exotic medicaments in Pliny's natural history. The "anti-exotic" position by the early eighteenth century is exemplified by Ludovicus 1710, a treatise on materia medica, written to educate polite clients in self-quackery. Opposing the trend toward exotic medicaments, Ludovicus proposed a series of healthier, indigenous substitutes such as turpentine, St. John's Wort, juniper, and "the leaves of rosemary and sage in place of tea, as the Chinese themselves recognize" ([Review of Ludovicus 1710] 1711, 902).[7] An economic self-presentation that legitimated access to global natural resources was thus open to criticism both at home and abroad. In writings defending the territorial rights of the French nobility, urban tastes for exotica were contrasted with the provincial cultivator's simpler lifestyle (D'Arcq 1756, 93–137; Boutroux de Montcresson 1770). In March 1709, near Valparaiso, Louis Feuillée (1714, 1:387) encountered some "savages" whose existence was threatened in different ways by globalization and new forms of wealth generation:

> I saw a cabin in a valley and went in, to inform myself of some Indians, which plants from their mountains were of most use in their diseases; in that little house I found an old woman with two Indians at her side . . . in rags. The compassion that I felt at seeing them in so miserable a state, led me to present a piastre to that woman, telling her in her language: *Poor woman, take this piastre*. Hardly had I spoken the words, . . . when, enraged, she rose to her feet and threw herself upon me furiously, ready to throttle me . . . reproaching me for the atrocious cruelties meted out to them by the Europeans, in ravishing their wealth and their treasure; she made me understand that I ought not to label her *poor*, saying that I was but a pauper myself, forced to leave my own country and undertake such long and difficult voyages, to come and steal their treasures; and that, besides, the Indians possessed more riches in a small corner of their Empire, than the Europeans in the whole extent of their greatest Realms. I tried to appease this harpy, explaining that my voyage was not undertaken to cause her any harm . . . but this Fury never would listen to reason, and threw my piastre in my face.

Where scientific discourses about the natural economy served to legitimate the expropriation of natural resources, resistance to the process could be bracketed as evidence of unreason. Feuillée made a rapid exit from the scene—not without first recovering his coin—and continued his mapping and natural historical activities, which were aimed at opening up the west coast of South America to French commercial and naval exploitation.

7. Another tea substitute was veronica (*Thé de l'Europe* 1704; [Review of *Thé de l'Europe*] 1704). On indigenous substitutes, see especially Koerner 1999, chaps. 5–6.

Two different models of economy were at stake in Feuillée's encounter. Included as an entertaining account of a misunderstood charitable transaction, the anecdote also reveals that the power relations governing both sides of the new mode of scientific endeavor were clearly recognizable, if differently interpreted on both sides: the official purposes of Feuillée's visit, the cataloging and arrogation of natural assets, were here apprehended as forms of economic conquest (Spary forthcoming, chap. 6). The legitimacy of scientific and commercial exploitation was thus one of the issues at stake in debates about natural productions as resources. Those who opposed global programs of natural-resource management might opt to present wealth quite differently, as legitimate only when locally generated. Thus, in a teaching text accompanying materia medica lectures at his private botanical garden, Noël Chomel's nephew Jean-Baptiste Chomel (1712, "Discours préliminaire") presented natural-historical learning as a form of good husbandry of the natural world, drawing his audience's attention to the localized nature of natural resources:

> Now let us see the advantage there would be in making use of plants that grow beneath our feet, and which, so to speak, breathe the same air that surrounds us. . . . Persons of excellent sense have often witnessed their surprise to me that the salutary plants that nature profusely supplies in our woods and countryside, should be crushed beneath our feet with such negligence and disdain; while foreign plants and drugs are sought out at great cost.

Chomel's image of wasted local natural resources trampled underfoot frequently recurs in the literature of materia medica and natural history from this period. Governing his account was a particular natural theological, medical, and commercial agenda. Attention to the local would make the French independent of the commercial ties that bound them to other parts of the world; it was, moreover, in keeping with God's plan for supplying nations with local cures for diseases:

> It would not be difficult for me to demonstrate that in a state of health we can find herbs and fruits at home that suit us just as well as Tea, Coffee, Pepper, Ginger &c., that in sickness the plants that arise in our mountains contribute as much to the virtue of our most famous compositions as those from the Orient, and that our fine and Aromatic herbs are better proportioned to our temperaments than the spices of

> Asia and America; in a word, one could demonstrate that France encloses within her bosom or on her frontiers all that is most necessary and useful to the health of her inhabitants.

This botany of the local minimized the claims of exotic pharmacy. It was underpinned by a theological biogeography characterizing the country as a natural unit in which virtuous commerce and consumption coincided with the mapping of local medicobotanical knowledge.

That a local focus was a specific epistemological strategy is revealed by the fact that neither Jean-Baptiste Chomel's uncle nor Tournefort, his teacher and predecessor in the chair of botany at the Jardin du Roi, the Parisian royal natural-history garden, had distinguished systematically between exotic and indigenous plants in print (Tournefort 1708, 1698). Chomel *neveu*, on the other hand, divided each chapter into two, beginning with local remedies and ending with foreign ones. Tournefort's and Chomel's works of materia medica were more than coincidentally similar: they shared the same anecdotes, similar descriptive terms, a virtually identical classificatory structure for types of remedies, and an emphasis on natural history as the means to discredit medical charlatans. But the shift in their approach to the location of plants is worthy of note, especially since the Académie Royale des Sciences's perpetual secretary Bernard Le Bovier de Fontenelle (1719, 5) had explicitly rejected local providence in discussing Tournefort's local history of Parisian plants: "It is the Botany of one's own native Country which ought to be chiefly studied; not that Nature has been so careful as to furnish each Climate with Plants appropriated to the Diseases of the Inhabitants, but that it is more convenient to employ what is near at hand; and what comes from remote and foreign Parts, is often found possessed of no superior Virtue." The work of Alix Cooper (1998, chap. 1) has explored the opposition between indigenous and exotic in materia medica from earlier centuries. Such literature remained valuable throughout the early modern period because it had direct relevance for disputes over national boundaries and national identity.[8] If Chomel and others still left scope in their work for praising certain outstanding exotic remedies, particularly ipecacuanha and quinquina, by the 1730s the question of local versus global economies of nature was perhaps more polarized. The widely read didactic natural theology of the abbé Noël-Antoine Pluche ([1732] 1763, 1:487–88; Trinkle

8. In his later materia medica, Geoffroy ([1743] 1757, 2:1–2) suggested distinguishing plants into indigenous and exotic, but did not structure his work accordingly.

1997) informed youthful readers, "According to a sentiment that is beginning to become widespread . . . God has placed in each Country the remedies for diseases that are usual there, and we have around us an infinity of plants that offer us their services, and that, were we more attentive and less impatient, might save us making recourse to foreign remedies, [which are] always very expensive, often ruined, and converted into poison by the avarice of Merchants, or deteriorated by age." The search for substitutes for exotic natural goods has here become a form of self-disciplining, an aspect of the moral development of character. Nature is the model of a good economist, supplying just enough and not too much, and God's benevolent providence is threatened by grasping individuals seeking to dominate the whole (natural and social) world.[9] However, Pluche stigmatizes not the individual character, but that of the nation as a whole: the French are too impatient and greedy, and their illnesses are the wages of indulgence in (exotic) luxuries.

Thus, in the same decades in which French trade in exotic natural productions was rising rapidly, a protest against global economies of nature was also gathering pace ([Mercier] 1781, 3; Willemet and Coste 1778, i–ii). Du Tot's comment about needs, with which I began, was not as straightforward as it appears at first sight. By the early eighteenth century, the claim that diseases were a product of luxury was already commonplace in health literature (Duncan 1705, chap. 1; Lémery [1701] 1705, 7). If diseases generally revealed the national degeneracy produced by luxurious living and overindulgence, new diseases, for which sufferers eagerly embraced foreign remedies, were a particular evidence of the evils of global commerce and exchange (Crosby 1972; Rousseau 1976; Porter 1994); thus syphilis was considered a disease specific to the New World, while many medical treatises warned of the adverse health effects of consuming exotic substances.[10] The ill health that drove individuals to seek out exotic medicaments was itself produced by failure to restrain one's desires, so that the state of the nation was implicated in the exploitation of the natural world. This put a different gloss upon the optimism expressed by writers like de Vallemont. The exploitation of exotic plants thus raised particular problems concerning the meaning

9. Compare the more moderate position of Mathieu Fabregou (1734, xx-xxii).

10. Crosby 1972 has become a classic work on the exchange of plants, animals, and diseases between Europe and the New World, but it is concerned not with the meanings of such exchanges for contemporaries, only with their consequences from a twentieth-century perspective.

of a “natural economy.” A “biogeography” of the indigenous went in tandem with a moral critique in which consumer relations with natural bodies fashioned the nation as a natural whole.

3. Plants as Luxuries, or the Trials of Botanical Virtue

Within a decade of the publications of Tournefort and Chomel, Louis XIV had died, the Treaty of Utrecht had been signed, and French military prestige was on the wane. French journalists were wont to produce soliloquies on why the Dutch, whose republican nation was almost as far as one could get from Louis XIV’s absolute monarchy, were so successful in commerce and colonization; they praised them as “skillful, patient, untiring, sober, contenting themselves with little, thrifty, yet liberal, but always appropriately and to their own profit,” and wondered how, surrounded by such colonial wealth, the Dutch remained self-disciplined, laborious, and above all inconspicuous. “The arbiters of so many Kingdoms,” gasped one awestruck commentator ([Review of *Recueil des voyages*] 1705; Morize 1970, 103–4), “do not rise above their initial condition, they remain confounded with the other merchants, their compatriots, and at Amsterdam one cannot distinguish the Sovereigns of a great part of India from the crowd of burghers.” This way of governing, in short, seemed to denote a break with early modern uses of display as a source of power (Burke 1992; Frijhoff 1992). At the same time, Dutch successes in battles ensured that the boundaries of their republic remained intact against French military encroachments. French authors read Dutch military and commercial superiority as evidence of the relative condition of absolutist France and the Dutch Republic as nations: “The great enterprises that these wise Republicans undertook have almost all succeeded; thus a small country uncovered to the sea, . . . a country whose ports all owe more to art than nature, which cannot feed its inhabitants, and whose only goods are butter, cheese, and earth suitable for making pottery, has become powerful enough to resist the forces of the house of Austria and France together” ([Review of *Le grand thresor*] 1714). National identity was also configured in these debates about the indigenous and exotic; or rather, the natural status that colonies could have for the metropolitan state.

In their appeals to ministers and other patrons, botanists ascribed the resounding successes of the Dutch in international commerce to Dutch programs for capturing and sometimes monopolizing "economic" natural productions. These were propagated and cultivated in the Dutch colonial botanical gardens, the first in the world to be founded (Stearn 1962; Wijnands 1988; [Review of *Praeludia Botanica*] 1707). The Dutch had succeeded in exploiting exotic natural productions to the benefit of their nation *and* without risking their national morality. Plants possessed economic potential in a different form from most other goods, above all by virtue of their power to reproduce themselves in new settings. Botanists sought to bridge the moral gap between the indigenous and the exotic by involving themselves in projects to naturalize "economic" plants, and in attempts to identify valuable exotic plants or their substitutes within the kingdom of France, including the colonies.[11] In such projects, the status of the "natural" was at stake. Jean-François Melon, author of the famous *Essai politique sur le commerce*, was a robe noble who worked for successive regimes as a financial *commis*, then a tax farmer. Previously, in 1712, he was a leading figure in founding Bordeaux's royal academy of sciences (Michaud and Michaud 1998, 27:588–89; Roche 1978, 1996, 131). Writing of the Dutch East India Company, he noted that its

> great successes are the result of luck that rendered [Holland] the sole Sovereign of trade in Cinnamon, Nutmeg, and Cloves. If the same luck or industry had offered some different Nation a terrain that yielded the same product, the Dutch Company would have found it hard to sustain the immense costs of the Government of so many Fortresses and smaller individual establishments. For some time now, several European Nations have rivaled [Holland] in the production of Pepper, which she no longer supplies to us. (Melon [1734] 1736, 64–65)

What happened in the case of pepper would be repeated for other valuable plant products during the century: coffee, cinnamon, cloves, and nutmeg, especially. But Melon's view that conquering this commerce was a result of luck or colonial policy tends to obscure the increasing importance of active botanical involvement in state-supported programs for the introduction, propagation, and acclimatization of economic plants. The first coffee plant and the first pineapple grown in France were grown

11. See Lafitau 1717. De Vallemont ([1701] 1709) described a new technique of propagating "exotic plants or [those] brought from distant countries"; a reviewer enthused: "Nothing is more useful than a Physics that leads to practices of this sort. This one might make it possible to grow plants from all countries of the world in France" ([Review of de Vallemont (1701) 1709] 1711, 710).

at the Jardin du Roi; and through the course of the eighteenth century, French colonial botanical gardens came to dominate the process of introducing and naturalizing new economic plants (Jussieu 1719, 291–99; Lochner 1716; Spary forthcoming).

Even in botany, Melon's argument ([1734] 1736, 108) about the value of luxury in encouraging industry, as well as his claim that the colonies were an example of the relative and contingent nature of luxury ("Sugar, Silk, Coffee, Tobacco, are but new Luxury, unknown to the Romans"), touched on a sensitive issue for contemporaries. Botanists undertook naturalization projects against a growing chorus of criticism between the 1730s and the 1750s. On the one hand, there were those who argued that gifts of nature constituted a distinct category of morally acceptable luxury; on the other were those who represented even exotic nature as morally suspect. In their guise as rare commodities, plants entered into debates about the legitimacy of luxury. Voltaire, one of the wealthiest commoners in eighteenth-century France, was constantly concerned with presenting himself as a virtuous consumer. *Le mondain*, his 1736 verse commentary on Melon's essay, explicitly embraced luxury along Melon's lines: "The superfluous, a very necessary thing, / Has united the two Hemispheres." Scoffing at historical accounts of Gallic ancestors living in primitive frugality, he declared, "For myself, I give thanks to wise Nature, / Who, for my own good, had me born in this age" (Morize 1970, 133). By the 1750s, however, after the death of his lover, Emilie du Châtelet, and the breakdown of his own health, Voltaire was in chastened mood. Moving to Geneva, he established himself first just across the French border, at Ferney, and later at a new country house, which he named "Pleasures" ("Les Délices"). While there is every evidence that Voltaire passed his time sustained by the most luxurious comforts that money could buy in food and drink, furniture and fabric, he was also concerned with issues of self-presentation. Writing to Jean-Robert Tronchin in January 1755 regarding the house he proposed to buy, he claimed: "It is a philosopher's palace with the gardens of Epicurus" (Voltaire 1950, 22). Over the succeeding months and years he devoted his time (and a substantial proportion of his income) to converting Les Délices into a productive smallholding, obtaining seeds and young plants from suppliers and keeping detailed accounts of the income from its farmlands and livestock (Besterman 1968). In April 1759 he boasted of the product of his labors: "I know that our expenditure is furious, but it gives me pleasure. And to that I know no reply. I shall lead a patriarchal life. No money, but plenty of hay, sheep, cattle; and peaches, which the patriarchs didn't have" (Voltaire 1950, 389).

In his journey from advocate of luxury to patriarch over twenty years, Voltaire's choice of the peach as a virtuous luxury is significant: for contemporaries this fruit, more perhaps than any other, represented the beneficial effects of labor upon cultivated plants ("Pêcher" 1751–72, 230–31; "Perse" 1751–72, 415–17; Tschudi 1778, 21). In the first decades of the century, such arguments filled the moral gap between exploiting the natural world according to nature's plan, and perverting the natural economy through the use of force to arrogate the fruits of other countries, which, anyway, were not physiologically suited to French bodies. But during the 1750s, thanks to the publication of Jean-Jacques Rousseau's *Discours sur les sciences et les arts*, a dispute began over what it meant to be "natural," which would end only with the French Revolution. In the botanical domain, it translated into a debate over the extent to which human agency had historically transformed the gifts of nature from their original state. As Rousseau (2000, 8:157) argued in 1774, "to know the pear and the apple of nature, it is necessary to look for them not in kitchen gardens but in forests. The flesh is not as large and as succulent, but the seeds ripen better, in multiplying more, and the trees are infinitely taller and more vigorous." Wild fruits possessed a moral purity that cultivated ones potentially lacked. It is hardly surprising, therefore, that Rousseau's writings united an attack on the sciences as technologies of despotism with a critique of institutionalized botany. "Altering the nature of this lovely study, [savants] transplant it to the middle of cities and academies where it withers no less than exotic plants in the gardens of connoisseurs," Rousseau (2000, 8:65) complained.

4. Natural History as a Science of Resources

Rousseau's ambivalence about the moral foundation of a science that combined "material interest" with systematics, the panoptical conquest of nature with the corruption of a primitive frugality, shows what was at stake in an eighteenth-century "economic" botany (Cook 1994). Consumption, management, and globalization were becoming integral parts of botanical practice at this time, in France as elsewhere (Koerner 1999; Drayton 2000). To treat the natural world as a set of resources entailed the commodification of plants and other natural productions, their conversion into the raw materials of profitable transactions. Organizations such as the East India companies are well known in this connection, but many merchants and scientific practitioners had networks of correspondents that tied them to distant parts of the globe. The boundaries between the pharmacopoeia, the dictionary of natural history, and the compendium of foodstuffs were indistinct in such writings, as for example in the *Encyclopédie*'s many botanical articles. Classificatory activity was revitalized from the start of the eighteenth century through the prominence of botanists such as Tournefort and Antoine de Jussieu—the same individuals seeking both to reform materia medica and to insert botanical expertise into colonial commerce (Tjaden 1977; Becker et al. 1957; Stroup 1990, chaps. 7–8).

To construct materia medica as part of *natural history* was to present a bold agenda in which botanical knowledge was fundamental to medical authenticity, and botanists participated in global networks for the exploitation of exotic natural resources. Botany provided a set of techniques for policing foodstuffs and medicaments, promised the medical practitioner a means of getting rich, and presented the natural world in tandem with the human moral and political world in discussions about resource management. Considering contemporary botanical uses of the term *économie* refutes any narrow definition of natural history as strictly a science of classification. Although naturalists' efforts to recruit commercial and political support for their enterprises were only sporadically successful prior to the 1760s, events in the decades preceding this reveal the strategies used by certain naturalists to insert themselves into the nexus between government and commerce. A complete picture of the reasons why some espoused global models of trade, while others rejected or minimized them, is still required; but by the century's end, the anti-exotic critique was largely articulated by those outside an institutional setting (Spary forthcoming).

Why is the involvement of botanists and agronomists in models of economy significant? One important response for the purposes of this volume must lie in the fact that French economic discourse throughout the eighteenth century foregrounded the problem of *natural* resources. Strictly speaking, works like those of Melon or Du Tot were probably only later assimilated to "economy," so that political economy as a genre lagged behind rural economy.[12] Yet historians of "economic thought" have rarely touched upon the fact that accounts of the natural world were

12. On the association of the term *économie* with writings on commerce and government, see Larrère 1992, 6–8.

often at stake in writings on political economy from the 1760s and 1770s (Meek 1962; Fox-Genovese 1976; Weulersse 1910, 1950, 1985; Larrère 1992, chap. 1). Physiocracy arose as a doctrine in which nature was the supreme resource, the only true source of productivity; the implications of this have occasionally gone overlooked in the effort to confirm Adam Smith's economic critique. Yet a typical physiocratic account of economic language, addressed to a polite female reader, began with natural history:

> Consider, Madame, the earth covered with its *natural* productions at the moment of harvest, collect together in your imagination all the beings of the three kingdoms that we can *appropriate* for our *enjoyment*, the animals of air, land, and water . . .; all the plants that grow on the surface of our globe, that man *seeks out* in places where the soil seems to produce them of itself, or that he *multiplies* by cultivation, all that he gathers, all he extracts, all he preserves in order to consume it; finally add all the subterranean and mineral matters that art withdraws from the bowels of the earth and the bosom of the rocks; gather together all that mass of Nature's benefits, received by man in the space of *one year*: that, Madame, is the *annual production* or the *total reproduction*, whose idea . . . is the first foundation of the Economic Table. ([Baudeau] [1776] 1967, 1–3)

In a century in which Rousseau and others attempted to use nature as a moral standard in order to control how nature was to be viewed as a resource, we cannot neglect the natural meanings of economy and the economic; it is in terms of their relationship to the natural that economic systems acquired moral and political force during this period.

References

[Baudeau, abbé Nicolas]. [1776] 1967. *Explication du Tableau économique, a Madame de ***. Extrait des Ephémérides de 1767 & 1768.* Paris: EDHIS.

Becker, G., et al. 1957. *Tournefort.* Paris: Muséum National d'Histoire Naturelle.

Besterman, Theodore, ed. 1968. *Voltaire's Household Accounts 1760–1778.* Geneva: Institut et Musée Voltaire.

Biron, C. 1703. *Curiositez de la nature et de l'art apportées dans deux voïages des Indes, l'un aux Indes d'Occident en 1698 & 1699 & l'autres aux Indes d'Orient en 1701 & 1702, avec une Relation abrégée de ces deux voyages.* Paris: Jean Moreau.

Bourde, André. 1967. *Agronomie et agronomes en France au XVIIIe siècle*. 3 vols. Paris: S.E.V.P.E.N.

Bourguet, Marie-Noëlle. 1997. La collecte du monde: Voyage et histoire naturelle (fin XVIIe siècle–début XIXe siècle). In *Le muséum au premier siècle de son histoire*, edited by Claude Blanckaert et al. Paris: Editions du Muséum National d'Histoire Naturelle.

Boutroux de Montcresson, Charles. 1770. *Le cultivateur a son fils, sur les inconvéniens du luxe et les avantages de l'agriculture*. Paris: Veuve Regnard.

Brockliss, Laurence, and Colin Jones. 1997. *The Medical World of Early Modern France*. Oxford: Clarendon Press.

Burke, Peter. 1992. *The Fabrication of Louis XIV*. New Haven, Conn.: Yale University Press.

Butel, Paul. 1990. France, the Antilles, and Europe in the Seventeenth and Eighteenth Centuries: Renewals of Foreign Trade. In *The Rise of Merchant Empires: Long-Distance Trade in the Early Modern World, 1350–1750*, edited by James D. Tracy. Cambridge: Cambridge University Press.

Charlton, D. G. 1984. *New Images of the Natural in France: A Study in European Cultural History, 1750–1800*. Cambridge: Cambridge University Press.

Chomel, Jean-Baptiste. 1712. *Abregé de l'Histoire des Plantes usuelles. Dans lequel on donne leurs noms differens, François & Latins. La maniere de s'en servir, la dose, & les principales compositions de Pharmacie, dans lesquelles elles sont employées. Avec quelques observations de pratique sur leurs usages*. Paris: Charles Osmont.

Chomel, Noël. [1709] 1740. *Dictionnaire Oeconomique, contenant divers moyens d'augmenter son Bien, et de conserver sa Santé avec plusieurs Remedes assurez et eprouvez, pour un tres-grand nombre de Maladies, & de beaux Secrets pour parvenir à une longue & heureuse vieillesse*. Paris: Veuve Etienne.

Cook, Alexandra. 1994. Rousseau's "Moral Botany": Nature, Science, Politics, and the Soul in Rousseau's Botanical Writings. Ph.D. diss., Cornell University.

Cook, Harold J. 1996. Physicians and Natural History. In Jardine, Secord, and Spary 1996.

Cooper, Alix. 1998. Inventing the Indigenous: Local Knowledge and Natural History in the Early Modern German Territories. Ph.D. diss., Harvard University.

Crosby, Alfred W., Jr. 1972. *The Columbian Exchange: Biological and Cultural Consequences of 1492*. Westport, Conn.: Greenwood Publishing Company.

D'Arcq, Philippe Auguste de Saint-Foix, chevalier. 1756. *La Noblesse militaire, opposée à la noblesse commerçante; ou le Patriote françois*. Amsterdam.

Daston, Lorraine, and Katherine Park. 1998. *Wonders and the Order of Nature 1150–1750*. New York: Zone Books.

Delaunay, Paul. 1906. *Le Monde médical Parisien au dix-huitième siècle*. Paris: Jules Rousset.

De Vallemont, abbé Pierre Le Lorrain. 1701. Lettre de M. l'Abbé de Vallemont. In Biron 1703.

———. [1701] 1709. *Curiositez de la Nature & de l'Art sur le Vegetation; ou l'Agriculture & le Jardinage dans leur perfection: où l'on voit le secret de la multiplication du blé, & les moyens d'augmenter considérablement le revenu des biens de la Campagne: De nouvelles découvertes pour grossir, multiplier, & embellir les fleurs & les fruits*. Paris: Jean Moreau.

Diderot, Denis. 1751–72. Economie rustique. In vol. 5 of Diderot and d'Alembert 1751–72.

Diderot, Denis, and Jean Le Rond d'Alembert, eds. 1751–72. *Encyclopédie, ou Dictionnaire raisonné des Sciences, des arts et des métiers*. Paris: Briasson.

Drayton, Richard. 2000. *Nature's Government: Science, Imperial Britain, and the "Improvement" of the World*. New Haven, Conn.: Yale University Press.

Duchet, Michèle. 1971. *Anthropologie et histoire au siècle des lumières: Buffon, Voltaire, Rousseau, Helvétius, Diderot*. Paris: François Maspero.

Duncan, Daniel. 1705. *Avis salutaire à tout le monde contre l'abus des choses chaudes, et particulièrement du Café, du Chocolat, & du Thé*. Rotterdam: Abraham Acher.

Du Tot, Charles Ferrère. 1738. *Réflexions sur le commerce et les finances*. Paris.

Elias, Norbert. 1978–82. *The Civilising Process*. Oxford: Blackwell.

———. 1983. *The Court Society*. Oxford: Blackwell.

Estienne, Charles, and Jean Liebault. [1567] 1659. *L'Agriculture et maison rustique, . . . reueuë & augmentée de beaucoup . . . Auec un bref recueil des Chasses du Cerf, du Sanglier, du Lieure, du Renard, du Blereau, du Connil, du Loup, des Oyseaux, & de la Fauconnerie: . . . y joint la fabrique & usage de la lauge, ou Diapason*. Lyon: Claude Riviere.

Fabregou, Mathieu. 1734. *Description des Plantes qui naissent ou se renouvellent aux environs de Paris avec leurs usages dans la Médecine & dans les Arts, le commencement & le progrès de cette Science, & l'Histoire des personnes dont on parlera dans l'ouvrage*. Paris: Jacques Lambert.

Feuillée, Louis. 1714. *Journal des Observations physiques, mathematiques et botaniques, faites par l'ordre du Roy sur les Côtes Orientales de l'Amerique Meridionale, & dans les Indes Occidentales, depuis l'année 1707. jusques en 1712*. Paris: Pierre Giffart.

Flückiger, Friedrich A., and Daniel Hanbury. 1874. *Pharmacographia: A History of the Principal Drugs of Vegetable Origin, met with in Great Britain and British India*. London: Macmillan.

Fontenelle, Bernard Le Bovier de. 1719. A short Account of Monsieur *Tournefort*'s Life and Writings. In *The Compleat Herbal: or, the Botanical Institutions of Mr. Tournefort, Chief Botanist to the late French King*, by Joseph Pitton de Tournefort. London: For R. Bonwicke et al.

Fox-Genovese, Elizabeth. 1976. *The Origins of Physiocracy: Economic Revolution and Social Order in Eighteenth-Century France*. Ithaca, N.Y.: Cornell University Press.

Frijhoff, Willem Th. M. 1992. The Dutch Enlightenment and the Creation of Popular Culture. In *The Dutch Republic in the Eighteenth Century: Decline, Enlightenment, and Revolution*, edited by Margaret C. Jacob and Wijnand W. Mijnhardt. Ithaca, N.Y.: Cornell University Press.

Geoffroy, Etienne-François. 1708. Extrait d'un discours de Mr. Geoffroy l'ainé, Docteur & Professeur Royal en Medecine, sur la connaissance des Remedes. In *Memoires pour l'Histoire des Sciences & des beaux Arts. Recueillis par l'Ordre de Son Altesse Serenissime Monseigneur Prince Souverain de Dombes*, 1825–27.

———. [1743] 1757. *Traité de la matiere medicale, ou de l'histoire des vertus, du choix et de l'usage des remedes simples*. Paris: Desaint & Saillant.

Gillispie, Charles Coulston. 1980. *Science and Polity in France at the End of the Old Regime*. Princeton, N.J.: Princeton University Press.

Goodman, Dena. 1994. *The Republic of Letters: A Cultural History of the French Enlightenment*. Ithaca, N.Y.: Cornell University Press.

Harris, Steven J. 1998. Long-Distance Corporations, Big Sciences, and the Geography of Knowledge. *Configurations* 6:269–304.

Haudrère, Ph. 1993. The "Compagnie des Indes" and Maritime Matters (c. 1725–1770). In *Ships, Sailors, and Spices: East India Companies and Their Shipping in the Sixteenth, Seventeenth, and Eighteenth Centuries*, edited by Jaap R. Bruijn and Femme S. Gaastra. Amsterdam: Neha.

Hobhouse, Henry. 1985. *Seeds of Change: Five Plants That Transformed Mankind*. London: Sidgwick & Jackson.

Hulme, Peter. 1990. The Spontaneous Hand of Nature: Savagery, Colonialism, and the Enlightenment. In *The Enlightenment and Its Shadows*, edited by Peter Hulme and Ludmilla Jordanova. London: Routledge.

Isherwood, Robert M. 1986. *Farce and Fantasy: Popular Entertainment in Eighteenth-Century Paris*. New York: Oxford University Press.

Jardine, N., J. A. Secord, and E. C. Spary, eds. 1996. *Cultures of Natural History*. Cambridge: Cambridge University Press.

Jussieu, Antoine de. 1718. *Discours sur le progrès de la Botanique au Jardin royal de Paris, suivi d'une introduction a la connoissance des plantes, prononcez a l'ouverture des demonstrations publiques, le 31 May 1718*. Paris: Etienne Ganeau.

———. 1719. Histoire du café. In *Histoire de l'Académie Royale des Sciences, 1713*. Paris: Imprimerie Royale.

Koerner, Lisbet. 1999. *Linnaeus: Nature and Nation*. Cambridge: Harvard University Press.

Lafitau, père Joseph-François. 1717. *Memoire presenté à son Altesse Royale Monseigneur le Duc d'Orleans, Regent du Royaume de France; concernant la precieuse Plante du Gin-seng de Tartarie, découverte en Canada*. Paris: Joseph Mongé.

La Roque, Antoine de. 1716. *Voyage de l'Arabie heureuse, par l'Ocean Oriental, & le Détroit de la Mer Rouge. Fait par les François pour la premiere fois, dans les années 1708, 1709 & 1710. Avec la Relation particuliere d'un Voyage du Port de Moka à la Cour du Roi d'Yemen, dans la seconde Expedition des années 1711, 1712 & 1713. Un Memoire concernant l'Arbre & le Fruit du Café, dressé sur les Observations de ceux qui ont fait ce dernier Voyage. Et un Traité historique de l'origine & du progrès du Café*. Amsterdam: Steenhouwer et Uytwerf.

Larrère, Catherine. 1992. *L'invention de l'économie au XVIII siècle: Du droit naturel à la physiocratie*. Paris: Presses Universitaires de France.

Lémery, Louis. [1701] 1705. *Traité des Aliments, où l'on trouve par ordre, et separement. La difference & le choix qu'on doit faire de chacun d'eux en particulier; les bons & les mauvais effets qu'ils peuvent produire; les principes en quoi ils abondent; le temps, l'âge & le temperament où ils conviennent*. Paris: Pierre Witte.

Lémery, Nicolas. 1697. *Pharmacopée universelle, contenant toutes les compositions de pharmacie qui sont en usage dans la medecine, tant en France que par toute l'Europe; leurs vertus, leurs doses, les manieres d'operer les plus simples & les meilleures*. Paris: Laurent d'Houry.

———. [1698] 1714. *Traité Universel des Drogues simples mises en ordre alphabetique. Où l'on trouve leurs différens noms, leur origine, leur choix, les principes qu'elles renferment, leurs qualitez, leur étymologie, & tout ce qu'il y a de particulier dans les Animaux, dans les Végétaux, & dans les Mineraux*. Paris: Laurent d'Houry.

Licoppe, Christian. 1996. *La formation de la pratique scientifique: Le discours de l'expérience en France et en Angleterre (1630–1820)*. Paris: Editions la Découverte.

Liger, Louis. 1700. *Oeconomie generale de la campagne, ou nouvelle maison rustique*. Paris: Charles de Sercy.

———. 1704. *Le Jardinier fleuriste & historiographe, ou la culture universelle des fleurs, arbres, arbustes & arbrisseaux Servans à l'embellissement des jardins. Ensemble la maniere de dresser toutes sortes de parterres, berceaux de verdures, pattes d'oye, colonnes, & autres pieces*. Paris: Damien Beugnié.

———. 1709. *Moyens faciles pour rétablir en peu de temps l'abondance de toutes sortes de graines & de fruits dans le Royaume, & de l'y maintenir toûjours par le secours de l'Agriculture*. Paris: Charles Huguier.

Lochner, Michael Friedrich. 1716. *Commentatio de Ananasa sive Nuce Pinea Indica, vulgo Pinhas*. Nürnberg.

Ludovicus, Daniel. 1710. *Traité du bon choix des medicamens*. Lyon: Antoine Boudet.

Meek, Ronald L. 1962. *The Economics of Physiocracy: Essays and Translations*. London: Allen & Unwin.

Melon, Jean-François. [1734] 1736. *Essai politique sur le Commerce. Nouvelle Edition augmentée de sept Chapitres, & où les lacunes des Editions précedentes sont remplies*. N.p.

[Mercier, Louis-Sébastien]. 1781. *Tableau de Paris*. London.

Michaud, Joseph-François, and Louis-Gabriel Michaud, eds. 1998. *Biographie universelle ancienne et moderne*. 45 vols. Bad Feilnbach: Schmidt Periodicals.

Morize, André. 1970. *L'apologie du luxe au XVIIIe siècle et "Le mondain" de Voltaire: Etude critique sur "Le mondain" et ses sources*. Geneva: Slatkine Reprints.

Pagden, Anthony. 1983. The Savage Critic: Some European Images of the Primitive. *Yearbook of English Studies* 13:32–45.

Pêcher. 1751–72. In vol. 12 of Diderot and d'Alembert 1751–72.

Perse. 1751–72. In vol. 12 of Diderot and d'Alembert 1751–72.

Pluche, abbé Noël-Antoine. [1732] 1763. *Le Spectacle de la Nature, ou entretiens sur les particularités de l'histoire naturelle qui ont paru les plus propres à rendre les Jeunes-Gens curieux, & à leur former l'esprit*. Paris: Frères Estienne.

Pomet, Pierre. 1694. *Histoire generale des Drogues, traitant des Plantes, des Animaux, & des Minéraux; Ouvrage enrichy de plus de quatre cent Figures en Taille-douce tirées d'aprés Nature; avec un discours qui explique leurs differens Noms, les Pays d'où elles viennent, la maniere de connoître les Veritables d'avec les Falsifiées, & leurs proprietez, où l'on découvre l'erreur des Anciens & des Modernes; Le tout tres utile au Public*. Paris: Jean-Baptiste Loyson et Augustin Pillon.

Pomian, Krszysztof. [1978] 1987. *Collectionneurs, amateurs et curieux*. Paris: Gallimard.

Porter, Roy. 1989. *Health for Sale: Quackery in England 1660–1850*. Manchester: Manchester University Press.

———. 1994. Consumption: Disease of the Consumer Society? In *Consumption and the World of Goods*, edited by John Brewer and Roy Porter. London: Routledge.

Porter, Roy, and George Rousseau. 1990. Introduction: Approaching Enlightenment Exoticism. In *Exoticism in the Enlightenment*, edited by Porter and Rousseau. Manchester: Manchester University Press.

Ramsey, Matthew. 1988. *Professional and Popular Medicine in France, 1770–1830*. Cambridge: Cambridge University Press.

Regourd, François. 1998. La Société Royale d'Agriculture de Paris face à l'espace colonial (1761–1793). *Bulletin du centre d'histoire des espaces atlantiques*, n.s., 8:155–94.

[Review of Chomel 1712]. 1713. In *Memoires pour l'Histoire des Sciences & des beaux Arts. Recueillis par l'Ordre de Son Altesse Serenissime Monseigneur Prince Souverain de Dombes*, 133–57.

[Review of Chomel (1709) 1740]. 1710. In *Memoires pour l'Histoire des Sciences & des beaux Arts. Recueillis par l'Ordre de Son Altesse Serenissime Monseigneur Prince Souverain de Dombes*, 906–12.

[Review of de Vallemont (1701) 1709]. 1711. In *Memoires pour l'Histoire des Sciences & des beaux Arts. Recueillis par l'Ordre de Son Altesse Serenissime Monseigneur Prince Souverain de Dombes*, 694–713.

[Review of *Le grand thresor historique et politique du florissant commerce des Hollandais dans tous les Etats du monde, quelle est leur maniere de le faire, son origine, leurs grands progrès, leurs possessions & gouvernement dans les Indes, comment ils se sont rendus maîtres de tout le commerce de l'Europe, quelles sont les marchandises convenable au trafic maritime, d'où ils les tirent, & les gains qu'ils y font*, by Pierre Daniel Huet.] 1714. In *Memoires pour l'Histoire des Sciences & des beaux Arts. Recueillis par l'Ordre de Son Altesse Serenissime Monseigneur Prince Souverain de Dombes*, 1–16.

[Review of Ludovicus 1710]. 1711. In *Memoires pour l'Histoire des Sciences & des beaux Arts. Recueillis par l'Ordre de Son Altesse Serenissime Monseigneur Prince Souverain de Dombes*, 899–904.

[Review of *Nova plantarum Americanarum Genera*, by père Charles Plumier]. 1703. In *Memoires pour l'Histoire des Sciences & des beaux Arts. Recueillis par l'Ordre de Son Altesse Serenissime Monseigneur Prince Souverain de Dombes*, 1343–46.

[Review of *Praeludia Botanica, ad publicas Plantarum exoticarum demonstrationes dicta in Horto Medico, cum Demonstrationes Exoticarum*, by Caspar Commelin]. 1707. *Journal des Sçavans* 1707.2:40–47.

[Review of *Recueil des voyages qui ont servi à l'établissement et aux progrès de la Compagnie des Indes Orientales, formées dans les Provinces Unies des Pays Bas*, by René Augustin Constantin de Renneville]. 1705. In *Memoires pour l'Histoire des Sciences & des beaux Arts. Recueillis par l'Ordre de Son Altesse Serenissime Monseigneur Prince Souverain de Dombes*, 1669–70.

[Review of *Thé de l'Europe* 1704]. *Journal des Sçavans* 1704:63–66.

Roche, Daniel. 1978. *Le siècle des Lumières en province: Académies et académiciens provinciaux, 1680–1789*. Paris: Mouton.

———. 1996. Natural History in the Academies. In Jardine, Secord, and Spary 1996.

Rosenthal, Jean-Laurent. 1992. *The Fruits of Revolution: Property Rights, Litigation, and French Agriculture, 1700–1860*. Cambridge: Cambridge University Press.

Rousseau, George S. 1976. Nerves, Spirits, and Fibres. *Studies in the Eighteenth Century* 3:137–57.

Rousseau, Jean-Jacques. 1751–72. Economie. In vol. 5 of Diderot and d'Alembert 1751–72.

———. 1972. *Les rêveries du promeneur solitaire*. Paris: Gallimard.

———. 2000. *The Reveries of the Solitary Walker, Botanical Writings*, and Letter to Franquières. In vol. 8 of *The Collected Writings of Jean-Jacques Rousseau*, edited by Christopher Kelly. Hanover, N.H.: University Press of New England.

Spary, E. C. 1996. Natural, Political, and Bodily Economies. In Jardine, Secord, and Spary 1996.

———. 2000. *Utopia's Garden: French Natural History from Old Regime to Revolution*. Chicago: University of Chicago Press.

———. Forthcoming. *Eating the Enlightenment: Food and the Sciences in France, 1680–1820*.

Stearn, William T. 1962. The Influence of Leyden on Botany in the Seventeenth and Eighteenth Centuries. *British Journal for the History of Science* 1:137–59.

Stroup, Alice. 1987. *Royal Funding of the Parisian Académie Royale des Sciences during the 1690s*. Philadelphia: American Philosophical Society.

———. 1990. *A Company of Scientists: Botany, Patronage, and Community at the Seventeenth-Century Parisian Royal Academy of Sciences*. Berkeley, Calif.: University of California Press.

Sturdy, David J. 1995. *Science and Social Status: The Members of the Académie des Sciences, 1666–1750*. Woodbridge, Suffolk: Boydell.

Le Thé de l'Europe ou les proprietez de la Veronique, tirées des observations des meilleurs Auteurs, & sur tout de celles de Mr. Francus, Medecin Allemand. 1704. Paris: Jean Boudot.

Tjaden, W. L. 1977. Sebastian Vaillant's Flora of Paris, Botanicon Pariense, 1727. *Journal of the Society for the Bibliography of Natural History* 8:11–27.

Tournefort, Joseph Pitton de. 1698. *Histoire des Plantes qui naissent aux environs de Paris, avec leur usage dans la Medecine*. Paris: Imprimerie Royale.

———. 1708. *Materia medica; or, a Description of Simple Medicines Generally us'd in Physick; Fully and accurately demonstrating their Uses, Virtues, and Places of Growth. As also, their Operating and Acting upon Human Bodies according to the Principles of the New Philosophy, Chymistry, and Mechanism. With an Appendix, shewing the Nature and Use of Mineral Waters*. London: J. H. for Andrew Bell.

———. 1717. *Relation d'un Voyage du Levant, fait par ordre du Roy. Contenant l'Histoire Ancienne & Moderne de plusieurs Isles de l'Archipel, de Constantinople, des Côtes de la Mer Noire, de l'Armenie, de la Georgie, des Frontieres de Perse & de l'Asie Mineure . . . Enrichie de Descriptions & de Figures d'un grand nombre de Plantes rares, de divers Animaux; Et de plusieurs Observations touchant l'Histoire Naturelle*. Paris: Imprimerie Royale.

Trinkle, Dennis. 1997. Noël-Antoine Pluche's *Le spectacle de la nature*: An Encyclopedic Best-Seller. *Studies on Voltaire and the Eighteenth Century* 358:93–134.

Tschudi, Jean-Baptiste-Louis-Théodore de. 1778. *De la transplantation, de la naturalisation, et du perfectionnement des Végétaux*. London: Lambert.

Viel, Claude. 1985. Duhamel du Monceau, naturaliste, physicien et chimiste. *Revue d'histoire des sciences* 38:55–71.

Voltaire, François Arouet de. 1950. *Correspondance avec les Tronchin*. Paris: Mercure de France.

Weulersse, Georges. 1910. *Le mouvement physiocratique en France de 1756 à 1770*. Paris: Félix Alcan.

———. 1950. *La physiocratie sous les ministères de Turgot et de Necker (1774–1781)*. Paris: Presses Universitaires de France.

———. 1985. *Les physiocrates à l'aube de la Révolution, 1781–1792*. Paris: Editions de l'E.H.E.S.S.

Whitaker, Katie. 1996. The Culture of Curiosity. In Jardine, Secord, and Spary 1996.

Wijnands, D. Onno. 1988. Hortus Auriaci: The Gardens of Orange and Their Place in Late Seventeenth-Century Botany and Horticulture. *Journal of Garden History* 8:61–86, 271–304.

Willemet, Remi, and Jean-François Coste. 1778. *Essais Botaniques, Chimiques et Pharmaceutiques, sur quelques Plantes indigènes, substituées avec succès, à des végétaux exotiques, auxquels on a joint des observations médicinales sur les mêmes objets*. Nancy: Veuve Leclerc.

The "Spirit of System" and the Fortunes of Physiocracy

Jessica Riskin

1. Physiocracy and Teleology

While debating the epistemological limits of mechanics, A. R. J. Turgot—philosophe, political economist, and finance minister to Louis XVI—wrote to the marquis de Condorcet, in a letter dated 18 May 1774, that impulsion could not account for the existence of movement in the universe because it presumed a prior source of motion. Any given push had to have been precipitated by a prior push. Moreover, daily experience established that matter in motion was always causally preceded by an act of will. Following the pushes back to their source, one invariably found an intelligence at work. Both to avoid an infinite regress and to be properly empirical, therefore, physics must ultimately arrive at teleological explanations. Turgot concluded, "The only principle that experience shows to be productive of movement is the will of intelligent beings . . . which is determined, not by motors, but by motives, not by mechanical causes, but by *final* causes."[1] Here was an interesting model of natural science to be espoused by one of the principal inventors of

Many thanks to Paul Christensen, Neil De Marchi, Margaret Schabas, and an anonymous reviewer for Duke University Press for incisive readings of earlier drafts of this essay, and to my coparticipants at the April 2002 *Oeconomies in the Age of Newton* conference at Duke University for invaluable responses to the work then in progress. The arguments in this essay are developed further in chapter 4 of my book, *Science in the Age of Sensibility: The Sentimental Empiricists of the French Enlightenment* (University of Chicago Press, 2002).

1. In Condorcet 1883, 172–73.

the so-called moral sciences, Enlightenment precursors of the modern social sciences. Turgot was closely connected with the circle of economists who named their moral science *physiocracy*, meaning "rule of nature," to suggest that political economy (and, by implication, each of the moral sciences) reduced to a natural science. Taking their cue from such gestures, historians writing on eighteenth-century economic theories in general, and on the ideas of the French physiocrats in particular, have often emphasized their naturalism.[2] But it is not enough to say that the physiocrats drew upon the methods of natural science, for these methods were themselves subject to heated controversy. One must therefore specify that the model for physiocracy was a certain kind of natural science, one that I will call "sentimental empiricism."

By this I mean a distinctive, Enlightenment mode of natural science that rooted knowledge, not in sensory experience alone, but in an inseparable fusion of physical sensation and moral sentiment, a union of experience and emotion residing in the Enlightenment ideal of sensibility.[3] Subscribers to this ideal assumed that to sense was to feel, and accordingly, around 1750, began to talk, write, and argue about the sentimental origins of knowledge. They supposed that nature was propelled, not by matter in motion, but by benign purpose. Therefore the science they promoted was antimechanist, and they found their foil in René Descartes's physics, which to sentimental empiricists epitomized a deplorably reductive, mechanist, dogmatic, and arrogant philosophy. A natural philosopher's business, they believed, was not to build ambitious rational systems, but to maintain a certain sensibility, an emotional sensitivity to nature's purposeful behavior. It was this sentimental view of nature and natural knowledge that informed physiocracy. Naturalism was common to the economic theories that arose during the latter part of the eighteenth century, particularly in France and Britain, a cluster of theories of which physiocracy was an early and influential member.[4] But naturalism in the sentimental-empiricist mode entered political economy through physiocracy, crucially shaping the theory and the surrounding controversy. According to the physiocrats' sentimental-empiricist logic,

2. See, for example, Fox-Genovese 1976, 9–10.

3. I have developed this argument more fully in Riskin 2002.

4. On the naturalism of classical economics in general and Adam Smith's economic thought in particular, see Mirowski 1994 and Ross 1995, 279–80. Sentimentalism was also a common feature. For an examination of the Enlightenment view that "economic life [was] . . . a matter of sentiment" and its implications for eighteenth-century economic theory, focusing on Condorcet and Smith, see Rothschild 2001.

tariffs, complex tax laws, industrial regulations, and currency manipulations constituted foolish attempts to impose an artificial, rational order on the economy.[5]

Using "sensibilist" science's nastiest word, they called mercantilist policy a "system." The phrase *spirit of system*, denoting the misguided inverse of sensibility, was drawn from the internecine battles of natural philosophers beginning around midcentury. In these battles, system-building—the construction of mathematical and mechanical systems to explain natural phenomena—had emerged as the evil opposite of a philosophy of sensitive responsiveness to nature's ways. Systems were arrogant, dogmatic attempts to impose one's own scheme on nature.

Actors' categories such as "spirit of system" and "system-builder" are difficult to read because they were polemical, not applied with rigor and consistency, but rather launched by everyone against everyone else. Their ubiquity reflects their power and the depth of the preoccupations to which they gave voice. Like most polemical phrases, these were neither straightforward descriptions of reality, nor utterly detached from actual practice. How, then, should intellectual and cultural historians treat them? If we cannot simply adopt them, we cannot dismiss them either: they are our raw materials. Actors' categories are both descriptions of a period and elements of it, and we must treat them in both ways simultaneously. Treating them as descriptions, we may accept what they tell us. But treating them as elements of the period they describe, we discover that their own position in that period undermines some of what they say. For example, according to actors' accounts, dogmatic system-building was a central tendency of Enlightenment science. But these same actors' accounts, by their very existence, indicate that an antipathy for rational systems was equally important. I therefore read the phrase *spirit of system* as the expression of a fundamental ambivalence at the heart of Enlightenment natural and moral science: as evidence, not only of their thoroughgoing rationalism, but also of an equally important countering tendency, sentimentalism. The two impulses, rational system-building and sentimentalist system-bashing, constituted a central dialectic of Enlightenment science.

The physiocrats beautifully exemplify this dialectic: they became primary targets of the epithet *spirit of system* though they had themselves been its original promulgators in political economy. They pronounced

5. "De l'état actuel" 1765, 220–21, 238; "Sur la prosperité" 1766, 3:2:266; "Réponse" 1767, 7:143.

mercantilism an "artificial system," a system with "no limits," a system "impossible to execute," a "system . . . [in which] all the errors touch and support one another." The abbé Baudeau, founder and editor of one of the main physiocratic journals, proclaimed that if such mercantilist "systems had never interfered, the ancient and primitive liberty . . . would still subsist; for it is evidently the natural state."[6] The spirit of system must give way, in the sciences of society as in natural science, to an empiricist sensitivity to nature's intentions.

François Quesnay, the physiocrats' founder, traced the origins of social life to primitive people's "*involuntary sensibility* to physical pleasure and pain," which induced them to provide for their own subsistence. To assure themselves of the "peaceful possession of the fruits of their labors," they needed "to live in society." Nature was therefore "the first teacher of social man." It was she who "wanted the reunion of men in society; it was she who dictated the essential conditions of this reunion; it is she finally who makes *sensible* to them the necessity of society, and that of the conditions to which they must submit in order for society to form and perpetuate itself" (Quesnay, in Mercier de la Rivière 1767, 610). Nature, the basis of sensibility and social life, should be the basis, too, of state policy.

How might nature govern the economy? Briefly, the physiocrats' "science" (as they called their economic theory) taught that all wealth originated in agriculture, and therefore in nature. Other areas of human endeavor, in particular manufacture and commerce, conserved value rather than creating it. In manufacture, the value of the inputs, raw materials and labor, equaled the value of the outputs, the resulting products. In commerce, products were exchanged for money or for other products of equal worth. Thus neither industry nor trade generated value—each merely transformed it.[7] Wealth originated exclusively in the agricultural surplus, which physiocrats termed the "net product," and the only way to suit taxation to the annual increase in wealth, and so be true to nature's

6. Mercier de la Rivière 1767, 527, 581, 575, 577, 560; Baudeau 1771, 716. See also Quesnay 1765, 744: "If each one reasons from his own particular point of view, the result is so many discordant systems harmful to the advancement of the science." The essay is written as a dialogue, and in this passage Quesnay adopted the voice of his adversaries.

7. "Here is the essential point, and the one most ignored or at least neglected in France: we have not even recognized the difference between the product of work that returns nothing but the price of the labor, and that of work that pays for the labor and procures revenues. As a result of this inattention we have preferred industry to agriculture, and commerce in manufactured goods to commerce in raw materials" (Quesnay 1757, 472).

rule, was to draw all taxes directly from the net product (Dupont de Nemours 1768, 550, 575–76).

Therefore the physiocrats advocated replacing the entire baroque tax structure of the Old Regime with an *impôt unique*, a single tax on land rent. A policy of taxing only land rent might seem disadvantageous to the proprietors, the very class who oversaw the generation of all new wealth according to physiocratic doctrine. But in fact, advocates of the *impôt unique* explained that the policy would benefit landowners first and foremost, as it would maximize their profits from the sales of their agricultural products.[8] The crucial physiocratic reform was the freeing of the grain trade (Quesnay 1757, 509). Until the mid-eighteenth century, the Crown imposed an elaborate array of restrictions on the market in grain: it prohibited export of grain to foreign countries, constrained its movement within the kingdom by means of permits and certificates, and disallowed its measurement, sale, or purchase outside of stipulated areas within each province. The Crown, towns, and provinces also levied tolls on the transit and sale of grain. The physiocrats proposed doing away with this whole structure of restrictions and tolls. They also espoused a mode of government by "legal despotism," in which the monarch and his administrators empirically derived and enacted the law as dictated by nature.[9] This doctrine was intended as a rebuke to the baron de Montesquieu's parliamentary theory of government, in which its functions were divided among mutually balancing bodies. The physiocrats judged such an arrangement of counterweights to be, like mercantilist economic policy, a "system"—"mechanical," artificial, and counter to the order of nature.[10]

To be sure, the physiocrats' policy recommendations did not spring fully formed from the brow of a philosophical movement. They responded to certain features of the Old Regime economy: first, that France was a predominantly agricultural country; second, that French agriculture was dominated by small-scale, impoverished, subsistence farming; and third, that the tax structure of the Old Regime had become increasingly chaotic, due largely to the nobility's successes at securing fiscal privileges and tax exemptions, and imposed an ever more crippling burden on peasants and on a new class whose interests the physiocrats sought

8. Fox-Genovese 1976, 58; Meek 1962, 25; Dakin [1939] 1965, 92–93.

9. See Mercier de la Rivière 1767, chaps. 18–21.

10. Quesnay 1767, 949; Turgot, letter to Dupont de Nemours, 10 May 1771, in Turgot 1913, 3:486–87. See also Weulersse 1910, 2:52–55.

to advance, reform-minded agricultural entrepreneurs. The physiocratic program accordingly had two purposes: to simplify fiscal policy and to channel resources into agriculture (Meek 1962, 23–27). However, if economic problems inspired physiocratic policy, it was the language and arguments of sentimental empiricism that provided the medium in which the physiocrats developed and defended their proposals. The ideals of sensibility shaped discussion of physiocratic reforms, not only among the philosophes but in court and in parlement, and defined the terms in which these reforms were both instituted and opposed.

At the heart of physiocratic doctrine was a naturalist theory of value. The wealth of the land was "annually reborn"; it was "renascent." Money was "sterile." It could not constitute the "true wealth of a nation" because "money does not breed money." Value could be bred, generated, born, but never made. This accounted for its unique origin in agriculture: "industry and mercantile trade" constituted "only an artificial realm."[11] In their naturalization of value, the physiocrats differed from their contemporaries, who located value in conventional, man-made bases: money, population, and—particularly after the 1776 publication of Adam Smith's *Wealth of Nations*—labor. Rejecting the labor theory of value, Quesnay (1766, 912) warned that it was artificial, abstract, a "system," a "vain and frivolous prejudice," and potentially "a dangerous and perfidious error."

Smith, for his part, frequently counseled against the spirit of system and insinuatingly called Quesnay a "very speculative philosopher."[12] Still, he deemed physiocracy "the nearest approximation to the truth" so far and may even have thought of dedicating *The Wealth of Nations* to Quesnay.[13] Nevertheless Smith rejected the physiocrats' central theoretical claim, that wealth originated in nature. For him, economic value was man-made. The naturalism of Smith's economy was thus of a more limited sort than the physiocrats' naturalism. Smith assumed an analogy between nature, governed by natural laws, and economic life, propelled

11. Quesnay 1767, 967–69. For a thorough examination of Quesnay's and the physiocrats' theory of value, and an argument that it encompassed notions of the exchange value of commodities despite its naturalism, see Vaggi 1987.

12. See Smith 1790, bk. 4, chap. 1, para. 11; bk. 6, sec. 2, para. 40; bk. 6, sec. 2, para. 42; and Smith 1789, bk. 5, chap. 1, para. 154, and bk. 4, chap. 9, para. 28 (on Quesnay as a "speculative philosopher").

13. Smith 1789, bk. 4, chap. 9, para. 39; Stewart [1793] 1854-60, sec. 3, para. 12; Ross 1995, 278–79.

by laws of human nature. But the physiocrats made their economy an integral part of the natural world, its naturalism literal and absolute.[14]

Wealth in physiocratic theory was a natural fluid similar to those with which contemporary physics was rife: electricity, magnetism, light, heat, gravitational ether.[15] Quesnay drew up a *Tableau économique* to show the flow of the natural fluid of wealth through the economy, originating in the agricultural surplus and conserved through every subsequent transaction. The *Tableau* made a great impression among reformist philosophes and became emblematic of physiocracy.[16] Observing that Quesnay was a doctor and surgeon who had, moreover, written several treatises on bloodletting, historians have often identified the circulation of the blood as the model for his theory of the circulation of money.[17] In fact, in the preceding century, even before William Harvey's demonstration that blood circulated, political economists already liked to call money the blood of the body politic (see Larrère 1992, 107–8). Physiocratic authors did revisit the old analogy, but only in passing (see, for example, Turgot [1766] 1997, sec. 68). Harvey's hydraulics of the circulatory system were not very useful to them.

Their wealth was a fluid more like Benjamin Franklin's electrical fire, which did not act mechanically, but instead pursued its own goals and tendencies, preferring, for example, water and metals to air and glass, and striving above all to maintain itself in a state of even and harmonious distribution.[18] The physiocrats were Franklin's first friends and promoters in France and were very impressed by his electrical physics, as was he, in turn, by their economic physics. This mutual admiration proved fruitful on both sides. For Franklin, it was an entrée into the field of political economy. And for the physiocrats, it provided something crucial to the development of their rigorously naturalist moral science: a

14. On Smith's rejection of the physiocratic principle that wealth originated solely in agriculture, and on the different, analogical naturalism of Smith's theory of value, see Ross 1995, 216–27, 238–39, 281–82.

15. On the so-called subtle fluids of eighteenth-century physics, particularly electricity, as sources of models for understanding wealth, see Schabas 2001. On the naturalism of Quesnay's *Tableau*, see Vaggi 2002, 81.

16. Quesnay 1758; Fox-Genovese 1976, 246.

17. See Barre 1966, 1:34–35; Banzhaf 2000, 517–51; and Foley 1973. For a thorough examination of the physiological and chemical models for Quesnay's theory of circulation, see Christensen 1994.

18. For a close analysis of equilibrium and disequilibrium in Quesnay's *Tableau économique*, see Eltis 2002. On Quesnay's theory of growth and its role in the development of the *Tableau*, see Charles 2000.

congenial model of nature and of natural science, one that ascribed moral purposes to nature and privileged these purposes in scientific explanation.[19]

Once born from the land, wealth spread itself through the economy "by an influence as rapid as electrical fire."[20] The chief natural purpose guiding the flow of wealth through Quesnay's *Tableau* was the same as that directing Franklin's electrical physics, namely to maintain an equilibrium. Pierre-Samuel Dupont de Nemours, another leading physiocrat, emphasized the necessary symmetry of commercial exchanges. "We will repeat incessantly," Dupont de Nemours (1764, 162) wrote, "that all trade assumes equilibrium, a balance of sales and purchases." Those who failed to understand this fact, and tried to buy without selling, were lucky "that the thing is impossible." When physiocratic authors did call upon hydraulic and mechanical analogies to explain such principles, it was not to reduce the economy to a machine but, on the contrary, to invoke the hidden operation of natural purpose even in mechanical arrangements. For example, Dupont de Nemours argued that buying and selling were inextricably connected as two sides of a single spring, which cannot restore itself to its proper state without simultaneously contracting the expanded side and expanding the contracted side (162).

Similarly insisting upon the tendency of the economy to seek a balance, Turgot wrote that although "the different uses of capital result in very unequal products," this inequality did not prevent the products from "establishing a kind of equilibrium, as between two fluids of unequal weight that occupy two branches of an inverted siphon." The fluids' appearance would be asymmetrical, but "the height of one could not augment without the other climbing as well" (Turgot [1766] 1997, sec. 87). Behind the operation of springs, siphons, and market exchanges lay nature's eternal tendency toward balance. The *Tableau* represented the "basis of moral order on earth," an "immutable" order from which "Sovereigns and Subjects can only stray . . . to their disadvantage." As Quesnay and his closest collaborator, the marquis de Mirabeau (1764, xviii), explained, "perfect government is not of human institution." Governments

19. For a fuller development of this argument regarding the mutual influence of Benjamin Franklin and the physiocrats, see Riskin 2002. On Franklin and the physiocrats more generally, see Chinard 1955 and Aldridge 1957.

20. Dupont de Nemours 1764, 120–21. Christensen (1994, 277) emphasizes the importance of "a highly subtle and active ether—the matter of fire" as a model for Quesnay's understanding of the movement of wealth.

must simply allow the natural flow represented in the *Tableau* to take place unimpeded. Wealth would then follow its own course from agriculture through industry and commerce, and back to agriculture to renew the cycle.

The physiocrats' naturalization of economic value provoked criticism even among their political allies. Etienne Bonnot de Condillac, for example, supported the same economic policies as they did; in particular, he favored freedom of commerce, but for opposite reasons. The physiocrats, as we have seen, argued for freedom of commerce on the ground that nature, through agriculture, was the source of all new wealth and must accordingly be allowed to determine the annual tax, which must therefore be drawn directly from the agricultural surplus. Condillac, in contrast, rooted value, not in nature, but in social convention.[21] He opposed the tendency to "regard value as an absolute quality, inherent in things independently of the judgments we make." The value of a thing, Condillac said, arose primarily from assessments of its "utility," the needs and uses people had for it. He therefore argued for free trade on the basis of the social, rather than natural, origins of value.

Condillac's conventional origin of value implied that commerce was not sterile, despite the claims of the physiocrats; exchanges between people who valued what they received over what they traded always maximized value. Taxes would inhibit such exchanges, and it was for this reason, and not the sterility of commerce, that Condillac opposed them.[22] Because judgments were at the source of all wealth, a proper general understanding of the economy would bring about a properly functioning economy. In Condillac's view, such an understanding was best achieved through a careful use of language. He insisted, for example, upon the distinction between "values" and "sums," the confusion of which allowed bankers to make their profits: equal sums had different values in different places, thus one could make a profit in value through an exchange

21. On the importance of "sociability" in Condillac's economic theory, see Larrère 1992, 66–69. On the subjectivity of Condillac's theory of value, see Knight 1968, 238–39. Others among the physiocrats' opponents, including the abbé Galiani and J.-J.-L. Graslin, gave similarly subjective definitions of value. Graslin (1767, 51) wrote, "Wealth is the thing to which value is attributed; the thing is not wealth except in proportion to this attribution. But the attribution of value is foreign to the nature of the thing; its principle is in man uniquely, it grows and shrinks with the needs of man and disappears with him." See Airiau 1965, 96–101.

22. Condillac 1776, 254–59, 249, 367, 320–21, 369–70. On this difference between Condillac and the physiocrats, and for an argument that the physiocrats missed an opportunity in categorically rejecting Condillac's views, see Eltis 1995, esp. 231–34.

of equal sums. Condillac surmised that "bankers affect an obscure language" in order to prevent "people from seeing their operations clearly."[23] Economic health lay in clarity of expression and public instruction, not, as the physiocrats would have it, in allowing nature to govern.

For similar reasons David Hume disapproved of the physiocrats, rather vehemently. In a 1769 letter to the abbé Morellet, a physiocratic fellow traveler though not an orthodox believer, he urged "thunder [the physiocrats], and crush them, and pound them, and reduce them to dust and ashes! They are, indeed, the set of men the most chimerical and arrogant that now exist."[24] The physiocrats so trusted nature over human judgment, Hume charged, that they were willing to sacrifice political to economic freedom with their doctrine of "legal despotism." In contrast, he associated a healthy economy with benevolent politics, not unhampered nature. Individual autonomy far outweighed natural facts like soil and climate. In fact, he maintained that barren soil and inclement weather had actually benefited English peasants because difficult conditions gave rise to an advantageous social system. Having a more complicated task than their French or Italian counterparts, English peasants received larger funds and longer leases. Their independence bred industry and inventiveness (Hume [1752] 1898, 297–98).

Like Condillac, who traced economic prosperity to clear language, and Hume, who located it in a social system that fostered autonomy, Jacques Necker, the Genevan banker who served as controller-general of finances during the 1770s and 1780s, also assigned a cultural rather than natural origin to economic value. In keeping with physiocracy, Necker denied that the accumulation of money was the measure of a state's strength (money was not a good in itself, but only a "sign of the good truly useful and agreeable to men"), but he then parted company with the physiocrats. He made the size of a state's population the index of its success and traced population growth to happiness, arguing that a population increased when there was "a happy harmony among the different classes in society." Lifting export barriers might maximize revenue, but not happiness. If wine were consumed at home rather than exported abroad, Necker surmised, the "French nation would not be less happy." To foster happiness, and an increased population, administrators should

23. Condillac 1776, 302–4, 308, 301. On John Horne Tooke's similar association of clarity of expression with political health, see Smith 1984, 110–53.

24. Cited in Skinner 1993, 247.

focus their efforts on perfecting domestic "political relations" through a harmonious distribution of goods (Necker 1775, 2:216, 219, 357–58).

In particular, their chief duty, described in a letter from Necker to Sartine dated 14 February 1778, was to insure subsistence: "The subsistence of the people is the most essential object that must occupy the administration."[25] During his three terms as finance minister, Necker introduced various social and administrative reforms—lifting the mortmain on royal domains, reducing the number of tax farmers,[26] introducing new provincial assemblies—but he did not relinquish his commitment to the principle that provisioning was the job of administration, not nature.[27]

Finally, Antoine Lavoisier—a tax farmer and economic theorist as well as chemist, academician, and gunpowder commissioner—also settled upon conventional rather than natural sources of prosperity. He had started off in search of natural ones. But after eight years of experimentation on his farm at Freschines, Lavoisier reported political rather than strictly agronomic findings to the Paris Society of Agriculture. He had begun with a principle informed by the new "agronomy," an experimental science of agriculture founded around midcentury by the chemist and botanist Henri-Louis Duhamel du Monceau:[28] successful farming required fertilization by manure, which meant animals. Lavoisier argued that French farmers had too few animals; the greater success of English agriculture was due to the English emphasis on raising and selling livestock rather than wheat. This allowed the English to plant clover and turnips every third year, which they could use profitably as nourishment for the animals, rather than leaving their fields to lie fallow. The English system had the further advantage of supplying farmers with plenty of manure to fertilize their crops. To increase the numbers of animals on his farm, in keeping with the recommendations of the new agronomy, Lavoisier had planted "artificial prairies" with grass for grazing. But his improvements produced few results, and he now said that he "recognized

25. Archives nationales, F11*1, fol. 258, cited in Kaplan 1984, 23. Kaplan writes that except "for two brief interludes, this commitment to the consumer-people of France was the uncontested tenet of public policy during the old regime. It was founded on the conviction that social stability could be guaranteed only by guaranteeing the food supply" (23).

26. Tax farmers (*fermiers généraux*) were members of the Tax Farm, the corporate body to whom the Crown contracted tax collection under the Old Regime.

27. On Necker's ministries, see Hardman 1995, 133–43, 162–67; and Harris 1979, 1986.

28. The seminal texts were Duhamel du Monceau 1750–56, 1762. On Duhamel du Monceau, the origins of agronomy, and the new agriculture, see Bourde 1953; Viel 1985, 55–71; and Dinechin 1999.

with pain" that no matter "what care, what economies" cultivators made, they could never hope for a return of more than 5 percent.

The problem was not insufficient food for the animals but "a moral obstacle, more difficult to vanquish than most physical obstacles." As he would repeat continually during the early years of the Revolution, Lavoisier now concluded that it was "principally from our institutions and our laws that arise the obstacles to the progress of agriculture." These obstacles included the arbitrary and fluctuating taille and the corvée, which "humiliat[ed] the taxpayer" and "punish[ed] industry"; feudal tithes that carried off more than half, and sometimes all, of the net yield of a region; the excise taxes on salt and tobacco, which involved "inhuman and indecent inspections that . . . tend to render odious the authority" of the Crown; monopolies on milling, which led to poor quality and loss of grain from faulty practices and subjected the people to the greed of the millers; and the prohibition on the export of grain, which "limit[ed] the industry of the cultivator and prohibit[ed] him, in a sense, from harvesting more wheat than the nation could consume."[29] Although Lavoisier identified the same impediments to prosperity as the physiocrats, he differed from them in that he assessed these obstacles as political not only in their origins, but in their effects. The physiocrats held that taxation and regulation impeded the operations of nature, but Lavoisier argued that these institutions distorted the social conditions necessary for the production of wealth.[30]

There were many, then, even among those who advocated some of the same reformist policies as the physiocrats, who did not harness their recommendations to an economic philosophy that naturalized wealth. This was the physiocrats' innovation. In making wealth a natural fluid like electricity, magnetism, light, and heat in contemporary physics, they armed themselves with the arguments of sentimental empiricism: that the economy was not a mechanical arrangement to be rationally grasped and deliberately manipulated, but an organic, balance-seeking process whose flow must be left unimpeded; that good administration was a matter of sensitivity to this organic process. These arguments shaped

29. In Lavoisier 1862–93: "Assemblée d'Orléans" (1788), 6:256–58, 260–61; "Instruction" (1787), 6:205, 248; "Expériences" (1788), 2:814–16, 819–21; "Encouragements" (1787), 6:218–19. On Lavoisier's identification of institutional obstacles to economic progress, and institutional remedies, see also Poirier 1996, chap. 14.

30. "What is interesting is that it should have been a scientist who came to these conclusions. For what could science do about any of these, the real problems?" (Gillispie 1980, 387; cf. Bensaude-Vincent 1993, 230).

the meaning of physiocratic policies such as freedom of commerce. In Condillac's hands, freedom of commerce expressed something quite different: a conviction that value was not an objectively measurable quantity but the product of subjective human needs, uses, and judgments. With Smith, freedom of commerce became something else again: a response to central tendencies of human nature. To the physiocrats, however—among the earliest advocates of a policy of free trade, and promulgators of what has remained that policy's slogan for over two centuries, "laissez-faire, laissez-passer"[31]—freedom of commerce was the policy of an administration sensitive to a purpose-driven natural world.

Extending the language and principles of sentimental empiricism to political economy, the physiocrats armed themselves with a powerful set of arguments. They also made themselves vulnerable to the same arguments in the hands of their enemies.

2. The "Spirit of System" and the Disgrace of Turgot

During his disastrous tenure as finance minister from 1774 to 1776, Turgot tried assiduously to enact physiocratic economic reforms but was hampered by an increasingly fervent opposition. The most common and damning accusation it leveled against him and the physiocrats was that they were guilty of the "spirit of system." Appropriating the physiocrats' best rhetorical weapon, their opponents made *system* their own catchword and rendered *physiocratic* synonymous with *systematic*. By the time of Turgot's disgrace, not only natural philosophers and economic reformers but the parlement and even the king spoke their arguments in the language of sentimental empiricism.

To understand the meaning of the epithet *system* during Turgot's battle with the parlement, we must begin with its emergence as a term of censure around midcentury. In the autumn of 1748 the Cartesian former secretary of the *Académie des Sciences*, Dortous de Mairan, addressed an indignant paper to the assembly. He had had his fill of the sudden vogue of system-bashing: "System and chimera seem to be synonymous today.

31. Quesnay, "Lettre de M. Alpha" (1767), in Quesnay 1958, 940. Quesnay's usage of the phrase was not the first, nor was Vincent de Gournay's (to whom Quesnay himself attributed it). But it was the physiocrats who transformed *laisser faire* into a slogan. On the history of the phrase, and the physiocrats' role in promulgating it, see Beer 1939, 89, 122; Oncken 1886; and Quesnay 1888, 671–72 n. 1.

'It's a system,' is often the whole criticism of a book, and to declare oneself against systems, and emphasize that what one offers the public is not one, has become a commonplace of prefaces." Mairan (1749, v, vii) identified a certain false modesty in protestations that the human intelligence was too feeble to achieve a rational understanding of nature: "Those who condemn us to an eternal ignorance of first principles, have they so perfectly seen the heart of things? . . . One must know a lot to decide thus the extent of human knowledge, present and future." The initial targets of the slur *spirit of system* had been the mechanical systems of Cartesian physics, but the field grew to embrace all branches of natural and moral science. The year after Mairan's speech, Condillac ([1749] 1798, 207–8) wrote, "If there is a field where we have been warned against systems, it is politics." When, in a letter to Gabriel Cramer on 21 September of the same year, Jean Le Rond d'Alembert described Montesquieu's *L'Esprit des lois* (1748) as "the physics of Descartes applied to politics," he clearly intended no compliment.[32]

Although even he occasionally used *Descartes* as an epithet, d'Alembert was worried about the vogue against systematic philosophy. In 1751 he urged the members of the *Académie* that "having learned to be suspicious of our industry, we must not carry our suspicions to an excess." Like Mairan, d'Alembert suggested that dogmatic skepticism was no better than other forms of dogmatism. It was "often as dangerous to pronounce upon what [the mind] . . . cannot do, as upon what it can" (d'Alembert 1751b, 6, 18–19). The first volume of Denis Diderot's and d'Alembert's *Encyclopédie* appeared in the midst of these polemics, and d'Alembert had the delicate task of writing its methodological preliminary discourse. He reached for compromise. The "spirit of system" invoked arbitrary metaphysical hypotheses, he conceded, and that was bad. But this pernicious tendency must be distinguished from the good "systematic spirit," which rigorously reduced as many phenomena to as few principles as possible. D'Alembert's attempts at conciliation often resulted in confusion. On the one hand, he wrote that "vain" geometry consisted of "mind games," its axioms empty tautologies. On the other hand, the mathematical sciences were the only source of certainty about nature. They alone were destined "always to perfect themselves."[33]

32. Cited in Hankins 1970, 81.

33. D'Alembert 1751a, 89, 92–93, 95, 91, 155–56. D'Alembert's insistence on the status of the mathematical sciences was polemical, since the debate over system-building was marked by an exodus away from mathematics. Buffon, Voltaire, and Diderot, all of whom had had an early

D'Alembert cited Condillac, who, like Mairan and d'Alembert himself, warned those who denounced system-building against falling "to the other extreme, and asserting that there is no knowledge at all to which we may aspire." Condillac had proposed pure mathematics and technical languages as good systems,[34] and d'Alembert (1751a, 155–56) followed suit, arguing that safety lay in rigorous calculation, which was "seldom found in those frivolous conjectures we honor with the name of systems." Throughout his articles in the *Encyclopédie*, d'Alembert sprinkled similarly mixed messages. In "Geometry" he wrote that although this science had "all kinds of detractors among us," its undeniable truths perhaps provided the only means for victims of despotism to "[shake] off the yoke of oppression" (d'Alembert 1757, 628). And in "Expérimental" he surmised that "this would be the place to make some observations on the abuse of calculations and hypotheses in Physics, if that object had not already been filled" amply by other writers. Perhaps some natural philosophers did misuse mathematical and mechanical reasoning, but "finally, what do men not abuse?" (d'Alembert 1756, 92–93).

Yet Mairan's, d'Alembert's, and Condillac's protestations fell upon deaf ears. Indeed, although Condillac's complaint in his *Traité des systèmes* was that most supposed systems were unworthy of the name, his contemporaries took the *Traité* as their rallying cry against the spirit of system.[35] Diderot, for one, was not pleased by d'Alembert's ambivalent and often approving attitude toward system-building.[36] *De l'interprétation de la nature* (1753) was Diderot's published rebuttal to d'Alembert's *Discours préliminaire*.[37] It began with a poetic celebration of raw experience: "It is about nature that I am going to write," Diderot announced, and to do so properly, "I will let the thoughts flow from my pen, in the same order in which the objects present themselves to my reflection." He identified his subject as "that phenomenon that seems to occupy all of our philosophers, and to divide them into two classes," the phenomenon of systematic speculation. Citing the naturalist Georges

interest in the discipline, became disenchanted with it in the years leading up to midcentury, and Diderot (1755, 49) reported "a general movement toward natural history, chemistry, and experimental physics." See Hankins 1970, 99.

34. Condillac [1749] 1798, 43, 329, 401; Hankins 1970, 107–8.

35. See "Système" 1765, 777; and Knight 1968.

36. Pappas 1972, 1235; Hankins 1970, chap. 4. Buffon disapproved of d'Alembert's discourse as well. See Roger 1989, 264–65.

37. Hankins 1970, 89–90; Pappas 1972, 1235.

Buffon, Diderot affirmed that mathematical truths were empty tautologies. He called mathematics a game, an affair of mere convention, and, notoriously, predicted the imminent demise of geometry.

Diderot exempted from eternal obscurity those "happy geometers" (d'Alembert) who maintained an interest in the beaux arts (Diderot 1753, 177–80). This was a concession to friendship, an attempt to find redemption in d'Alembert's mostly systematic spirit. Some years later, in *Le rève de d'Alembert*, Diderot made a fictional d'Alembert, lost in a philosophic dream, recognize the unsystematic vitality of a swarm of bees as the basis of all things in nature, animate and inanimate. In the lucidity of his dream, the d'Alembert character accepts Diderot's principle of "sensibility," as a "general and essential quality of matter," with its implication that even a "stone feels."[38] The systematic mind was closed to this vibrant truth, Diderot implied: the capacity of all things in nature to feel.

It is an old theme of Enlightenment historiography that the philosophes used natural-philosophical words, especially *nature* and *reason*, as coded promotions of social and political reform.[39] But this observation does not do justice to the complexity of the exchange between natural and moral science. To start with, terms and models traveled in both directions. The physiocrats and their fellow travelers provide countless examples of this mutual borrowing: Franklin's theory of negative and positive electricity, which so influenced the physiocrats, was itself shaped by a mode of moral reasoning in terms of conservation of harms and goods;[40] Lavoisier's new chemical language, which served as a model at the end of the century in discussions of civic education, was founded in his own and others' (notably Condillac's) reflections on pedagogy;[41] and Turgot, as noted at the beginning of this essay, emphasized in a letter to Condorcet of 18 May 1774 that in physics, as in daily life, mechanical causes must ultimately give way to final causes, "motors" be preempted by "motives."[42]

38. Diderot 1767b, 291–92; 1767a, 257–58.

39. Cassirer 1951, 248; Gay 1966–69, 2: chap. 3; Baker 1990, 159. For a contrasting view of the relation between scientific explanation and political authority, see Gillispie 1980, 549.

40. I discuss the moralism of Franklin's electrical theory in Riskin 1998a and 2002, chaps. 3 and 4.

41. I treat the relation among Lavoisier's new chemical nomenclature, revolutionary theories of civic education, and the controversies surrounding each in Riskin 1998b and 2002, chap. 7.

42. In Condorcet 1883, 172–73. See Riskin 2002, chap. 4.

Thus, language and models traveled both directions between natural and moral science. One must also take account of the versatility of these borrowings and, in this instance, of political rhetoric drawn from the language of natural science. For one thing, by the 1770s, all wanted nature on their side, so the arguments of natural science served both ends of the political spectrum, reformers and conservatives alike.[43] For another, this language included negative slogans that were at least as powerful as the positive ones; witness the word *system*. Natural philosophers' terms of opprobrium for themselves and one another were effective, and they spread quickly from philosophy to politics. Peter Gay (1966–69, 1:4–5) has called the philosophes a bickering family whose criticisms of one another provided the counter-Enlightenment with its most persuasive claims. The central family quarrel of the second half of the century, the quarrel over sensibility and system-building, provided political slogans that were both potent and versatile, serving the needs of reformist administrators and of their critics as well.

Turgot's tenure as controller-general of finances from 1774 to 1776, the first years of Louis XVI's reign, was the philosophes' moment of closest involvement with the court and the height of their political power. Turgot had served as intendant of the Limousin, one of the poorest regions of France, for the previous thirteen years. There he had established a laboratory of enlightened political economy and administration, successfully enacting the essentials of the physiocrats' program.[44] He had reformed the tax system, compiling a land register and lifting feudal taxes (the taille, from which the clergy and nobility had been exempt, and the corvée, a tax of labor on unlanded peasants for the maintenance of roads). He had also maintained a local free trade in grain through difficult conditions with good results.[45]

In 1763 and 1764, successive finance ministers had issued decrees freeing first domestic and then foreign commerce in grain. These were initially well received, but beginning in 1765, there was a sequence of bad harvests, and grain prices began to rise. High prices brought

43. Kaplan (1976, 2:696) wrote that in the political history of grain regulation, "parlementary politics" were "much more nuanced than is generally supposed." Parlementarians treated "political, social and economic questions without reference to the narrow range of motives usually ascribed to them."

44. Concerning Turgot's intendance in the Limousin, see Dakin [1939] 1965 and Maurepas and Boulant 1996, 345–46.

45. For a discussion of these enlightened administrative measures, see Dakin [1939] 1965, chap. 7.

extensive popular resistance to the free commerce laws, disobedience on the part of municipal authorities, and opposition by the Parlement of Paris and by provincial parlements, all of whom demanded a return to the old laws. This opposition to a free market in grain culminated in 1770 in a resumption of traditional trade restrictions. But Turgot received a special dispensation from the court to continue enforcing the free commerce laws of 1763 and 1764 in the Limousin, where the bad harvests had brought famine. In order to bring grain into the region, Turgot offered incentives to the merchants: he insured their losses, guaranteed their capital advances, and, in addition, promised them bounties. The result was that 800,000 livres worth of grain were brought into the Limousin during the famine years of 1769 and 1770 and sold at a loss of 5 percent as compared with a 30 percent loss on grain transactions in Paris.[46] Thus Turgot had supplied the physiocrats and other reformist philosophes with a modest but significant track record. In 1774, with the death of Louis XV and the accession of his adolescent grandson to the throne, reformist administrators such as the comte de Maurepas, then minister of state, saw the chance for Turgot to apply their program on a grander scale.

One of Turgot's first acts as finance minister, in 1774, was to issue an edict freeing domestic commerce in grain. The edict left in place all restrictions on foreign trade and on trade in Paris and was essentially a reenactment of the 1763 law.[47] Like the 1763 law, Turgot's edict was initially quietly received in parlement and in the provinces. But once again, in 1774, a poor harvest sent prices up, and, as had been the case a decade earlier, high prices brought widespread opposition to free commerce, which culminated in the spring of 1775 in the bread riots known as the *guerre des farines*. Turgot responded in part by offering bounties to merchants who agreed to import grain and by announcing an amnesty for those rioters who returned home. However, he also threatened to arrest those who did not—almost six hundred people were arrested and two were publicly executed—and quartered troops in the towns to enforce his edict. Where inducement failed, he fell back on force and used

46. See Dakin [1939] 1965, 104–10; and Poirier 1999, 125–32. Meanwhile, Turgot also established a system of social welfare in his region. He issued a decree requiring each parish to convene an assembly to organize poor relief. These assemblies were to set up voluntary subscription lists or taxes to provide the poor with food, money, and work. Turgot himself set up soup kitchens and public works projects, including a road works that produced three hundred miles of roadway (Dakin [1939] 1965, 112–17; Poirier 1999, 127–28).

47. See Morilhat 1988, 39–40; and Dakin [1939] 1965, 177–79.

it unflinchingly. When the *guerre des farines* was over, he proceeded to expand the free trade in grain with twenty-three new regulations eliminating taxes and suppressing the privileges that created monopolies.[48]

In the meantime, however, the Parlement of Paris had begun to oppose Turgot and his policies, demanding that the king reduce and fix the price of grain (Dakin [1939] 1965, 185–88). The members of parlement had abundant reason to dislike Turgot, with his repeated insistence upon free commerce against parliamentary opposition and his affiliation with the antiparliamentarian physiocrats. In the heated atmosphere of the *guerre des farines*, they, and others, began a campaign against him. Turgot's opponents, both within and outside the parlement, shared a common language: they accused Turgot of being "systematic," lost in a dogmatic dream of how the economy should operate, insensitive to the nuance and complexity of the real world. By common consensus among his contemporaries, Turgot was a system-builder. This verdict pursued the physiocrats and Turgot throughout his ministry and into his fall from power, becoming the slogan of the campaign against him.[49]

As early as the summer of 1774, when Maurepas first proposed Turgot to the new king for the position of controller-general of finances, Louis XVI replied doubtfully that he feared Turgot was "quite systematic." Maurepas responded with irritation that "none of those you might ask would be exempt from this criticism. . . . You will perhaps see that his systems reduce to ideas you find correct." Then, during the period before his official appointment, Turgot's close friend and advisor, the abbé Véri, promoted him by seeking occasions for him to "purge himself of the coloring of a man of systems."[50]

These accusations took on new force in the wake of a treatise by Necker, criticizing the physiocrats' economic philosophy in general and

48. Dakin [1939] 1965, 181–90; Baker 1975, 61; Rudé 1964, 30.

49. "The opposition," according to Weulersse (1950, 223; 1985, 349), incessantly "reproached the Economists for their spirit of system." Poirier (1999, 280–81) similarly observes that by the end of 1775, a profusion of "songs, pamphlets, and epigrams described [Turgot] as an encyclopedist, a man of systems, a stubborn type capable of driving the state to its demise rather than renouncing his ideas." Ironically, while the physiocrats' allies were often practitioners (proprietors or grain traders) rather than theoreticians, the physiocrats' enemies, those who so deplored the spirit of system, tended to be philosophes. Diderot, for example, was a stern critic of the physiocrats and their friends, accusing them of "abstract" reasoning (Kaplan 1976, 2:687–88, 697, 608).

50. Véri [1774–81] 1928, 1:160, 173–74 (entries for 9 and 13 August 1774).

Turgot's (limited) implementation of it in particular, entitled *Sur la législation et le commerce des grains*. Necker's attack was published with Turgot's overconfident blessing in 1775, at the height of the *guerre des farines*.[51] In the work, Necker (1775, 212–13) decried "men who meditate in their study" and contended that truth "refuses any simple or general notion, surrounding itself with exceptions, reservations, and modifications." The abbé Morellet summed up Necker's work as a tissue of "middling and moderate opinions, and some declamations against the spirit of system, that is the whole work." Another critic concurred: "M. Necker is like all Writers who combat systems, destroying much more easily than he builds."[52] But others found the treatise persuasive, and it became enormously popular.[53] "Wherever our steps carry us in a rioting city," Mirabeau wrote during the *guerre des farines*, "everywhere there is bitterness . . . against people of system."[54] Véri observed that a "furious cry" had arisen among "a class of people in the capital" labeling the freedom of commerce a "*dangerous system, a famishing system*," and that the same people were calling to Maurepas to save "the State against a systematic head."[55]

Finally the abbé Baudeau, a physiocrat and friend of Turgot, having tired of all the talk of systems, published the following anecdote in his *Chronique secrète*: when a lady in the court accused Turgot of system-building, Baudeau retorted, "Yes, Madam, he is systematic, that is to say his ideas are well examined and joined by principles; as that is what the word *systematic* means. Ah! Do you believe, then, that to govern a realm like France, one must have ideas that are desultory?"[56] His words had been foreshadowed over a decade earlier by Turgot's own lament that "any man who thinks has a system," and yet "this name, 'man of systems,' has become a sort of weapon."[57] *Man of systems* would become Turgot's political epitaph. Shortly after his disgrace, a memoir writer

51. Véri [1774–81] 1928, 1:283 (entry for 10 May 1775).

52. Morellet 1988 (for the year 1775), 202; Bachaumont 1780–89, 8:19 (entry for 10 April 1775).

53. Baker (1975, 63) calls Necker's treatise "a patiently undogmatic appeal for a more pragmatic approach to matters of social legislation than Turgot's rational convictions would allow."

54. Mirabeau, "Discours de la rentrée," 1776, cited in Weulersse 1950, 35.

55. Véri [1774–81] 1928, 1:286 (entry for 26 May 1775), 412 (entry for 20 February 1776).

56. Baudeau, *Chronique secrète*, 7 July 1774; cited in Weulersse 1950, 35.

57. Turgot 1759, 618–19. In Dupont de Nemours's edition of Turgot's works, the second part of the quote is replaced by "a man without a system or any linkage in his ideas could only be an imbecile or a lunatic" (Turgot 1759, 619 n).

reported that "Turgot's enemies do not stop letting loose against him" and insisting that his "views" were "too systematic."[58]

Historians have echoed contemporary analyses of Turgot's disgrace.[59] But this is worth reexamining. It was Turgot, after all, who recommended in a letter to Condorcet of 27 October 1772 that natural philosophers look beyond nature's "motors" to her "motives." It was he again who wrote, in another letter to Condorcet (13 November 1772), that geometry would never capture the atomic structure of matter, just as mechanism could never explain motion.[60] Nor did Turgot ever entirely accept the physiocrats' system, although he was sympathetic to the essentials of their program.[61] He was often severe with his friend Dupont de Nemours for his orthodoxy, criticizing, in a letter of 18 November 1767, Dupont's *La physiocratie* as "too systematic, too tight, too abridged by essential omissions."[62]

Turgot also mocked Dupont de Nemours's loyalty to the physiocrats' "master," Quesnay. In a letter to Dupont of 26 December 1769, Turgot wrote irreverently that "criticism based upon facts is not the strength of the Master" and deplored the publication of one treatise by Quesnay as "truly the scandal of scandals, it's the Sun crusting over!"[63] Turgot reviled the physiocratic doctrine of "legal despotism" to ensure proper

58. Bachaumont 1780–89, 9:86 (entry for 16 April 1776).

59. See, for example, Gillispie 1980, 16–17; and Cornette 1995, 64. Cf. Dakin [1939] 1965, 282–85. Dakin defended Turgot against charges of system-building, writing that Turgot was a sensationalist who succeeded in giving "to sensational philosophy a richer and . . . less ambiguous meaning than that with which Locke and many of his followers had endowed it." Lockeans, seeking to make the thin database of "immediate experience" support the full weight of their philosophy, inevitably fell back upon theoretical presuppositions in their interpretations of experience. According to Dakin, Turgot's broader conception of "experience," embracing the experience of the past as well as the immediate experience of the senses, was better able to found philosophical understanding without recourse to dogma. Another, more recent defense of Turgot is to be found in Poirier 1999. Poirier describes Turgot as "driven by a concern for the public good and social justice," as a "technocrat" and liberal reformer who nonetheless made concessions to the contemporary political and social realities by incorporating *dirigiste* measures into his reforms, and as the "most brilliant advocate" of a set of sweeping social reforms ultimately put in place by the *constituants* in 1789 (371, 368–69, 374).

60. In Condorcet 1883, 101, 106.

61. Dakin [1939] 1965, 302. Morilhat (1988, 209) wrote that Turgot's central difference from the physiocrats was his distaste for their systems, arising from his sensationist-empiricist impulses: "Sensationist empiricism was the principle of Turgot's theoretical position in regard to the Physiocratic school."

62. In Turgot 1913, 2:677.

63. In Turgot 1913, 3:78. Turgot referred to Quesnay's *Recherches philosophiques sur l'évidence des vérités géometriques*, which was published in 1773.

taxation, which "incessantly dirtie[d] the works of the economists" (letter to Dupont de Nemours, 10 May 1771).[64] Although he advocated a single tax on land, he did not admit the exclusive productivity of agriculture. He supported the liberty of commerce and believed the economy would seek its own balance, but not as a consequence of the agricultural origins of wealth. He also distrusted Quesnay's *Tableau économique*.[65]

Neither as a mechanist, nor as a mathematician, nor as a physiocrat, therefore, was Turgot systematic in his commitment. What then was the spirit of his system-building? Charles Gillispie (1980, 16–17) has diagnosed a certain dogmatic rigidity that rendered Turgot unable to reconcile the demands of efficient administration with those of diplomacy. Yet consider Turgot's response to the cattle plague that began during his first year as finance minister. Henri Bertin, secretary of state for agriculture, had recommended the slaughter of infected animals as the safest method for containing and ending the plague. But Turgot hoped for a less drastic approach and requested a commission from the Academy of Sciences to look into the matter. In his correspondence with commissioners and local notables in the plague-stricken areas, Turgot continually cited the limits of human control and of his own knowledge, and the importance of remaining sensitive to the farmers' suffering.

In one letter to the archbishop of Narbonne dated 1 January 1775, he explained his recommendation of slaughtering only the first eight or ten sick animals. If more than that number were infected, he reasoned, the whole parish must be written off, "in which case it could be humane not to take from the Proprietors the feeble glimmer of hope that they might save those still alive." Moreover, Turgot added, "I pray you to remember that I am very far from the center of the evil, and . . . believe I can do no better than to yield my judgment to those who are better established to see the effects of the harms and remedies."[66]

Turgot was authoritarian in the enforcement of his policy of limited free commerce in grain. But authoritarianism is not the same thing as system-building. Keith Baker (1975, 61) has noted that Turgot found nothing "more to be feared and repressed than the irrational disposition

64. In Turgot 1913, 3:486.

65. See Turgot 1759, 595; and Fox-Genovese 1976, 67. Concerning Turgot's emphasis, distinguishing him from the physiocrats, on "moral causes over physical causes" in political economy, see Fontaine 1997 (esp. 3).

66. Archives nationales, F12 151. Charles Gillispie (1980, 28) has called it "characteristic" of the results of liberal reform during that period that Turgot and his commission "ended by ordering slaughter far more widely than Bertin had imagined."

of the inflamed and ignorant mob." It was this fear, which Turgot shared with many of his enlightened contemporaries, and not an attachment to abstract principles or an imperviousness to real-world complexities, that drove his response to the popular resistance against his policy of free trade. Answering a worried subordinate who wrote to say that the people of Dijon continued to oppose the liberty of commerce, Turgot replied that it was "not the people that should guide you, but the Law." He authorized severity in enforcing it "to make an example that intimidates the people and serves to contain them." True, Turgot's belief in free commerce seemed unshakable. He insisted that the local inspectors, by visiting bakeries to investigate the hoarding of grain, had themselves caused all the "tumult." Urging them not to manage the market but to allow it to right itself, Turgot insisted that free trade would make the prices "as low as they can be." In any event, he maintained, even if the prices did remain high, "they themselves [would] calm the alarms they cause" by attracting wheat from other regions to ensure provisioning. On the other hand, as we saw earlier, Turgot helped the forces of "nature" with a scheme of incentives for merchants and, in the Limousin, with an extensive new apparatus for poor relief. He also noted in his correspondence with local authorities that his instructions were "not a rule to follow scrupulously in all its particulars; but an indication of what can be done and how one can proceed; and I yield to your prudence for whatever you believe needs to be changed."[67]

Free commerce in grain was a policy that Turgot was neither the first nor the last to institute, and his version of it was comparatively moderate.[68] He made important concessions. The "Marseillaise du blé," Turgot's 1774 edict freeing the commerce in grain, was significantly limited, applying only to the domestic trade and only outside Paris.[69] Over the opposition of Hue de Miromesnil, Louis XVI's keeper of the seals, Turgot also acceded to demands that the clergy be exempted from the general tax with which he proposed to replace the corvée.[70] On the evidence,

67. Turgot, "Commerce des grains en Bourgogne," Archives nationales, H 187, nos. 108, 110, 111, 119.

68. Three finance ministers under Louis XV, Jean-Baptiste de Machault d'Arnouville (1745–54), Henri-Léonard-Jean-Baptiste Bertin (1759–63), and Clément-Charles-François de Laverdy (1763–68), had pursued policies of liberalizing the grain trade. Turgot's immediate predecessor, Joseph-Marie Terray (1769–74), had reinstituted taxes and restrictions. See Maurepas and Boulant 1996, 346–37.

69. See Morilhat 1988, 39–40. The quote is from Jules Michelet.

70. Véri [1774–81] 1928, 1:423 (entry for March 1776).

then, just as Turgot was not especially rigid in his commitment to theoretical systems—quite the contrary—he was also not unusually "systematic" (although he could be dictatorial) in his implementation of policies. Certainly he was not utterly flexible, but neither was he hopelessly doctrinaire. Like most administrators, he was somewhere in between.

Turgot's problems may have been exacerbated by a diplomatic and social incompetence. He was described as shy, awkward, and brusque.[71] "There is currently much noise on the subject of M. Turgot," wrote one observer of the court in the spring of 1775, who professed to offer his readers "the exact truth of what one must think of this Minister." He reported that Turgot's fellow courtiers found him "inflexible," and even his friends judged him to be "too severe" (Métra 1787, 1:268). Véri frequently cautioned Turgot about his overconfident temperament. "Without regard for persons, without consideration of the ignorance in which you might be of a thousand details," Véri scolded, "you pronounce your judgment . . . you never pronounce a word that might signify the slightest hesitation." Sometime later Véri demanded, "Will you never learn to condescend to an evil" for the sake of diplomacy? Turgot's response was all good-natured humility. "I agree with you on all the points of your sermon," he teased. Still, after Turgot's fall from power, Véri judged that his "character . . . had more to do with his dismissal than any other cause." His "considerable" faults all bore upon his "qualities as a courtier and a colleague."[72] Louis XVI's ultimate decision to dismiss Turgot in disgrace in 1776 seems to have resulted mainly from his alienation of many people at court, especially Marie-Antoinette and her entourage, who resented the economies Turgot tried to impose on the royal household.[73]

That system-building was the loudest, commonest, and longest-lived charge against Turgot says as much about the charge as it does about Turgot. The physiocrats themselves had brought the language of sensibility from natural philosophy into political economy in their invention of a natural-moral science, and their critics responded in kind. The philosophes had long used *spirit of system* to associate qualities of

71. See Faure 1961 and Hardman 1995, 50–51.

72. Véri [1774–81] 1928, 1:319, 328, 331, 392, 446 (entries for June 1775–May 1776).

73. Hardman 1995, 50–51; Maurepas and Boulant 1996, 348–49; Cornette 1995, 69; Poirier 1999, 252–63. Even Turgot's enemies at court accused him of system-building. One of Marie-Antoinette's allies against Turgot, the Baron de Besenval ([1805–7] 1987, 187), wrote in 1776 that Turgot was an "*homme d'esprit*, but systematic from having long worked in a study, through which he arrived at speculations mostly false or impracticable, the usual pitfall for people given to a metaphysical theory who always go astray in administration."

character—solipsism, arrogance, insensitivity, authoritarianism—with a quality of intellect, extreme rationalism. Turgot's critics reversed the relation, associating the flaws of character they discerned in Turgot—arrogance and insensitivity—with a type of intellect, the system-builder. Rationalism was insensitivity, and insensitivity, rationalism. In the same way, historians have understood Turgot's dictatorial enforcement of free trade as system-building, eliding the political evil with an intellectual one.

Toward the end of Turgot's tenure as finance minister, he became embroiled along with Louis XVI in a major struggle with the Parlement of Paris concerning the registration of the so-called Six Edicts, with which Turgot intended to enact a new set of reforms. The most important of the edicts replaced the corvée with a tax on all landowners except the clergy; another abolished guilds; and the remaining four eliminated various dues and offices. The parlement received the Six Edicts from the king in February 1776 and refused to register them. Instead, it issued two remonstrances, one against the edict eliminating the corvée and the second against the other edicts. Upon receiving these the following month, Louis XVI forced the parlement to register all six edicts in a *lit de justice*.[74]

The remonstrances were written in a language that was, by then, familiar. Against the proposed tax to replace the corvée, the parlement cited the "natural right" to property, a "law of the Universe that, despite the efforts of the human mind, maintains itself in each empire." The remonstrances continually referred to free commerce as a "system" and relied upon the following arguments: generalities belied the diversity of nature and human society; Paris was not like the provinces, the grain trade was not like other commerce, and these distinctions must be reflected in fiscal policy; the economists had only speculative "knowledge without practice"; their indifference to practical concerns had transformed mere opinions into systems; whereas an isolated opinion might easily be forgotten, systems, by their very nature, were evil.[75] When the parlement referred to pernicious "systematic opinions," Edgar Faure

74. Flammermont 1888–98, 3:275–77, 326–56; Cornette 1995, 68. A *lit de justice* was a special session of parlement in which the monarch arrived in person to reclaim his supreme legislative authority. The parlement in turn expressed its opposition to the law by recording it as registered "at the express command of the king." See Hardman 1995, 263.

75. Flammermont 1888–98, 3:277–324. The parlement also neatly inverted the physiocrats' argument against regulation, that it gave the state undue control over a natural process; the parlement claimed that *freeing* the grain trade made the state responsible, in the eyes of the

(1961, 486), chronicler of Turgot's disgrace, has noted "the word 'systematic' indicated Turgot from a mile away."

It is a poignant detail that the parlement appropriated these arguments, not just from the writings of the philosophes in general, but from Turgot himself. Searching for weapons to use against him, parlementarian researchers studied his early discourses at the Sorbonne and circulated a passage from his *Discours sur les avantages que l'établissement du christianisme a procuré au genre humain* (1750). The passage began: "Sorrow to those nations in which the spirit of system has directed the legislators" (Métra 1787, 3:26–27).

In the midst of the struggle between Crown and parlement, a supporter of Turgot, Pierre-François Boncerf, added fuel to the fire by publishing a pamphlet entitled *Les inconvénients des droits féodaux* (Francaleu 1776), in which he advocated the elimination of seigniorial privileges. The prince de Conti, a supporter of the queen and enemy of Turgot, called the parlement's attention to the pamphlet, and the parlement promptly ordered it shredded on the great staircase of the Palais de Justice. After the ceremonial shredding, the parlement intended to interrogate Boncerf and Pidansat de Mairobert, the censor who had permitted publication of the pamphlet, but Louis XVI put his foot down, forbidding any further hostilities. Here was an occasion for a third Turgot-related remonstrance (Flammermont 1888–98, 3:356–64).

This one was in the full flower of sentimental empiricism, with warnings against the hubris of rationalism and the dangerous detachment of mind from natural experience. Boncerf's pamphlet was—what else?—"purely systematic." The parlement warned the monarch, "There are limits that nature prescribes to man; there is, so to speak, a wall of separation that she forbids him to breach." Having arrived at this limit, with "nothing more to discover," the "simple progress of spirit" gave way to "subtleties of mind." Man began to "blame that which exists" and to substitute for it "systems built upon sophisms." Thus, the parlement concluded, "the multiplicity of systematic writings in a nation is almost always a sign of decadence . . . and . . . of revolution."[76] In a final remonstrance in response to the *lit de justice* at which the Six Edicts

---

people, for fluctuations in price and supply that had previously been blamed upon seasonal variation alone. See Kaplan 1976, 2:446–47.

76. "Remontrances sur l'interdiction des poursuites, dirigée contre l'auteur de la brochure sur les inconvéniens des droits féodaux" (March–April 1776), in Flammermont 1888–98, 3:362–63.

were registered, the parlement warned against "purely speculative" principles and wrote, "Your Majesty will doubtless see in the totality of all these edicts, the branches of a system that destroys ceaselessly." When Louis XVI received the remonstrance in May, he had already fired his ill-starred finance minister (Flammermont 1888–98, 3:374, 384, 368). J. E. B. Clugny, Turgot's successor, repealed his reforms. The corvée, the guilds, and the old restrictions on the grain trade would now survive until the Revolution (Dakin [1939] 1965, 264).

That the parlement had successfully appropriated its targets' own sources of uncertainty and ambivalence is reflected in Mirabeau's mournful and self-accusatory assessment of the physiocrats' position in 1776: "Always," he wrote, "the greatest number, even while following our principles and profiting from our work, will say that the Economists were . . . people of imagination and of systems, who dazzled and caused illusions because they suffered from them themselves. . . . They'll say that, Messieurs, and they won't be wrong."[77] The philosophes' self-directed admonitions against system-building had spread during Turgot's tenure as finance minister to permeate the language of the court, the king, and the parlement.[78]

Common sense might seem to dictate that any slogan launched in support of all sides of a controversy cannot have been a significant force in determining its outcome. On the contrary, however, by its very ubiquity, the phrase *spirit of system* indicates one of the most powerful, widespread, governing assumptions of the moment. While administrators, parlementarians, and reformists differed in where they identified system-building, they were unanimous in condemning it. This seems to me, in closing, worth emphasizing: the points of disagreement are the most apparent features of a dispute, but they are not necessarily the most telling. Historians looking back upon a controversy can learn as much from what the disputants agreed upon as from their divergences. A current example is that every Western politician would describe him- or herself as "pro-democratic." This does not mean that claims of democracy are empty, but on the contrary, that they are the most powerful claims

77. Mirabeau, "Discours de la rentrée" (1776), cited in Weulersse 1950, 46.

78. There are many examples of parlementary and royal appropriations of Enlightenment vocabulary. In one, Antoine-Louis Séguier, *avocat du roi*, told the king, "You have all around you ministers whose . . . enlightenment inspired hope for the end of these disgraces and the restoration of the old magistrature" ("Lit de justice pour le rétablissement du Parlement" [12 November 1774], in Flammermont 1888–98, 3:238–39).

available. One cannot understand any political dispute of our age without understanding their power. Similarly, one cannot understand any dispute in natural or moral science during the Age of Sensibility without recognizing the force of the argument against a rational, systematic epistemology, and for sensitivity to nature's purposeful behavior as the true basis of knowledge and social life.

References

Airiau, Jean. 1965. *L'opposition aux physiocrates à la fin de l'ancien régime*. Paris: Libraire générale de droit et de jurisprudence.

Aldridge, Alfred Owen. 1957. *Franklin and His French Contemporaries*. New York: New York University Press.

Bachaumont, Louis Petit de. 1780–89. *Mémoires secrets pour servir à l'histoire de la république de lettres en France*. 9 vols. London: John Adamson.

Baker, Keith. 1975. *Condorcet: From Natural Philosophy to Social Mathematics*. Chicago: University of Chicago Press.

———. 1990. *Inventing the French Revolution: Essays on French Political Culture*. Cambridge: Cambridge University Press.

Banzhaf, Spencer. 2000. Productive Nature and the Net Product: Quesnay's Economies Animal and Political. *HOPE* 32.3:517–51.

Barre, Raymond. 1966. *Economie politique*. Paris: Presses Universitaires de France.

Baudeau, Nicolas. 1771. *Introduction à la philosophie économique*. In Daire 1846.

Beer, M. 1939. *An Inquiry into Physiocracy*. London: G. Allen and Unwin.

Bensaude-Vincent, Bernadette. 1993. The Balance: Between Chemistry and Politics. *Eighteenth-Century Theory and Interpretation* 33.3:217–37.

Besenval, Pierre Victor de. [1805–7] 1987. *Mémoires du Baron de Besenval sur la cour de France. Introduction et notes de Ghislain de Diesbach*. Paris: Mercure de France.

Bourde, André. 1953. *The Influence of England on the French* Agronomes *1750–89*. Cambridge: Cambridge University Press.

Cassirer, Ernst. 1951. *The Philosophy of the Enlightenment*. Translated by Fritz Koelln and James Pettegrove. Princeton, N.J.: Princeton University Press.

Charles, Loïc. 2000. From the *Encyclopédie* to the *Tableau économique*: Quesnay on Freedom of Grain Trade and Economic Growth. *European Journal of the History of Economic Thought* 7.1:1–21.

Chinard, Gilbert. 1955. *L'apothéose de Franklin*. Paris: Librairie orientale et américaine.

Christensen, Paul. 1994. Fire, Motion, and Productivity: The Proto-Energetics of Nature and Economy in François Quesnay. In Mirowski 1994.

Condillac, Etienne Bonnot de. 1776. *Le commerce et le gouvernement considérés relativement l'un à l'autre*. In Daire 1847–48.

———. [1749] 1798. *Traité des systèmes*. In vol. 2 of *Oeuvres complètes*, edited by Arnoux and Mousnier, 23 vols. Paris: Houel.

Condorcet, Marie-Jean-Antoine-Nicolas Caritat, marquis de. 1883. *Correspondance inédite de Condorcet et Turgot*. Edited by Charles Henry. Paris: Charavay Frères.

Cornette, Joël. 1995. Turgot, ou la dernière chance de la monarchie. *L'histoire* 191:64–69.

Daire, Eugène. 1846. *Physiocrates: Quesnay, Dupont de Nemours, Mercier de la Rivière, l'abbé Baudeau, le Trosne, avec une introduction sur la doctrine des physiocrates, des commentaires et des notices historiques*. Paris.

———, ed. 1847–48. *Mélanges d'économie politique. Précédés de notices historiques sur chaque auteur, et accompagnés de commentaires et de notes explicatives, par Eugène Daire et G. de Molinari*. 2 vols. Paris.

Dakin, Douglas. [1939] 1965. *Turgot and the Ancien Régime in France*. New York: Octagon.

D'Alembert, Jean Lerond. 1751a. Discours préliminaire. In vol. 1 of Pons 1986.

———. 1751b. *Réflexions sur la théorie de la résistance des fluides*; *Lues dans l'Assemblée publique de l'Académie des Sciences du 13 Novembre 1751*. Paris.

———. 1756. Expérimental. In vol. 1 of Pons 1986.

———. 1757. Géometrie. In vol. 2, bk. 7 of Diderot and d'Alembert 1751–72.

De l'état actuel des Sciences et des Arts. 1765. In vol. 2, bk. 2 of *Les Éphémérides du citoyen; ou, Bibliothèque raisonnée des sciences morales et politiques*.

Diderot, Denis. 1753. De l'interprétation de la nature. In Diderot 1986.

———. 1755. Encyclopédie. In vol. 2 of Pons 1986.

———. 1767a. Entretien entre d'Alembert et Diderot. In Diderot 1986.

———. 1767b. Le rève de d'Alembert. In Diderot 1986.

———. 1986. *Oeuvres philosophiques*. Edited by Paul Vernière. Paris: Garnier.

Diderot, Denis, and Jean d'Alembert, eds. 1751–72. *Encyclopédie, ou, Dictionnaire raisonée des sciences, des arts et des métiers*. Paris.

Dinechin, Bruno Dupont de. 1999. *Duhamel du Monceau: Un savant exemplaire au siècle des lumières*. Luxembourg: Connaissance et mémoires européennes.

Duhamel du Monceau, Henri-Louis. 1750–56. *Traité de la culture des terres*. Paris: H.-L. Guerin.

———. 1762. *Eléments d'agriculture*. Paris: H.-L. Guérin.

Dupont de Nemours, Pierre Samuel. 1764. De l'exportation et de l'importation des grains, mémoire lû à la Société royale d'agriculture de Soissons. In Dupont de Nemours 1979.

———. 1768. *De l'origine et des progrès d'une science nouvelle*. In Dupont de Nemours 1979.

———. 1979. *Oeuvres politiques et économiques*. 2 vols. Nendeln: KTO.

Eltis, Walter. 1995. L'Abbé de Condillac and the Physiocrats. *HOPE* 27.2:217–36.

———. 2002. How Quesnay's *Tableau Economique* Offered a Deeper Analysis of the Predicament of France. *Journal of the History of Economic Thought* 24.1:39–53.

Faure, Edgar. 1961. *La disgrâce de Turgot*. Paris: Gallimard.

Flammermont, Jules, ed. 1888–98. *Remontrances du Parlement de Paris au XVIIIe siècle*. 3 vols. Paris: Imprimerie nationale.

Foley, V. 1973. An Origin of the Tableau Economique. *HOPE* 5.1:121–50.

Fontaine, Philippe. 1997. Turgot's "Institutional Individualism." *HOPE* 19.1:1–20.

Fox-Genovese, Elizabeth. 1976. *The Origins of Physiocracy*. Ithaca, N.Y.: Cornell University Press.

Francaleu [Pierre-François Boncerf]. 1776. *Les inconvénients des droits féodaux*. Paris: Valade.

Gay, Peter. 1966–69. *The Enlightenment: An Interpretation*. 2 vols. New York: Norton.

Gillispie, Charles. 1980. *Science and Polity at the End of the Old Regime*. Princeton, N.J.: Princeton University Press.

Graslin, Jean-Joseph-Louis. 1767. *Essai analytique sur la richesse et sur l'impôt, où l'on réfute la nouvelle doctrine économique qui a fourni à la Société Royale d'Agriculture de Limoges les principes d'un programme qu'elle a publié sur l'effet des Impôts indirects*. London.

Hankins, Thomas L. 1970. *Jean D'Alembert: Science and the Enlightenment*. Oxford: Clarendon.

Hardman, John. 1995. *French Politics, 1774–1789: From the Accession of Louis XVI to the Fall of the Bastille*. London: Longman.

Harris, Robert D. 1979. *Necker, Reform Statesman of the Ancien Régime*. Berkeley, Calif.: University of California Press.

———. 1986. *Necker and the Revolution of 1789*. Lanham, Md.: University Press of America.

Hume, David. [1752] 1898. Of Commerce. In *Essays Moral, Political, and Literary*, edited by T. H. Green and T. H. Grose. London: Longman.

Kaplan, Steven. 1976. *Bread, Politics, and Political Economy in the Reign of Louis XV*. 2 vols. The Hague: Martinus Nijhoff.

———. 1984. *Provisioning Paris: Merchants and Millers in the Grain and Flour Trade during the Eighteenth Century*. Ithaca, N.Y.: Cornell University Press.

Knight, Isabelle. 1968. *The Geometric Spirit: The Abbé de Condillac and the French Enlightenment*. New Haven, Conn.: Yale University Press.

Larrère, Catherine. 1992. *L'invention de l'économie au XVIIIè siècle*. Paris: Presses Universitaires de France.

Lavoisier, Antoine. 1862–93. *Oeuvres de Lavoisier*. Edited by J. B. Dumas and Edouard Grimaux. 6 vols. Paris: Imprimerie impériale.

Mairan, Dortous de. 1749. *Dissertation sur la Glace, ou Explication physique de la formation de la Glace, et de ses divers phénomènes*. Paris: Imprimerie royale.

Maurepas, Arnaud de, and Antoine Boulant. 1996. *Les ministres et les ministères du siècle des lumières (1715–1789)*. Paris: Christian.

Meek, Ronald. 1962. *The Economics of Physiocracy*. Cambridge: Harvard University Press.

Mercier de la Rivière, P. F. J. H. 1767. *L'ordre naturel et essentiel des sociétés politiques*. In Daire 1846.

Métra, François. 1787. *Correspondance secrète, politique et littéraire, ou, Mémoires pour servir à l'histoire des Cours, des Sociétés et de la Littérature en France, depuis la mort de Louis XV*. London: John Adamson.

Mirabeau, Victor de Riquetti, marquis de. 1764. *Philosophie rurale, ou économie générale et politique de l'agriculture, réduite à l'ordre immuable des loix physiques & morales, qui assurent la prospérité des empires*. Amsterdam: Libraires Associés.

Mirowski, Philip, ed. 1994. *Natural Images in Economic Thought*. Cambridge: Cambridge University Press.

Morellet, André. 1988. *Mémoires de l'Abbé Morellet*. Edited by Jean-Pierre Guicciardi. Paris: Mercure de France.

Morilhat, Claude. 1988. *La prise de conscience du capitalisme*. Paris: Méridiens Klincksieck.

Necker, Jacques. 1775. *Sur la législation et le commerce des grains*. In Daire 1847–48.

Oncken, August. 1886. *Die Maxime Laissez faire et laissez passer*. Bern: K. J. Wyss.

Pappas, John. 1972. L'esprit de finesse contre l'esprit de géometrie: Un débat entre Diderot et d'Alembert. *Studies on Voltaire and the Eighteenth Century* 89:1229–53.

Poirier, Jean-Pierre. 1996. *Lavoisier: Chemist, Biologist, Economist*. Translated by Rebecca Balinski. Philadelphia: University of Pennsylvania Press.

———. 1999. *Turgot: Laissez-faire et progrès social*. Paris: Perrin.

Pons, Alain, ed. 1986. *Encyclopédie, ou, Dictionnaire raisoné des sciences, des arts et des métiers (articles choisis)*. 2 vols. Paris: Flammarion.

Quesnay, François. 1757. Grains. In Quesnay 1958.

———. 1758. *Tableau économique*. In Quesnay 1958.

———. 1765. Mémoire sur les avantages de l'industrie et du commerce. In Quesnay 1958.

———. 1766. Sur les travaux des artisans. In Quesnay 1958.

———. 1767. Maximes générales du gouvernement économique d'un royaume agricole. In Quesnay 1958.

———. 1888. *Oeuvres économiques et philosophiques*. Edited by August Oncken. Frankfurt: J. Baer.

———. 1958. *Textes annotés*. Vol. 2 of *François Quesnay et la physiocratie*. Paris: Institut National d'Etudes Démographiques.

Réponse à l'oeuvre intitulé Principes de tout Gouvernement. 1767. In vol. 7 of *Les Éphémérides du citoyen; ou Bibliothèque raisonnée des sciences morales et politiques*.

Riskin, Jessica. 1998a. Poor Richard's Leyden Jar: Electricity and Economy in Franklinist France. *Historical Studies in the Physical and Biological Sciences* 28.2:301–36.

———. 1998b. Rival Idioms for a Revolutionized Science and a Republican Citizenry. *Isis* 89:203–32.

———. 2002. *Science in the Age of Sensibility: The Sentimental Empiricists of the French Enlightenment*. Chicago: University of Chicago Press.

Roger, Jacques. 1989. *Buffon: Un philosophe au Jardin du Roi*. Paris: Fayard.

Ross, Ian Simpson. 1995. *The Life of Adam Smith*. Oxford: Clarendon.

Rothschild, Emma. 2001. *Economic Sentiments: Adam Smith, Condorcet, and the Enlightenment*. Cambridge: Harvard University Press.

Rudé, Georges. 1964. *The Crowd in History, 1730–1848*. New York: Wiley.

Schabas, Margaret. 2001. David Hume on Experimental Natural Philosophy, Money, and Fluids. *HOPE* 33.3:411–35.

Skinner, Andrew S. 1993. David Hume: Principles of Political Economy. In *The Cambridge Companion to Hume*, edited by David Fate Norton. Cambridge: Cambridge University Press.

Smith, Adam. 1789. *An Inquiry into the Nature and Causes of the Wealth of Nations*. 5th ed. Philadelphia: Thomas Dobson.

———. 1790. *The Theory of Moral Sentiments*. 6th ed. London: Strahan & Cadell.

Smith, Olivia. 1984. *The Politics of Language, 1791–1819*. Oxford: Clarendon.

Stewart, Dugald. [1793] 1854–60. Account of the Life and Writings of Adam Smith LL.D. In *The Collected Works of Dugald Stewart*, edited by Sir William Hamilton. Edinburgh: T. Constable and Co.

Sur la prosperité du commerce. 1766. In vol. 3, bk. 2 of *Les Éphémérides du citoyen; ou Bibliothèque raisonnée des sciences morales et politiques*.

Système. 1765. In vol. 15 of Diderot and d'Alembert 1751–72.

Turgot, Anne Marie Robert. 1759. Eloge de Gournay. In vol. 1 of Turgot 1913.

———. 1913. *Oeuvres de Turgot et documents le concernant*. Edited by Gustave Schelle. 5 vols. Paris: Félix Alcan.

———. [1766] 1997. *Réflexions sur la formation et distribution des richesses*. In *Formation et distribution des richesses*, edited by Joël-Thomas Ravix and Paul-Marie Romani. Paris: Flammarion.

Vaggi, Gianni. 1987. *The Economics of François Quesnay*. London: Macmillan.

———. 2002. Quesnay and the Road to Modernity: Technology, Markets, and Polity. *Journal of the History of Economic Thought* 24.1:73–89.

Véri, abbé Joseph Alphonse de. [1774–81] 1928. *Journal de l'Abbé de Véri*. Edited by Baron Jehan De Witte. 2 vols. Paris: J. Tallandier.

Viel, Claude. 1985. Duhamel du Monceau: Naturaliste, physicien et chemiste. *Revue d'histoire des sciences et de leurs applications* 38:55–71.

Weulersse, Georges. 1910. *Le mouvement physiocratique en France*. 2 vols. Paris: Félix Alcan.

———. 1950. *La physiocratie sous les ministères de Turgot et Necker (1774–1781)*. Paris: Presses Universitaires de France.

———. 1985. *La physiocratie à l'aube de la Révolution, 1781–1792*. Paris: Ecole des Hautes Etudes en Sciences Sociales.

The Agricultural Foundation of the Seventeenth-Century English Oeconomy

S. Todd Lowry

The extensive literature and cultural traditions associated with agricultural production in the seventeenth century have been undeservedly slighted in discussions of the agricultural economy. A revolution in agricultural production has been associated traditionally with the latter half of the eighteenth century and the beginning of the Industrial Revolution. The scientific revolution in agriculture is associated with the mid-nineteenth century emergence of soils chemistry after Justus von Liebig (Fussel 1971; Wilmot 1990). However, recent work has further documented an earlier revolution in agricultural productivity around the beginning of the seventeenth century (Kerridge [1967] 1968; Allen 1992). Two aspects of the increases in agricultural yields are striking. First, the guiding literature on agricultural practices was surprisingly constant from the sixteenth through the eighteenth century. Incongruously, despite the increase in agricultural productivity during this period, the agricultural manuals are frequently dismissed as pedestrian and nonscientific.

Second, a cooler climate afflicted northern Europe from around 1300 to after 1900 (Andersen and Borns 1994; Briffa and Osborn 2002). David Grigg (1982, 85, 88) dates the period of poorest climate from 1550 to 1700, with cold winters, wet summers, and shorter growing seasons. Yet this was the very period in which English agriculture doubled its yields per acre, according to R. C. Allen's (1992) statistical study of the Midlands (see also Kerridge [1967] 1968). Perhaps a retrospective overemphasis on the growth of commerce and the mathematization of science have limited our appreciation of the importance of the agricultural base of the economy and its instructional and legal components (Cipolla 1980).

I focus my analysis on the dominant economic concerns of the vast majority of the population of that day and on the reflective thought that paralleled their concerns. Emphasis must be on the physical realities of early modern agriculture. The best data indicate that, in the sixteenth century, 70 to 90 percent of the population lived on the land. This base of the population pyramid struggled to provide for itself and to supply a material surplus to support the political, military, clerical, and commercial superstructure of the society. In the prologue to his agricultural manual of 1534, Mayster Fitzherbert likened the society to the game of "chesse," with the pawns equivalent to the yeomanry. A best estimate for England in 1520 is that it took 100 families on the land to support 106 families. This indicates that roughly 94 percent of the population worked in agriculture at that time (Wrigley 1986, 136). By 1800, it is estimated that 100 families on the land could support a total of 138 families, including themselves. This indicates that over 70 percent of the population was still on the land, but there had been a sixfold increase in the economic superstructure supported by domestic agriculture and augmented by food imports (136). To put this background in perspective, compare it with modern agricultural practices. Less than 5 percent of the population in the United States is still on the land, and much agricultural production is devoted to industrial crops rather than food. The hidden distinction in such an overview is the difference between production per acre and production per laborer. The former is vital in subsistence agriculture; the latter, in capitalist agriculture.

The economic and cultural importance of basic agriculture during the 1600s can be underlined by some consideration of famine. Late medieval grain yields ran from three to five times seed in normal times. Planters used about two bushels of seed per acre, and this had to be held back from the meager harvest for the following year. In this period, bread was figuratively "the staff of life." Barley, however, was frequently malted and made into beer to improve its palatability. Altogether, the four grains (barley, oats, and wheat or rye bread) made up the foundation of the English diet. It was supplemented with a little cheese, beef, or mutton and peas, beans, turnips, or cabbage. In the early seventeenth century, one farm ration was two pounds of bread per day plus four pints of beer and some meat, fruit, and vegetables. Generally, a peck of wheat a week (eight quarts) in bread and near that in barley, mostly in beer, was the basic adult ration. This ran to as much as two "quarters" (sixteen bushels) of grain a year (Kerridge [1967] 1968, 332–35). The protein count in the small grains runs from wheat down to rye, oats, and barley. Considering that fields were left fallow every third year as part of the late medieval tradition, and the need for a few acres for hay plus the burden of paying rent to the landlord, a tenant on a half "yardling" (around fifteen acres) would live at bare subsistence in good years. With a full yardling (thirty acres) with as much as fifteen acres of it in grain, in a lean year averaging three times seed (four bushels per acre above seed), a family would have only a small surplus even with some benefit from grazing animals on the commons (Thirsk 1967).

The moral stamina inherent in the requirement to retain seed after a poor harvest must have been formidable. Such a deeply ingrained sense of thrift and investment in basic subsistence would be tested most profoundly when two famine years occurred back to back, something that happened every fifteen to twenty years (Braudel 1981, 1:73–78.) It should also be kept in mind that the cost of transportation of grain in the absence of access to waterways was so high that localized crop failures could not be relieved by surpluses a few score miles away. Both the lack of monetary reserves among the rural poor and the absence of organization such as that found in medieval cities resulted in a rigorous cultural training in thrift and seed preservation as capital for future planting. This issue is not discussed in the agricultural manuals, mostly written by the gentry, despite the unmitigated reality of such material imperatives.

Another revolution, or at least a major reorientation in the economy during the seventeenth century, was the diminution in the rate of population growth and the increase in urbanization. Although the statistics are not dependably precise, comparable inaccuracies probably affect all the figures, so it is the general picture that counts. The population of England was roughly 2.4 million in 1520. By 1600 it was around 4.1 million—a 71 percent increase. By 1700 the population had risen to 5.06 million—only about a 23 percent increase over 1600. By 1800, the population had jumped to 8.66 million—more than a 72 percent increase over 1700, with most of the increase coming in the latter half of the century (Wrigley 1986, 128, table 2). At the same time, the city of London grew from a population of 55,000 in 1520 to 200,000 in 1600, to 575,000 by 1700, to 675,000 by 1750, and to 960,000 by 1801. This plateau in population growth for England in the 1600s and the concentration of almost 40 percent of the curtailed growth in the city of London alone calls for explanation, particularly since it occurred during a period of climatic stress on agriculture, political unrest, and bad harvests in the early 1630s, 1650s, 1660s, and 1690s. This also appears to have been a period of general increase in the standard of living and diversion of cropland to pasture for meat production and dairying. In the following pages, I will explore these anomalies aided by a reading of the agricultural literature of the sixteenth and seventeenth centuries, and by an overview of the legal theory and policy that elucidated and directed the institutional structure of the economy from 1550 to 1750.

The relevant economic literature of the agricultural economy of the seventeenth century comprehended tenures, rents, improvements, and profits. The evolving legal system represents an institutional superstructure framing the organization and technology of production. Given the importance of organization in a production system, however, it should also be thought of as a sort of social technology invented by a dynamic judiciary with shifting ideological and class allegiances.

The Land and Its Control

Utilization, however, is our primary interest. After 1066, William the Conqueror imposed a basic feudal system on the land dividing it into over 60,000 "knight's fees." This was an expression of the military economy of feudalism under which the king or dominant feudal authority organized the land—the basis of the economy—into units designed to support military service. Each knight's fee was obligated to provide, on call, support for the king. The royal domain, realm, or kingdom was the property of the Crown, but this "royal estate" or "real estate" (realty) was parceled out to many dukes, earls, and barons who held it in a hierarchical structure with the knight's fee as the underlying unit. In addition, the king held extensive estates directly for his own support. The military aspect of the organization rapidly evolved into a manorial economy with nonmilitary services due to the Crown or overlord. In the early seventeenth century, Sir Edward Coke identified the standard knight's fee as 680 acres, a little over a square mile (640 acres) (*Coke on Littleton*, 69a). These tracts incorporated Anglo-Saxon villages with their own traditions, and the knight's fee became the basis of the manorial economy of the late Middle Ages and early modern times.

The Black Death or plague of 1348 depopulated the countryside by as much as 30 percent in some areas. Although such figures are little more than guesses, the practical result was documented by the shift in relationships between the actual husbandmen on the land and their landlords. In order to hold husbandmen on the land, they were given rights as "copyholders" that were recorded on the "rolls" kept by the manor lord or his steward. Obligations were reduced to token contributions and money rents in most cases. Although copyholds were commonly "tenancies at will," that is, terminable by the landlord at the end of the year, the "customs of the manor" became an important consideration over the years. A. Macfarlane (1978) has cogently argued that there was a high degree of individualism among the early English rural population and that the technical definition of *peasantry*, a village-controlled system of land allocation, did not apply. The existence of small freeholds and copyholds antedated the Black Death, but it proliferated afterward. This individualism manifested itself in the fifteenth and sixteenth centuries (Aylmer 1980; Baack 1979).

Much of the economic thought and practice of the times is documented in the legal and organizational developments of the late Middle Ages. With tenants living at little more than bare subsistence and rents low, landlords found two ways of increasing their incomes. One was by selling off land as "freeholds." The power of freemen to sell lands or tenements had been established by statute in 1290 (Macfarlane 1978, 83). The other way to increase income was to put the demesne lands, that part of the manor not held by tenants, into "sheep walks" and take advantage of the more remunerative wool trade. Tenants-at-will could be thrown off the land, but many copyholders held life estates, and some held rights of inheritance subject to an entry fee or "fine" to be paid by the heir. Where such rights had become a matter of presumption as "customs of the manor, for time out of mind," copyholders, in the fifteenth century, had begun to enforce them in chancery courts where equity was applied. The chancellor or king's chaplain, "keeper of the king's conscience," heard pleas for special decrees where it was alleged that justice could not be obtained at common law. By the middle of the 1500s, aggressive copyholders were getting protection of their customary rights at common law as well as in chancery (Reid 1995, 245–50). This pattern of customary and contractual rights, life estates, leaseholds, and heritable copyholds persisted into the late seventeenth century (Clay 1985, 198–229).

In order to appreciate the burgeoning scientific spirit of the sixteenth century, it should be noted here that the common law was developing a philosophical basis of natural reason and systematic rationality that formed and reflected part of the broader movement of the age. It should also be observed that the common law, as a social science that drew from practical reality and formulated operational policy to guide the economy, relied heavily on maxims to articulate its principles (Sommerville 1999, 81–83). Maxims and moralistic adages had long been the stock-in-trade of the chancery courts freely asserting principles of equity or justice. This use of maxims marks an extension of formal thought to a marginally literate society and conversely a reaching for a broader conceptual principle in customary sayings. Consider, for instance, "The best dung on the land is the footprints of the master!" This maxim dates back to ancient Greece and was repeated in the Roman agricultural writings. Its appearance in the agricultural manuals of the sixteenth century represents a succinct indictment of absentee ownership and an emphasis on good, flexible management. In a comprehensive study of the changes in agrarian thought in the sixteenth and seventeenth centuries, A. McRae has identified a distinct shift from a moral to a rational outlook in the mid-sixteenth century. A clerically endorsed idealization of paternalistic stewardship over the land was replaced by a rationalistic production-oriented attitude. McRae (1996, 168) describes this transitional century as follows: "The discourse of agrarian improvement had by the middle of the seventeenth century revolutionized the ways in which the English might envisage their land. . . . Ideals of manorial order had given way to the desire for 'profit'; the honest ploughman had been displaced by the thrifty freeholder; and cries for economic freedom and rationalism were driving an assault on the authority of custom."

This revolution at the broader level of society is further characterized by McRae as "an emergent orientation toward the standards and imperatives of a market culture." He goes on to specify the full significance of this paradigmatic change in the institutions or relations of production: "The principal interest group behind the movement was the rural 'middling sorts': the small freeholders and rising yeomen who were prepared to embrace the new world of commerce" (168). In the context of McRae's thorough and authoritative analysis of the literature of the sixteenth and seventeenth centuries, it is appropriate to try to understand the development and role of the agricultural manuals in the setting of this fundamental social change. It is necessary, however, as a foundation for such an inquiry, to understand the nature of land tenure and economic choice that underwrote this agrarian revolution.

The Agricultural Manuals

Probably the earliest agricultural manual in England was Walter of Henley's *Husbandry*, written in the late 1200s. It circulated in manuscript and is of interest to us because of its formal rationalism. For example, it compared the costs and advantages of oxen and horses as draft animals. In his essay on the use of horses and oxen in medieval England, J. Langdon (1982, 31) reproduces Walter's columns showing comparative costs of feed, winter and summer, for oxen and horses, and he adds the cost of shoeing for horses. Langdon points out that oxen were a cheaper source of plow power, but for the small independent freeholder, horses were more versatile. One horse could plow and serve as both packhorse and riding horse. Our interest in this document is attracted by its use of a formal arithmetical tabulation illustrating a rationalistic tradition in agriculture. This late medieval competence can also be illustrated by the formal administrative record keeping by monasteries such as the Cistercians (Baeck 1994, chap. 5). We should, however, keep in mind that this arithmetic rationality and administrative formalism goes back to the Roman agricultural writers and Xenophon's *Oeconomicus*. The onset of widely distributed manuals, however, came only after printing became well established in the early 1500s. McRae (1996, 302–18) lists a printed edition of Walter of Henley's *Boke* in 1508 along with over seventy-five other husbandry manuals between 1500 and 1660. There are also more than a dozen texts on surveying in his bibliography of sources.

One of the best known, and among the earliest, of the manuals was *The Boke of Husbandry*, first published by Mayster Fitzherbert in 1523. Some contend that it was written by Sir Anthony Fitzherbert, a leading jurist and author of significant works on English law. However, in the same year, his brother, John, published a book on surveying. Authorship of the work on husbandry is sometimes attributed to him. In any event, this formidable book, 172 pages in length, went through several editions and was in circulation for many years, the last edition appearing in 1598.

The only suggestion of a political or economic orientation in Fitzherbert's book, other than technical efficiency, appears in its prologue. After beginning with two Latin renditions of scripture and his accompanying translation—"man is ordeyned and borne to do labour" and "he that laboureth not, shulde not eate"—he goes on to justify the hierarchy of society that performs necessary functions. Fitzherbert illustrates this division of labor with the game of "chesse" and notes that a book could be written about the contributions of each of the six ranks: king, queen, bishop, knight, judge, and yeoman. Fitzherbert ([1534] 1965, 2) states his objective: "And in so moche the yomen in the sayde moralytyes and game of the chesse be set before to labour, defende, and maynteyne all the other hyer estates, the whiche yomen represent the common people, as husbandes and labourers, therefore I purpose to speake fyrste of husbandrye."

This can hardly be touted as an idealization of the gentry. We should also keep in mind that *husbandman* and *to husband* have the traditional meaning of a householder with a family as the basic tiller of the soil who conserves or efficiently manages his resources. This being said, it is difficult to know the breadth of audience Fitzherbert anticipated for his book. In his topic 141, "A shorte information for a yonge gentylman, that entendeth to thryue," he recommends that the husbandman read this book twice thoroughly and read timely parts of it to his servants. He reveals a rustic empiricism when he goes on to assure the reader with a Latin adage that he translates as, "It is better the practiue or knowledge of an husband-man well proued, than the science or connynge of a philosopher not proued, for there is nothynge touchyng husbandry, and other profytes conteyned in this presente booke, but I have hadde the experyence thereof, and proued the same" (90–91).

An emphasis on practical experimentation not only characterizes Fitzherbert's book but is consistently echoed in the plethora of agricultural manuals that were published through the 1600s. It accords with Peter Dear's (1995; 2001, chap. 2) description of the thought of the sixteenth century as dominated by an Aristotelian emphasis on observation and consensus. Dear is intent on excluding this tradition of observationally opinionated archaism from the Newtonian revolution in science. Fitzherbert is an inappropriate target, since his emphasis on observation and experiment follows the Roman agricultural manuals rather than Aristotle.

The Roman agricultural manuals by Cato, Varro, Columella, and Palladius were all available in Latin in the sixteenth century and were very influential (Fussell 1947; Thirsk 1992; McRae 1996, 136). Varro is the only one actually cited by Fitzherbert. Dear does not deal with this dominant sector of the economy and its scientific impetus, which differs from the more esoteric orientations of the Aristotelian tradition as it was invoked at the time. Varro (1936, 1.18.8.231–33), for example, generalized, "Nature has given us two routes to agriculture, experiment and imitation." He continues, "We ought to do both—imitate others and attempt by experiment to do some things in a different way, following not chance but some system." Varro follows this abstraction with the example of evaluating the frequency and depth of plowing for summer weed control and "dust mulching"—a practice used in Mediterranean agriculture to preserve the previous winter's soil moisture during a summer fallow in preparation for a fall grain planting. He also rejects two traditional programming standards that propose optimum combinations of men, yokes of oxen, and land area, on the grounds that every piece of land has unique characteristics that should be considered. If Varro had framed a mathematical "system" as a reference base for his experimentation, he would probably have satisfied Dear's characterization of Newtonian science. However, Varro preempted such implied criticism by pointing out that in the science of specific decisions in agriculture, experiment produces specific conclusions appropriate to unique conditions, although in the context of an overall system, in short, general principles.

A peculiarity of Fitzherbert's manual is that it avoids any treatment of institutional considerations, the relational aspects of production. However, the detailed thoroughness with which he covers all aspects of the technical elements of agriculture is impressive. His discussions range through the making of a plow, hay rake, and pitchfork, to veterinary medicine, planting techniques, rates of seeding, soil amendment, and manuring. It is interesting that he avoids discussions of personnel management and human capital that form the core of Xenophon's *Oeconomicus*, which had appeared in English translation in the middle of the sixteenth century (McRae 1996, 136, 138). The technical aspect of the efficient ordering of work is implicit in Fitzherbert's analysis of programming. In recommending that a young gentleman make a routine tour of his holdings, as mentioned above, he says, "For a man alwaye wanderynge or goinge aboute somewhat, findeth or seeth that is a-mysse, and wolde be amended" (Fitzherbert [1534] 1965, 92). Such a practice institutionalizes the search for problems that one does not know exist.

The formulation of abstract efficiency in organizing work is carried to a high point in topic 146 of Fitzherbert's book. After listing household duties for a wife, he elaborates:

> May fortune sometime, that thou shalt have so many thinges to do, that thou shalt not well knowe where is best to begyn. Than take hede,

> which thing shuld be the greatest losse, if it were not done; and in what space it wold be done: than thinke what is the greatest losse, & there begyn. But in case that thynge, that is of greatest losse, wyll be longe in doynge, and thou myghteste do thre or foure other thynges in the meane whyle, thanne loke well, if all these thynges were sette together, whiche of them were the greatest losse; and if all these thynges be of greater losse, and may all be done in as shorts space, as the other, than doe thy many thynges fyrst. (97)

The economic content of this analysis of comparative cost-benefit with emphasis on quantity and time is self-evident. Such passages are often dismissed as banal or irrelevant to economic science because they occur outside a formal system of analysis. We should keep in mind, however, that earlier cultures had their own comprehensive systems. The cited passage in Fitzherbert echoes a similar discussion of comparative programming found in Varro immediately before and after his discussion of experimentation mentioned earlier. A similar type of analysis appears toward the end of Xenophon's *Banquet* (7.1–5), where the advice to a Syracusan impresario on marginal efficiency is represented as an example of professional abstract thought (Lowry 1987, 81). Anachronistic quibbles over definitions or priorities are not particularly important, however. Instead, my concern is to examine the character and limitations of the agricultural instructional literature.

What emerges when one reads the agricultural manuals is their near unanimity in dealing solely with technical improvements and practices that enhance soil productivity. The term *improvement* and the commendation of someone as an "improver" reflect the evolution of this term as meaning an increase in the value of the land. The term *profit* also had a traditional meaning in land law, referring to a benefit to be derived from land. More specifically, it meant a right to some resource such as a mineral deposit. A "charge" on land meant a capital cost that had to be justified by increased production. The manual literature has been amply surveyed by G. E. Fussell (1947) and by Joan Thirsk (1983, 1985c) and analyzed by McRae (1996). What stands out, though it has been little emphasized, is the narrow intensity with which these manuals follow the format of the Roman classics that influenced them (Thirsk 1992). They treat *manuring* in its original connotation of *any* manual efforts to improve the soil with additives. They understand the problems with, and advantages of, heavier clay soils (fat land) and how to amend them with sand. The practices of carrying sea sand by packhorse to improve clays and adding lime in the form of crushed shell were limited economically to a few miles, but a clear picture is painted of the labor-intensive problem of the transport and spreading of soil amendments. Marl (calcareous clay) was found in local deposits, and limestone was burned to produce lime for the fields, following Roman advice. The importance of lime and marl was recognized, although their role in "base exchange" was not understood until the twentieth century. It raised pH, that is, it lowered the acidity of the soil and made other minerals more readily available. Another innovation was called "denshiring," possibly a corruption of "Devonshiring," also known as "paring" (Campbell 1942, 173). To counter an excessive accumulation of organic matter or "peatification," sods were turned up with a mattock, allowed to dry, and then burned, and the ash spread back over the fields. This practice, which lowered the acidity of the soil and made calcium and potassium available while reducing excess water retention in the soil, is one of many impressive labor-intensive efforts undertaken to improve the soil.

What Audience Did the Manuals Reach?

Only rarely does one find anything that is agronomically questionable in these manuals. What is noteworthy, however, is their repetitive character. It suggests a widening audience, as printing and literacy interacted with the growing numbers of small leaseholders, copyholders, and freeholding yeomen. Gervase Markham, for example, published ten different books on husbandry in the second and third decades of the 1600s, according to McRae's (1996) bibliography.

The interesting undercurrent in many of the manuals, although not particularly explicit in Fitzherbert, is their emphasis on "natural bounty." The Greek tradition, as transferred by Xenophon's *Oeconomicus*, emphasized the human factor and the importance of personnel management, leadership, and training for increasing wealth. These aspects seem to have been completely ignored in the manuals, and the more technical agronomic orientation of the Romans was followed with their naturalistic overlay. The titles of several speak for themselves, such as Hugh Plant's *The Jewell House of Art and Nature* ([1594] 1979) and Gabriel Plattes's *A Discovery of the Treasure Hidden since the Worlds Beginning* (1638). These sentiments are conspicuous examples of an ideological emphasis on the infinite wealth to be extracted from the earth, properly fertilized and amended.

The ideological focus on the land as the primary source of increased wealth and the "jewel box" metaphor parallel the development of physiocratic thought in France, as elaborated in Alix Cooper's contribution to this volume. They also accord with the prevailing view of most economic writers through Adam Smith and into the middle of the nineteenth century. D. McNally (1988) has described the reverse side of this pattern of emphasis in pre-Smithian thought, namely, that in competitive commercial exchange, no surplus can be accumulated—only payment made for the use of capital. The only source of surplus to promote investment in new commercial and industrial development was assumed to come from rent that was necessarily accumulated solely by the landlord class (see also Caton 1985). While in Xenophon's *Ways and Means* this infinite wealth perspective was applied to the Athenian silver mines, there is no echo of Xenophon in either the Roman or English agricultural writers. However, the *Ways and Means* was accepted as advice on economic administration and was appended to the 1698 edition of Charles Davenant's work on trade, and later to the 1751 edition of William Petty's *Political Arithmetick* (Lowry 1987, 49).

Our problem is to identify the audience for the agricultural manuals of the late sixteenth and seventeenth centuries and to evaluate their impact. There was clearly a large class of those involved in agriculture that were designated as "yeomen" or "copyholders" or both. In the late-fifteenth- and early-sixteenth-century struggle between landlords and tenants, the Crown and the courts supported the interests of the copyholders. The enclosures of this period converted arable land to sheep walks and reduced rural population. In this context, enclosures disturbed the Tudor monarchy, although later enclosures for better management of cropland were accepted. At the same time, rising grain prices and falling wool prices during the sixteenth century were leading manor lords to move from copyhold tenancies to leaseholds, where rents could be raised more freely as grain prices rose. Macfarlane (1978, 83) estimates that a third of the land in England was held under copyhold tenures at the beginning of the seventeenth century. We can only guess at the amount held as freeholds by husbandmen not classified as knights, gentlemen, or esquires. The small freeholders were a growing class, the yeomanry, but many copyholders of inheritance held titles that were equally secure. There was no public registry of land titles through the seventeenth century, and thus records are based on surviving legal documents. It is easy for moderns to forget the importance of a social definition of land titles that makes the public record a reliable source of one's legal rights. As a result, an unrecorded deed held by a third party is legally irrelevant. Public provision of an absolute reference for title plus the modern U.S. practice of requiring documentation of prices paid combine to create a reasonably informed market in land.

Allen's (1992, 207–8) statistically oriented study of the Midlands documents a doubling of agricultural production during the period from around 1500 to 1700. He attributes this increase in production to improved seed and the yeomen's adoption of improved agricultural practices. His study includes copyholders as yeomen. Allen characterizes the increase as the first or yeoman's agricultural revolution, to be distinguished from the more widely recognized upsurge in agricultural production after 1750, which he identifies as the landlord's agricultural revolution (231).

Allen uses the term *yeoman* to designate the small independent farmer who aggressively implemented the improved agricultural methods and raised productivity during the late sixteenth and early seventeenth centuries. The group included freeholders and copyholders with estates for life, frequently held by "the custom of the manor." It also included leaseholders with long leases, who would have had some interest in improving the land.

Technically, the yeoman had been identified as a freeholder with an income of forty shillings a year and over. This had been the requirement for enfranchisement in a statute of 1429 that permitted the yeomanry to participate in the election of representatives to parliament. By the early 1600s, inflation had made forty shillings a much lower threshold. In the early seventeenth century, the operative distinction was a matter of economic control. What was critical was whether the small farmer could control his land either through freehold status or through copyhold on a manor where enclosure permitted him to benefit from practices not followed by his neighboring tenants. Mildred Campbell (1942, 12) derived insights on the yeoman class from her extensive perusal of muster roles, parish records, and lawsuits. They indicate that the yeomanry was still considered a class in the early 1600s, falling below "gentleman" and "esquire," but above "husbandman" and "labourer." Each village had several prosperous yeomen who were adding to their estates and who were taking on local civic duties eschewed by the gentry (354–56).

In the latter part of the 1500s, landlords were motivated to regain control over the manor lands tied up in copyhold tenures through illegal enclosures of common grazing land and harassment of copyholders. Manor lords did not necessarily focus on introducing sheep walks. With inflation, contractual rents on life estates by copyhold were quite low. Although the wool trade was no longer so inviting, much higher rents could be obtained from leasing land. Alternatively, revenue could be derived from outright sales as freeholds (Reid 1995, 245–46).

A sermon by Hugh Latimer provides a picture of the intellectual state of the yeomanry. Given before Edward VI in the middle of the sixteenth century, it decries the ineffectuality of protests and statutes designed to protect the "comeners." Latimer goes on: "For if ye bryng it to passe, that the yomanry be not able to put their sonnes to schole (as in dede universities do wonderously decaye all redy) . . . I say ye plucke salvation from the people and utterly distroy the realm. . . . For by yomans sonnes, the fayth of Christ is, and hath bene mayntained chefely. Is this realme taught by rich mens sonnes? No, no" (quoted in Reid 1995, 254 n. 138). This speech suggests a generally accepted awareness of rising literacy among the yeomanry and a sense of class mobility. Moreover, it implies that the concept of "yeoman" at this time included prosperous copyholders whose tenures were being assaulted.

The local clergyman and schoolteacher were frequently draftsmen for copyholder complaints. Hugh Latimer was himself the son of a yeoman. There is no good source of information on the literacy level of the yeomanry, but Campbell (1942, 263–76) finds over 60 percent of them could sign their names on some surviving muster roles, and some diaries and wills indicate personal libraries—mostly religious books. To fill out the picture, we should note that Shakespeare's father was listed as a yeoman, as was Sir Isaac Newton's. The students at Oxford between 1567 and 1622 were identified by social class. Fewer than half were sons of the gentry, nobility, and clergy. The majority, over seven thousand, were mostly listed as "plebeians" and included less than a thousand unclassified (271).

We can surmise that a significant percentage of the ambitious and energetic yeoman farmers of the late sixteenth and early seventeenth centuries could read. Campbell cites what she considers a conservative estimate from an early-seventeenth-century scholar, Thomas Wilson, that in England, around 10,000 yeomen (freeholders) had incomes of three hundred to five hundred pounds per year or better, and some 60,000 had lesser incomes. These data were drawn from sheriffs' jury lists of freeholders, not including copyholders and leaseholders. At the end of the seventeenth century, Gregory King estimated that England held 40,000 wealthier and 160,000 less wealthy freeholders (Campbell 1942, 219).

A more precise image of the yeoman as a nascent agricultural capitalist is drawn by Macfarlane (1978, 177) from the writings of Sir Thomas Smith's *De Republica Anglorum* of 1565. Comparing the French and English, Smith emphasized class mobility in England: "[They] do their business, and travail to acquire riches; these be (for the most part) farmers unto gentlemen, which with grazing, frequenting of markets, and keeping servants not idle as the gentleman doth, but sich as get both their own living and part of their masters, by these means do come to such wealth, that they are able and daily do buy the lands of unthrifty gentlemen." He goes on to say that they send their sons to the universities to study law or such and become free from labor.

Although some scholars have contended that only the gentry were functionally literate, the many agricultural manuals and their repeated editions suggest a wide readership among a newly literate section of the population. While Fitzherbert's *Book of Husbandry*, first published in 1523, was formally addressed to young gentlemen taking up the management of estates, we note that all Latin phrases were followed by English translations. In addition, he provides suggestions for those who cannot write. For example, when making a weekly tour of the land, a stick could be carried and notched as a reminder of things noticed that needed attention. We can compare this with writings such as Gerard Malynes's tracts from the early seventeenth century, which were liberally salted with Latin phrases and asides that were presumed to be intelligible to the merchant audience.

Among the people of Appalachia and the upland South in the United States, many Elizabethan words and phrases survive along with well-documented folk ballads. The image of the dog-eared, well-thumbed remnant of an instructional manual that had passed from hand to hand is caught by the expression, referring to a knowledgeable person, "What he don't know was tore out."

Agriculture and Formal Science in the Age of Newton

The Newtonian revolution in science as it is usually portrayed cannot be shown to have any significant influence on the "revolutions" in agricultural production of the early seventeenth and late eighteenth centuries.

Sarah Wilmot's (1990) study of agricultural science in Britain between 1770 and 1870 shows that the increased yields of the late 1700s came from crop rotations, drainage, and livestock breeding. The agricultural research program of the period emphasized field trials, magazines, and livestock shows. The research did little more than extend early-seventeenth-century knowledge and practices. Soils chemistry during the 1700s was irrelevant or erroneous as a contribution to the improvement of agricultural productivity. Only Justus von Liebig's contributions to soils chemistry in the 1840s placed the field on a sound scientific course. Another half-century had to pass before this new level of knowledge had significant influence on agricultural production (Wilmot 1990, 22–30). The eighteenth- and early-nineteenth-century problem was the practical implementation of what was already known. Many of the problems were institutional. Other problems were primarily with the dissemination of technical information. Wilmot summarizes this period of developing capitalist agriculture: "In practical terms the landlord's role in the late-eighteenth and early-nineteenth centuries was as provider of fixed capital. . . . In this respect [Arthur] Young, firstly, urged the nobility and gentry to 'act like merchants'; . . . [raise capital] 'and this capital once raised should be sacred to the intended purpose'" (56).

The problem was articulated as far back as Fitzherbert that tenants holding at will or with short leases avoided making capital or long-term improvements to the land for fear of having their rents raised as the value of the land increased. Francis Home, a prominent researcher in the mid-eighteenth century, urged that the distinction be kept clear that revenue from the inherent fertility of the land and from increases in productivity belonged to the landlord as rent, but that increased yields resulting from the skill of the tenant should belong to him (Wilmot 1990, 56–57). Such a division implies that the landlord should provide funds for liming and manuring the land to its potential. Others decried the practice of some landlords of refusing long leases in order to maximize control over their tenants. However, leases usually included control by the landlord over cropping practices and the tenant's equipment (56–57). This friction between the interests of landlord and tenant during the "second" agricultural revolution is also elucidated by E. P. Thompson's (1975) study of the conflict between small freeholders and the new capitalist farmers in the 1740s. However, the political and economic overtones of the early-seventeenth-century and late-eighteenth-century agrarian revolutions need to be developed separately, as does the consideration of what C. J. Reid (1995) has called the "landlord's revolution."

Returning to the seventeenth-century agricultural manuals themselves, their narrow technical agronomic focus was broadened somewhat by the acceptance of turnips, clover, and other legumes as rotation crops in lieu of fallowing the fields. This was partially tied to the development of enclosures, freeing the copyholders from the open field system. When the fields were thrown open to common grazing after grain harvest and during fallow, a farmer could not justify planting clover or turnips as soil improvers, only to have them overgrazed or destroyed by other people's livestock. Clover and other legumes are nitrogen-fixing; they make high-quality hay, while turnips have a deep taproot that opens the subsoil to improve internal drainage and can be plowed under to add organic matter to the soil. Turnips could also be pulled for winter livestock feed. Grazing sheep, however, can eat the bulb of the turnip in the ground and defeat the potential of the crop for storage as winter fodder. Varro recommended plowing a crop of lupines under as "green manure," but such practices did not spread into England on a significant scale until the mid-1600s. The use of turnips and legumes was well developed in the Netherlands, however.

Some scholars place the increase in yields in the latter half of the 1600s and attribute it primarily to clover and turnips (Jones 1965). They dismiss "up and down" or "convertible husbandry," but this view misdates the period of increased productivity.

The emphasis on clover and turnips as the backbone of the increases in agricultural production is highly overrated, according to Eric Kerridge ([1967] 1968). These crops were not suited to all lands and were introduced toward the middle of the seventeenth century, while the great increase in yields came much earlier, in the latter 1500s and early 1600s. Kerridge attributes the progress in English agriculture to the indigenous developments of "up-and-down husbandry" and "the floating of water meadows" (chaps. 3 and 6). Although field-use data is scarce, Kerridge finds sufficient references to the discontinuation of the practice of fallowing on continually cropped grain land and replacing this custom with alternations between grain and pasture grasses. This practice, up-and-down husbandry, raised grain yields per acre markedly. Also, diverting streams to flood meadowlands at intervals fertilized them with silt and led to multiple increases in hay yields.

Equally important to the increased production of the early 1600s was the obsessive culture of fertilization—lime, marl, dung, and everything else organic that could be swept, scraped, scavenged, or pilfered to plow into the fields (Kerridge [1967] 1968, chap. 5; Woodward 1990). References to "loads" or "sacks" of lime or marl are difficult to evaluate, since even traditional measures vary from region to region. Some data suggest, however, that the farmers were dealing in tons rather than hundredweights of lime, marl, and other soil amendments. Anyone familiar with the dramatic impact that fertilization has on "cropped-out" land knows that neighbors could not help but take notice and imitate. Kerridge ([1967] 1968, xx–xxi) also points out that the excessive concern over the open field system and enclosures is misplaced. Tenants on manors with open field systems could negotiate "severaltry" agreements, specifying lands to be withheld from common grazing. This could be done by trading rights or paying a small fee to the other tenants for "severalty." In his detailed history of the copyholders' struggle with the landlord on the extensive Ombersley Manor, Peter Large (1990) recounts that, toward the end of the seventeenth century, the copyholders made oral land-exchange arrangements to block up holdings for individual practices. The problem was to avoid any record that would support possible fines or questions over legal rights to make such arrangements.

In the middle of the 1600s we observe an intriguing interlude in agricultural thought when academic scientists became interested in agronomy. The most influential was Samuel Hartlib, who published several books on agriculture in the 1650s, advancing the concept of an agronomic cornucopia and advocating the cultivation of clovers (Thirsk 1985b). Hartlib, Robert Boyle, and others, including the physician-cum-economist Sir William Petty, were designated by Boyle in 1646 as the "Invisible College." This group of London scientists evolved into the Royal Society for the Advancement of Science in 1660. They were, however, primarily natural philosophers and academics. Some of them introduced a rather mystic tone into their interest in agricultural production.

Before formal academic agronomy became obsessed with the role of "vegetable salts" in soil fertility, there were some sound examples of more abstract field trials. Boyle, in particular, was skeptical of Paracelsean, Arabic, and Aristotelian elements and alchemical influences: "He demonstrated the need for experiment and observation as the foundation on which to build, . . . His work was a turning point in agricultural chemistry," although some of his theories were off the mark (Fussell 1971, 78).

Nicholas of Cusa (mid-1400s) made one of the first well-framed experiments by growing a plant in a carefully weighed tub of earth and then weighing the plant and the earth after it had grown. He determined that the plant must have obtained some mass from the air since the loss of weight of the earth did not account for the weight of the grown plant (44). The experiment was repeated by Johannes Baptista van Helmont (1577–1644) with a willow tree in a tub (56, 60). Van Helmont followed Paracelsus's system but believed that the two operative elements were air, or gasses, and water. Paracelsus's influence emphasized the balance between the elements—the Aristotelian earth, air, fire, and water, and the Arabic sulfur, mercury, and salt—as the basis of health. He brought botany and medicine into a common focus so that medical science embraced botany and nascent chemistry.

The late Tudor and early Stuart scientists were unhelpfully influenced by the alchemists and searched for a single general principle of plant growth. This was identified as "vegetable salt," present in various animal dungs in varying quantities and understood by scientists, as well as by farmers, to leach into the ground from uncovered manure piles. G. E. Fussell (1971, 59–60) quotes one historian to the effect that "the whole scientific world extolled in extravagant terms the virtues of a compound the true nature of which it had yet failed to grasp." Meanwhile, as Fussell reminds us, "Farmers of this period, both high and low, had one main worry, manure, . . . They dared not neglect any source of supply, however minute, . . . They were willing to undertake the labours of Hercules to build a sufficient dunghill or compost heap" (61).

A somewhat more practical experiment, similar to some of Francis Bacon's fertilizer and seed germination comparisons, was Walter Blith's set of test plots with a control. As reported in his book, *English Improver Improved* (1653), he applied dung, pond muck, marl, and "fold muck" (sheep droppings) to different plots and monitored the crop yields on them over several years. He noted which inputs performed better, observing that the marled land perpetuated its improved performance longer. However, he did not record specific yields (Fussell 1971, 68–69). Blith's failure to be specific about yields also characterizes other manuals, mostly written by gentlemen observers following the Roman pattern, which emphasized manuring for improvement. The academic science group, although formally emphasizing "observation and experiment," as with Boyle, seemed steeped in the Paracelsean tradition, looking for "the primal essence" of plant growth. This limited their concern for yields or productivity.

After the Invisible College evolved into the Royal Society in 1660, those interested in agriculture formed the "Georgics Committee." The name, of course, drew on the Roman tradition, specifically, Virgil's *Georgics*, his work on agriculture. These men understood that "the major industry of the time was food production," and their scholarly leisure was largely dependent on "the exploitation of their landed possessions" (Fussell 1971, 76). One of the first and most interesting efforts of the Royal Society was an attempt to survey farming practices across England. It was based on the circulation of "an exhaustive questionnaire." The returns were apparently poor or lost; however, some of them survive. Their focus on manuring practices and farming methods was consistent with the premise of the time, namely, that agricultural productivity was to be improved by extracting more wealth from the land (76–77).

Two other interesting studies, however, were actually published by the Royal Society. The best known of these agriculturally oriented publications is John Evelyn's book, *Sylva*, brought out in 1664, on forest trees and "the propagation of timber." The book included a supplement on pomology advocating the development of the "red strake" apple of Herefordshire, among other fruit trees, as a cider crop.

The other agricultural publication of the Royal Society seems to have fallen on deaf ears and serves as a prime example of the frequent dominance of cultural over rational influences. In 1662 the Royal Society appointed a committee to study the use of the potato as food for the masses (Salaman 1985, 447). This resulted in the 1664 publication of John Forster's *Englands Happiness Increased, or A Sure and Easie Remedy against all succeeding Dear Years*. "England's happiness" was to be achieved by planting the "roots called Potatoes." While new crops such as hops had been introduced in the 1580s, and turnips and clovers through the first half of the 1600s, potatoes, a New World crop, were primarily accepted as curiosities in house gardens in seventeenth-century England. Strangely, the crop had been adopted by the common people in Ireland at the end of the 1500s. The Irish people had found that British troops, in their sweeps through the country, burning or trampling down crops, ignored the potatoes. The survivors, hiding in the forests, could subsist on potatoes left in the ground after the troops moved on. What was ultimately so impressive about this crop was its yield per acre, which is what prompted Forster's book. Wheat and barley production rose, but good barley crops ran, at best, twenty-five bushels per acre, and wheat, under twenty. Potatoes, however, which weigh about the same as grain (fifty-five to sixty pounds per bushel), yielded over two hundred bushels per acre. Although only some 25 percent of the potato is dry matter, potatoes still yielded at least two to three times the basic food per acre as the small grains. Irish country folk successfully reared large families on little more than an acre of potatoes and a milk cow. R. N. Salaman (1985, 260) cites yields of 6.5 tons per acre at the beginning of the 1700s. Potatoes were only grudgingly accepted as a basic foodstuff in England after Irish laborers brought them into some areas in the 1700s, and English industrialists began to push them as a way to lower the subsistence wage of workers (Salaman 1985, chaps. 24–26). Salaman points out that regardless of the rational advantages of potato culture, the English farm and industrial workers were and remained "bread eaters." Even during the series of very poor harvests between 1793 and 1815, the working class clung to bread despite extremely high prices.

Conclusion

An overview of the accepted pattern of events during the 1500s and early 1600s in England produces a convincing picture of a major agricultural transition. Plow land was being sacrificed to sheep walks during the 1400s and early 1500s at a time when grain farming barely produced a 5 to 10 percent surplus over the subsistence needs of the people on the land. The question to be resolved is quite clear: How, in the face of these constraints, did the population increase some 70 percent between 1520 and 1600, and urbanization increase markedly in the following century? Furthermore, how can we explain this gross increase in agricultural capacity to support an increased population in the face of a documented deterioration of the climate during this particular period? At the same time, there was a significant increase in the commercial and naval superstructure of the society, which placed an additional burden on the agricultural base with no major imports of food. The simple arithmetic of the situation requires a significant increase in per-acre grain production in England. In this setting, the role of technical innovations in production is very convincing despite the paucity of data on yields per acre and gross production.

Kerridge's ([1967] 1968) analysis of an indigenous shift away from continuous cropping of grain lands with a third-year fallow is agronomically convincing. Independent farmers began a practice of planting grain on their good land for three or four years, then putting it in pasture for four or five. This practice, "up-and-down farming" or "convertible husbandry," resulted in much higher grain yields per acre and the plowing of previous pastureland. Also, "water meadows," the flooding of lowland meadows, produced great increases in hay crops for wintering livestock. Allen's (1992) careful statistical study of the Midlands in the early 1600s gives us a supporting picture of improved land management and farming techniques with accompanying higher yields. These land management practices went hand-in-glove with an enhanced program of fertilization.

Increased agricultural surpluses can be documented not only by the development of markets for agricultural produce, but also by increased rents on leaseholds and on short-term copyhold lands. This commercial influence appears to have stimulated a tremendous increase in heavy fertilization and soil amendment. Liming, marling, manuring, and amelioration of heavy clays with sand, or sandy soils with clays or humus, could be justified when significant increases in yields provided marketable surpluses.

McRae (1996) has documented the broader cultural spirit of rationalism that replaced a moralistic tradition during the 1500s. In agriculture, this rationalistic tradition is best exhibited in the emergence of an emphasis on surveying. This commitment to quantification became a form of agrarian accounting in such treatises as John Norden's *The Surveiors Dialogue* of 1618, where a survey included an identification of the various soil types and recommendations for optimal land use. This concern for quantification and resource development was carried to a "perambulation" of the national timber supply by A. Standish (1612) and by John Evelyn (1664).

The shift toward rationalism coincided with the proliferation of instructional manuals on agricultural topics. Supported by the newly developed printing press, cheap reading matter and increased literacy appear to have been mutually reinforcing developments. The agricultural manuals were repetitious and went through multiple editions, suggesting that the publishers failed to anticipate the extent of the market demand. Although they emphasized fertilization and soil amendment plus some planting techniques, these manuals seem all cut from the same cloth. They echo the high-quality technical advice on liming, manuring, and soil amendment found in the Roman agricultural texts that were part of the literature available to the educated gentry (Fussell 1972). Their mantra was "observation and experiment," and their orientation was toward the earth as the source of increased wealth (Schaffer 1997). The premise that the land was the only source of real wealth supported an assumption that investment was derived from rents. This assumption dominated economic thought up to the time of the physiocrats and the writings of Adam Smith (McNally 1988; Caton 1985; Smith [1759] 1976, 1:219–20).

At the same time, formal academic science was generally irrelevant to agriculture or even erroneous in many cases. As late as 1757, Francis Home, a leading Edinburgh chemist, could make the following comment on the failure of agricultural research to keep up with the advances in all other sciences during the previous 150 years. Referring to agriculture, Home wrote, "It seems to be little better understood . . . at present, than amongst the ancients; and I believe Virgil and Columella may still be reckoned the best authors on this subject" (Fussell 1971, 117). Although Fussell considers Home's observation a bit of an overstatement, it is a valid comment on the sophistication of the Roman agricultural writers and on the pedestrian progress of agriculture through the seventeenth century.

The institutional aspect of this episode in agricultural productivity needs to be more systematically correlated with the technical developments. The yeoman class, made up of small freeholders, grew in the aftermath of the Black Death and the disintegration of the manorial system during the 1400s and early 1500s. At the same time, many copyholders on the manors had acquired, under "the custom of the manor," inheritable estates and money rents fixed at very low levels before the inflations of the early 1500s. These groups could take advantage of commercial agricultural opportunities by implementing long-term land improvement and management plans. Although Campbell (1942) and Macfarlane (1978, 1988) have been conspicuous in emphasizing the yeomanry component in the agricultural revolution of the early 1600s, it is even more explicit in Allen's work. The full story of the erosion of the role of the yeomanry, which came to include relatively independent copyholders, involves a complex evolution of legal and political reversals. Estimated to control more than half the agricultural land in England in the early 1600s, the freeholders and copyholders lost their economic edge in the latter half of the 1600s. Copyholders' petitions to get their titles converted to freeholds were ignored by parliaments in the Interregnum of the 1650s. After the Restoration of 1660, the legal climate changed, copyholders lost legal support, and their rights tended to lapse. The surviving gentry adjusted to the new standards of agricultural productivity and markets for grain and livestock. With hired labor and "rack rents," that is, rents that extorted full potential value from the land, leaving the tenant in a subsistence position, the manorial system gained a new lease on life (Beckett 1990). This process provided the setting for capitalist agriculture and the grand manorial estates with impressive "landscape gardens" of the eighteenth century and the second agricultural revolution of the late 1700s. The spontaneous vitality of the yeomanry of the 1500s and early 1600s was dissipated; though some of the more prosperous became gentrified, others hung on as smallholders, trying to protect their rights against large influential agricultural investors. This conflict was pictured by Thompson's (1975) account of the "Black Acts" of the 1740s. Most former yeomen became renters, laborers, or craftsmen, or drifted to the growing urban centers. In retrospect, it remains for historians to give full credit to the yeoman episode in providing the agricultural foundation for the early flowering of English commercial and protoindustrial expansion. The yeoman role in institutionalizing the agricultural techniques that undergirded the capitalist agriculture of the eighteenth century and the second agricultural revolution also deserves more attention.

References

Allen, R. C. 1992. *Enclosure and the Yeoman*. Oxford: Clarendon Press.

Andersen, B. G., and H. W. Borns, Jr. 1994. *The Ice Age World: An Introduction to Quaternary History and Research with Emphasis on North America and Northern Europe during the Last 2.5 Million Years*. New York: Oxford University Press.

Aylmer, G. E. 1980. The Meaning and Definition of "Property" in Seventeenth-Century England. *Past and Present* 86 (February): 87–97.

Baack, Ben. 1979. The Development of Exclusive Property Rights to Land in England: An Exploratory Essay. *Economy and History* 22:63–74.

Baeck, L. 1994. *The Mediterranean Tradition in Economic Thought*. London: Routledge.

Beckett, J. 1990. Estate Management in Eighteenth-Century England: The Lowther-Spedding Relationship in Cumberland. In Chartres and Hey 1990, 55–72.

Braudel, Fernand. 1981. *The Structures of Everyday Life: The Limits of the Possible*. Vol. 1 of *Civilization and Capitalism: 15th–18th Century*. New York: Harper and Row.

Briffa, K. R., and T. J. Osborn. 2002. Blowing Hot and Cold. *Science*, 22 March, 2227–28.

Campbell, Mildred. 1942. *The English Yeoman under Elizabeth and the Early Stuarts*. New Haven, Conn.: Yale University Press.

Caton, H. 1985. The Preindustrial Economics of Adam Smith. *Journal of Economic History* 45:833–53.

Chartres, J., and D. Hey. 1990. *English Rural Society, 1500–1800: Essays in Honour of Joan Thirsk*. Cambridge: Cambridge University Press.

Cipolla, C. M. 1980. *Before the Industrial Revolution: European Society and Economy, 1000–1700*. 2d ed. London: W. W. Norton.

Clay, C. 1985. Landlords and Estate Management in England. In Thirsk 1985a, part 2, 119–251.

Dear, Peter. 1995. *The Mathematical Way in the Scientific Revolution*. Chicago: University of Chicago Press.

———. 2001. *Revolutionizing the Sciences: European Knowledge and Its Ambitions, 1500–1700*. Princeton, N.J.: Princeton University Press.

Evelyn, J. 1664. *Sylva or a Discourse of Forest-Trees, and the Propagation of Timber in his Majesties Domain*. London: Council of the Royal Society of London for the Improving of Natural Knowledge.

Fitzherbert, Mayster. [1534] 1965. *The Book of Husbandry*. Edited and with an introduction, notes, and a glossarial index by W. W. Skeat. Vaduz: Kraus Reprint.

Forster, John. 1664. *Englands Happiness Increased, or A sure and Easie Remedy against all succeeding Dear Years; by A Plantation of the Roots called Potatoes*. London: for A. Seile.

Fussell, G. E. 1947. *The Old English Farming Books: From Fitzherbert to Tull, 1523 to 1730*. London: Crosby Lockwood and Son.

———. 1971. *Crop Nutrition: Science and Practice before Liebig*. Lawrence, Kans.: Coronado Press.

———. 1972. *The Classical Tradition in West European Farming*. Cranbury, N.J.: Associated University Presses.

Grigg, David. 1982. *The Dynamics of Agricultural Change: The Historical Experience*. New York: St. Martin's Press.

Jones, E. L. 1965. Agriculture and Economic Growth in England, 1660–1750: Agricultural Change. *Journal of Economic History* 25.1:1–18.

Kerridge, Eric. [1967] 1968. *The Agricultural Revolution*. New York: Augustus M. Kelley.

Langdon, J. 1982. The Economics of Horses and Oxen in Medieval England. *Agricultural History Review* 30:31–40.

Large, Peter. 1990. Rural Society and Agricultural Change: Ombersley 1500–1700. In Chartres and Hey 1990, 105–38.

Lowry, S. T. 1987. *The Archaeology of Economic Ideas: The Classical Greek Tradition*. Durham, N.C.: Duke University Press.

Macfarlane, A. 1978. *The Origins of English Individualism: The Family, Property, and Social Transformation*. Cambridge: Cambridge University Press.

———. 1988. The Cradle of Capitalism: The Case of England. In *Europe and the Rise of Capitalism*, edited by J. Baechler, J. A. Hall, and M. Mann, 187–203. Oxford: Blackwell.

McNally, D. 1988. *Political Economy and the Rise of Capitalism: A Reinterpretation*. Berkeley, Calif.: University of California Press.

McRae, A. 1996. *God Speed the Plough: The Representation of Agrarian England, 1500–1660*. Cambridge: Cambridge University Press.

Norden, J. [1618] 1979. *The Surveiors Dialogue*. Amsterdam: Theatrum Orbis Terrarum.

Plant, Hugh. [1594] 1979. *The Jewell House of Art and Nature*. Norwood, N.J.: Walter Johnson.

Plattes, Gabriel. 1638. *A Discovery of the Treasure Hidden Since the Worlds Beginning*. London: I. L. for George Hutton.

Reid, C. J., Jr. 1995. The Seventeenth-Century Revolution in the English Land Law. *Cleveland State Law Review* 43:221–302.

Salaman, R. N. 1985. *The History and Social Influence of the Potato*. Rev. ed. by J. G. Hawkes. Cambridge: Cambridge University Press.

Schaffer, S. 1997. The Earth's Fertility as a Social Fact in Early Modern Britain. In *Nature and Society in Historical Context*, edited by M. Teich, R. Porter, and B. Gustafsson. Cambridge: Cambridge University Press.

Smith, Adam. [1759] 1976. *The Theory of Moral Sentiments*. Edited by A. L. Macfie and D. D. Raphael. Glasgow edition. Oxford: Oxford University Press.

Sommerville, J. P. 1999. *Royalists and Patriots: Politics and Ideology in England, 1603–1640*. London: Longman.

Standish, A. 1612. *The Commons Complaint, newly corrected and augmented*. London: William Stansby.

Thirsk, J. 1967. *The Agrarian History of England and Wales, 1500–1640*. Cambridge: Cambridge University Press.

———. 1983. Plough and Pen: Agricultural Writers in the Seventeenth Century. In *Social Relations and Ideas: Essays in Honour of R. H. Hilton*, edited by T. H. Aston et al., 295–318. Cambridge: Cambridge University Press.

———, ed. 1985a. *Agrarian Change*, part 2 of *1640–1750*, vol. 5 of *The Agrarian History of England and Wales*. Cambridge: Cambridge University Press.

———. 1985b. Agricultural Innovations and Their Diffusion. In Thirsk 1985a, 533–88.

———. 1985c. Agricultural Policy: Public Debate and Legislation. In Thirsk 1985a, 298–388.

———. 1992. Making a Fresh Start: Sixteenth-Century Agriculture and the Classical Inspiration. In *Culture and Cultivation in Early Modern England: Writing and the Land*, edited by M. Leslie and T. Raylor, 15–34. Leicester: Leicester University Press.

Thompson, E. P. 1975. *Whigs and Hunters*. New York: Pantheon Books.

Varro, M. T. 1936. *On Agriculture*. Translated by W. D. Hooper. Loeb Classical Library. Cambridge: Harvard University Press.

Wilmot, Sarah. 1990. *The Business of Improvement: Agriculture and Scientific Culture in Britain, c. 1770–c. 1870*. Historical Geography Research Series, no. 24. Bristol, U.K.: Historical Geography Research Society.

Woodward, Donald. 1990. "An Essay on Manures": Changing Attitudes to Fertilization in England, 1500–1800. In Chartres and Hey 1990, 251–78.

Wrigley, E. A. 1986. Urban Growth and Agricultural Change: England and the Continent in the Early Modern Period. In *Population and Economy: Population and History from the Traditional to the Modern World*, edited by R. I. Rotberg and T. K. Rabb, 123–68. Cambridge: Cambridge University Press.

Epicurean and Stoic Sources for Boisguilbert's Physiological and Hippocratic Vision of Nature and Economics

Paul P. Christensen

> The soul of the new system is of doing only what is in concert with the people and in relation to the true interests of all the public.
> —Pierre Le Pesant Boisguilbert (1705)

Pierre Le Pesant Boisguilbert (1646–1714) is known as a great precursor of physiocratic, classical, and Keynesian lines of analysis, one of the first writers to base the "hidden processes" of the economic order on a seventeenth-century theory of natural order (Spengler [1966] 1984), and the first to articulate the "liberal vision" of laissez-faire generally credited to François Quesnay and Adam Smith (Hecht 1989).[1] These anticipations are embedded in a remarkable theory of economics that treated production and "consumption as the [twin] drivers of economic prosperity," the requirements for equilibrium between asymmetric sectors and markets, and the causes of "economic disequilibrium, crisis, misery, and social disorder" (Carbon 1989; Faccarello [1986] 1999). The range and fecundity of a theory encompassing so many thinkers and

Special thanks to Jacqueline Hecht for her invaluable suggestions on the state of Boisguilbert research and affirmation of the importance of the connection to Fontenelle (Hecht 1996); Hal Cook for aid on developments in Holland and the role of Seneca in the rise of Epicureanism; Christian Strube for early help with references; and Christine Virol for access to her work on Vauban. I gratefully acknowledge invaluable critical readings by the editors, an anonymous referee, and Jessica Riskin, none of whom is responsible for my not making better use of their help.

1. He provides, Hecht (1989, 468) notes, "the germ of a great number of the contributions later developed . . . by Cantillon, Quesnay, Smith, Malthus, Say, Ricardo, Marx, Walras, and Keynes."

schools that are today at each other's throats suggest the existence of a deep and generative connection to a powerful philosophical and scientific system.[2]

For mainstream historians of economics, Boisguilbert's theoretical vision was a product of the theological and scientific matrix of Jansenism and Cartesian occasionalism (Perrot [1984] 1992). Joseph Spengler ([1966] 1984) credits his idea of natural order to his younger cousin, the "Cartesian Fontenelle." A few years in a Jansenist school reinforced by the moral and social theories of Blaise Pascal, Pierre Nicole, and Jean Domat are seen to forge an Augustinian vision of a human nature driven by "self-love, interest, lust and deceit" but masked by a ruse of concern for others (Perrot 1989; Faccarello [1986] 1999). With the addition of the political absolutism of Jean Bodin and Cardinal Richelieu "there emerges a Boisguilbert who is a Cartesian, an absolutist and an Augustinian" (Facarello [1986] 1999, 11). All this separates him from the English preclassicals and places him securely within the amour propre tradition of the French moralists, which those who consider Boisbuilbert a Cartesian occasionalist consider the main road to economic theory.

Although not without important strengths, this interpretation presents major difficulties. First, the occasionalist denial of nature's active powers and attribution of all motion to God's intervention are inconsistent with the central role Boisguilbert gives to nature's activity in economic and social life. Second, this thinking assumes an automatic connection between Cartesianism and Jansenism.[3] Third, Boisguilbert's insistence on evidence and hostility to speculative systems fit uneasily with Cartesian rationalism. Fourth, Bernard de Fontenelle's scientific and philosophical views were not Cartesian but those of a radical Epicurean (Niderst 1972, 1991). Lastly, this interpretation neglects Boisguilbert's links to the physiological production ideas of Thomas Hobbes and Sir William Petty, who have joined the ancient physics to William Harvey's new circulation physiology (Christensen 1989).

Boisguilbert's striking technical knowledge of the culture of grains and the obvious production underpinning of his asymmetric model of

2. Boisguilbert's treatment of changing expectations in the context of market disequilibrium, Facarello ([1986] 1999, 142) writes, appears to be so modern as to render suspect the historian's retrospective analysis.

3. Scholars now recognize that only a few Jansenist philosophers were closely identified with Cartesianism and that Antoine Arnauld, who was bitterly critical of Nicolas de Malebranche, was a significant exception. According to Jacques Roger (1971, 403), Pascal is much nearer to Pierre Gassendi than to Descartes.

agricultural and artisanal markets suggested an investigation of his possible connections to the emerging sciences of botany and natural history in France. This led to the great research projects of plant and animal anatomy conducted by the new Royal Academy of Sciences and to the publications of its leading scientists that set out an epistemology of experience and conception of an organic world unified and maintained by a continuous flow of active and nutritive materials through the kingdoms of nature.[4] The ties of these ideas to the Epicurean respiration chemistry of Harvey's English disciples (Frank 1980), the influence of Pierre Gassendi's epistemological and conceptual vision of science on the new academy and its research program, and Fontenelle's Epicureanism suggested a Gassendian influence on Boisguilbert. A parallel inquiry into Hippocratic ideas of nature and medicine as a source of Boisguilbert's ideas of "letting nature alone" led in its turn to the medical, political, and economic ideas of Gassendi's leading disciple, François Bernier, and the neo-Hippocratic medicine of the Gassendian physicians.[5] All this suggests that Boisguilbert's scientific ideas are closer to the Gassendians than to the Cartesians.

Section 1 offers a brief look at Boisguilbert's early life, the intellectual resources available in Rouen, and the theoretical alternatives they might have provided. Section 2 explores the academy's work on plant and animal physiology as sources of epistemological ideas and for a "physiological" model of economics. Section 3 sketches Boisguilbert's model of the production and circulation of agricultural and artisanal goods, the sectoral conditions of balance (on the point of a sword), and the unfortunate propensity of these asymmetric markets to fall into disequilibrium, as well as the relation of these ideas to the new theories of physiology and nature. Section 4 examines Gassendi's system with its ideas of nature and self-regulation in physics, physiology, and psychology as a source for Boisguilbert's view of nature, providence, and self-healing. Section 5 takes up the relation of Gassendian ethics and politics and its themes of "life, liberty, property, and the pursuit of happiness" to Boisguilbert's social-economic vision.

4. See especially Salomon-Bayet 1978, 109–29, which emphasizes the sustained concern with physiological function in the academy's research in relation to the circulation and the "heritage of Harvey" (129).

5. The daunting task of taking up this line of investigation has been made possible by the explosion of scholarship on Gassendi and Bernier opened by Bloch 1971. See Brundell 1987, Joy 1987, Darmon 1994, Darmon 1996, Duchesneau 1998, Murr 1997, Osler 1991, and Sarasohn 1996.

1. Family, Religious, and Intellectual Background

Boisguilbert was the second son of a high noble family in Rouen, related through his father to the dramatists and poets Pierre and Thomas Corneille.[6] He spent four years at the prestigious Jesuit College de Bourbon in Rouen before being sent to the Jansenist Port Royal school at Chesney (closed by the state in 1660, when Boisguilbert was fourteen years old).[7] The severity of the pedagogy, designed to separate children from parental influence, shaped a confident but difficult personality. Boisguilbert studied law (which he hated) in Paris, attaining the grade of advocate.

Before taking up legal practice, he "gave free rein to his strong taste for history and literature" (Hecht 1966a), publishing two translations of Roman history from the ancient Greek and a historical romance, *Mary Queen of Scots* (which had two editions and an English translation). In 1674, he was named a councilor to the Rouen parliament. Was he abandoning a literary career entirely or adopting the more prudent career path of his uncles, who early on combined the security of law and remuneration of public office available to his class with leisure for literature (soon replaced by science)?[8] Was it this connection to the model of his uncles, whose work was anathema to the Jansenists, that fueled the break with his parents? When his older brother was killed in battle, the main family estates and hereditary rank were passed to his younger brother. Angry and intensely competitive, Boisguilbert married a wealthy widow and applied himself to the study and practice of farming and commerce. The acute understanding of the culture of grains he displays in his treatises is described by the leading historian of French agronomy, Andre Bourde (1967, 1:129), as "more exact and precise than any agricultural manual of his epoch."

In 1678, Boisguilbert purchased the office of judge of Montevilliers, which introduced him to the intense poverty and misery of the

6. The Le Pesant family of Marthe Corneille and Boisguilbert's father had been advocates and officeholders for generations. Both Corneille uncles went to the Jesuit College in Rouen and were advocates. On the exceptional importance given to Marthe Le Pesant and the law in the family history by Thomas Corneille and Fontenelle, see Le Gall 1997.

7. It had been thought that the decision to send the Boisguilbert children to Port Royal schools was due to the influence of the Corneille uncles. Jacqueline Hecht (1996) reports new evidence that indicates it was Boisguilbert's father who was close to the Jansenists.

8. On the uncles' career path, see Le Gall 1997. Theirs was the path, Niderst (1991, 19–21) suggests, that was followed by Boisguilbert and urged on Fontenelle, who instead chose the insecurity of geometry over the confusion of the law.

countryside, problems that became central concerns in his work. Together with the great Protestant merchant Thomas Legendre,[9] he undertook an ambitious program to collect statistics, analyze the causes of the disastrous state of the French economy, and provide a program of fiscal reform that would relieve the peasants of their heavy financial burdens and thereby restore the economy to health.[10] Boisguilbert's theoretical and policy program is first laid out in his *Le détail de la France* ([1695] 1966), whose prepublication circulation may have influenced his appointment in 1690 as *lieutenant-général* of Normandy under Louis Pontchartrain, the controller general of France, minister of finance (Colbert's former office).[11]

From 1691 until his death in 1714, Boisguilbert sent a stream of letters, short papers, and treatises to Ponchartrain and his successors attempting to convince the ministers of his radical solutions for reform of the finances and economy. After *Le détail* appeared anonymously, he was prohibited from publication. Despite the ban, *Le détail* appeared in some fifteen editions during his life. In 1707, he brought out *Le détail*, *Factum de la France*, and *Traité de la nature . . . des grains* under Vauban's name and was sentenced to a short but costly exile. A more complete edition of his works was made in 1712. His work was obviously known by the physiocrats and by Smith but otherwise neglected outside France until Marx—a neglect that continues in English outside a few specialist histories (see Groenewegen 2001).

We do not know the path Boisguilbert followed to the study of the "new system of nature" and its foundation for a vision of economics and society. It is quite possible his agricultural investigations led him to the "new vegetable physiology" produced by the botanists and chemists of the Academy of Science, which would have led in turn to the ideas about nature's inherent powers of productivity and conservation that are

9. Legendre is said to have responded to Jean-Baptiste Colbert's query of what to do about the economy with the "well-known remark . . . '*laissez nous faire*'" (Turgot, cited in Castelot [1925] 1987, 116).

10. Le Maréchal de Vauban has generally been connected with the inception of this project. Virol 2002 shows that Vauban became involved only later. His project, the *Dîme royale* (an income tax of one-twentieth), published in 1707, was coordinated and assembled by Vauban's associate, the Jansenist abbé Ragot de Beaumont, who borrowed considerable material from Boisguilbert's research and writing. Boisguilbert favored a tax on agricultural earnings and was very critical of the *Dîme*.

11. *Le détail* was written some ten years before its publication. Boisguilbert knew Jérome Ponchartrain, the controller general's son, who would soon be appointed to head the ministry of maritime affairs (Niderst 1991).

central features of his work. A second possibility was that his early literary career, inspired by the example of his uncles, led him from the Christian humanism of the uncles, through the historical reconstruction of the literary and philosophical knowledge of antiquity undertaken by their erudite friends, to the study of the new sciences, which were being built on ancient foundations. This was the path that might have beckoned once he engaged the uncles' commitment to the "precious culture of antiquity," the moral virtues of the Roman Republic, and the philosophy of the Stoics (Poirier 1984). A third possibility is that his main introduction to the new ideas awaited the pioneering contributions of his younger cousin to the popular communication of science in the mid-1680s.

Now let us briefly explore the implications of a connection to the uncles and their friends. This connection makes sense of his early concern with translations of Roman history from the ancient Greek and provides his introduction to the Stoic philosopher Seneca, who had a special importance for him. Seneca opened the door to Epicureanism by his sympathetic presentation of Epicurus and the passions as positive forces in contrast to the negative value they had in Jansenist morality.[12] Boisguilbert's family connections also help account for the very strong attraction that he has for the theater, the place he gives to comedy as the "highest" of the professions, and the use he makes of Jansenist expressions such as "the arrow of God" as literary devices in the manner of Pierre Corneille rather than as signs of adhesion to Jansenist doctrine.[13] Nicole's vicious attack on Pierre Corneille's plays in 1667—which accused him of "poisoning the souls of the faithful"—and the wounds it inflicted on Corneille make it unlikely that Boisguilbert would have been on the Jansenist side in this affair.

A movement from history and literature to science would have been facilitated by the friends and supporters of the Corneilles, especially Emeric Bigot, a scion of a great Protestant legal family and dedicated

12. On the important role played by Seneca in the transition from the neo-Stoic hostility to the passions as the enemy of reason to an acceptance of the passions as a regulative guide for human activity in Holland, see Cook 2002. A heavily annotated book of Seneca is all that remains of Boisguilbert's library (Hecht 1996).

13. Pierre Corneille notes the capacity of comedy to bring pleasure and enlightenment to a broader audience than can tragedy. The fact that comedians had been put on the list of persons excluded from communion in 1654 (Le Gall 1997, 465) suggests that Boisguilbert was not being lighthearted. For Corneille's frequent use of Jansenist religious tropes such as the "arrow of God" and the insistence that they do not implicate him in Jansenist beliefs, see Ferreyrolles 1985.

Hellenist who had devoted his life to books. Bigot sponsored the regular thematic discussions for the young advocates of Rouen in which Fontenelle would later participate (Niderst 1991). He was part of a circle of erudites, historians, and translators that included Gilles Ménage, who dedicated his translation of *Diogenes Laertes* to Bigot. This would provide another important introduction to Epicurean philosophy and ethics and open the pathway that led from the historical and philosophical interests of late humanists to the doorstep of Gassendi's great edifice of an empirically and theoretically oriented philosophy and science.

Given Boisguilbert's economic interests, we expect he encountered Bernier's *Travels in the Mongol Empire* ([1670–71] 1916) and its analysis of the economic decline of authoritarian political systems rather early on. This would bring to his attention Bernier's ([1684] 1992) *Abrégé* of Gassendi and its extensive coverage of ideas of nature, providence, and the common interest. Hobbes and Petty would likewise reinforce the connections between the new economics and Epicureanism.

All of these links would have enabled a deeper appreciation of Fontenelle's *Conversations on Other Worlds* ([1686] 1790), which would not have been obvious to the uninitiated reader. Certainly the first message of this work, with its use of vortices to explain planetary motion and its comparison of the universe to a watch whose operations "are conducted by regular movements and depend on the arrangement of the parts" (20), is Cartesian.[14] Descartes and his cosmology are praised. But as L. Marsak (1959, 15) points out, an important distinction is present between the mechanics of physical motion and a living world of prodigious fecundity and magnificence that display purpose, intelligence, and God's providential concern for his creatures. Apart from his fidelity to the physics and the idea of a general mechanism at work in nature and human art, the bulk of the references to Descartes, Niderst (1972, 276) argues, are superficial and even misleading. The deeper debts to Bernier and Gassendi are unacknowledged. Nature makes everything by capacities inherent in matter (Fontenelle [1686] 1790, 2:135); nature is designed to work harmoniously, she keeps in view the needs of all living beings (2:130), has much of mind (2:86), and displays a vitalism and purpose in her capacity for regulation and conservation. These ideas appear to come directly from Bernier (2:280).

14. Gottfried Leibniz will critique the comparison of the universe to a clock. Fontenelle responds in *Lettres galantes* (letter 12) with a "remarkable" critique of the Cartesian animal machine based on Gassendi (Roger 1971, 346). Niderst (1991, 67) calls this work a "breviary of radical Epicureanism."

It was Gassendi (1658) who made the arguments about nature's magnificence and economy well before Leibniz and Malebranche debated these issues. Nature makes all things "with a certain harmony and *convenance* [fitness and expediency]" (Bernier [1684] 1992, 4:254). The terms *order of nature* and *laws of nature*, which historians of economics attribute to Cartesianism, are in their turn found in the methodological treatise of the Gassendian physicist Edme Mariotte ([1678] 1992, 23, 32). It is these ideas about nature that permeate Boisguilbert's writing.

2. Production and Circulation in the New Vegetable Physiology

Starting from the proposal of Claude Perrault that all the members of the newly established Royal Academy of Sciences engage in a common project studying "the anatomy and knowledge of plants," the academy's scientists produced a new "vegetable physiology" and, in conjunction with a parallel study of animals, a new conception of unity of organisms and organic nature based on the linked nutritional requirements of plants and animals. A basic feature of this nutritional model was the analogical extension of Harvey's model of the circulation of the blood to plants, an imperfect model to be sure, but one that spotlighted the central importance of plant production in supplying nutrients to animals. The result was a model, conceived in terms of the chemical combination, use, and reassembly of basic elements taken from the soil, sun, and air. All nature was linked together in a material chain of transformations and circulations that a sustained chemical analysis would somehow eventually reveal (Salomon-Bayet 1978, 77–87; Stroup 1990).[15] It is this conception of an organic nature maintained in a state of reciprocal and "mutual need" by the continuous production and circulation of nutritive materials that we see at the center of Boisguilbert's theory of economics production, circulation, and consumption.

The methodological ideas presented in the early natural histories published by the academy are of particular interest.[16] Perrault queried the

15. Delaporte 1982 attributes the new interest in plants to a leveling by Cartesian mechanics that gives plants the same status with animals as machines. But the philosophical inspirations of Marchello Malpighi, Nehemiah Grew, and John Ray, as well as the scientists of the early Royal Academy, were not Cartesian. In fact, Cartesians were excluded from the academy in the early decades.

16. The early anatomical studies were presented in two *Mémoires*, the first on animals (Perrault [1671] 1676) and the second on plants (Dodart 1676). Each volume was republished many

place of principles and experience and insisted on the sovereignty of facts, exact observations, and experience, an emphasis that Alberto Tenenti (1953, 305) sees as separating itself from the Cartesian method of philosophizing deductively from a few principles and examples. One proceeds, Perrault ([1671] 1676) wrote, "by the multiplication of detail" to move toward more general notions. Theoretical assumptions are, of course, imbedded throughout; the central notion being "provided by the word 'nature' which is always employed to designate an ensemble characterized by necessity and finality and which is always wise, industrious, provident, and farsighted" (in Tenenti 1953, 306). The relevance of this for Boisguilbert is evident and may have influenced his choice of title for his first work, *Le détail de la France*.

Perrault presented the first paper on plants (on the circulation of the sap) in January 1667. He proposed an initial preparation in the soil by the heat of the sun and a second in the roots. The resulting sap is carried by the "arteries" in the woody parts to nourish the branches and leaves. Exhausted of its powers, it is returned to the roots by the "veins" in the bark, to be replenished and circulated anew (Perrault [1680–88] 1721). Perrault ([1680–88] 1721, 110) insists on a distinction between a "physical circulation that perfects the sap" and a mechanical circulation of an unchanged liquid by a pump.[17]

Perrault drew the conclusion that all the parts exist in the interior of the organism in a state of "mutual need" and of cause and effect (79). Circulation prepares the nutrients for assimilation and assures the continuity of the dissimilar yet necessary parts of the organism, none of which is privileged. The implications in the following passage for a theory of organic unity and nutrition in the human economy cannot have escaped the attention of an alert reader (the vitalism here may be compared to what we saw in Bernier and what reappeared in Fontenelle): "The

times, including by Fontenelle (1733, vols. 3 and 4). I have been unable to study Dodart's volume. Stroup 1990 reports Dodart's interest in nutrition, his chemical approach (99), and his concern with elaborating methodological issues (87), although she gives no indication of their epistemological content. Dodart was a devout Jansenist but not apparently a Cartesian. He does not seem to have been an occasionalist (see footnote 25).

17. The report of the initial paper is in Keller 1974. Perrault published his paper in a collection he entitled *The Mechanics of Animals* (in [1680–88] 1721). He insisted that animals are not pure machines but beings with sentiment and capacities of exercising the functions of life by "the principle of the soul" (3:329). He rejected the (Cartesian) view that animals are automatons and based his theory on the view of "some ancient philosophers" that the animal body is animated by subtle and volatile particles provided by respiration (4:517–20).

sympathy and mutual conspiracy which all the philosophers recognize in the parts of living bodies, and which distinguish them from the inanimate have never been so . . . clearly explained as they are by the commerce that the heart and all the other parts have together by means of the circulation" (79).

Perrault's model of the sap was challenged in July 1668 by the physicist Edme Mariotte, a new member of the academy.[18] He argued that the "principles" taken from the earth by the roots were too thin and "not suited for nourishing . . . the plant." He placed the crux of nutrient preparation in the leaves, where additional materials are absorbed and the heat of the sun perfects the sap as it passes through the small tubes. Mariotte ([1679] 1923, 82) considered this part of the process analogous to "animal vegetation," where "the blood is perfected in the small vessels of the lungs, liver, and glands." This more nutritive humor flows to the flowers, fruits, and other parts by tubes in the outer ring of the stem, which are the true "arteries" of plants.[19]

Features of Mariotte's model of the circulation of the sap that made it especially appropriate for a model of the human economy were the localization of production within the plant and its spatial separation in two sites, the site of initial elaboration (primary production) and the site where the initial materials were brought to perfection (secondary production). These were connected to each other by two distinct circuits, one carrying the primary product and the second the perfected or finished product. This contrasted with the animal circulation, where the blood continuously circulated, picking up and dropping off an inflow of nutrients and outflow of waste. Partly because Harvey insisted on a vitalistic unity of the blood, the separation between the blood and the nutrients took time to clarify. The plant model put nutrition and the distinction between material nutrients and the active substances responsible for vital activity in clear relief.

Mariotte's *Vegetation of Plants* ([1679] 1923) also elaborates a simple chemical theory of the composition of plants. His atomistic hypothesis

18. The verbal report of Mariotte's paper is given in Heller 1986. It does not substantively differ from the published version. Mariotte is an atomist and chemist whose "critical and skeptical rationalism" reflects Gassendi (Roger 1971, 201). He wrote an important methodological treatise ([1678] 1992) designed in part to counter the Port Royal logic of Nicole and Pascal.

19. Mariotte's paper was challenged by the physician Du Clos and the chemist Bourdelin, both "impregnated with medieval conceptions." The result, despite Perrault's coming over to Mariotte's view, was a decision of the academy to rest the debate. Contestation is easier, Heller (1986, 191) notes, than clinching new results. Mariotte published his paper independently of the academy, a pattern followed by other leading researchers (see Stroup 1990).

is that the gross principles (compounds) are composed of three or four principles that are in turn composed of even smaller particles (the elements or atoms). In plant production, the basic principles are combined in different proportions to make the great variety of plant substances. This is a likely source for the analogy Boisguilbert draws between the four elements of chemistry and the four basic commodities from which all the rest are made.

We may suppose that Boisguilbert was also familiar with Mariotte's important 1678 book on logic and scientific method. This book developed a conception of a "system of science" emphasizing a combination of deductive and empirical principles (34), stated the principle of the conservation of matter as holding that matter is neither gained nor lost in chemical combinations (92), and extended the logic of scientific principles to morals by sketching a moral calculus of utility based on comparisons of the utility of different goods and bads. This neglected work links back to Gassendi and Bernier and is another possible source for Boisguilbert's utilitarian ideas.[20]

3. Boisguilbert's Physiological Economics

A very important but neglected part of Boisguilbert's own theoretical contribution to economics is his remarkable treatment of the physical side of production. *Le détail de la France* ([1695] 1966), begins with a discussion of the fall in the country's output of goods after 1660. France, he argued, was producing with one-half of its forces, the other half suspended by a superior power (bad policy), which works indirectly to stop the exercise of its full force. The powers of the richest kingdom in Europe should be able to produce all sorts of things necessary to life in great abundance.

He began his consideration of the production of wealth with an analogy to matter theory: "As the four elements are the principles of all species of things, and it is from these that everything is formed, the entire foundation and the cause of all the wealth of Europe are the wheat, the wine, the salt, and the cloth, which are abundant in France; and one can only procure the other things in proportion as one has more than one needs of these" (Boisguilbert [1695] 1966, 583). Boisguilbert also offered a "historical" sketch of the development of the productive forces. At the commencement of the world, wealth was simple nourishment and

20. See Heller 1986. Boisguilbert's utilitarianism is discussed in Rothkrug 1965.

clothing produced by two classes: farmers and shepherds. Each class procured its needs "by a natural circulation whose movement begins with the products of the fields" (584). With the multiplication of needs and crafts, a simple and immediate exchange no longer suffices (Boisguilbert [1705] 1966b, 888), and money is introduced to "enable the goods that have been produced to pass by an infinity of hands until its circuit is achieved" (Boisguilbert [1695] 1966, 584). Thereafter, resources and goods move via monetary exchange.

While Boisguilbert's central concern was with how this circulation is disrupted and diminished, we wish to emphasize his conception of a physical circulation that "starts in the fields" and provides the products that nourish all the other classes. The first leg of this circuit ends at the workshops, which elaborate and transform the primary materials. His description echoes the circulation of sap in conception and language when he characterizes the professions as an "efflorescence of a hundred" trades and services. From the workshops the second part of the circulation begins, which carries the products of the artisans and professions around to other trades, to consumers, and back to the farmers. Each item carried in this physical circulation is matched by a reverse "passing" of money, which moves the material inputs and products in a continuous flow that can never cease.[21]

The source of this flow of wealth is the land, its products, and those who engage in agriculture and commerce. Echoing Hobbes, Boisguilbert ([1695] 1966, 624) calls "agriculture and commerce . . . the two breasts of all the republic." The distinction between agricultural and industrial goods is ever present: "All the goods of France are divided in two species, the goods of the fields and the goods of industrial revenue" (583). But there is more: the first category is embodied in the second, which becomes the basis of a proportionality of prices that must be maintained. And it is the productivity of agriculture (the surplus of wheat over subsistence requirements) that sets the total of the other goods that can be produced:[22] "The latter [the industrial goods] contain three times more

21. Historians of economic theory have missed the physical circuits of production and exchange. Faccarello ([1986] 1999, 177) sees two types of "circuit" in Boisguilbert's analysis: a natural circuit, which makes "reference to the process of the appearance of professions," and a "social" circuit "relating to the circulation of revenues between the idle class and the rest of the economy." The appearance of the professions is an evolutionary process through time, not a circuit. The circulation of revenues requires the physical circulation of material necessities and artisanal goods.

22. Boisguilbert's concept of the surplus likely builds on Petty [1662] 1899 (see Aspromourgos 1986). There is a hint of the surplus idea in Hobbes. For an excellent discussion of

of the world than the former, and increase or decrease in (physical) proportion to the first, so that the excrescence of the fruits of the earth produce the lawyers, doctors, entertainers, and the least artisans according to whatever art or skill they can be, to an extent which one sees very little in the sterile countries" (624). In addition to the idea here that everything depends on the productivity of agriculture, there is also an understanding that the materials and nutrients of the earth are physically embodied in the industrial goods (the conservation of matter applies) in particular proportions, a proportionality that Boisguilbert seems to be suggesting affects the formation of equilibrium prices as it does in the classical cost of production prices. This understanding is lost in neoclassical theory, which treats all goods as produced from "original factors of production."

Agricultural goods are "the essential fruits [or] capital that produce France" (Boisguilbert [1704] 1966b, 830) without which the other goods and the two hundred or so professions that follow cannot exist. All of the latter, laborers and masters, thus have a common interest in a continuous and mutual exchange at the appropriate prices. This proportionality of prices ensures that the industrial and professional classes can continue "producing their art," whose total depends on physical inputs of "the fruits of the earth." Each of these different kinds of production and their subsequent consumption together form "a chain of opulence composed of many links," where a breakdown of one renders the rest useless or at least very imperfect, since they can only subsist by a common maintenance (830).

The basic condition for maintaining this opulence is a "good price" for grains that covers expenses and maintains the proper cultivation and care of the earth.[23] Prices that are too high or low (fluctuations due to changes in short-run supply conditions) endanger prosperity by setting off dangerous swings in grain prices and production. The immediate effect of prices that have been bid up by a run on stocks of grain is to curtail the purchases and thus the production of industrial goods, which reduces in turn the consumption of the industrial workers. This then produces a

the recognition and use of the concept of the surplus in the English agronomy literature, see Lowry, this volume.

23. These expenses include the levels and types of investment and culture required in different agricultural activities, the various rotations and fallows, and the returns to investment discussed in Bourde 1967. Grain, Boisguilbert insists, is not like manna or truffles. The soil, like the best vineyards, does not give its best products gratis. It is only the sustained enterprise and skill of the workers that can make the state rich and produce public wealth.

long fall in agricultural prices, whose effect will be to curtail the agricultural investment needed to maintain productivity:[24]

> In effect, extreme dearness makes labor yield a profit on the worst lands and produces such great abundance that a fall in price then follows if there is not an evacuation [as provided by a bleeding]; the result is that even on the best lands there is a loss, which leads to a neglect of the greater part of the lands, at least as regards their fertilization, because these are costly expenses. The least sterility [loss of productivity] thus brings a frightful disorder. (Boisguilbert [1705] 1966c, 707)

Short-run crises can have long-run implications (this is not the reversible world of equilibrium mechanics). Only the continuous flow and exchange of agricultural necessities and manufactured products and services going from person to person, trade to trade, region to region, kingdom to kingdom can maintain the state and its parts. As in the body, all this must work without cessation or interference. But given the terrible blindness of market participants who work for their own advantage, harmony "is only maintained on the point of a sword by buying and selling": "The public opulence that furnishes the nourishment to all the subjects only subsists by a superior Providence, which sustains it as she makes fruitful the productions of the earth; there is never a moment nor a single market where it is not necessary for her to act, since there isn't a single encounter where war is not declared against her" (Boisguilbert [1704] 1966a, 986). The reference to providence in this passage has been used by historians to indicate Boisguilbert's Jansenist and occasionalist commitments, in which all activity is attributed to God (Perrot 1989, 154).[25] This interpretation neglects the coupling of "nature or Providence" that

24. A reader points out that Adam Smith would disagree. When the terms of trade favor agriculture, the real value of the agricultural surplus is greater and results in more purchases of manufactured goods. But this is an equilibrium argument and embodies the mistake of Say's Law. In the short run, the high prices go to classes whose composition of demand is different from the present consumers who must reduce their consumption of manufactured goods immediately. A multiplier effect is thus set in motion that can swamp price effects. Boisguilbert also knows that prices in manufacturing are relatively inflexible in the short run and behave differently in agricultural markets. See Faccarello [1986] 1999 for a discussion.

25. Jansenism is not necessarily implicated in this occasionalist belief in God's direct and continuous intervention in the world. The Jansenist biologist Denis Dodart remarks in regard to the preexistence of germs that "it is more philosophical to think that God has created all things in time. It is not [philosophical] to introduce the Creator into the machine [i.e., the order of nature] but to discover where He is through a deep investigation of nature" (in Roger 1971, 353).

is always implied: "Nature is nothing other than Providence" (Boisguilbert [1704] 1966b, 829); "it is only due to nature that order and peace are maintained." It is "nature hence, or Providence that can alone establish this justice" (Boisguilbert [1704] 1966a, 992). Thus the conclusion, "one must *laisser faire la nature*" (993). The argument is not about God's direct activity in nature or markets but rather about how nature's design (providence) works. Nature has the capacity to maintain and regulate itself, to restore the balance when it is disturbed. We will return to these ideas below.

The interdependence (and absence of easy reversibility) in social and economic processes is more organic than mechanical. This is evident in Boisguilbert's characterization of the profusion of professions that emerge through time. Once introduced, these "take root and become a part of the substance of the state so that they cannot be removed or severed without immediately altering the entire body" (986). The necessity of nutritional subsistence extends to the reciprocal dependence of artisans on supplies and purchases from other sectors. When everyone is making purchases and sellers receive a price that covers costs and sustains investments, prosperity reigns and the condition of the state is one of opulence. But a disruption of the balance anywhere along the circuit can set a self-reinforcing cycle in motion that is transmitted to the other links leading to disruption and hardship for the entire society.

Boisguilbert's acute understanding of how an economic cycle works reflected important asymmetries in the structure of production and price behavior in agricultural and industrial sectors. He speaks frequently of a balance (Boisguilbert [1704] 1966b, 859, 862), but it is a balance disrupted that tips all to one side. The misery caused by too high a price of grain or too great a fall is like a dagger or poison. These are illnesses that take the same course in "their birth, progress, and end" and that we see time and time again (847). Boisguilbert suggests reservoirs be established for the storage of surpluses to be used in time of dearth and compares the "management of a reserve body" of wheat to the slow evacuation by bleeding that is necessary to save the patient from death (Boisguilbert [1705] 1966c, 706).

His analysis expresses the neo-Hippocratic conception of a natural course of diseases, causes, and treatments, which emphasizes exact observation and letting nature do its work—healing.[26] In economics as in

26. On the Hippocratic idea of nature and the natural course of diseases see Duchesneau 1998. In contrast to the more empirical focus of English Hippocratic medicine (chap. 8), neo-Hippocratic medicine in France put considerably more emphasis on a theory of nature. This

Hippocratic medicine, the wise physician sets out the proper regime to achieve and maintain the health of the body but is prudent in her interventions.

4. Epicurean and Stoic Physics

Boisguilbert's physical and physiological ideas and emphasis on the active role of nature are difficult to square with the Augustinian occasionalism of Descartes and Malebranche, in which nature does nothing and everything is due to God. Recent scholarship gives strong support to the view of Jacques Roger (1971) and others that Gassendi provided the main alternative to Cartesian doctrine in this period. Gassendi intended his rehabilitation of ancient physics and ethics to be a replacement for Aristotelian natural and social philosophy, which he considered to be not only inconsistent with Copernican astronomy and Galileo's new mechanics but also unsatisfactory from the view of Christian doctrine. He sets out an exceptionally broad program. While his contribution to "establishing the first great empiricist philosophy of knowledge and promoting the corpuscular hypothesis as the foundation of natural philosophy" is well known, F. Duchesneau (1998, 85) notes, his central contributions to the early development of the biological sciences are considerably less appreciated (although this is rapidly changing). The same can be said for his role in shaping the politics and ethics (and economics) of the (early) modern world.

The atoms that Gassendi uses as the foundation of his theory were not the eternal atoms of antiquity but created by God and, in contrast to the passive matter of standard mechanism, endowed with the inherent and active powers required to construct and run the natural world. These active elements were linked to an emerging chemical theory of the elements, which was separated from alchemy's mystical and hermetical past. This provided a conception of inanimate matter built by the chemical combination of atoms (elements) and a conception of organic "molecules" whose construction embodied a very active and subtle matter of fire. The latter provided the seminal and dynamic principles of a materialist biology (Bloch 1971, chap. 8; Rey 1997; Duchesneau 1998).

Gassendi's physical theory drew heavily on ancient atomism and a mechanistic theory of contact and motion. When he moved from physics

appears to have been shaped by the connection Gassendi reestablished between Hippocratic and Epicurean ideas (chap. 3). See also Grmek 1990 and Rey 1997.

to an account of life processes he adopted the Stoic versions of Epicureanism, in which nature was established on an orderly plan and exhibited purpose in its behavior (Brundell 1987, 51).[27] He likewise rejected Aristotle and Harvey's epigenetic approach to generation to return to the Hippocratic idea that the male and female equally contributed the seminal materials generating the organism. This permitted the hypothesis that a fetal soul—formed by the seeds of the parents from matter endowed with the potential of perception, sensitivity, and thought—had a form of consciousness that directed the nutrition, animation, and formation of all the organic parts. This awareness and protoknowledge, Duchesneau (1998, 110) observes, is extended by Gassendi and Bernier into "a propensity to conserve, repair, and mechanically reproduce the same organic totality." This notion of conservation and repair was closely linked to the revival of a "true" Hippocratic medicine.[28]

Gassendi transposes the capacity for regulation and healing of individual organisms to nature as a whole using the ancient idea of "the soul of the world," which he had earlier criticized in the work of Platonists, Pythagoreans, and others as confused and impious (Darmon 1994). He opposed the use of an immaterial substance or principle to explain a material process, not the idea itself. He rejected an "immanentist" idea of God's direct and active presence in the world and also an idea of a nonmaterial secondary cause of things. Only corporal bodies can be the cause of physical actions. In nature, the physical cause of motion and activity is the igneous substance that is cause of heat and fire. Animals obtain this substance from the nutritive materials assimilated by vegetables from the soil, the air, and the subtle matter plants take from sunlight. This active matter provides the energetic explanation of motion, the material account of sensation in living things (the animal soul), and, by extrapolation, the operation of a world soul.

The world soul carries out the design of the world. God is copresent in the world as a designer and director but is not actively present in terms of being the efficient or immediate cause of things. The concept of world soul also designates the *heat* or *fire* that Hippocrates, Democritus, Aristotle, and other ancient philosophers believed provides the second

27. Brundel (1987, 51) notes that Gassendi draws on the versions of Epicurean teachings presented in "the writings of Diogenes Laertius, Seneca, and Cicero."

28. That is, "true" in connecting empiricism to theory (Grmek 1990). The main figure in the "return" to the Hippocratic emphasis on clinical observation and a prudent therapeutics was the physician Charles Barbeyrac, who "found a decisive inspiration in atomism" (291, 296). He was well known to the young Epicurean physicians.

cause of things (Gassendi 1658, in Darmon 1994, 536). The reasoning is analogical. We observe the self-healing properties of organisms and the communities of living things. Since these capacities are part of the design of nature's parts (God's providential concern for the well-being of creation), these capacities were assumed to extend to nature's operation as a whole.

Bernier ([1684] 1992, 2:71–72) gave a detailed summary of Gassendi's argument. The agency by which God designed and conserved the world (the heat or subtle matter) provides the "seeds of Sentiment, and of the Soul." Hippocrates, Aristotle, and many others, he argues, all teach the same idea of "a certain Heat diffused, and expanded through the world, from which all the requisite dispositions are produced, . . . [that] engenders living things, . . . [and that] includes the Vegetative, or Sensitive, or Reasonable Souls."[29] Bernier then reported conversations with Gassendi in which the master supposed that "the earth, just as any Animal, would have an inclination for its own conservation, and that it would know that the separation of parts would be pernicious to it" (2:75); thus the gravitational force that keeps everything from flying off.

According to Lisa Sarasohn (1996), Gassendi's (1658) vision of nature's order and harmony is particularly beholden to Seneca, whose ideas are reset within a Christian view of a created world. This world, God's creation, is his providence, that is, nature. Providence is "nothing other than the natural causes . . . that act . . . in accordance with the force planted by God" (Gassendi 1658, 59–60). Bernier's insistence on a clear distinction between God and providence, creator and creation, and first and second causes is even stronger than Gassendi's (Darmon 1994).

The distinction is obviously important for clarifying Boisguilbert's use of the terms *nature* and *providence*. G. Coulombeau (1989, 349), for example, attributes to him a direct identification of God and nature: "There only exists One Single and True God: 'Nature, which is none other than Providence.'" The passage she cites, however, contains no mention of God: "One has already remarked that nature, which is nothing different from Providence, does not treat men in a manner less favorable than it does animals; and as there are none for which she has

29. The idea that a subtle matter (or fire or heat from the sun) is the source of the motion and activity in nature and the substance that constitutes the sensitive and animate souls is a basic part of physiology in this period in John Mayow, Thomas Willis, John Locke, Guillaume Lamy, and Claude Perrault (Frank 1980; Wright 1991). This joins the ancient atomism to the new chemistry and to the physiology of respiration. Lamy's ([1675] 1996) very clear exposition of these ideas was published in Rouen and well known.

not prepared nurture and put it in the world, she assuredly supplies the same toward all the people . . . unless they engage in a species of outrage which [she] will punish" (Boisguilbert [1704] 1966b, 869–70).

The idea that nature punishes outrage against her appears to reflect the ancient Stoic idea found in Seneca that nature exacts retribution to restore a lost equilibrium. The identification of nature and providence as an active cause also applies to the interpretation of the passage about the working of providence in markets (sec. 3, 115–16), which has been used as a sure sign of Boisguilbert's adhesion to Malebranche's occasionalism.

5. Neo-Epicurean Politics and Ethics

Although Gassendi is known today primarily for his physics, he viewed the ethics as an equally important part of his system. As in Epicurus, pleasure is viewed as the highest good, although Gassendi extends its application from the private domain to the public sphere. A central feature of this extension is the constitutional and political framework it provides for facilitating individual freedom and social well-being. His defense of individual liberty and natural rights was one of the first in the modern period. At the same time, Gassendi emphasizes the welfare of the community and the protection of the weak. The concept of the protection of individual rights and interests is evident in the political prudence and restraint the state must observe; the welfare of all the community is behind the justice the state must vigilantly enforce. Private property is established and protected to harness individual and social initiative; at the same time, the weaker members of society must be protected from the strong and the wicked.[30]

Gassendi's central concern was the quest for happiness in relation to the moral life, which presumes a positive valuation of pleasure. The desire for pleasure and aversion to pain, he argued, are physiologically implanted in living things as part of the providential plan to ensure the survival and prosperity of the individual and reproduction of the species (Sarasohn 1996, 60–61, 134–35). The needs of the body and the experience of pleasure produce a desire for new experience and result in new desires. From intrinsic needs, desires, and satisfactions, the human

30. Gassendi's idea of the social contract builds, Sarasohn (1996, 155) writes, on medieval and sixteenth-century Jesuit thinking and on the older dual contract of Lucretius. The latter captures a critical advance missing in other seventeenth-century contract theories (Darmon 1996).

imagination creates new desires, pleasures, and needs (189–90).[31] The desire for pleasure spurs people to action and work and promotes an incipient sociability, group activity, and the formation of political units (64). The natural inclinations of the passions are the "invisible hand" of God, guiding individuals toward ordained paths without denying them the use of free will.[32]

Gassendi's positive valuation of the passions and an expanding loop of desires, pleasures, and wealth (broadly distributed in the population) appear to have a considerable resonance with Boisguilbert. The latter's ([1695] 1966) insistence that wealth is not money but "no other thing than the power of procuring a commodious maintenance of life, as much by necessities as by the superfluous" emphasizes both the desirability and the distribution of material goods. His declaration that "money is not the end but a means and path, and the goods useful to life are the end and the goal" (618) carries us from Gassendi and Hobbes forward to Adam Smith, who stressed that consumption is "the sole end and purpose of production."

Gassendi regarded the protection of property rights as so important that he built them into the social contract. His version of the contract involved three successive agreements (Darmon 1996). The first establishes private property, defines the boundaries for "yours and mine," and requires that each individual forgo an unlimited right to all things. The second transfers the right of defense from the individual to the group. Noting the need to protect the rights and goods of the weaker against the superior force of the more vigorous, it establishes a constitutional guarantee to protect basic rights and punish violators. The third pact transfers sovereignty to a single person or body of persons as society grows larger and collective governance becomes more difficult. Putting this pact last obligates the sovereign power to defend property and rights (134–36).

While property rights are fundamental for Gassendi, their justification is the interests of the community. A law is not just if its consequences do

31. Gassendi's "incorporation of Greek eudaemonist theory in its Epicurean form . . . anticipates Benthamite hedonism" (Sarasohn 1996, 61). His work also closely parallels Hobbes's treatment of desire in *Leviathan*. Democritus's anthropology is an obvious source for these ideas (Cole 1967).

32. Gassendi's use of the "invisible hand" in the context of a providentially designed psychology of desire and self-interest is obviously part of a long theological and philosophical tradition. Jean-Claude Perrot ([1984] 1992) traces the idea to Pascal's explanation of a "visible nature" by an "invisible God" and a "hidden will." Roger's (1971) view that Pascal is closer to Gassendi than Descartes raises a question about whether Augustinianism is the source of this idea.

not conform to this larger interest. The main criterion by which the economic system is to be judged is not the increased production of goods but social well-being. Natural justice has two conditions: first, that it increase the common well-being and security, and, second, that it has the sanction of the common accord. Boisguilbert also insists on these two features. His concern with the common interest is readily seen in the epigraph cited at the head of this essay.

Bernier ([1684] 1992, 7:349) made it clear that inequality not only exists but will continue to exist, since "civil society has made certain things necessary according to the rank that each one takes in this society." But it does not follow that there is "according to nature a necessity for some to suffer hunger, thirst, or cold." The solution he proposes is a combination of moderation in needs and a confidence in the fecundity of nature, which he considers "a mother nourishing all the animals" (2:214). In the same vein, Boisguilbert ([1704] 1966b, 868) cited Seneca that "nature never refuses the necessities." He also adds nature's protection: "Nature and Providence," he notes, "are charged with the maintenance of justice." Yet in the setting of market encounters where each individual pursues his or her self-interest to the greatest degree possible, the extent of the protections offered the weak from the strong are the "retreats and the means" nature provides to protect the feeble animals from the fangs of the predators who live by carnage (891). This is cold comfort to those ravaged in the competitive struggle.

Bernier's passive acceptance of inequality needs to be seen in the context of his well-known critique of the socioeconomic implications of oriental despotism (Bernier [1670–71] 1916), which by implication he extended to France. His well-known "Letter to Monseigneur Colbert" described the political and military powers of the eastern empires and explained why these states were "an abyss for gold and silver." Despite their continuous intake of treasure, they suffer an appalling inequality, poverty, and despair because the gold and silver they receive through trade is hoarded as jewelry or buried in the ground and ceases to circulate. Why? Because property rights and state protections are entirely absent, leaving holders of wealth prey to the almost unlimited power of military officials and governors to confiscate whatever wealth they see (223). Under this arbitrary power, the peasants especially, but also the artisans and merchants, are subject to an unimaginably cruel and oppressive power. Instead of being able to live in increased comfort, anyone acquiring wealth must hide it and affect indigence.

Authoritarianism and injustice together yield a downward spiral of wealth. Countries once fertile, well cultivated, and populated are now desolate. Apart from the commerce serving the elites, there is little stimulus to the arts, no incentives for schools, and a general ignorance. By contrast a government that protects private property and the rights of its citizens and encourages the arts, education, and formation of skills fosters the production of goods and the accumulation of wealth, which stimulate more needs and effort.

This analysis was directly relevant to Boisguilbert's concern with the decline of wealth in France. As in the eastern countries where a "miserable system of government" (in France, a miserable system of taxation) produced a decline in commerce, the only way to raise money for military and government expenses is to squeeze the peasant even harder. This set in motion a negative and reinforcing cycle of decline and increased fiscal exactions. The underlying cause is the absence of any "idea of the principle of mine and yours relative to land or other real possessions . . . which is the basis of all that is good and useful in the world." The result is inevitably "tyranny, ruin, and misery" (232).

In the context of Louis XIV's disastrous military adventures, tax farming, persecution of the Jansenists, and revocation of the Edict of Nantes, Bernier's analysis helped galvanize a wide spectrum of political opposition in France (see Rothkrug 1965). This included Jansenists, those with friendships and commercial ties to the Protestants, and the "left-wing Colbertists" such as Fontenelle and his friends (Niderst 1991).

Boisguilbert's critique of the tax system, and the inequality it fostered, provided a powerful extension of these ideas. I will focus here on the indictment of the inequality of wealth and power that he made under the heading of the "four articles of politeness," which are especially pernicious in their consequences for both the smaller producers and greater interests of the state (Boisguilbert [1705] 1966a, 764–67). These are, first, the extraordinary magnificence of the houses being built and the vast amounts being spent on luxuries that marked a lavish lifestyle "new to France." Second, these items of display are obtained from only a few select merchants, where the willingness to spend exempts sellers from any real competition. The third article is the great distance between this world and the ordinary merchants and artisans who lack for markets and work because of the great inequality in income distribution. The rich, Boisguilbert observes, will have no commerce with these ordinary persons, although they are "the only ones who enrich the state." The fourth concept is the continual disguise of true feelings and betrayal of conscience and truth in all affairs, which he again connects to the court and the pursuit of fortune. This lack of honesty destroys "the lines of communication" between the government officials and subjects. The high ministers act as if they are "infallible in matters of fact" and fail to gather evidence on the effects of their policies, insisting on a sycophancy where all who work under them "must act as if they are so persuaded" or otherwise be severely punished.[33]

The negative consequences Boisguilbert sees in the immense economic inequality and distance between the classes amplify Bernier's analysis of political and social systems that serve the few. Two immediate observations drawn from the Orient suggest a dialogue with his source: the difference he marks between Turkey, where "it is not extraordinary for a man who has filled a place of the first degree of eminence to become a simple particular," and the great abyss that now exists (in France) and approaches the situation existing in China (Boisguilbert [1705] 1966a, 766). This further supports the relation of his ideas to the work of Bernier and Gassendi.

6. Conclusion

Starting from the physiological production economics initiated by Hobbes and Petty and the new ideas of plant and animal physiology, circulation, and nutrition developed by the scientists at the academy of sciences, Pierre Boisguilbert makes a powerful extension of the production current of "preclassical" theorizing that will be taken up by physiocratic and classical economists. As earlier noted, his work provides a breadth of ideas, particularly regarding the possibilities for disequilibrium behavior, that are missing from his physiocratic, classical, and neoclassical successors, whose beliefs are ultimately based on the equilibrium ideas of classical mechanics. The range and depth of his theory of economy and society may be traced to the less reductive scientific and intellectual currents from which he drew and the capacity of the biological ideas to provide relevant analogies and models for understanding economic activity.

33. Boisguilbert's ([1705] 1966a, 767) comment that the "high ministers should know it is only God who is infallible in matters of fact" is taken as a sure sign of his Jansenism (Perrot 1989, 150). He may be using the Jansenist vocabulary, however, only as a literary device to make a point.

While Jansenism no doubt shaped his modes of expression, his ideas about human behavior and psychology, and his intense concern with poverty and the general welfare, I have found no support for the occasionalist view of nature's impotence and God's provision of all motion and activity in the world (the Augustinian and Cartesian heritage that other scholars have attributed to him). Boisguilbert's conception of nature's active powers and pervasive role in economic operations and regulation appear to be drawn from the great synthesis Gassendi assembled from ancient, scholastic, and early modern natural, moral, and political philosophy. Although a survey of Cartesian biology has not been made here, there is little evidence in Boisguilbert of Cartesian ideas as described in major secondary sources (e.g., Roger 1971). The use of mechanics in his treatment of equilibrium was more Archimedean than Cartesian, and such ideas were well known. The more important influence was the biological idea of equilibrium and coordination between constantly adjusted material flows, which was characteristic of Hippocratic notions of equilibrium or balance in living bodies.

The physiological ideas that Boisguilbert developed in his emphasis on the reciprocal relations that must be maintained between all the parts of the economy owe a considerable debt to the work of the academy of sciences and its leading members. This influence presents itself in his epistemology of experience; his model of the production and exchange of agricultural materials and artisanal products in two distinct circuits of transmission between production sites; his emphasis on the requirements imposed by nutritional needs for the continual circulation of vital and nutritive substances; his sectorial model of the two basic goods (agricultural and artisanal) whose quite different production conditions and price quantity behavior contribute to the unusual disequilibrium dynamics of these two basic markets; and his ideas about the physical investments and price proportions that must be maintained between the different sectors in order to maintain the balance and health of the economy.

The most obvious source for the methodology of the academy's science and for Boisguilbert was Gassendi's synthesis of empiricism, skepticism, and theory construction. The open-ended framework Gassendi provided for the sciences included contributions to an emerging corpuscular chemistry, an energetic theory of activity in nature based on an active and subtle matter provided by the sun, and "seminal molecules" of perception and sensitivity, which establish a Hippocratic "biology" of generation and conservation. The extension of Hippocratic ideas of regulation and healing via the Stoic idea of a world soul to all of nature provided the idea of nature we find in Bernier and Fontenelle, which Boisguilbert boldly extended to economic activity. Gassendi's Epicurean psychology of pleasure and self-interest and model of prudential ethics in turn provided key ideas for economic motivation and for the structural relations between government and economic agents. The Epicurean idea that human behavior is best understood in terms of the positive role of the passions and self-interest provided a dynamic account of the development of wants and desires and a model of reciprocal exchange based on the subjective comparison of the utility of goods that became a central feature of the classical lineage of economic theory.

The Hippocratic ideas advanced about nature's nurturing, regulating, and healing powers have a particular importance for Boisguilbert's economic theory. The role he gives to nature goes well beyond a belief that the economy is subject to the necessary operations of natural laws. There is a powerful recognition of the beneficial effects of economic competition. But competition's positive role depends on the active hand of nature, which alone can bring order to the whole. The healing powers evident in organisms and the harmonious operations of the new natural history are the obvious models for this conception. But there is an underlying belief in a providential design that allows Gassendi and his disciples to regard nature in general as capable of sensing what is harmful to itself and engaging in corrective and healing action. This is the model that Boisguilbert, for good and ill, extends to the inner operations and ultimate direction of the economy. We can hardly escape the conclusion that the early formulation of the invisible hand idea was closely tied to a metaphysical vision of nature and divine design and was not a product of Boisguilbert's vision of the intrinsic operations of market forces or laws alone.

References

Aspromourgos, Tony. 1986. Political Economy and the Social Division of Labour: The Economics of Sir William Petty. *Scottish Journal of Political Economy* 33 (February): 28–45.

Bernier, François. [1670–71] 1916. *Travels in the Mogul Empire: AD 1656–1668*. 2d ed. New York: Oxford University Press.

———. [1684] 1992. *Abrégé de la Philosophie de Gassendi*. 2d ed. 7 vols. Lyon: Anisson, Posuel et Rigaud.

Bloch, Olivier. 1971. *La philosophie de Gassendi: Nominalisme, matérialisme, et métaphysique*. La Haye: Martinus Nijhoff.

Boisguilbert, Pierre. [1695] 1966. *Le détail de la France: La cause de la diminution de ses biens. . . .* In Hecht 1966b, 2:581–662.

———. [1704] 1966a. *Dissertation de la nature des richesses, de l'argent et des tributes. . . .* In Hecht 1966b, 2:973–1012.

———. [1704] 1966b. *Traité de la nature, culture, commerce et intéróst des grains. . . .* In Hecht 1966b, 2:827–78.

———. [1705] 1966a. *Factum de la France, contre les demandeurs en délay. . . .* In Hecht 1966b, 2:741–98.

———. [1705] 1966b. *Factum de la France, ou Moyens très facile. . . .* In Hecht 1966b, 2:879–956.

———. [1705] 1966c. *Mémoire sur l'assiette de la taille et de la capitation. . . .* In Hecht 1966b, 2:663–740.

Bourde, Andre. 1967. *Agronomie et agronomes en France au XVIIIe siècle*. Paris: S.E.V.P.E.N.

Brundell, Barry. 1987. *Pierre Gassendi: From Aristotelianism to New Natural Philosophy*. Dordrecht: D. Reidel.

Carbon, Luc Bourcier de. 1989. L'analyse fondamentale de Boisguilbert et le système économique de son temps. In Hecht 1989, 45–57.

Castelot, E. [1925] 1987. Laissez-faire, Laissez-passer, History of the Maxim. In vol. 3 of *The New Palgrave: A Dictionary of Economics*, edited by John Eatwell, Murray Milgate, and Peter Neuman, 116. New York: Stockton Press.

Christensen, Paul. 1989. Hobbes and the Physiological Origins of Economic Science. *HOPE* 21.4:689–709.

Cole, Thomas. 1967. *Democritus and the Sources of Greek Anthropology*. Cleveland: Western Reserve University Press.

Cook, Harold J. 2002. Body and Passions: Materialism and the Early Modern State. *Osiris* 17:25–48.

Coulombeau, G. 1989. Boisguilbert: Le sens d'une mission. In Hecht 1989, 347–76.

Darmon, Jean-Charles. 1994. Gassendi contra Spinoza selon Bayle: Ricochets de la critique de l'âme de monde. *Archives de philosophie* 57:523–40.

———. 1996. Prudence politique et droit de propriété privée selon Bernier: Pour une analyse utilitariste de la décadence des états du Grand Mogol. In vol. 3 of *Libertinage et philosophie au XVIIe siècle*, organized by Antony McKenna and Pierre-François Moreau, 123–42. Saint-Etienne: L'université de Saint-Etienne.

Delaporte, F. 1982. *Nature's Second Kingdom*. Cambridge: MIT Press.

Dodart, Denis. 1676. *Mémoires pour servir à l'histoire des plantes*. Paris: Imprimerie Royale.

Duchesneau, F. 1998. *Les modèles du vivant de Descartes à Leibniz*. Paris: J. Vrin.

Faccarello, G. [1986] 1999. *The Foundations of Laissez-Faire: The Economics of Pierre de Boisguilbert*. London: Routledge.

Ferreyrolles, Gérard. 1985. "Attila" et la théologie du fléau de Dieu. In *Pierre Corneille: Actes du colloque à Rouen*, edited by Alain Niderst, 535–44. Paris: Presses Universitaires France.

Fontenelle, Bernard de. 1733. *Mémoires de l'Académie Royale des Sciences depuis 1666 jusqu'à 1699*. Vols. 3–4. Paris: Compagnie des Libraries.

———. [1686] 1790. *Entretiens sur la pluralité des mondes*. In vol. 2 of *Oeuvres de Fontenelle*, 1–172. 8 vols. Paris: Bastien.

Frank, Robert G. 1980. *Harvey and the Oxford Physiologists*. Berkeley, Calif.: University of California Press.

Gassendi, P. 1658. *Sytagma philosophicum*. In *Opera omnia*. Lyon.

Grmek, M. 1990. *La premier révolution biologique*. Paris: Payot.

Groenewegen, Peter. 2001. Boisguilbert's Theory of Money, Circular Flow, Effective Demand, and Distribution of Wealth. *History of Economics Review* 33:33–43.

Hecht, Jacqueline. 1966a. La vie de Pierre le Pesant, Seigneur de Boisguilbert. In Hecht 1966b, 1:121–244.

———, ed. 1966b. *Pierre de Boisguilbert ou la naissance de l'économie politique*. 2 vols. Paris: Institut National d'Etudes Démographiques.

———, ed. 1989. *Boisguilbert parmi nous: Actes du colloque*. Paris: INED.

———. 1996. Conversation with the author, May.

Heller, R. 1986. Mariotte et la physiologie végétale. In *Mariotte, Savant et philosophe 1684: Analyse d'une renommée*, edited by René Taton, 185–203. Paris: J. Vrin.

Keller, A. G. 1974. Claude Perrault. In vol. 10 of *Dictionary of Scientific Biography*, edited by C. C. Gillispie, 519–21. New York: Scribner's.

Lamy, G. [1675] 1996. *Discours anatomiques*. In *Discours anatomiques* and *Explication méchanique et physique des fonctions de l'âme sensitive*, edited by Anna M. Belgrado. Oxford: Voltaire Foundation.

Le Gall, André. 1997. *Pierre Corneille*. Paris: Flammarion.

Mariotte, Edme. [1679] 1923. *Discours de la nature de l'air, De la végétation des plantes; Nouvelle découverte touchant la vue*. Paris: Gauthier Villars.

———. [1678] 1992. *Essay de logique contenant les principes des sciences. . . .* Paris: Librairie Arthème Fayard.

Marsak, L. 1959. Bernard de Fontenelle: The Idea of Science in the French Enlightenment. *Transactions of the American Philosophical Society*, n.s., vol. 49, pt. 7, pp. 1–64.

Murr, Sylvia, ed. 1997. *Gassendi et sa postérité en France et en Europe, 1592–1792*. Paris: J. Vrin.

Niderst, Alain. 1972. *Fontenelle à la recherche de lui-même (1657–1702)*. Paris: A.-G. Nizet.

———. 1991. *Fontenelle*. Paris: Plon.

Perrault, Claude. [1671] 1676. *Mémoires pour servir à l'histoire naturelle des animaux*. Paris: Imprimerie royale.

———. [1680–88] 1721. *Essais de physique; ou recueil de plusieurs traités touchant les choses naturelles*. In *Oeuvres diverses de physique de méchanique*. 5 vols. Leiden: Pierre Vander Aa.

Perrot, Jean-Claude. 1989. Portrait des agents économiques dans l'oeuvre de Boisguilbert. In Hecht 1989, 141–56.

———. [1984] 1992. La main invisible et le Dieu caché. In *Une histoire intellectuelle de l'economie politique*. Paris: Editions de l'Ecole des Hautes Etudes.

Petty, Sir William. [1662] 1899. *A Treatise of Taxes and Contributions. . . .* In vol. 1 of *The Economic Writings of Sir William Petty*, edited by C. H. Hull, 1–97. Cambridge: Cambridge University Press.

Poirier, Germain. 1984. Corneille et la vertu de prudence. Geneva: Libraire Droz.

Rey, Roselyn. 1997. Gassendi et les sciences de la vie au XVIIIe siècle. In *Gassendi et sa postérité en France et en Europe, 1592–1792*, edited by Sylvia Murr. Paris: J. Vrin.

Roger, Jacques. 1971. *Les sciences de la vie dans la pensé française du XVIIe siècle*. 2d ed. Paris: Armand Colin.

Rothkrug, Lionel. 1965. *Opposition to Louis XIV: The Political and Social Origin of the French Enlightenment*. Princeton, N.J.: Princeton University Press.

Salomon-Bayet, Claire. 1978. *L'institution de la science et l'expérience du vivant: Méthode et expérience à l'Académie royale des sciences: 1666–1793*. Paris: Flammarion.

Sarasohn, Lisa T. 1996. *Gassendi's Ethics: Freedom in a Mechanistic Universe*. Ithaca, N.Y.: Cornell University Press.

Spengler, Joseph. [1966] 1984. Boisguilbert's Economic Views Vis-à-Vis Those of Contemporary *Réformateurs*. *HOPE* 16.1:69–88.

Stroup, Alice. 1990. *A Company of Scientists: Botany, Patronage, and Community at the Seventeenth-Century Parisian Royal Academy of Sciences*. Berkeley, Calif.: University of California.

Tenenti, Alberto. 1953. Claude Perrault et la pensée scientifique française dans la seconde moitié du XVIIe siècle. In *Eventail de l'histoire vivante: Hommage à Lucien Febvre*, edited by Ferdinand Braudel, 2:303–16. Paris: Armand Colin.

Virol, Michèle. 2002. Publier le conseil au prince: La dîme royale de Vauban. In *De la publication entre renaissance et lumières*, edited by C. Jouhaud and A. Viala. Paris: Fayard.

Wright, John P. 1991. The Embodied Soul in Seventeenth-Century French Medicine. *Canadian Bulletin of Medical History* 8:21–42.

"The Possibilities of the Land": The Inventory of "Natural Riches" in the Early Modern German Territories

Alix Cooper

In 1728, the court physician Franz Ernst Brückmann published a "Subterranean Thesaurus of the Duchy of Braunschweig," or, as he subtitled it in German, "Braunschweig with Its Underground Treasures and Rarities of Nature." This work, a survey of the mineral world of the Braunschweig area, was far from unique; from the late seventeenth century onward, such localist mineralogical works had begun to appear with increasing frequency from German presses. But Brückmann's "Subterranean Thesaurus" is of special interest because of an intriguing congratulatory poem that opens the volume. This poem, penned by Albrecht Ritter, administrator of the gymnasium at Ilfeld and a fellow devotee of the mineral world, displays a striking preoccupation with issues we might term economic and with the concept of natural wealth in particular. The poem begins: "Mortals often squander their treasuries [*thesauros*], for when they decide what to gather up, they find poverty in riches" (Brückmann 1728, 11). Here Ritter invokes a trope that, by the time he wrote, had become a commonplace in local mineralogies: namely, the contention that many lands possessed natural "riches" that had, up until then,

Among the people I'd like to thank are Pamela Smith, with whom I shared a stimulating conversation early on; the panelists and audience at an American Historical Association session where I presented an early version of this article; all the participants in and organizers of the delightful workshop resulting in this volume, for their helpful comments; an anonymous referee; Margaret Schabas, Neil De Marchi, and the staff at *HOPE*; Donna Sammis at SUNY–Stony Brook Interlibrary Loan and Tom Ford and Denison J. Beach at the Houghton Library; and, for some final crucial pieces of the puzzle, Martin Mulsow, Andre Wakefield, and last but not least, the intrepid Denise Phillips.

been neglected or seen as worthless, but that could be redeemed if their true nature were recognized. In his poem, however, Ritter gives this theme a surprising twist. He enumerates various different ways of seeking wealth—alchemy, mining, and trade, among others—and dismisses them all as problematic and uncertain. In contrast to these popular Renaissance and Baroque modes of wealth-seeking, Ritter argues that Brückmann's project of describing natural riches is far more simple and sound: "You act far better and more prudently, most experienced man, when you reveal treasures to mortals that are true and beneficial, that are constant, that are true and beneficial, since they lead us to the recognition of God" (11–12). For Ritter, Brückmann's undertaking of documenting his territory's possession of *natural* riches, of a different kind than men at court had previously looked for, would lead not only to a sound natural theology, but to a better understanding of the true "value" of nature.

The goal of this article will be to explore the connection between ideas of political economy and the emergence of new forms of natural description in the German territories of the late seventeenth and early eighteenth centuries. This period saw the origins of several new genres of writing in natural history that crossed the boundaries, in various ways, between the new sciences and statecraft. The late-seventeenth-century emergence of local mineralogies, such as that of Brückmann, provides an example of one such development; another may be seen in the early-eighteenth-century arrival of works purporting to provide the complete "natural history" of a territory in all of its dimensions, animal, vegetable, and mineral. An examination of these genres shows that, while drawing on the model of the local floras, or lists of "indigenous" plants, that had begun to appear several decades earlier (Cooper 1998), they reveal a new and considerable preoccupation on the part of their authors with ideas of "natural wealth." It will be the purpose of this article to examine the origins and implications of this concern with "natural wealth" and to show the ways in which, while expressing clear affinities with central European politico-economic literature of the time, authors of these new localist inventories of the natural world came to develop their own distinctive interpretations of the "value" of nature.

Over the course of the past several decades, scholars of the Scientific Revolution and those of early modern Europe have moved closer together. Historians of science no longer focus entirely on "pure knowledge," on the internalist discussion of abstract ideas, though this remains an extremely important part of the history of science. But what has been most noteworthy in recent years is the way in which scholars have begun to reintegrate the study of early modern "science" into the study of early modern "society" and "culture," spheres that in an earlier era had, for the sake of disciplinary convenience, been kept all too separate. Realizing that the very use of the term *science* in early modern contexts tends toward anachronism and a certain kind of presentism, historians have worked to rediscover the ways in which early moderns themselves viewed their rapidly expanding knowledge of the natural world: through categories, for example, like "natural philosophy," "natural history," "physick," "experimental philosophy," and the "new science" or "new philosophy."

In the process of rediscovering these "actors' categories," of paying close attention to the ways in which early moderns conceptualized their various activities in pursuit of knowledge, historians have come to realize that ideas about the natural world in the seventeenth and eighteenth centuries were often, in fact, very closely tied together with ideas about political economy: namely, ideas about how early modern societies worked and, in some cases, how contemporaries thought they might, through the "useful knowledge" potentially provided by the sciences, be reformed to work even better.[1] The famous "theses" propounded by Max Weber and Thomas Merton, however, which argued for close causative connections between science, culture (in the form of religion), and the origins of modern capitalism, have long served more to deter this necessary discussion than to advance it, with many scholars reluctant to plunge into the morass of debate generated by these theses. Likewise, the early attempt by Soviet scholar Boris Hessen to link early modern science (through Isaac Newton as its figurehead) with nascent capitalist concerns is generally agreed to have foundered on the author's crude Marxism (Hessen 1931; Graham 1985).

Given this situation, then, one of the most promising areas of recent inquiry has been undertaken within the context of central European economic ideas, which—with concerns differing somewhat from those of the more "advanced" economies of the western European states of the time—admit of few such simplistic or Whiggish links with the rise of modern capitalism. In her pathbreaking study of Johann Joachim Becher's

1. A panel on "Political Economies of Science in Early Modern Europe" at the American Historical Association 1999 annual meeting, with contributions by Andrea Rusnock, Mary Fissell, Alix Cooper, and Harold J. Cook, presented a discussion of these issues in a comparative European context.

career as alchemist and entrepreneur at the early modern German courts, for example, Pamela Smith (1994) has shown the extent to which his natural-philosophical ideas reflected his involvement in a specific and contextualized set of politico-economic doctrines, those of central European cameralism. Similarly fruitful work has recently been undertaken in the area of natural history, particularly in the investigation of the career of the famous Swedish naturalist Carl Linnaeus, one of its "founding fathers." Lisbet Koerner (1999) has demonstrated the centrality of cameralist ideas in Linnaeus's thinking and, through him, in the entire subsequent project of eighteenth-century natural history, which he came to influence so greatly. Staffan Müller-Wille (1999), meanwhile, has argued that Linnaeus, if he is to be understood in economic terms at all, is better linked with a different set of discourses than those of cameralism, namely, more general eighteenth-century concerns about international trade. While these authors may disagree on the precise relations between scientific and economic ideas, clearly such connections can now be seen as highly relevant to our understanding of how early moderns conceptualized—and created—natural knowledge.

This article will argue that, in fact, concerns with "natural wealth" had become central to the practice of natural history in the German territories long before the arrival or eventual triumph of the Linnaean system. As naturalists examined the products of their own territories, localist works came to constitute much of the bulk of the natural-historical literature produced in the Holy Roman Empire during the late seventeenth and eighteenth centuries. These pre-Linnaean inventories of nature rarely appeared as mere lists; rather, their discursive format offered their authors ample room to expand on the meanings of the natural objects they described, which they did liberally, drawing on ideas ranging from the natural-theological to those reminiscent of the *Hausväterliteratur*, or early modern German household manuals. They also revealed, in the ideas of "natural wealth" they developed, strikingly similar preoccupations to those of the cameralist literature, and it will be their resonance with this particular literature that will form the focus of this article.

It may be worthwhile to make one difficulty clear at the outset: local natural histories, like many other works from this period, were notoriously lacking in direct citation of their influences, and thus in only one case (discussed later in this article) is it possible to prove that an author of local natural histories actually *read* any of the more famous cameralist treatises. Nonetheless, the concerns articulated in these works with the revaluation of natural objects, with territorial self-sufficiency, and with the role of nature in producing wealth do show remarkable affinities with cameralist thinking. Rather than attempting to make the case for any direct influence of specific economic thinkers on local naturalists, then, the article will concentrate on exploring the economic implications of the concepts local naturalists used. As the article will attempt to show, authors of local natural histories availed themselves of ideas in wide circulation at the time to come up with their own interpretations of the significance of "natural wealth" for natural knowledge. The article will argue that if we hope to understand subsequent linkages between nature and the state, we need to understand local natural history and local naturalists' interpretations of "natural wealth."

Natural Treasures

In the years following the conclusion of the Thirty Years' War and the Peace of Westphalia, a new kind of natural-historical writing began to appear in the German territories. Today we might call the resulting works "local mineralogies" or "regional geologies"; at the time, however, they were more commonly labeled "oryktographies" (from the Greek word for *rock*). These books purported to survey the mineral world or, as they more often termed it, the mineral "wealth" of a given territory. In doing so, they departed in many ways from the lengthy heritage of the mining literature produced by centuries of extractive enterprise in the Germanies. Whereas traditional works on mining had tended to concentrate most heavily on such obviously valuable metals as gold and silver—the foundations of medieval and early modern European currency systems, and thus of much discussion as well, culminating in the common seventeenth-century obsession with the stockpiling of these materials—the new local mineralogies of the German territories cast a much wider net. As their authors boasted, these compendia claimed for the first time to survey comprehensively *all* the mineral productions of a territory, including not only those most obviously of economic value, but also those that had previously been seen as worthless and unimportant. Even the latter had value, if only it could be recognized; and they, too, could contribute to a territory's "natural riches" and "natural wealth."

If a single concern united these local mineralogies, it was indeed this preoccupation with the idea of "natural wealth." This concept recurred again and again in the ways authors described their works, in the imagery they used, and in the goals they set for themselves. Brückmann's use of the term *thesaurus*, or treasury, to title his book provides only one of the most obvious examples. Local mineralogies referred to rocks as "natural treasures" and "natural riches" (*Naturschätzen, Schätzen der Natur, Reichtum der Natur*) among other similar phrases. They repeatedly employed imagery of the collection of natural abundance, alluding both to books and to territories as "storehouses" heaped full of precious objects. In so doing, they drew on an early modern tradition that posited books and other cultural productions as repositories of one sort or another, declaring books to be treasuries, gardens, libraries, labyrinths, *gazophylacii*, and so forth. But they used this imagery consistently, not haphazardly, to support a central theme: that of nature as a source of previously ignored riches. In the process, the local natural history acquired as its key mission the search for natural treasures even in places of seeming barrenness, proving that even apparently "common" natural objects could possess significant value.

In arguing that any natural object could be seen as inherently valuable, requiring only human attention to discover that value and to put it to use, authors of local mineralogies can indeed be seen as making claims very similar to those of central European cameralists at the time. Many scholars have drawn a distinction between "mercantilism," as a system of widely shared early modern assumptions about the necessity of regulation and state intervention in economies throughout Europe, and, as a subset of this, "cameralism," the particular shape that these ideas came to take in the German territories and in Scandinavia. Though these categories have proved notoriously difficult to define, in large part because of the wide diversity of views they encompass (cf. Tribe 1978, 80–85), nonetheless they are helpful in suggesting some of the ways in which economic ideas reflected specific contexts. In this view, whereas mercantilist authors based in such western European colonial powers as England, France, and the Netherlands focused primarily on the importance of gaining wealth (in particular gold bullion) through trade, central European cameralists instead tended to favor the pursuit of territorial self-sufficiency as the most direct route to economic success (Heckscher [1935] 1983; Coleman 1969; Small 1909; Brückner 1977).[2] Central

2. This account of western European mercantilism is, of course, somewhat of an oversimplification, given the range of views represented under the term; there also exists considerable difference of opinion on where the stress should lie. I am grateful to Carl Wennerlind for his helpful point that for many English mercantilists, gold as a precious metal was far less the issue

European authors thus placed particular emphasis on the more generally held belief at the time that rather than importing expensive foreign goods, states would do far better to further production of similar goods or alternatives at home, boosting local economies while reducing the inflow of dangerous luxuries. And the cameralist ideologies these authors developed concentrated renewed attention on the territory as a unit and on making the fullest use of that territory's own resources, natural, human, and otherwise.

The origins of cameralist ideas can, if necessary, be traced chronologically quite far back, for example to the intersection of administrative and natural-theological concepts in sixteenth-century German courts, where new advisors began to apply the model of the prince's chamber (*Kammer*; literally, *room*) to territorial governance more generally (Small 1909, vii, 2). However, cameralism first came to real prominence during the period following the Thirty Years' War. Court advisors throughout the Holy Roman Empire examined the economic proposals developed by ambitious projectors and entrepreneurs like Johann Joachim Becher, as cash-strapped rulers sought to make full use of their territories' resources to provide badly needed funds for their treasuries. Books such as Johann Rudolf Glauber's *Teutschlands Wolfahrt* (1656), Veit Ludwig von Seckendorff's *Teutscher Fürsten-Staat* (1665), and Becher's *Politischer Discurs von den eigentlichen Ursachen deß Auf- und Abnehmens der Städt, Länder und Republicken* (1668) in their various ways each promoted the intensive development of local enterprise to make use of raw materials at hand. Examples of proposed projects included the construction of factories and workshops to take advantage of concentrations of particular resources in territories; the establishment of mines for the extraction of specific materials; the reclamation of wastelands; and experiments with ways of increasing agricultural productivity (Troitzsch 1966; Nielsen 1911; Zielenziger 1914; Gray 2000). Though some of these proposals were not much more than utopian sketches, their authors framed them as attractive tools for court treasurers and administrators faced with the task of maximizing revenue, to offset increasing expenditures for armies and for the upkeep of courts in an age of emulation, luxury, and absolutism. A key consideration thus became the maintenance of the greatest possible degree of self-sufficiency in economic, and natural, matters. In

than the monetizing of society as a whole. On cameralism, see also Wakefield 1999, 1–43, for a lucid interpretation of its historiography.

keeping with this, princes were urged to pay closer attention to the contents of their territories. For example, Seckendorff (1665) counseled territorial rulers to have thorough surveys of their territories completed as a first and fundamental step in governance. Only a prince who had full command of the details of his territory's natural products could hope to command his people properly.

Even if the authors of local mineralogies may not have actually read Seckendorff—they were generally, by profession, university-educated physicians, and cameralism had not yet made its way into the universities as an academic subject—the works that they produced show strong evidence that they were, indeed, intrigued by the same kinds of bureaucratic ideals that Seckendorff expressed. Most notably, authors of local mineralogies strove to claim a similar comprehensiveness and exhaustiveness for their mineral surveys. And just as cameralist treatises urged princes to put every resource in a territory to use, arguing for the desirability of an economic self-sufficiency verging in some cases on total autarky, local mineralogies took a similar path, as they sought to establish the presence in each territory of every single mineral kind then known. Friedrich Lachmund (1669), for example, in his local mineralogy of the area around Hildesheim, systematically proceeded through all possible mineral categories one by one, demonstrating Hildesheim's possession of the mineral in question and carefully recording its location. Another author, Johann Jakob Baier (1708, 93), discussing the Nuremberg area, noted that some minerals did indeed seem to be absent from the area but optimistically declared these as merely "yet to be found"—in other words, suggesting the hope that his own region would be found to possess a full complement of every kind of natural object, if only the search were conducted vigorously enough.[3]

Likewise, local mineralogies echoed cameralist insistence on the necessity of *transforming* natural objects, in one way or another, to release their value. "Hidden" in the earth, a mineral was indeed useless; only when its presence was made public and brought to human attention could its ends be fulfilled (cf. Schütte 1720, preface).[4] Just as wastelands

3. As has been pointed out, efforts to become self-sustaining in any aspect were not really practicable for the majority of German states, which were quite simply too small (cf. Cameron 1993, 144). Nonetheless, the goal of territorial completeness seems to have persisted as an ideal (though combined with a fair amount of flexibility when it came to trade arrangements).

4. It is worth noting that whereas other early modern writers sometimes made distinctions between "natural" and "artificial" wealth, with the latter term understood to refer to wealth created primarily by human effort in industry and manufactures (cf. Mun 1664), German local

could be reclaimed for human use, so, too, could entire arrays of natural objects. This can be seen on a practical level; for example, compilers took pains to point out cases of minerals where some serviceable application could, they thought, be made and often suggested potential uses to which minerals could be put. Baier (1708) in Nuremberg was typical in the mix of uses he found for the minerals he discussed, recounting folk and popular uses as well as those in mining, industry, and medicine, and on occasion suggesting new uses of his own; though the German-speaking authors of local mineralogies at this early stage rarely used the language of "improvement" that had become so popular over on the other side of the English Channel (cf. Schaffer 1997), their interest in demonstrating each mineral's "use" often forced them to improvise in this direction.[5] But authors of local mineralogies made their case about the value of each and every mineral on a symbolic level as well. As they repeatedly maintained, their actions in publishing information about a territory's full complement of natural objects were intended to transform their readers' *perceptions* of the value of these objects.[6] Through the very act of setting out to describe local nature with such thoroughness, authors of local mineralogies called for a more general revaluation of that nature.

This interest in revaluing nature on a symbolic as well as a practical level can be seen most clearly in the issue of hierarchy. Both mineralogical and cameralist works sought to persuade their readers to look beyond the most obvious sources of wealth and to reconsider their hierarchies of value more generally. Popular conceptions of the natural world had, traditionally, been full of these hierarchies. Some plants, for example, were commonly regarded as nobler and more refined—those that stretched up higher toward the sky—while others were seen as coarser and lower, like mosses huddled on the ground (Grieco 1992). But even more definite hierarchies existed in the world of minerals and metals. Nowhere may this be seen more clearly than in the long German tradition

mineralogists did not make this distinction; rather, they presented human utilization of a natural object as *fulfilling* that object's "natural" potential.

5. The fact that these authors concerned themselves only with issues of production, never with those of any *demand* that might have existed for the products they proposed, again suggests a mindset quite different from that of the classical economists.

6. One author of a local mineralogy, for example, quoted another on the "holy simplicity," not to mention "ignorance" of the Germans in recognizing the true value of things and cited what he claimed to be a German mining proverb: "One often throws a stone at a cow, when the stone is actually worth more than the cow" (Schütte 1720, unpaginated preface).

of mining literature, where "noble" metals such as gold and silver had always warranted reverential attention, with "common" or "base" substances dismissed in a sentence, or not mentioned at all.[7] The authors of oryktographies were most definitely familiar with this mining literature, which they cited liberally.[8] But while they often adopted its terminology of *noble* and *base*, they frequently did so in ironic fashion, insisting, for example, that "common" minerals were every bit as much worthy of interest as "noble" ones—such as the very gold and silver to the accumulation of which some seventeenth-century balance-of-trade theorists devoted so much attention (Coleman 1969). By granting roughly comparable amounts of space and attention to most of the substances they treated, oryktographies tended to have a leveling or equalizing effect. As inventories or annotated lists, they set all natural objects on the same plane, collapsing hierarchies so as to examine and extol the merits of each and every natural production. This collapsing of hierarchies has been seen as a feature of Enlightenment political thought, at both its radically democratic and absolutist extremes; but in fact we see a similar phenomenon occurring in the description of the *natural* world during the early Enlightenment. Thus Baier (1708, 94), for example, cheerfully conceded that there were no "noble" metals in the Nuremberg area. In the imperial free city of Nuremberg, lacking any resident court, Baier could make such a claim with no hint of apology, while writers of more lavish tomes, explicitly aiming to please princes, operated under different constraints. Nonetheless Peter Wolfart (1719, 17, 22), writing for the *Landgraf* of Hessen, ended up dividing the rocks he discussed into "precious" and "vulgar, or less precious," suggesting something less than an absolute hierarchy. Even "vulgar" rocks might themselves possess something "precious" about them, and Wolfart set out to prove this through his ample description of their value and uses.

In this evolving constellation of ideas, where every different rock was seen as possessing its own intrinsic value, we can see a strong emphasis on "variety" in natural history. Certainly an interest in the "diversity" of the natural world was long-standing in European culture, dating back at least to the medieval period; but much of this interest seems to have

7. For an accessible introduction to the vast mining literature (both primary and secondary), see Long 1991.

8. As Hamm (1997) and Wakefield (1999) have argued, knowledge of mining practices was relatively widespread among German intellectuals, particularly those serving administrative functions at courts—or attempting to train others to do so, after universities began to establish chairs in *Kameralistik* from 1727 onward.

been linked to the concept of the "diverse" as strange, as a quality to be found in the East, rather than at home (Park 1997). More recently, authors of local floras or plant catalogs had concerned themselves with such issues as well, on occasion counting the number of different species they were able to list and boasting about their sheer quantity, just as they had boasted about the number of exotic species they had successfully established in their botanical gardens (Cooper 1998). But this concern with the diversity of nature's productions became especially marked in the local mineralogy. Authors here boasted not so much of sheer numbers of natural kinds, but rather of their "variety" more generally. The compiler of one tome on subterranean Saxony, for example, gushed over the fact that "so many kinds of stone [were] to be found deep in the earth" (Mylius 1709, preface), while another author rhapsodized about his Hessian landscape as "nature's richest treasure chest, crammed with such a multitude and variety of things" (Liebknecht 1730, preface).

One reason the mineral realm was seen as so varied and diverse was, of course, the inherent difficulty in reducing some rock finds to previously known natural kinds or species. Unlike the plant specimens cataloged in local floras, which might be seen as representing regional variations but which could usually be assigned to some "type" or other, mineral specimens frequently *were* unique—they matched no preexisting pattern. In particular, "figured stones," rocks bearing images from beyond the mineral kingdom (what we might today call "fossils" but what were at the time as frequently ascribed to the play of nature, *lusus naturae*), challenged their finders' cataloging abilities (Laudan 1987, 27; Gohau 1990, 57–59; Oldroyd 1996, 52; and of course Rudwick [1972] 1976). Authors of local mineralogies celebrated the individuality of these "figured stones," which mere words could not describe adequately; they often undertook the expense of commissioning illustrations—even in otherwise unillustrated books—so as to more adequately demonstrate to the reader this individuality. Figured stones offered authors of local mineralogies ample opportunities to speculate on broader natural processes, such as the universal deluge many of them believed the rocks attested to; yet here, too, they returned to the local, presenting each specimen in question as yet another proof of the natural wealth of their region, of riches not so much monetary as rather spiritual (see, for example, Liebknecht 1730). Here, too, then, we see an expanded definition of natural "riches," as offering not only practical but also symbolic benefits to the areas in which they were located.

And just as the diversity of natural objects came to acquire new importance in the local mineralogy, so, too, did that of places and entire environments. Writers of local mineralogies headed up the slopes of hills and mountains, in the footsteps of writers of local plant catalogs, to discover not only the wild and varied flora that often grew there, but also the various inorganic materials to be found on or beneath the surface (cf. Baier 1708, preface; Volkmann 1720, 4–5). A particularly vivid example of the exploration of new terrains may be seen in the case of caves. Whereas miners had long worked amid the terrors and mysteries of underground passageways, developing their own protective folklore in the process, naturally formed caves were in the seventeenth century still often shunned. Gateways to subterranean worlds, and possibly hells, they were also dangerous places to visit. Those that had been canvassed in search of metals, and subsequently abandoned, commonly were the sites of legends about demons and evil spirits. Yet over the course of the seventeenth and eighteenth centuries we see a gradual introduction of what might be termed a learned tourism of sorts—though one practiced by relatively few, mainly academics—in these precarious locations. By the early eighteenth century, academicians such as Albrecht Ritter went on regular spelunking expeditions in the Harz mountains (see, for example, Ritter 1741–43, 30), while even those less accustomed to wild landscapes, such as Baier in Nuremberg, felt it their duty to overcome their "dread" (Baier 1708, 23; Schütte 1720, 50) and to check out local caves for any possible treasures—of the learned kind. For there was no question of any search for gold or silver here. Professors searched caves as much for the marvelous forms of their stalactites and stalagmites as for any explicitly "useful" minerals (cf. Lachmund 1669, 62). All were presented as equally of interest. In calling attention to these "uses," authors of local mineralogies thus seem to have had in mind not merely economic utility, but rather a broader concern for recognizing places' and objects' hidden possibilities. For compilers of local mineralogical inventories, the endeavor to locate and publicize previously unknown natural riches was inseparable from the larger project of attempting to develop and fulfill their natural potential.

The Nature of the Territory

In the early eighteenth century, a new style of doing natural history began to emerge in the German territories. While local floras and mineralogies continued to be written along the lines developed in the previous century, writers in various corners of the empire also began to experiment with writing full "natural histories" of entire territories. In the works they composed, we see a set of aspirations toward what they saw as a novel and exciting way of doing natural history. Though these authors were scattered across the Holy Roman Empire, they held several key goals in common. First, they shared a vision of their aim, in writing "natural history," as the description of *all* of "nature," breaking down traditional disciplinary divisions of botany, zoology, or mineralogy, inherited from antiquity, to which previous localist authors had confined themselves. Second, they aimed their works at a "public" beyond the university, in most cases publishing in German rather than Latin so they could be understood by the "locals" themselves. They saw natural history as an enterprise not only conducted for the public good, but also requiring public involvement: an enterprise no one person could hope to encompass, but that instead needed the assistance of many. And finally, unlike the authors of local mineralogies, they went so far as to make explicit their appeals to princes and noble patrons for an understanding of natural history as essential to the proper administration of their realms. They often failed in their attempts to secure patronage, as is evident from the number of projects that were begun but never completed; nonetheless, the resulting works yield considerable insight into the mindset of their writers.

While a number of colorful characters involved themselves with this new form of natural history, this article will focus in its remaining pages on the career of just one of these, an obscure, medically trained projector named Urban Gottfried Bucher, because of his exceptional status: of all those who engaged in local natural history during the late seventeenth and eighteenth centuries, he demonstrated most clearly an *explicit* (as opposed to implicit) familiarity with the actual literature of cameralism. During the early 1720s, Bucher wrote a series of works in which he attempted to sell his skills as a "physicist," naturalist, and expert evaluator of territories' "natural wealth." Relatively little is known about Bucher's life, beyond his publications—but these are of considerable interest. For Bucher authored not only a "report" on the "natural things" in a prince's Black Forest domains (1720), as well as a "natural history" of the entire territory of Saxony many miles away (1722b, subsequently revised and expanded in 1723), but also a biographical account of the prominent early German cameralist and projector discussed earlier in this article, Johann Joachim Becher himself (1722a).[9] In the reasons Bucher gave for his admiration of the early cameralist, and in the ways in which he appropriated his predecessor's legacy to develop his own natural-historical projects, we can gain new insight into the relations between nature, economy, and early Enlightenment ideas of "natural wealth."

Bucher's choice, in the early 1720s, of Johann Joachim Becher as a biographical subject was a striking one. Becher had, after all, pursued his polymathic career within the German courts of the 1660s and 1670s, half a century earlier, and he had died in 1682 in English exile. Bucher had thus never met the man and (as he admitted) was forced to rely almost entirely on his subject's own published writings for biographical information (Bucher 1722a, unpaginated preface). The range of these writings, not to mention the character of the individual who had produced them, was, furthermore, extraordinary. In addition to his well-known contribution of the *Politischer Discurs* (1673) to what would subsequently become the cameralist canon, Becher had also written literally dozens of treatises on topics alchemical, chemical, medical, philological, pedagogical, moral, colonial, technological, and miscellaneous—with only a tiny amount of the "natural history" that would so interest Bucher thrown in. And, as Pamela Smith (1994) has pointed out in her own more recent, and much more definitive, biographical study, Becher had, in the process of integrating "theory" and "practice" through his various schemes, achieved a somewhat dubious notoriety within the court circles in which he moved. Why then would an early-eighteenth-century physician choose to write about such a man?

In Bucher's *Das Muster eines Nützlich-Belehrten in der Person Herrn Doctor Johann Joachim Bechers* (1722a) we can find some clues. Bucher presented Becher as, literally, "the model of a useful scholar" (or,

9. In addition to the works mentioned above, Bucher is also listed as respondent on the title pages of two medical dissertations, one dating from his early studies at Wittenberg (Bucher 1700) and the other from his completed degree under Friedrich Hoffman at Halle (Bucher 1707). The authorship of a controversial medical-philosophical treatise on the soul (*Zweyer guten Freunde* 1713) has also been ascribed to him; for an attempt from the former German Democratic Republic at a Marxist interpretation of this work, as well as selected extracts from it, see Stiehler 1966, 7–35, 177–99. More recently, Martin Mulsow (forthcoming) has analyzed this treatise in the context of the complex interplay of ideas and influences in Wittenberg and Halle during the early German Enlightenment; I am grateful to Dr. Mulsow for sharing with me in a personal communication the information he has gathered about Bucher's life. A reprint edition of the treatise in question, edited by Dr. Mulsow, will shortly be appearing in the series "Philosophische Clandestina der deutschen Aufklärung."

alternatively, a "usefully learned man").[10] Becher, his biographer argued, had displayed in his career "a particular affection toward the common German good" (25).[11] And Becher had displayed this public-mindedness by repeatedly offering his services to princes of the Holy Roman Empire, just as Bucher was doing in the 1720s. Bucher seems to have seen in Becher a kindred spirit, someone who through his career had paved the way for Bucher's own. Like Bucher, Becher had gained important status through a medical degree (though one acquired despite his avowed autodidacticism; see Smith 1994, 15–17). And also like Bucher, Becher had sought, persevering through the frivolity and intrigue of the German courts, to put his knowledge of *physis* or nature, the physician's hallmark, to broader use. In his treatise, Bucher defended Becher's polymathy, his mixing of the "medical" and the "political" (among other categories). Becher had, he maintained, successfully proven that "a physician (*Medicus*) was also useful in state affairs" (Bucher 1722a, 4–5, 81; see also Smith 1994, 69). Outlining his predecessor's numerous projects—including not only his famous efforts to set up German colonies overseas, but also his more prosaic attempts to invent saw- and water mills, textile machinery, and ovens (cf. Bucher 1722a, 55–59)—Bucher presented them all as motivated by the same admirable spirit of public service. Becher, as a "clever *Politicus* or *Cameralist*" (Bucher 1722a, unpaginated preface) had sought to find a productive use for his natural knowledge at the German courts; for his biographer, Becher presented a "model" that *could* in many ways still be followed.

Yet Bucher, writing in the 1720s, seems also to have felt obliged to distance himself somewhat from his predecessor. While he praised Becher's zeal in conducting "observations and experiments" (51), like the practitioners of the new sciences, Bucher also scrupulously noted assorted flaws in Becher's character, devoting an entire chapter to a disapproving assessment of his forerunner's "Conduite," or conduct (34–40). Some of Becher's habits, he mused, such as that of making extreme

10. Some catalogs list the title as reading *Gelehrten*, not *Belehrten*. Although the copy I read used the latter spelling (and thus might also potentially be interpreted as meaning "a usefully *trained* man," rather than a scholar or *Gelehrte*), the term *Gelehrte* is in fact the one used throughout the book, and the substance of Bucher's argument in the book itself suggests that he did see this new kind of intellectual as not just passively trained but rather actively participating in creating new knowledge; thus, I prefer the two translations given in the body of the article.

11. For the significance and usefulness of the idea of the *gemeinen Wohl* or *Besten*, a phrase gaining increasing popularity among central European academics and bureaucrats at this time, see Merk [1934] 1968 and Walker 1971, 171.

claims, had perhaps contributed to his being viewed in the eyes of many as a mere "gold-maker" (*Goldmacher*), an alchemist either deceitful or deluded by his own hopes (39). This was far from a rousing condemnation of alchemy in itself; in the early eighteenth century when Bucher wrote, the pursuit of alchemy was still alive and well at some German courts. In Saxony, for example, where Bucher would publish his local natural history that same year, the Elector August II's personal alchemist Johann Frederick Böttger had only recently died (from the aftereffects of toxic fumes) after repeatedly failing to produce gold but successfully concocting the first European porcelain instead (Gleeson 1998). But Bucher's attitude toward Becher's alchemy was ambivalent. While he went on actively to praise and expound Becher's chemical doctrines in some detail (Bucher 1722a, 60–74), he presented these as based on "physical principles," not the search for the philosopher's stone. And in the remainder of the book, he likewise presented a relatively sanitized version of Becher's schemes, largely cleansed of associations with alchemy or with their creator's poor "Conduite" at court. Rather than emphasizing Becher's alchemical "art," Bucher chose instead to emphasize his predecessor's interests in "nature." Here, he seems to have felt, was the area where his model most lived up to the image of a "usefully learned man."

Bucher thus ended up presenting an image of his predecessor that was, in some ways, tailored to his own hopes and prospects. Nowhere can this be more clearly seen than in his attitudes toward natural wealth. What Bucher appears to have been most impressed by in Becher's schemes was the latter's model of nature as constituting a "factory in the earth" (*Werckstadt in der Erde*), a source for all of the goods that humans could possibly need, should they only apply their own industry to the extraction and proper manufacture of these goods (71). While Becher had himself downplayed the significance of "natural" wealth per se, for example that of agriculture, in favor of the "made" wealth that could be created through alchemy and the mechanical arts (cf. Smith 1994, 215),[12] Bucher in contrast seems not to have seen any distinction between natural and artificial wealth, viewing the latter (much as authors of local mineralogies had done) rather as a "natural" extension of the former. Likewise, while Bucher noted on several occasions that Becher's version of cameralism was one that strongly stressed promoting

12. It should be noted, however, that Becher saw this "made" wealth as arising from the *imitation* of natural processes (Smith 1994, 203, 207).

trade or "commerce" between different areas, for example through the colonies he unsuccessfully tried to establish (Bucher 1722a, 4, 13)—a stance that set him somewhat apart from other early central European cameralists, with their greater emphasis on territorial self-sufficiency—Bucher seems to have found no contradiction between this endeavor and his own goal, through his concurrent ventures into natural history, of discovering and converting the "natural riches" of a territory into economically useful products. Thus, for example, it is revealing that while discussing Becher's interest in promoting Austrian trade with other countries, Bucher chose to focus not on the mechanisms Becher had elaborated for such trade, but rather on the natural products that would be involved, each of which Bucher listed and explained (21). What Bucher himself seems to have seen as most "useful" for his own purposes in Becher's example was the latter's insistence on discovering and converting natural potential into actuality, an enterprise for which Bucher felt natural history to be eminently suited.

Bucher thus appropriated Becher's "model" as support for his own natural-historical efforts of the early 1720s. Though it was written two years before his biographical sketch of Becher was published, his treatise titled *Der Ursprung der Donau in der Landgraffschafft Fürstenberg* (1720), for example, already reveals a very similar interest in the idea of useful knowledge—and in the contention that natural history could provide such knowledge. As its title suggests, *Der Ursprung der Donau in der Landgraffschafft Fürstenberg* (which Bucher, not surprisingly, dedicated to the count of Fürstenberg) was framed in the form of an argument. Natural evidence, argued Bucher, could be shown to prove that the count's own Black Forest domains were the ultimate source for Europe's greatest river—an honor for land and prince alike. And Bucher did indeed devote the first several pages of his book to the service of this politico-symbolic mission. Yet seen as a whole, the book strays far from this stated brief, assembling a wide series of facts and observations about the territory in question that, in sum, suggest some of Bucher's broader goals. In his subtitle, for example, Bucher hinted to his readers that the book would also involve a description of "the land's qualities and possibilities . . . with relevant physical remarks and also a few economic reflections." And in his dedication, he chose to label the book even more broadly, describing its contents as "a recension of natural things, occurring in the county of Fürstenberg." Likewise, toward the book's end, he similarly described it as a "report" (*Bericht*) about "natural history" (*historiae naturalis*) (83). Defending his investigation of "the often humble-appearing things within it [the book]," Bucher argued that the investigation of natural objects, far from being a lowly enterprise, provided a worthy topic for the economic *and* intellectual enrichment of a prince interested in learning "the useful things hidden in the land for the benefit of his subjects" (83–84).

Bucher's broader interests are obvious from the contents of the book itself. Bucher wrote not only about the Danube's course, but about the atmospheric and meteorological features of the surrounding area, the quality of its land, farming and agricultural products, its trees and wild game, its natural resources, mineral baths, and "materials" in general. Bucher thus earnestly took the new sciences—physical and mathematical, not only natural-historical—as his model, just as Becher had. Disparaging the qualitative methods of previous writers on the area, for example, he approvingly cited the quantitative measurements of those modern "physici," like Johann Jakob Scheuchzer in Switzerland, who had begun to take instrumental readings of natural phenomena like atmospheric pressure and the height of mountains (1; see Scheuchzer 1706–8).[13] One of the reasons Bucher placed particular emphasis on questions of measurement was, of course, his need to establish the altitude of the area, so as to construct a logical argument for his prince's realm as the source of the Danube. But Bucher did not confine himself merely to proving this one symbolic point. He emphasized repeatedly that he did not see his goal in the book as merely to look at the "legal rights of the dynasty (*Haus*)," but rather to explore the "situation of nature in the land" (22). And thus he ranged far beyond hydrological questions, giving detailed analyses of the current arrangements of men, meadows, forests, and livestock.

But the land as it was was not the only thing that interested Bucher. He had visions for the "possibilities of the land" (*die Vermögenheit des Landes*), how the land could potentially be—if only "improved" (*verbessert*) with full attention to its economic "potential" (*Vermögenheit*). To prevent the flooding of hay fields, for example, Bucher proposed a "projected canal," whereas discussing the different kinds of crops that could and could not grow on the land, he argued for the strategic use of those crops best adapted to the area. Bucher was concerned about the poor

13. Bucher (1720, 6) also cited Becher in this portion of the treatise, mentioning the latter's *Physica Subterranea*. For a discussion of some of Bucher's many other influences, see Mulsow forthcoming.

condition of local forests and, indeed, of much of the Black Forest, owing to the chopping down of trees and the consumption of their wood for industry as well as for heat. His proposed remedy for the fuel shortage, or "lack of wood" (*Holtz Mangel*), rested mainly in the protection of the woods, not only from their human population but also from the cattle and wild game whose grazing harmed the trees. Condemning the stopgap solutions proposed by other economic advisors, he argued instead for the systematic reseeding of some areas (40, 46–47, 52, 57). In his proposals for these and other "projects," Bucher allied himself with the improving spirit of Becher himself.

Yet Bucher's proposals also displayed clear affinities with those of contemporary local natural histories, both the new histories of entire territories and previous local mineralogical works. These may be seen perhaps most clearly in his discussion of the various mineral resources of the Fürstenberg lands. Bucher maintained that the lands' mountainous terrain should be seen not as a drawback, but rather as an opportunity for the exploration of mineral wealth. Bucher was confident that the area, in fact, possessed a full complement of natural resources. He stressed that the economically minded observer must not ignore those objects "otherwise held as being limited" and must not "pass by those truly useful," lest he miss the true value of a territory's natural wealth (61). He enthusiastically listed the numerous minerals to be found in the territory, stressing, for example, that *Kalckstein* was so abundant that the castle had been built with it, while *Gyps* was to be found in numerous places. He pointed out that there were promising mineral waters that had not yet been developed. Likewise he noted that the region had an abundance of different kinds of iron, scattered in different places. Although this local iron had previously not been used as much as it could have, because it was considered too brittle, Bucher felt that all that was needed would be to find a good "*Tractament*" for it, that is, a treatment or procedure that would enable good iron to be formed from it; technology could be set to work to make previously useless objects useful. Finally, he concluded by arguing that it was not yet known whether other metals were in existence in the territory, and he urged the local miners to set to work to figure out what metals *could* be found (61–62, 65, 69–75, 73). Bucher thus parlayed the diversity of natural resources that, he maintained, were readily available into a set of arguments for the *diversification* of the territory's economy. For Bucher, then, economy and natural history formed a perfect match, each complementing the other and enabling him to generate his proposals for realizing the "possibilities of the land."

In his other natural-historical project of the early 1720s, Bucher likewise took many of the claims for the utility of natural knowledge that he had attached to Becher's work and applied them to his own. In his *Sachßen-Landes Natur-Historie* (originally published as an extremely slim treatise in 1722, then revised, expanded, and reissued a year later), Bucher took on the task of describing the "natural history" of a much greater German principality than in his previous book, namely that of Saxony in its entirety. This work was far less systematic than *Der Ursprung der Donau*; Bucher set it up as a series of "stories" (*Erzehlungen*) or "reports" (*Berichten*), each describing a different aspect of Saxon "nature," from its overall configuration, to the particular situation of the Saxon capital Dresden and the surrounding Elbe valley (where he included a discussion of Meissen porcelain), to the potential of mineral baths on the territory's outskirts, and even to an outbreak of the supernatural in a case of suspected witchcraft in a nearby mining town (which Becher painstakingly showed to result from *natural* causes).[14] Though the collection grew from two of these chapters to five in the 1723 edition, and though Bucher (1723, sig. A4^{R}) claimed in the latter edition that the first had met with some "approbation," no further installments seem to have appeared.

Nonetheless, although the book took a very different form than its Black Forest–based predecessor, in it, too, Bucher declared the pursuit of the "natural" to be the key to useful knowledge about a territory. In the preface to both editions, Bucher offered the following reason for his decision to write a "natural," and not a conventional civil "Historie" of Saxony: "For how little one really knows about the changes among nations, and about their governance, and about their old boundaries. The detailed investigation of such things, in my opinion, brings little of use." In contrast, he argued, natural history was definitely of use, since it provided a kind of knowledge that he believed was stable and reliable, knowledge that was based on a seemingly unchanging "nature," and that thus would not shift arbitrarily over time (Bucher 1722b, sig. A2^{R}; 1723, sig. A4^{R}). Unlike boundaries, which were human constructions, *Natur* endured and

14. In this last "story," examining a series of witchcraft reports centered on the Saxon mining town of Annaberg, Bucher (1723, 55–80) took an "enlightened" stance, laboriously explaining each piece of evidence in question as having a natural cause and triumphantly concluding that with this demonstration, "superstition" (*Aberglauben*) had been banished from that corner of Saxony.

offered power to the person who could comprehend it in its various manifestations, as Becher had understood. Saxony had plenty of "excellent gifts of nature, not to be found elsewhere" (Bucher 1723, sig. $A8^R$); all that was needed was to understand how they might be made of use.

And here Bucher made yet again an explicit connection, in his 1723 edition, between *Natur* and *Oeconomie*. Natural history had, he acknowledged, not always been fully grounded in the phenomena it purported to describe; he cited the case of the ancient naturalist Pliny, renowned for his credulity and "disgusting excesses." These "excesses," Bucher promised, he would replace in his own natural history with "oeconomic reflections" (sig. $A8^R$). In this staged battle between the ancients and the moderns, Bucher effectively equated *Oeconomie* with modernity. As "the practical part of physics," which concerned itself with the "use and usefulness of the things, which grow in a land, or are to be found there" (sig. $A8^R$), this territorially oriented *Oeconomie* set yet another check on knowledge. For natural history, it ensured its usefulness. For Bucher, it ensured that he, too, could claim himself, as he did Becher, to represent a "usefully learned man."

Several conclusions may be drawn from the materials discussed above. First, late-seventeenth- and early-eighteenth-century authors of local natural histories in the German territories developed distinctive conceptions of "natural wealth," which they used to justify and to frame their projects for the inventory of local nature. In doing so, they helped to shape the intellectual climate in which Linnaeus's subsequent formulations of natural history could be propounded and then ultimately widely accepted in central Europe and beyond. Second, the local natural histories of this period seem to have provided an arena in which the discourses of natural history and of cameralism, otherwise still separate during this period, could begin to converge. The results of this convergence would only become evident later in the eighteenth century, as natural history became folded into the university study of *Kameralistik*, and as professors of this subject began to generate works labeled "economic natural histories" in a steady stream that would ultimately lead into the production of *Statistik* (cf. Wakefield 1999; Köhler 1993; Rassem and Stagl 1980; Tribe 1988; Lindenfeld 1997). But that is a story that would lead beyond the confines of this study. What the local mineralogies and territorial natural histories of the late seventeenth and early eighteenth centuries reveal is a world in which the study of "natural riches" has come to seem newly meaningful; and in which the inventory of local nature has become an avenue for discussing issues with implications far beyond the local, issues of the ultimate value of natural objects themselves.

References

Appleby, Joyce Oldham. 1978. *Economic Thought and Ideology in Seventeenth-Century England*. Princeton, N.J.: Princeton University Press.

Baier, Johann Jakob. 1708. *Oryktographia Norica*. Nuremberg: Impensis Wolfgangi Michahellis, Bibliopolae.

Becher, Johann Joachim. 1668. *Politischer Discurs von den eigentlichen Ursachen deß Auf- und Abnehmens der Städt, Länder, und Republicken*. Frankfurt: Johann David Zunner.

Brückmann, Franz Ernst. 1728. *Thesaurus Subterraneus, Ducatus Brunsvigii, id est: Braunschweig mit seinen Unterirdischen Schätzen und Seltenheiten der Natur*. Braunschweig: Verlegt durch Johann Christoph Meisner, Hochfl. Braunsch. Lüneburgisch. Wolffenbüttelschen privilegirten Buchhändler.

Brückner, Jutta. 1977. *Staatswissenschaften, Kameralismus und Naturrecht*. Munich: Beck.

Bucher, Urban Gottfried. 1700. *Dissertationem medicam de catalepsi*. Wittenberg: Ex Officina Goderitschiana.

———. 1707. *Dissertatio inauguralis medica leges naturae in corporum productione et conservatione*. Halle: J. Gruner.

———. 1720. *Der Ursprung der Donau in der Landgraffschafft Fürstenberg, samt des Landes Beschaffen- und Vermögenheit, untersuchet, und mit andern hierzu dienenden Physicalischen Anmerckungen auch einigen Oeconomischen Reflexionen*. Nuremberg: bey Johann Daniel Taubers sel. Erben.

———. 1722a. *Das Muster eines Nützlich-Belehrten in der Person Herrn Doctor Johann Joachim Bechers*. Nuremberg: bey Johann Daniel Taubers sel. Erben.

———. 1722b. *Sachßen-Landes Natur-Historie, oder Beschreibung der Natürlichen Beschaffenheit und Vermögenheit der zu Sachßen gehörigen Provinzen*. Pirna: druckts Georg Balthasar Ludewig.

———. 1723. *Sachßen-Landes Natur-Historie. In Welcher Dieses Landes, und der darzu gehörigen Provintzen Natürliche Beschaffenheit, Vermögenheit und Begebenheiten, in unterschiedenen Erzehlungen vorgestellet werden. Erste Erzehlung*. Dresden: bey Johann Christoph Krausen.

Cameron, Rondo. 1993. Economic Nationalism and Imperialism. In *A Concise Economic History of the World*, 130–61. Oxford: Oxford University Press.

Coleman, D. C., ed. 1969. *Revisions in Mercantilism*. London: Methuen.

Cooper, Alix. 1998. Inventing the Indigenous: Local Knowledge and Natural History in the Early Modern German Territories. Ph.D. diss., Harvard University.

Eamon, William. 1994. *Science and the Secrets of Nature*. Princeton, N.J.: Princeton University Press.

Glauber, Johann Rudolf. 1656. *Teutschlands Wolfahrt*. Amsterdam: Gedruckt bey Johan Jansson.

Gleeson, Janet. 1998. *The Arcanum*. New York: Warner Books.

Gohau, Gabriel. 1990. *A History of Geology*. Translated by Albert V. Carozzi and Marguerite Carozzi. New Brunswick, N.J.: Rutgers University Press.

Graham, Loren R. 1985. The Socio-political Roots of Boris Hessen: Soviet Marxism and the History of Science. *Social Studies of Science* 15:705–22.

Gray, Marion W. 2000. *Productive Men, Reproductive Women: The Agrarian Household and the Emergence of Separate Spheres during the German Enlightenment*. New York: Berghahn.

Grieco, Allen J. 1992. The Social Politics of Pre-Linnaean Botanical Classification. *I Tatti Studies: Essays in the Renaissance* 4:131–49.

Hamm, E. P. 1997. Knowledge from Underground: Leibniz Mines the Enlightenment. *Earth Sciences History* 16.2:77–99.

Heckscher, Eli F. [1935] 1983. *Mercantilism*. Translated by Mendel Shapiro. New York: Garland Publishing.

Helwing, Georg Andrea. 1717. *Lithographia Angerburgica, sive, Lapidum et fossilium, in Districtu Angerburgensi & ejus vicinia, ad trium vel quatuor milliarium spatium*. In *Montibus, Agris, Arenofodinis & in primis circa Lacuum littora & fluviorum ripas, collectorum brevis & succincta Consideratio*. Königsberg: Literis Johannis Stelteri.

Hessen, Boris. 1931. The Social and Economic Roots of Newton's "Principia." In *Science at the Crossroads*, edited by N. I. Bukharin et al., 151–212. London: Kniga.

Koerner, Lisbet. 1999. *Linnaeus: Nature and Nation*. Cambridge: Harvard University Press.

Köhler, Sybilla. 1993. Zur Sozialstatistik im Deutschland zwischen dem 18. und 20. Jahrhundert. Ph.D. diss., Dresden.

Lachmund, Friedrich. 1669. *Oryktographia Hildesheimensis*. Hildesheim: Sumptibus autoris, Typis viduae Jacobi Mülleri.

Laudan, Rachel. 1987. *From Mineralogy to Geology: The Foundations of a Science, 1650–1830*. Chicago: University of Chicago Press.

Lerche, Johann Jakob. 1730. *Oryktographiam Halensem sive fossilium et mineralium in agro Halensi descriptionem*. Halle: Typis Joh. Christiani Hilligeri Acad. Typogr.

Liebknecht, Johann Georg. 1730. *Hassiae Subterraneae specimen clarissima testimonia diluvii universalis*. Giessen: Apud Eberh. Henr. Lammers.

Lindenfeld, David F. 1997. *The Practical Imagination: The German Sciences of State in the Nineteenth Century*. Chicago: University of Chicago Press.

Long, Pamela O. 1991. The Openness of Knowledge: An Ideal and Its Context in Sixteenth-Century Writing on Mining and Metallurgy. *Technology and Culture* 32:318–55.

Merk, Walther. [1934] 1968. *Der Gedanke des gemeinen Besten in der deutschen Staats- und Rechtsentwicklung*. Darmstadt: Wissenschaftliche Buchgesellschaft.

Müller-Wille, Staffan. 1999. *Botanik und weltweiter Handel. Zur Begründung eines natürlichen Systems der Pflanzen durch Carl von Linné (1707–1778)*. Berlin: VWB.

Mulsow, Martin. Forthcoming. Säkularisierung der Seelenlehre? Biblizismus und Materialismus in Urban Gottfried Buchers *Briefwechsel vom Wesen der Seelen* (1713). In *Säkularisierung der Wissenschaften*. Berlin: Akademie-Verlag.

Mun, Thomas. 1664. *Englands Treasure by Foreign Trade. Or, The Balance of our Forraign Trade is The Rule of our Treasure*. London: J. G. for Thomas Clark.

Mylius, Gottlob. 1709. *Memorabilium Saxoniae subterraneae, i.e. Des Unterirdischen Sachsens seltsamer Wunder der Natur*. Leipzig: In Verlegung des Autoris, zu finden bey Friedrich Groschuffen.

Nielsen, Axel. 1911. *Die Entstehung der deutschen Kameralwissenschaft im 17. Jh.* Jena: Gustav Fischer.

Oldroyd, David R. 1996. *Thinking about the Earth: A History of Ideas in Geology*. London: Athlone.

Park, Katharine. 1997. The Meanings of Natural Diversity: Marco Polo on the "Division" of the World. In *Texts and Contexts in Medieval Science: Studies on the Occasion of John E. Murdoch's Seventieth Birthday*, edited by Edith Sylla and Michael R. McVaugh. Leiden: Brill.

Rassem, Mohammed, and Justin Stagl, eds. 1980. *Statistik und Staatsbeschreibung in der Neuzeit, vornehmlich im 16.-18. Jahrhundert*. Paderborn: Schöningh.

Ritter, Albrecht. 1732. *Epistolica oryctographia Goslariensis ad excellentissimum experientissimumque virum August. Johannem Hugo*. Helmstedt: Litteris Buchholzianis.

———. 1734. *Commentatio epistolaris I de fossilibus et naturae mirabilibus Osterodanis*. Sondershausen.

———. 1741–43. *Specimen I-II oryctographiae Calenbergicae, sive rerum fossilium quae sub adpellatione rerum naturalium plerumque veniunt et in ducatu electorali Brunsvico-Luneburgico Calenberg eruuntur historico-physicae delineationis*. Sondershausen: n.p.

Rudwick, Martin J. S. [1972] 1976. *The Meaning of Fossils: Episodes in the History of Palaeontology*. 2d ed. Chicago: University of Chicago Press.

Schaffer, Simon. 1997. The Earth's Fertility as a Social Fact in Early Modern Britain. In *Nature and Society in Historical Context*, edited by Mikuláš Teich, Roy Porter, and Bo Gustafsson, 124–47. Cambridge: Cambridge University Press.

Scheuchzer, Johann Jakob. 1706–8. *Beschreibung der Natur-Geschichten des Schweizerlandes*. Zürich: In Verlegung des Authoris.

Schütte, Johann Heinrich. 1720. *Oryktographia Jenensis, sive fossilium et mineralium in agro Jenensi brevissima Descriptio*. Leipzig: Sumptibus Josephi Wolschendorfii, Typis Hermannianis.

Seckendorff, Veit Ludwig von. 1665. *Teutscher Fürsten-Staat*. Frankfurt: In Verlegung Thomas Mattiae Gotzens.

Small, Albion W. 1909. *The Cameralists: The Pioneers of German Social Policy*. Chicago: University of Chicago Press.

Smith, Pamela. 1994. *The Business of Alchemy: Science and Culture in the Holy Roman Empire*. Princeton, N.J.: Princeton University Press.

Spary, E. C. 2000. *Utopia's Garden: French Natural History from Old Regime to Revolution*. Chicago: University of Chicago Press.

Stiehler, G., ed. 1966. *Materialisten der Leibniz-Zeit: Ausgewählte Texte*. Berlin: VEB Deutscher Verlag der Wissenschaften.

Tribe, Keith. 1978. *Land, Labour, and Economic Discourse*. London: Routledge and Kegan Paul.

———. 1988. *Governing Economy: The Reformation of German Economic Discourse, 1750–1840*. Cambridge: Cambridge University Press.

Troitzsch, Ulrich. 1966. *Ansätze technologischen Denkens bei den Kameralisten des 17. und 18. Jahrhunderts*. Berlin: Duncker & Humblot.

Volkmann, Georg Anton. 1720. *Silesia subterranea, oder Schlesien mit seinen unterirdischen Schätzen*. Leipzig: Verlegts Moritz Georg Weidmann, Sr. Königl. Maj. in Pohlen und Churfürstl. Durchl. zu Sachsen Buchhändler.

Wakefield, R. Andre. 1999. The Apostles of Good Police: Science, Cameralism, and the Culture of Administration in Central Europe, 1656–1800. Ph.D. diss., University of Chicago.

Walker, Mack. 1971. *German Home Towns: Community, State, and General Estate, 1648–1817*. Ithaca, N.Y.: Cornell University Press.

Wolfart, Peter. 1719. *Historiae naturalis Hassiae inferioris, Pars prima . . . i.e. Der Natur-Geschichte der Nieder-Fürstenthums Hessen Erster Theil*. Kassel: Gedruckt bey Heinrich Harmes.

Zielenziger, Kurt. 1914. *Die alten deutschen Kameralisten: Ein Beitrag zur Geschichte der Nationalökonomie und zum Problem des Merkantilismus*. Jena: n.p.

Zweyer guten Freunde vertrauter Brief-Wechsel vom Wesen der Seele. 1713. Haag: bey Peter von der Aa.

Nature as a Marketplace: The Political Economy of Linnaean Botany

Staffan Müller-Wille

1. Oeconomia, Natural Science, and the Economy

Carl Linnaeus is well known to disciplinary historians as the "father of systematics," and yet it is only recently, in Lisbet Koerner's *Linnaeus: Nature and Nation* (1999), that he was considered in the context of his own time and place.[1] Koerner argues convincingly for a relation between his economic ideas and his science. Linnaeus saw science as the prime tool in pursuing an economic ideal of national autarky through import substitution, and correspondingly he carried out ambitious research projects aimed at substitution of imports, especially of plants and plant substances, and based on shifting assumptions about the feasibility of cultivating exotic plants in his own home country or substituting them with domestic plants of analogous virtues.

Beyond guiding research projects, Linnaeus's economic contentions also found expression in his engagement for educational and administrative reform. Thus he urged at several occasions that "oeconomia"—which he understood not as a science of human economic action and behavior, but as a science of natural products and their "use" for humans—should be included as a compulsory part of university teaching

1. Before, in a curious case of inverse anachronism, Linnaeus had been classified as an "Aristotelian" (see Larson 1971). It should be noted, however, that there exist important publications in Swedish that put Linnaeus in his contemporary economic (Heckscher 1942) as well as theological (Malmeström 1926) context.

and that respective chairs of oeconomia should be created at Swedish universities (see Rausing, this volume). Another project of reform in which Linnaeus was involved was the foundation of the Royal Swedish Academy of Science at Stockholm in 1739, which by public lectures and demonstrations, as well as the edition of a scientific journal and a popular almanac, both in the vernacular, aimed to "serve the growth and development of useful sciences, economy, trade, and manufactures" (Liedman 1989; Eriksson 1989). In short, Linnaeus viewed oeconomia—the "new science" as he liked to call it—not only as a source of information for state elites, but also as a pedagogic instrument that could provide a broad, disciplined basis of local assistants—parsons, physicians, and engineers—to an administrative state machinery furthering national prosperity by systematic resource allocation and exploitation (cf. Liedman 1989, 28–31; Tribe 1988, 19–34).

With this conception of science as an instrument for rational development, one should expect a close conformity between Linnaean oeconomia and natural science. And indeed, in Linnaeus's eyes, oeconomia was about hardly anything more than natural history plus information on the uses made of its diverse objects in technology. Conversely, Linnaean natural history was thoroughly designed to serve its function as a practical and simple tool to explore natural resources. Thus binomial nomenclature, the main innovation for which Linnaeus is remembered today, was developed within the context of one of his "patriotic" projects: as a tool for shorthand designation to be used by a group of students who followed cows, pigs, and sheep to observe which plants they fed upon (Stearn 1959). In a sense Linnaeus's version of oeconomia reduced economics to technology and science to a technicality serving technological goals (Koerner 1999, 101–4).

Despite these conformities, however, some economic propositions surfacing in Linnaeus's botanical publications are not readily reconciled with the economic persuasions he expressed in his "patriotic" writings. Most conspicuously, as Koerner noted herself, Linnaeus's conception of an "economy of nature"—on which, after all, human economics depended in his view—was based on "notions of equilibria" as "checks and balances and feedback loops," while he "modeled . . . the economy of the nation on mechanistic notions of force" (102). The theoretical framework of Linnaeus's natural science, expressed in economic metaphors of balance and exchange, thus seems to have conflicted with the economic contentions on which he built his oeconomia.

The key to developing an understanding of these conflicts lies in Linnaeus's classification of sciences, which did not result in a dichotomy of natural science versus oeconomia, as one might expect, but in a tripartition. In a programmatic contribution to the first volume of the journal of the Royal Swedish Academy of Science, Linnaeus distinguished "physics" from "natural science" (encompassing botany, zoology, and lithology), and each of them from "oeconomia." The latter was defined as "the science teaching us the application of the elements [i.e., "earth, water, air, and fire"] to natural bodies in serving our needs," while "physics" simply emerged as the science "rendering the properties of elements" and "natural science" as the science "teaching us the knowledge of natural bodies," both together providing the foundation for oeconomia (Linnaeus 1740, 411–12).[2] Linnaeus explained the common ground for this tripartition in the following paragraph: "All that man can use for his needs, must be at hands on this globe; that is either elements or natural bodies. Elements can neither feed nor clothe man, for that he must use natural bodies primarily; however, these in themselves are often raw, unless they have been prepared by the elements for the purpose that man enjoys from them" (412).

What can be discerned in this explanation is an abstract distinction that in itself is economical: Human production always involves the application of certain agents (elements) to certain materials (natural bodies), the latter preexisting the production process itself, as they always have to be procured from elsewhere. "Physics" is thus separated from "natural science" along a dividing line that approaches the modern distinction between "forces of production" and "commodities," or, to put it more generally, between a sphere of production and a sphere of exchange. However, in its abstract generality this distinction was (and still is) anything but trivial. To see this, one only has to think of the premodern opposition of oeconomia and chrematistics—Linnaeus's own economic ideal of (national) autarky being a reflection thereof—which identified the dividing line between (re)production and exchange with the concrete border of the individual "household" (cf. Tribe 1988, 23–25). And indeed, it is hard to see why water and earth should be conceived exclusively as agents (and not as materials also, as Aristotle originally had it), and minerals, plants, and animals exclusively as materials (and not as agents also).

2. Translations, if not otherwise stated, are my own.

If it is difficult to understand the content of Linnaeus's distinction of "elements" and "natural bodies," it is even more difficult to see where it derived from. Though economic in itself, it did not result from, but was presupposed by his oeconomia, as it provided the background for his general classification of sciences. In this article I will argue that this fundamental abstraction derived from Linnaeus's involvement in the collection and exchange of plant specimens among botanists, an involvement that dates back to his short stay in the Dutch Low Countries from 1735 to 1738. A closer analysis of this practice will then help me to explain the centrality of notions of balance and exchange in Linnaeus's "economy of nature."

2. The Market of Botany

When Linnaeus arrived in Holland in 1735 to get his degree as a medical doctor, he was quick to establish close relations with leading botanists there, namely, Johan Friedrich Gronovius and Hermann Boerhaave at Leiden, and Johan Burman at Amsterdam. These contacts soon proved rewarding: Not only did these men promote the publication of all the major works of Linnaeus, but they also secured him a position as a curator for a large private botanical garden, that of James Clifford, former director of the Dutch East India Company. This position allowed Linnaeus to visit other European centers of botany, such as Paris, London, and Oxford. Linnaeus saw himself in the center of the botanical world, both in an "economical" sense, as botanical exploration still largely depended on international trade, and intellectually, as the network of academic patronage and recognition had its center in Leiden during the first half of the eighteenth century (Stearn 1962).

Linnaeus reflected this position self-consciously in a distinction of "true" from "amateur" botanists (*botanophili*) that he presented in one of his first publications, the *Bibliotheca botanica* of 1736. The exclusion of "amateurs" was justified with surprisingly few words by Linnaeus and in a seemingly odd reference to linguistic categories: "Amateurs do not deal with names," as "true" botanists do, "but with the various attributes of plants" (Linnaeus 1736, 1). Yet if one takes into account the central function that plant names had as a means of communication among botanists, the distinction of "true" and "amateur" botanists begins to make some more sense. Linnaeus (1737a, 204) explained this function with the help an interesting economic metaphor:

> The generic name has the same value on the market of botany, as the coin has in the commonwealth, which is accepted at a certain price—without necessitating a metallurgic examination—and is received by others on a daily basis, as long as it has become known in the commonwealth.

Even if this passage does not witness a really determinate and precise "theory of money"—price and value are not clearly distinguished, and exchange is conceptualized in a rather awkward, unilateral way—it nevertheless makes one thing very clear: to Linnaeus, the function of plant names depended upon an institutionalized practice of exchange peculiar and restricted to the community of botanists. It was this practice that his *Bibliotheca botanica* explored by presenting an elaborate "division of (botanical) labour" (Heller [1970] 1983). As I have argued elsewhere (Müller-Wille 2001b), this division rested upon a common hinge, the existence of specialized institutions, botanical gardens namely, that separated those who extended the periphery of the known plant world by discovering and documenting "new" species ("collectores" in Linnaeus's classification of botanical authors), from those who presided over the centers in which these "new" species were accumulated and stored for purposes of research and education ("methodici"). On an additional level, botanical gardens were interrelated by networks of correspondence accompanied by the exchange of seeds and specimens, a network that served the *methodici* to further augment their collections by sharing in the findings of others. In the course of the seventeenth and eighteenth centuries, alongside the expansion of colonial trade, this network of exchange reached a truly global scale (cf. Stearn 1961; Wijnands 1988; Miller and Reill 1996; Drayton 2000, 32–37; Spary 2000, 61–78).

Thus botany seems indeed to have formed a kind of "sphere of exchange," as Linnaeus supposed in its definition as a "natural science." Yet to understand the effects that this had on the conceptual content of Linnaean botany, including the fundamental abstraction that provided the basis for Linnaeus's classification of sciences, it will not be enough to describe the general outlines of this exchange and its embedding in contemporary developments of worldwide commerce. The geographical distances spanned by this exchange alone cannot help to see how it effectively brought about such abstractions. A closer look at the inner mechanics of this exchange is needed instead, and the letters that accompanied it may provide material for that investigation.

3. Gifts and Pledges, Seeds and Names

On 28 June 1754, just a few months after his return from a four-year trip to Senegal sponsored by the Compagnie des Indes and promoted by leading French naturalists, among them Bernhard de Jussieu (Nicolas 1963, 16–30), Michel Adanson directed a letter to Linnaeus that was accompanied by a package of seeds gathered in Senegal, which, as announced in the letter, included "as much as nine new genera."[3] After briefly introducing himself and mentioning his promoter Jussieu, Adanson explained that he sent the seeds "in order that you and other botanists may judge from them how much still remains to be done in botany" and expressed his hope that they might "suffice as pledges of my strong attachment to you, until time has come to send more." Linnaeus, who had been informed by Jussieu on Adanson's Senegal travel and, moreover, had already received some seeds and dried specimens from the collections Adanson had sent to Jussieu (Nicolas 1963, 31–32), was quick to "return due thanks for the seeds You sent" in a letter from 1 October 1754. Acknowledging the value of the seeds received, the letter ended with the following statement: "Thus I had known You from Your gifts, before anyone wrote about You, except that illustrious Jussieu." The terminology with which both Adanson and Linnaeus referred to the seeds traded—"pledges" (Adanson) and "gifts" (Linnaeus)—indicates that they understood this as some kind of gift exchange. And indeed, the two letters witness every feature characteristic of it.[4]

First, the acts of giving and returning were separated in the transaction, that is, Adanson did not send his specimens with an explicit expectation for immediate and proportionate return. Yet his gifts carried with them an obligation for return, and Linnaeus recognized that obligation, offering to "gladly return others, if I should possess some that can please you," and adding that he had "recently received a whole Palestine and Egyptian herbarium" containing "various plants hitherto obscure and many new ones." Moreover, he accepted that some kind of intellectual ownership remained tied to the new plants discovered by Adanson and acknowledged this by giving one of the Adansonian plants that he had

3. The two letters between Linnaeus and Adanson discussed in this section are quoted from Linnaeus 1916, 1–3. My translation is partly based on Smith 1821, 465–67.

4. I am basing my analysis of botanical seed exchange on Mauss [1924] 1997 and its elaboration by Sahlins (1972, chap. 5) and Gregory (1982, part 1). I will use their distinction of gift and commodity exchange for purely analytic purposes. For a thorough critique of tendencies to view the distinction as an essential one between more or less primitive economies, see Thomas 1991.

received earlier from Jussieu and grown in his garden in Uppsala the name of "Adansonia" (cf. Hagstrom [1965] 1972, on intellectual ownership in science). In this sense, therefore, the objects of exchange were recognized as *inalienable*.

Second, the exchange rested upon and established relations between the transactors rather than between the objects transacted: Adanson's approach to Linnaeus had been prepared by Jussieu, Adanson's promoter, and it was motivated by Adanson's wish to establish similar relations with Linnaeus. The exchange occurred among transactors who were socially *dependent* on each other: Adanson on Linnaeus "and other botanists" for "judging" the significance of his findings; Linnaeus on Adanson for more specimens of "new" species (on the dependence of botanical exchange on patronage networks, see Spary 2000, 61–88).

And yet there is something peculiar in the workings of this gift exchange. The relation of mutual dependence existed between Adanson and Linnaeus *only* with respect to the transaction of seeds. In all other respects, Adanson and Linnaeus were socially *independent* from each other. Correspondingly, Linnaeus defined the roles of "collector" and "methodicus" purely in regard to the exchange of specimens: "Collectores" were those who simply contributed to the "number of species," while "the most consummate botanist," the one who had access to "most species," was in the best position to classify plants (see Müller-Wille 2001a, 36–37).

In regard to the inalienability of the objects exchanged, there appears to be another peculiarity in the way botanical "gifts" were compensated: Instead of compensating gifts "like-for-like" (in kind, not in terms of identity; see Gregory 1982, 46, on this point), botanical "gifts" were strictly and exclusively compensated "unlike-for-unlike." As Linnaeus's reaction shows, Adanson expected a return not in plants of the same kind as the "new" ones he had sent, but rather others that might be new to him. The objects of exchange were evaluated, or rather ranked, by Adanson and Linnaeus according to their newness, a wholly subjective (and not quantifiable) measure, as what might occur "new" to one of them was definitely "old" to the other. Thus, in effect, the object given was *alienable*, a duplicate or "supernumerary specimen" as Linnaeus called it in addressing Adanson for some more specimens.

The exchange that underlay botany as Linnaeus and his contemporaries understood and practiced it thus combined aspects of gift exchange with aspects of commodity exchange in a way that I would like to call "global exchange," with respect to the consequences it had for transactors and objects transacted alike. In regard to the former, it is to be observed that the way in which botanical exchange worked as a gift economy guaranteed that "collectors" could be recruited for Linnaean botany across all existing cultural, political, and social boundaries (cf. Pratt 1992, 27; Secord 1994). Adanson already furnishes a good example for this, as he in fact disagreed with Linnaeus on all fundamental points of botanical theory (Stafleu 1963, 228–37). A further example is provided by the plant *Quassia*, which Linnaeus named after a Suriname slave (see Rausing, this volume). Allowing for such extravagant alliances, it comes as no surprise that Linnaeus portrayed the community of botanists as a "free republic," whose inhabitants enjoyed free speech and were subject to self-imposed laws only (Linnaeus 1737a, Lectori).

While the gift aspect of global exchange had consequences for the community of its transactors, its commodity aspect had consequences for the relations established among its objects. As in gift exchange, these relations emerged as a classification of exchangeable goods (cf. Lévi-Strauss 1962, chap. 2), with the important difference, however, that this classification was not restricted to the economy of a particular group occupying a particular territory, but was a universal one. A central passage in Linnaeus's response to Adanson witnesses this: In reporting on the seeds he had already received (via Jussieu), Linnaeus informed him that "also the species of Acacia with white bark is growing from Your seeds." The plant in question, which Jussieu had praised as a "new" one to Linnaeus, is designated here by a name for a plant genus ("Acacia") and the feature that differentiates it from all other plants under that genus ("with white bark"). Simultaneously, Linnaeus pointed out to Adanson that this distinctive feature had been reproduced in his garden, despite the species' translation from Senegal via Paris to Uppsala. The transaction of a "new" species—its adding up to the "number of species" in the collection of a "most consummate botanist"—was successful if, and only if, it retained its specificity throughout all transactions and did not turn out to be another plant already known ("old," or "supernumerary") on its way. By this simple mechanism, the realm of botanical "goods" was fragmented into a coherent classification of mutually exclusive "spheres of exchange," encompassing universally reproducible, alienable (as duplicates), and thus universally exchangeable plants of a certain, distinguished kind.

The conjunction of gift and commodity aspects peculiar to the practice of Linnaean botany occurred at a crucial point in the institutional history of natural history: While Renaissance natural history had been a "product of the patronage culture of early modern Europe" (Olmi 1993; Findlen 1994; Smith and Findlen 2002), and while the nineteenth century would see the usurpation of that culture by such institutions as the British Museum and Kew Gardens (Miller and Reill 1996; McCracken 1997, chap. 3) and a corresponding formal codification of botanical exchange (McOuat 1996), Linnaeus united the functions of both patron and institution through which every specimen of a species had to run to become accepted as a "new" one (cf. Sörlin 2000). How this conjunction played out on all levels of Linnaeus's natural science, including his "economy of nature," will be discussed in the next section.

4. The Economy of Nature

The most notorious theoretical contribution of Linnaeus was his definition of species as eternally immutable "forms." A close look at it now can reveal how much this definition was in line with the "economy" of his botany rather than with any philosophical traditions (which, after all, had always conceded the possibility of transmutations; see Zirkle 1959):

> There are as many species as different forms produced by the Infinite Being in the beginning. Which forms afterward produce more, but always similar forms according to inherent laws of generation; so that there are not more species now than came into being in the beginning. Hence, there are as many species as different forms or structures of Plants occurring today, those forms (varieties) rejected which place or accident exhibits to be less different. (Linnaeus 1737b, Ratio operis, sec. 5)

There are two features peculiar to this definition that betray its indebtedness to the "market of botany." First, it tells its reader not so much what it is that makes a plant belong to a species, but rather how many species there are. And botanical exchange turns around the number of species, as seen in the previous section. Second, the definition furnishes a criterion to decide which "forms or structures"—that is, aggregates of characters—distinguish species and which do not. This criterion is simply the reproducibility of forms: those that "produce more, but always similar forms according to inherent laws of generation" do distinguish, those that "place or accident exhibits to be less different" do not. In other words, features that distinguish a plant from other plants at a certain location or under certain circumstances but do not do so when that plant is reproduced at another location or under different circumstances cannot serve to distinguish that plant at the species level (they distinguish it as a variety only). This was a criterion that could be applied, made sense, and was of paramount importance only if plants were indeed exchanged globally (Müller-Wille 1998; cf. Spary, this volume).

It is on this basis, also, that one can see why Linnaean botany should be a science of "names," as mentioned before. In the last instance, it is only the name of a species, that rigid, designatory relation established in exchange, that can remain unchanged throughout all possible transactions. All other features, including "form or structure," may be dependent on local contexts. This is also the sense in which Linnaeus compared names with coins: as the coin does not need "a metallurgic examination" to serve its function of mediating exchange, thus the name of a plant does not need an etymological examination to serve its communicative function. Coining plant names in honor of their "first discoverers" illustrates this point: while such a name is permanently and rigidly attributed to the plant kind in question, in whatever contexts it might be referred to later, the name itself does not say anything about the actual plant, the circumstances of its discovery, or even the personality of its discoverer. And yet it is precisely because names are thus reduced to linguistic expressions stripped of all contextual meaning that they can remain unchanged throughout any conceivable context. Names, in this sense, are the hallmark of global exchange.

This understanding of names can also elucidate the characterization that Linnaeus gave of true botanists dealing with "names," and not with "attributes" as botanical amateurs did. Botanical amateurs included, besides anatomists and pharmacologists, gardeners. As Linnaeus "rejected" varieties from the scope of "true" botany, all research into the agents that produced plant variety—for example, certain physical factors like temperature, moisture, soil composition, and so on—was equally excluded from it. Thus horticulture—which of course was basic to Linnaean oeconomia and which he knew very well (Stearn 1976)—was explicitly removed from botany, not because it did not count as a science—Linnaeus ([1754] 1759, 210) did call it a science—but because, as he put it, "gardeners only aim to produce more luxurious, bigger, and earlier plants, so that their experience in fertilization is of no use in botanical gardens"

(Linnaeus 1739, 5). In other words, gardeners were interested in producing varieties and identifying the means to effect such productions, not in identifying species by names (Linnaeus 1751, 255–57). Likewise, anatomy dealt with the causes of "vegetation," and pharmocology with the effects of plants on the human body such that both addressed causal rather than taxonomic relations. All three sciences thus formed branches of "physics," dealing with the "elements" as agents as such, as "universal tools," rather than branches of botany as a "natural science," a science of "universal commodities" (Müller-Wille 1999, chap. 5). This separation, far from being the outcome of a mere professional ideology, depended on the institution of global exchange among botanical gardens, in which the (re)production of plants at certain localities and their circulation among these localities were set apart from each other inasmuch as that which was produced only locally appeared as not exchangeable, and that which was exchanged among the gardens appeared as not locally produced, but essentially and universally given—in the last instance given by names, once "coined," and not by any physical feature.

This fundamental separation also played out in Linnaeus's philosophy of nature. Under the title *Oeconomia naturae*, it has long since attracted the attention of historians of ideas for its "conception of a purposeful interaction among natural bodies, by which an inviolable equilibrium is maintained through time" (Limoges 1972, 9). What has been missed so far, however, is a curious and unusual distinction that Linnaeus ([1749] 1787, 2–3) drew when outlining his *oeconomia naturae*:

> Whoever directs his attention to those things, that occupy our terraqueous globe, will finally admit, that it is necessary, that all and each are arranged in such a series and in such mutual nexus, that they aim at the same end. . . . So that natural things may last in continued series, the wisdom of the highest Being has ordained, that all living beings perpetually work for the production of new individuals, and that all natural bodies reach out a helping hand to their neighbor for the conservation of each species, so that what serves the ruin and destruction of one of them, serves the others restitution. (translation partly based on Linnaeus [1749] 1762)

This passage demonstrates how Linnaeus distinguished two dimensions in the economy of nature, a temporal one termed *series* and a topological one termed *nexus*. The former simply consisted in local relations of mutual consumption ("destruction") and production ("restitution") of individual beings. The terminology used—*nexus*, with its legal and religious connotation of a personal obligation implied by the contractual transfer of goods (Mauss [1924] 1997, 229–32) —witnesses remnants of gift economy. The "continued series" could be seen as the mere reproductive resultant from the local relations of production and consumption implied by the nexus. But why, then, would it be set off terminologically as a dimension in its own right?

The answer lies in the species definition of Linnaeus quoted above, in which the reproduction of living beings was said to follow "inherent laws of generation," according to which they "produce more, but always similar forms" independently of "place or accident." If such "laws" did not exist, the economy of nature would indeed be exhausted by local relationships of domination and servitude determining life-forms. As they do exist, however, according to Linnaeus's species concept, each individual enters these relations determined independently of any other species by the "laws of generation" governing its species' form. And as, moreover, according to these laws, not only similar, but always "more" individuals of a given species are produced, Linnaeus's economy of nature included a portrayal of nature as a system of mutually independent contractors exchanging alienable goods—namely, the products and services organisms offer to each other by way of their very own, prolific nature. What particularly puzzled Linnaeus in his *Oeconomia naturae* were instances of overproduction in offspring, which were apparently generated only to be devoured immediately by other species. This, in his eyes, could be explained by assuming that "providence aimed at not only sustaining, but also keeping a just proportion among all the species" (Linnaeus [1749] 1787, 119). In devouring prey, predators do not only receive their nourishment, but in fact, by checking their number, also confer a service to the species preyed upon in return. At the end of the passage quoted from Linnaeus's *Oeconomia naturae* above, the economy of nature can therefore turn out as a cyclical (instead of hierarchical) model of mutual (instead of unilateral) benefaction and indulgence.

In Linnaeus's conception of an economy of nature we thus find the same peculiar interlocking of gift and commodity exchange as in the botanical practice of global exchange. Moreover, this exchange seems to have been the only possible source of its balance and circulation aspects. In local reproduction aiming at autarky, at whatever social level—family, parish, or nation—it is pursued, trade will always appear as a unilateral move and thus potentially as a damaging loss of resources, and Linnaeus indeed understood it as such in regard to his own nation. In global exchange, on the other hand, the careful balancing of "trade relations" was the only way to establish and reproduce oneself as a reputed botanist. It was thus vitally important for Linnaeus both to understand the system of specimen circulation among botanical gardens (as he very well did) and to take advantage of it by establishing strategic exchange relations with such collectors who offered the best chances for sending him "new species," which he then could use, by reproducing them in his own garden, to recruit new exchange partners by sending them duplicates, for instance. Only by following this strategy could Linnaeus hope to establish himself as "the most consummate botanist" in successive bargains of specimens representing "new" species (cf. Latour 1987, 219–57, on accumulation in science).

Nowhere did Linnaeus's conception of cyclical and balanced exchange as the basis for life become more explicit than in his *Politia naturae* ([1760] 1764). This essay is known mainly for its comparisons of "ecological" relations with relations of political dominance (see Spary 1996, 178–81). However, it opened with a metaphor that pointed surprisingly far beyond these similes in a cyclical model that combined domestic reproduction and market relations into one circulatory movement: at first sight, as Linnaeus argued in the very first paragraph, nature might appear in a state of war, as one sees "one animal tear to pieces the other in astonishing tyranny." After closer observation one had to admit, however, that

> it is difficult, if not impossible, to discern beginning and end in divine works. In a circle, namely, runs everything. No less than on weekly markets. At first one only sees how a great mass of people spreads out in this or that direction, while nevertheless each of them has his home, from where he approached and to which he will proceed. (Linnaeus [1760] 1764, 18)

5. A Laboratory for Economic Forms

In view of the last quote, it is difficult to resist the temptation of modifying Karl Marx's (1965, 319) statement on François Quesnay and his *Tableau économique*: that Linnaeus was one of the first to have identified circulation as a form of biological reproduction. And yet it is not necessary to assume that Linnaeus was "influenced" by Quesnay or any other economist of his time. To my knowledge, there is no evidence that he ever read any of the economic works of his day (cf. Koerner 1999, 2). Rather the converse seems probable, that Quesnay knew the work of Linnaeus and other naturalists of his time: the background of Quesnay's *Tableau* in contemporary medicine and natural science is well known (Banzhaf 2000), and influences of contemporary conceptions of an "economy of nature" on him have been discussed (Christensen 1994); John Locke had a medical background as well and kept a herbarium (Coleman 2000); Jean-Jacques Rousseau practiced botany late in his life and was a devoted admirer of Linnaeus (Cook 1994); and Adam Smith was "studying Botany" as a pastime while writing his *Inquiry into the Nature and Causes of the Wealth of Nations* (cf. Smith 1987, 252; Schabas, this volume).

Yet it is equally unnecessary to postulate any "influence" in this converse direction, as both Linnaeus and the "economists" just mentioned had a sufficiently common background in belonging to a scientific community that shared certain methodological vantage points, both in theory and practice. In Linnaeus, these were twofold: On the one hand, he followed the analytic-synthetic method—shared by Thomas Hobbes, Locke, Smith, Rousseau, and Sir Isaac Newton (cf. Freudenthal 1986)—in explaining the "economy of nature" on the basis of the principle that a system consists of elements (in this case, species) whose essential properties are given independently of the system of which they are part (in this case, by "laws of generation"). On the other hand, Linnaeus shared the standpoint of the medical profession to which he belonged and which, in the course of the eighteenth century, began to attend less to the working and healing of the individual body than to the working and healing of entire populations (cf. Foucault 1991 and Spary 1996; on the medical background of Linnaeus, see Hövel 1999). Linnaeus's theoretical accomplishments as well as his projects for political and economic reform had their background in these vantage points.

With this in mind, however, Linnaean "natural science" must be seen not so much as following particular political and economic agendas, but as a modernizing force in itself, which promoted a change not only in science but also in the institutions and practices of social life at large. The scientific activity in which Linnaeus engaged was a sort of "laboratory" for new social and economic forms, joining the unrelated—such as a Surinamese slave and a Swedish university professor—and yielding the unexpected—such as an African herb in Uppsala (cf. Pratt 1992, 24–37).

The ideal of a society of mutually independent contractors, which Linnaeus both envisioned in "the republic of botany" and, correspondingly, portrayed as nature's general form in his "economy of nature," was far from materializing in his own time and place, as Linnaeus's persuasions about how to foster his own country's economy prove. But it was certainly being promoted, if only inadvertently, by the peculiar codification it experienced in the theory and practice of Linnaean botany—which may also explain the astonishing career that his botany had as a "popular science" among the bourgeoisie in the late eighteenth and nineteenth centuries (cf. Stevens 1994, chap. 9; te Heesen 2001).

This raises again the question of the relation between Linnaeus's "natural science" and "oeconomia" and the tensions this relation exhibited. As quoted at the beginning of this essay, "natural science" was conceived by Linnaeus as one of the "two foundations" (alongside "physics") of oeconomia. As Koerner (1999, 55) rightly argues, this implies that "natural science" had to be designed as a "tool" that could further the aims of oeconomia, and many Linnaean innovations can indeed be explained along this line. But it also means that Linnaeus's peculiar program of creating national autarky by pursuing oeconomia was possible and conceivable only on the basis of these "tools." In a certain sense it originated from them, not vice versa. The global identifications of natural products that Linnaeus's natural science achieved could therefore serve other modernization strategies as well as his own "cameralist" one. Taken as such, they might equally well have served and promoted contemporary colonial or even free trade strategies. And indeed, Linnaean botany became especially well institutionalized in Great Britain, not the least by the foundation of the Linnaean Society in 1781, which devoted itself exclusively to the study of natural history according to the rules and methods laid down by Linnaeus (see Smith 1791; cf. Stafleu 1971, chap. 7, as well as Duris 1995 on the different fate of Linnaean doctrines in France, where they became popular only after the Revolution).

The modernization strategy that Linnaeus pursued for his own country—"creating a miniaturized mercantile empire within the borders of the European state," as Koerner (1999, 188) so aptly expressed it—thus turns out to have been only one particular option among others conceivable on the very same basis of a taxonomy of "universal commodities." That Linnaeus declared this option as an absolute solution to welfare problems—probably because he, as a naturalist who did not follow the developments in "physics," was blind to the prospects that the development of manufacture could offer for a positive trade balance (Liedman 1989)—finally explains why tensions existed between the economic contentions appearing in his "oeconomic" and his botanical writings. The very same scientific "tools" in which Linnaeus put his hope for achieving national autarky actually transcended the latter's limitations, and indeed all limitations of particular modernization strategies.

References

Banzhaf, H. Spencer. 2000. Productive Nature and the Net Product: Quesnay's Economies Animal and Political. *HOPE* 32.3:517–51.

Christensen, Paul P. 1994. Fire, Motion, and Productivity: The Proto-energetics of Nature and Economy in François Quesnay. In *Natural Images in Economic Thought: "Markets Read in Tooth and Claw,"* edited by Philip Mirowski. Cambridge: Cambridge University Press.

Coleman, William. 2000. The Significance of John Locke's Medical Studies for His Economic Thought. *HOPE* 32.4:711–31.

Cook, Alexandra. 1994. Rousseau's "Moral Botany": Nature, Science, Politics, and the Soul in Rousseau's Botanical Writings. Ph.D. diss., University of Michigan.

Drayton, Richard. 2000. *Nature's Government: Science, Imperial Britain, and the "Improvement" of the World.* New Haven, Conn.: Yale University Press.

Duris, Pascal. 1995. *Linné et la France (1780–1850).* Geneva: Droz.

Eriksson, Gunnar. 1989. The Academy in the Daily Life of Sweden. In *Science in Sweden: The Royal Swedish Academy of Sciences 1739–1989*, edited by Tore Frängsmyr. Canton, Mass.: Science History Publications.

Findlen, Paula. 1994. *Possessing Nature: Museums, Collecting, and Scientific Culture in Early Modern Italy.* Studies on the History of Society and Culture, vol. 20. Berkeley, Calif.: University of California Press.

Foucault, Michel. 1991. Faire vivre et laisser mourir: La naissance du racisme. *Les temps modernes* 535:37–61.

Freudenthal, Gideon. 1986. *Atom and Individual in the Age of Newton: On the Genesis of the Mechanistic World View.* Translated by Peter McLaughlin. Dordrecht: Reidel.

Gregory, Chris. 1982. *Gifts and Commodities.* Edited by John Eatwell. Studies in Political Economy. New York: Academic Press.

Hagstrom, W. O. [1965] 1972. Gift-Giving as an Organizing Principle in Science. In *Sociology of Science: Selected Readings*, edited by B. Barnes. Harmondsworth: Penguin Books.

Heckscher, Eli F. 1942. Linnés resor—den ekonomiska bakgrunden. *Svenska Linné-Sällskapets Årsskrift* 25:1–11.

Heller, John Louis. [1970] 1983. Linnaeus's *Bibliotheca botanica.* In *Studies in Linnean Method and Nomenclature.* Frankfurt: Lang.

Hövel, Gerlinde. 1999. *"Qualitates vegetabilium," "vires medicamentorum," und "oeconomicus usus plantarum" bei Carl von Linné (1707–1778)*. Braunschweiger Veröffentlichungen zur Geschichte der Pharmazie und der Naturwissenschaften, vol. 42. Stuttgart: Dt. Apotheker-Verl.

Koerner, Lisbet. 1999. *Linnaeus: Nature and Nation*. Cambridge: Harvard University Press.

Larson, James L. 1971. *Reason and Experience: The Representation of Natural Order in the Work of Carl Linnaeus*. Berkeley, Calif.: University of California Press.

Latour, Bruno. 1987. *Science in Action: How to Follow Scientists and Engineers through Society*. Cambridge: Harvard University Press.

Lévi-Strauss, Claude. 1962. *La pensée sauvage*. Paris: Plon.

Liedman, Sven-Eric. 1989. Utilitarianism and the Economy. In *Science in Sweden: The Royal Swedish Academy of Sciences 1739–1989*, edited by Tore Frängsmyr. Canton, Mass.: Science History Publications.

Limoges, Camille. 1972. Introduction. In *Charles Linné: L'équilibre de la nature*. Paris: Vrin.

Linnaeus, Carl. 1736. *Bibliotheca botanica*. Amsterdam: Salomon Schouten.

———. 1737a. *Critica botanica*. Leiden: Wishoff.

———. 1737b. *Genera plantarum*. Leiden: Wishoff.

———. 1739. Rön om växters plantering grundat på Naturen. *Kungliga Svenska Vetenskapsakademiens Handlingar* 1:5–24.

———. 1740. Tanckar om Grunden til Oeconomien genom Naturkunnogheten ock Physiquen. *Kungliga Svenska Vetenskapsakademiens Handlingar* 1:411–29.

———. 1751. *Philosophia botanica*. Stockholm: Kiesewetter.

———. [1754] 1759. Horticultura academica. In *Ammoenitates academicae*. Stockholm: Laurentius Salvius.

———. [1749] 1762. The Œconomy of Nature. In *Miscellaneous Tracts*. Translated by Benjamin Stillingfleet. 2d ed. London: R. & J. Dodsley.

———. [1760] 1764. Politia naturae. In *Ammoenitates academicae*. Stockholm: Laurentius Salvius.

———. [1749] 1787. Oeconomia naturae. In *Ammoenitates academicae*. Erlangen: Jo. Jacobus Palm.

———. 1916. *Bref och skrifvelser af och til Carl von Linné. Andra Afdelningen. Utländska Brefväxlingen. Del I*. Edited by J. M. Hulth. Uppsala: Akademiska Bokhandlen.

Malmeström, Elis. 1926. *Carl von Linnés religiösa åskådning*. Stockholm: Svenska Kyrkans Diakonistyrelse Bokförlag.

Marx, Karl. 1965. Theorien ueber den Mehrwert. Erster Teil. In vol. 26 of *Marx Engels Werke*. Berlin: Dietz.

Mauss, Marcel. [1924] 1997. Essai sur le don: Forme et raison de l'échange dans les sociétés archaïques. In *Sociologie et anthropologie*. Paris: Quadrige/PUF.

McCracken, Donald P. 1997. *Gardens of Empire: Botanical Institutions of the Victorian British Empire*. London: Leicester University Press.

McOuat, Gordon. 1996. Species, Rules, and Meaning: The Politics of Language and the Ends of Definitions in Nineteenth-Century Natural History. *Studies in History and Philosophy of Science* 27.4:473–519.

Miller, Philip D., and Hans P. Reill, eds. 1996. *Visions of Empire: Voyages, Botany, and Representations of Nature*. Cambridge: Cambridge University Press.

Müller-Wille, Staffan. 1998. "Varietäten auf ihre Arten zurückführen." Zu Carl von Linnés Stellung in der Vorgeschichte der Genetik. *Theory in Biosciences* 117:346–76.

———. 1999. *Botanik und weltweiter Handel. Zur Begründung eines Natürlichen Systems der Pflanzen durch Carl von Linné (1707–1778)*. Studien zur Theorie der Biologie, vol. 3. Berlin: Verlag für Wissenschaft und Bildung.

———. 2001a. Carl von Linnés Herbarschrank. Zur epistemischen Funktion eines Sammlungsmöbels. In *Sammeln als Wissen*, edited by Anke te Heesen and Emma C. Spary. Göttingen: Wallstein.

———. 2001b. Gardens of Paradise. *Endeavour* 25.2:49–54.

Nicolas, Jean Paul. 1963. Adanson, the Man. In vol. 1 of *Adanson: The Bicentennial of Michel Adanson's "Famille des plantes,"* edited by George H. M. Lawrence. Pittsburgh, Pa.: Hunt Botanical Library.

Olmi, Giuseppe. 1993. From the Marvellous to the Commonplace: Notes on Natural History Museums (Sixteenth to Eighteenth Centuries). In *Non-Verbal Communication in Science Prior to 1900*, edited by Renato G. Mazzolini. Florence: Leo S. Olschki.

Pratt, Mary Louise. 1992. *Imperial Eyes: Travel Writing and Transculturation*. London: Routledge.

Sahlins, Marshall. 1972. *Stone-Age Economics*. Chicago: Aldine.

Secord, Ann. 1994. Corresponding Interests: Artisans and Gentlemen in Natural History Exchange Networks. *British Journal for the History of Science* 27:383–408.

Smith, Adam. 1987. *Correspondence of Adam Smith*. Vol. 6 of *The Glasgow Edition of the Works and Correspondence of Adam Smith*, edited by Ernest Campbell Mossner and Ian Simpson Ross. Indianapolis, Ind.: Liberty Fund.

Smith, James Edward. 1791. Introductory Discourse on the Rise and Progress of Natural History. *Transactions of the Linnean Society of London* 1:1–55.

———, ed. 1821. *A Selection of the Correspondence of Linnaeus, and Other Naturalists: From the Original Manuscripts*. London: Longman, Hurst, Rees, Orme, and Brown.

Smith, Pamela H., and Paula Findlen, eds. 2002. *Merchants and Marvels: Commerce, Science, and Art in Early Modern Europe*. London: Routledge.

Sörlin, Sverker. 2000. Ordering the World for Europe: Science as Intelligence and Information As Seen from the Nothern Periphery. In *Nature and Empire: Science and the Colonial Enterprise*, edited by Roy MacLeod. Chicago: University of Chicago Press.

Spary, Emma C. 1996. Political, Natural, and Bodily Economics. In *Cultures of Natural History*, edited by Nicholas Jardine, James A. Secord, and Emma C. Spary. Cambridge: Cambridge University Press.

———. 2000. *Utopia's Garden: French Natural History from Old Regime to Revolution*. Chicago: University of Chicago Press.

Stafleu, Frans A. 1963. Adanson and His "Familles de plantes." In vol. 1 of *Adanson: The Bicentennial of Michel Adanson's "Famille des plantes,"* edited by George H. M. Lawrence. Pittsburgh, Pa.: Hunt Botanical Library.

———. 1971. *Linnaeus and the Linneans: The Spreading of Their Ideas in Systematic Botany, 1735–1789*. Utrecht: A. Oosthoek for the International Association for Plant Taxonomy.

Stearn, William T. 1959. The Background of Linnaeus's Contributions to the Nomenclature and Methods of Systematic Biology. *Systematic Zoology* 8.1–4:4–22.

———. 1961. Botanical Gardens and Botanical Literature in the Eighteenth Century. In vol. 2 of *Catalogue of Botanical Books in the Collection of Rachel McMasters Miller Hunt*, edited by J. Quinby and A. Stevenson. Pittsburgh, Pa.: Hunt Botanical Library.

———. 1962. The Influence of Leyden on Botany in the Seventeenth and Eighteenth Centuries. *British Journal for the History of Science* 1.2:137–59.

———. 1976. Carl Linnaeus and the Theory and Practice of Horticulture. *Taxon* 25.1:21–31.

Stevens, Peter F. 1994. *The Development of Systematics: Antoine-Laurent de Jussieu, Nature, and the Natural System*. New York: Columbia University Press.

te Heesen, Anke. 2001. Vom naturgeschichtlichen Investor zum Staatsdiener. In *Sammeln als Wissen. Das Sammeln und seine wissenschaftsgeschichtliche Bedeutung*, edited by Anke te Heesen and Emma C. Spary. Göttingen: Wallstein.

Thomas, Nicholas. 1991. *Entangled Objects: Exchange, Material Culture, and Colonialism in the Pacific*. Cambridge: Harvard University Press.

Tribe, Keith. 1988. *Governing Economy: The Reformation of German Economic Discourse 1750–1840*. Cambridge: Cambridge University Press.

Wijnands, D. Onno. 1988. Hortus auriaci: The Gardens of Orange and Their Place in Late-Seventeenth-Century Botany and Horticulture. *Journal of Garden History* 8:61–86, 271–304.

Zirkle, Conway. 1959. Species before Darwin. *Proceedings of the American Philosophical Society* 103.5:636–44.

Underwriting the Oeconomy: Linnaeus on Nature and Mind

Lisbet Rausing

In its full brittle complexity, nature today exists only on our sufferance. Around us and in our company relatively few life-forms thrive: our hybrid crops and infantilized companions such as the domestic dog, our parasites and microbes, the tramp flora invading the soils we ravage, and those generalist omnivores living from our refuse, such as houseflies, cockroaches, crows, pigs, and rats. The key distinction between our nature, which is to say modernity's nature, and the nature of the eighteenth-century enlightened improvers, is nicely captured by how we today describe those small fragments remaining as pristine ecosystems—our "refuges," "wildlife corridors," "reserves," "sanctuaries," "parks," and "set-asides."

These terms hark back to our self-image as stewards and guardians, and to the earth as our garden, as well as to medieval legal terminology of outlaws. A "sanctuary" was originally a place, usually a church, where criminals were safe from the law. So is a "refuge." And the Massachusetts Audubon Society defines their "set-asides" as places "without permanent improvements," even as the very existence of these places fundamentally questions that notion of improvement. As one writer of the deep-ecology movement, Bill McCormick, has put it, nature is now dead—not as a natural fact, but phenomenologically, as an entity existing independently of us.

Historians sometimes write of a specifically Western dysfunctional relation to nature (typically contrasted with non-Western peoples' supposedly custodial guardianship). This story is written in Freudian terms, as a repetition-compulsion. The Fall is acted out as people assert in action the power over nature that God granted them in Genesis. In this account, the story of the Fall is what constitutes the Fall.

I argue in this article that Christian theologies addressing nature (its constitution and its relation to humans) are more complex and varied. I have chosen one example: the natural theology of the Swedish botanist Carl Linnaeus (1707–78) and his students. Linnaeus and his followers, I argue, regarded nature as a benign and self-regulating superorganism, cyclically self-replicating its own perfection through "policing" mechanisms such as—if I may be permitted to use problematically modern terms—hydraulic cycles, successor plant communities, and predator-prey relations.

This is why, of course, some historians have dubbed Linnaeus the father of ecology, together with English naturalist parsons such as John Ray (1628–1705) and Gilbert White (1720–93). As I have argued in earlier publications, however, Linnaeus himself stands outside that more general reception of his thought, whereby Adam Smith imports the cybernetic concepts governing Linnaeus's natural theology into his own economics of the "invisible hand," and Charles Darwin in turn reimports Smithian conceptions of the economy and its autoregulatory features into the realm of nature (Koerner 1999). But Linnaeus *did* regard humankind as an integral part of his finely balanced nature (and as the worshipful mediator to its ultimate creator, God). In turn, this theology—which involved a far-reaching naturalization of humanity—underwrote Linnaeus's economics.

To help the uninitiated reader, I first sketch the practice and institutes of the Linnaean science of "oeconomy." In the bulk of the article, however, I address its theoretical constructs, analyzing how Linnaeus and his students conceptualized—by way of their natural theology—the relation between nature and economics. I pay particular attention to how their intertwining involved a claim to universality, of both nature and mind. That claim in turn resulted in an intriguing if not rigorously elaborated epistemology of cross-cultural knowledge formation, which looped back into, and ultimately depended on, Linnaean natural theology. The article concludes that Linnaeus's mind mirrored the nature he constructed not only in terms of his concepts of the naturalized human mind, but also in terms of the cycles and interdependence of its epistemologies.

"This era, when Sweden's age-old joy in battles and fighting games was tempted to turn instead in earnest to peaceful heroics, also led to a strong tending of the public [*allmänna*] and the private household. The Oeconomy was encouraged, and Sweden had the honor of being the first [country] to bring it to a proper science [*vetenskap*] and graft her onto Academic exercises" (Odhelius 1780, 15).

Or so explained the speaker at Pehr Kalm's memorial service in 1780, as his academician peers gathered to honor the old Linnaean student, America traveler, and professor of economics at Åbo University. In 1773, a speaker at another memorial service, this time for Linnaeus's closest friend, the court physician Abraham Bäck, at Uppsala University, noted that by the 1720s, and after the defeats of the Northern Wars,

> in Sweden people were beginning to get tired of the Warfaring life. We no longer succeeded in conquering new provinces, and coming home with rich bounty; instead we clearly felt the destructive results of War. There was no other possibility, except to try to do the best with what we already owned and had. Prosperity could only be had, by work and perseverance, and for that they needed a different kind of thinking and a bigger population. People found, that a pure Warrior People need a different kind of education to be able to feed itself. (Schulzenheim 1773)

As I have discussed in earlier publications, the Swedish school of economics was an elaborately crafted form of national economics (Koerner 1999). Patriotic subjects of a now minor Baltic country, Linnaeus and his peers dreamt of utilizing their natural knowledge in building a self-sufficient nation. They aimed to reconstruct their *fädernesland* after the traumatic loss of Gustav II Adolf's transnational Lutheran empire. But already by 1773, five years before Linnaeus's death, and certainly by 1780, this economic project seemed distant to most educated Swedes. Seen most broadly, it lasted from 1718, when Karl XII died, to 1773, when Gustav III reintroduced absolutist rule. But its heyday was from 1739, when the mercantilist Hat party came into power, to 1765, when the Hat party fell and with it much of the funding for the elaborate state apparatus devoted to economic projects.

By the later eighteenth century, other sciences were beginning to be favored by the Swedish state machinery and particularly its ever more important court. In 1788, for example, the enlightened despot Gustav III gave a Swedenborgian alchemist, August Nordenskjöld, a salary as well as a laboratory in the gardens of the royal castle of Drottingholm. Great secrecy was imposed. Outside the laboratory, Nordenskjöld was forced to wear peasant clothing and a long beard. To safeguard his persona as "gardener," he was not allowed to swim—a pursuit of the urban bourgeoisie—in the sea ringing the castle. Not surprisingly, he ran away after a year, and on the first anniversary of the fall of Bastille was seen dancing on its ruins.

A decade earlier, in 1778, August's brother Ulrik had presented the Swedish finance minister with plans for Swedish trading companies to Guiana and, in a pamphlet of 1776, Swedish colonies "in the Indies and in Africa." In a manner typical to this later period in Swedish economic thinking, he argued that Sweden's purported trade deficit was caused by her lack of tropical tributaries. A few years later, in 1782, he felt his argument was bolstered when he discovered that Emanuel Swedenborg had drawn (and this surely was a sign) a map of Africa in his *Diarium spirituale*. In 1784, Sweden did indeed acquire a (miniature) West Indian colony, St. Bart's. Two years later her first West Indian Company was formed, and in 1787, Gustav III secretly financed an exploration of Senegal by one of Linnaeus's students, Anders Sparrman. Once in Africa, the expedition acquired a few plots of land for the Nordenskjöld brothers and other Swedish Swedenborgians in Sierra Leone's "Province of Freedom," founded in 1787 by Henry Smeathman as a country for freedmen.

A little later, in a 1790 article in a Swedenborgian magazine, *Allmänna Magazinet*, Carl Fredrik, the last of the three Nordenskjöld brothers, outlined a new "Last Judgment," when enlightenment would stalk the earth and the middle classes rule (*medelklassen*, a term he coined in Swedish in that very article). He so stressed "utility" that even his vision of heaven was that of hardworking angels, laboring away in celestial libraries, workshops, and offices. Carl Fredrik Nordenskjöld's vision turned on humanity's duty to restore earth to order by cultivating nature. He imagined three classes in his utopia: *productors*, who fashion raw materials out of wild nature, manufacturers, and—lowest of all—merchants. In his all-powerful governing body of twenty-four men, twelve would be *productors*, eight manufacturers, and only four merchants. Here was a vision close to orthodox physiocracy, although Nordenskjöld added miners and fishermen into the class of farmers (Ambjörnsson 1975–76).

More broadly, of course, the Nordenskjöld brothers and their fellow Swedes followed a broad thought-tradition—running from Aristotle to Thomas Aquinas to Karl Marx and Georg Simmel, and along the way taking in the Linnaean economists—in their conviction that material production was the only source of value; that profits were suspect; that prices might need to be legislated; and that the use of money transformed *Gemeinschaft* to *Gesellschaft*.

The court of Gustav III was interested in esoteric sciences: alchemy and ancient mysteries, for example. A generation earlier, the utilitarian and practical-minded Linnaeans—who worked within a parliamentary system—drew on both English mercantilist and German cameralist theory, noting (correctly) their many similarities. Both creeds regarded trade and finance as largely parasitic on agriculture and the crafts. They believed that precious metals had an intrinsic value that went beyond use-value and market price. And they had a zero-sum view of the international economy, arguing that the chief economic goal of government was a perpetually positive national trade balance. The difference between the two comes at the level not of ideology, but of strategy. Mercantilists, who inhabited transoceanic empires, hoped to secure a positive trade balance by depot trading (the turnaround export of colonial imports) and by adding value to imported raw materials and exporting them as finished goods. Cameralists, who inhabited landlocked states, instead advocated import substitution (local production of imports).

The Swedish economic thought-world to which Linnaeus belonged—which broadly and in many variants held sway in the mid-eighteenth century—thus profoundly differed from later eighteenth-century English theories of individual choice, foundational for classical economics and political liberalism. Ultimately because of geopolitical realities (it theorized its own existence as a postimperial nation-state at the northern edge of Europe), it borrowed its aim from cameralism, or German seventeenth-century theories of how the protomodern police state could maximize tax revenues. Both cameralism proper and what I here shorthand as "Linnaean economics" saw the state as the privileged vehicle for economic development. But the Swedish school of economics in addition drew on English mercantilist theory in emphasizing the problem of negative trade balances, measured in flows of bullion. And in its emphasis on farming it foreshadowed, even if it did not influence, the French physiocrats of the 1750s.

Linnaean economics garnered additional moral force from its attempt to forge a new identity for the "pure Warrior People" of Sweden. This patriotic endeavor was not particularly advanced, however, seen from the viewpoint of later nationalisms. In 1804, traveling through Sweden, the German Romantic Ernst Moritz Arndt operated with ideas like *Geist des Nordens*, *nordischen Karakter*, and *Nationalgeist*. He searched for *unverdorbenen Gegenden*, where people were still blond, and adhered to *die alten frommen Gebirgsitten* (Arndt [1804] 1806, esp. 284). By contrast, half a century earlier, Linnaeus describes his own and his students' "nationalities" in terms of the medieval provinces that to this day constitute Uppsala student dormitories: "Smolandus" and "Ostro-Gothus" (Linnaeus 1961, 17, 33). When he spoke of his "dear Fatherland," he was as apt to mean Smolandium as Sweden (Linnaeus [1728] 1888, 57).

On the other hand, Linnaeus condemned Baltics' imitation of foreign mores. "When we are home, we walk about like Turks in a long wide nightgown, red slippers, and white cap: smoke our tobacco and drink our coffee" (student note on lecture by Linnaeus, 1747, KB, Ms. X.55, 96). He disliked "the Swedish monkey," "*Suecus Simia*, for he eats like an Englishman, drinks like a German, dresses like a Frenchman, builds like an Italian, smokes like a Dutchman, takes snuff like a Spaniard, and gulps down aquavit like a Russian" (Linnaeus 1907, 152). The cure against such influences he imagined in proto-Romantic terms—that is, in terms of a return to "Gothic" mores, the Goths being a tribe of pagan Sweden whose name still lives on in three Swedish counties, Västergötland, Östergötland, and Gotland, as well as in the name for the southern third of the country, Götaland.

But more importantly, as Linnaeus and his followers saw it, the reconstruction of the Swedish economy depended on a regulatory state machinery and particularly on import bans. "I am happy to admit," one correspondent to a Stockholm magazine wrote in 1769, "that the Manufactures can't do well or thrive in a country, as long as foreign pieces can be imported and sold." To ban such trade, he continued, was a matter of urgency. Swedish manufactures "increase our population . . . keep workers' salaries within our realm, decrease begging." Therefore, *husvisitationer*—unannounced raids in people's homes by customs and excise—were necessary even in a *fritt land* (*Posten* 1769). For the alternative, the export of specie to China, was worse. As Linnaeus put it, contemplating what he imagined to be the immense gold hoards of the Chinese emperor: "et sic perit labor Europa" (student note on lecture by Linnaeus, 1747, KB, Ms. X.55, 189).

Linnaean economists, and not least those in the Academy of Science, regarded labor-saving devices with suspicion. They noted, for example, that winnowing and sowing machines would deprive people of work. There was a widespread consensus that the goal of the manufacturers subsidized by the Hat party was *not* to make production processes more efficient through the use of machinery. This would employ fewer people, and so negate the whole point. Much more importantly, the idle poor needed to be put to work, be they beggars, children, or even wild animals: the academy, noting that "in the dense forests, elk can be seen wandering about, doing nothing," even offered a premium for tame breeding elks (Liedman 1989, 39–41). This interest in engaging people in work led to the academy's most lasting achievement: its population statistics. From 1748 on, the Office of Tables, having rejected methods of sampling and averaging, and using parsons as their laborers, counted each individual inhabitant of Sweden.

Through the academy, the Linnaean weltanschauung, and its views on nature and nation, had a surprisingly wide reach, although we know practically nothing about its reception among rural folks. From 1747 to 1972, the academy held a monopoly on printing almanacs. Selling—at country fairs, mostly—in editions of between 150,000 and 200,000 a year, these financed the academy's activities. Next to Luther's *Small Catechism*, they were the most widely read text in later eighteenth-century Sweden—already a largely literate, if still rural, nation, thanks to the *husförhör*, the Lutheran clergy's farm-by-farm literacy exams. This allowed academicians to popularize their science. A good example is Linnaeus's 1746 almanac essay on Chinese tea, which summarizes his views on the dangers of foreign trade. Another way to reach the populace was through parsons reading decrees in parish churches (church attendance was compulsory). Here, too, Linnaean science occasionally reached, as when Linnaeus's recipes of edible wild flora were read out in churches across Sweden in the great famine year of 1756.

Linnaeus's and his Swedish contemporaries' *vision* of modernity, then, was most typically that of a regulated *Ständesstaat*, which they described in terms of society emulating nature's police, so as to become the police of nature. Their vision had little to do with the Enlightenment's self-organized modes of sociability, such as coffeehouses, clubs, and academies, where a more fluid and open civil society had begun replicating itself, even though Linnaeus and his followers as a matter of *fact* involved themselves in these emerging communities—and their print equivalences such as periodical literature, pamphlets, magazines, and lending libraries. Instead they imagined that the future would be brought about through a Lutheran civil service, and that therefore, they themselves were key agents of historical change.

Traditionally, historians understand *natural history* as loosely encompassing what later became the life sciences, geography, anthropology, and the earth sciences. That is how we moderns have looked at natural history: as the source of a series of disciplines such as geology, physical anthropology, pharmacology, and mineralogy. Indeed, Thomas Kuhn, in his *Structure of Scientific Revolutions* (1962), arguably the single most influential book in the history of science, invokes natural history as his key example of a preparadigmatic science—that is, one where random facts are collected in a desultory fashion and hobbled together with ad hoc theories. Unguided by theory, or so Kuhn argued, natural historians were unable even to begin to select which natural phenomena, among the observable infinitude of nature, they should privilege. But the Linnaeans did not see it this way, and not only because they fundamentally did not believe what Kuhn posits as a natural fact, namely, an infinitude of natural facts. They saw the world as finite and knowable, and they regarded themselves as masters of a well-defined discipline.

Linnaeus's claim to provide a set of workable principles for what we may term "naturalized economics" is nicely illuminated by the iron manufacturer Anders Borgström's 1759 donation of an Uppsala University chair in "practical economics," which was intended to counteract the Uppsala professor in cameralism's pernicious influence on his students, as Linnaeus and his friend Borgström saw it. This professor, Anders Berch—whose chair was modeled on Europe's first chairs in cameralism at Halle (1727), Frankfurt-am-Oder (1729), and Rinteln in Hessen (1730)—did excellent work on improving ploughs and surveying methods for population statistics and economic output (Liedman 1989, 38, 44). To this Linnaeus did not object. But he disliked how Berch criticized his hopes for a self-enclosed local economy: Berch clamored for Swedish colonies in the tropics, where slaves and criminals would purchase the woolen cloths and silk brocades of Sweden's state-subsidized textile manufactures (Rydberg 1951, 136). This hope Linnaeus saw as chimerical, and his students, traveling to London, reinforced his doubts about Sweden's chance to become a transoceanic force by warning him of the English's "unnatural bragging over their military successes, so that one hears nothing, but that the English can conquer the whole world if they want" (Daniel Solander, letter to Linnaeus, 5 February 1761, LSL).

Elicited and negotiated by Linnaeus, Borgström's donation chair—like the ones Linnaeus fundraised for, and placed students at, at the universities of Åbo (1747) and Lund (1760)—combined the teaching of mineralogy, zoology, botany, and chemistry with that of trade, mining, manufacturing, fishing, and farming. At Uppsala, the students would even be taught (or so Borgström stipulated in his letter of donation, which was probably dictated by Linnaeus) on an experimental farm outside the townlet of Uppsala. On this farm the professor would both live and conduct his research. The farm, which was also donated by Borgström, was probably modeled on Löfwsta, Baron Sten Carl Bielke's model estate in the same county, Uppland, and the new professor's role would emulate that played by Linnaeus's student Pehr Kalm, when he was inspector at Löfwsta.

The farm never came into use, however, since the man Borgström chose—in accordance with the then academic custom that donors appointed the first professor—died early. His first five years as the Borgström professor were spent, like Borgström's donation letter dictated, traveling through Swedish provinces at Borgström's expense to discover economically useful plants, animals, and manufactures—this, of course, in obvious emulation of Linnaeus's *landskapsresor* of the previous two decades.

At the German university of Göttingen, too, a student of Linnaeus, Johann Beckmann, taught economics, beginning in 1766. His "economics" followed the Linnaean recipe: it was an amalgam of mineralogy, mining, farming, cameralism, and technology (a term he coined in 1772). From 1769, the professor in natural history and medicine, Johann Andreas Murray, was also an erstwhile student of Linnaeus. And through Göttingen, as much as through the Swedish universities, such teachings reached the high nobility of Sweden and its former Baltic realms: student rolls of the period include boys from families such as Lewenhaupt, de la Gardie, Bonde, Wrangel, von Essen, Brahe, Wachtmeister, Taube, and Piper (Callmer 1956).

Linnaeus, then, had considerable success in institutionalizing economics as an academic discipline, although he could not always control, of course, what was taught by the professors he helped install. Apart from creating chairs, and placing his students, he also managed to make his own lectures obligatory to Uppsala theology students (and thus most students), and he convinced the Swedish East India Company to employ naturalists he had trained as ships' parsons.

Nonetheless, as I discuss in *Linnaeus: Nature and Nation* (Koerner 1999), this newfound discipline left no lasting heritage. There were many reasons for this, not all of which were linked to Linnaean economics as such. There were also problems of universities' insistence on religious orthodoxy; their habit of making professorships—formally or informally—hereditary; their paying of teachers in fixed quantities of grain, which meant their salaries fluctuated wildly depending on harvests; and the much higher pay of theology professors (not to mention the chances of bishoprics that those chairs carried), which encouraged clever men to jump ship.

Also, the natural theology that was Linnaean economics' philosophical cornerstone—and to which we return below—quickly became a jargonized and stereotyped genre. Stockholm newspapers, with their more urban (and urbane) readers, soon began to joke about these provincial academic dispositions, written mainly to secure their authors parsonages. One such review devastatingly mocked a physico-theological thesis entitled "On God's Miracles in Nature" by noting simply that among such miracles, "this work however can hardly be counted" (Ehnmark 1931, 57).

Linnaeus was an Enlightenment empiric and utilitarian, who assembled around himself the propagandizing tools of a "new era," to be marked by that confluence of science and modernity that today irreversibly constitutes modernity. He positioned himself as a scientist-intermediary between the natural world and government planning. Like the more studied Newtonian philosophers, the Linnaean naturalists promised a useful science. Indeed, that utility was vast and, in its instrumentation, ambitious. For as I discuss in *Nature and Nation*, the goal of Linnaeus was nothing less than to render ecological divides—and hence, both mercantile colonies and free trade—economically and politically irrelevant.

Yet while it helped legitimize a catch-up modernization doctrine, Linnaeus's "new science" ultimately effected only incremental changes of Sweden's premodern agricultural economy. One reason can perhaps be found in how he tried to make his science serve his group aspirations. As an eighteenth-century civil servant, Linnaeus was in many ways a rent-seeker. Of course, Linnaeus never formally articulated this dilemma of group privilege versus national interest. But he and his followers prolonged the life of an old-fashioned economic doctrine—cameralism—that was itself tailor-made for rent-seeking by displacing its theoretical bonus from the management of people to the constitution of the natural world.

Already by the 1760s, the Swedish state elites were beginning to notice that the economic payoff promised by Linnaeus and his colleagues in the Swedish Academy of Science was not forthcoming (Frängsmyr 1989, 10). The results from global travels Linnaeus had sponsored and promoted, and the hopes of bringing new crops, animals, and technologies to Sweden, were especially disappointing. One Linnaean traveler to India came back—or so a student of Linnaeus bitterly noted—"with the interesting Information, that the Trees in India are green, that birds sit in them and monkeys, that the earth bore rare plants and everywhere Insects buzzed and Lizards crawled about" (Sandblad 1970, 262). This report is reminiscent of Columbus's famous logbook, where he noted on entering Hispaniola that he saw "green things and parrots." Another student of Linnaeus, en route to China, recorded that while on sea he could observe "only 2 Elements and 2 Naturalia nam. Air and water, Whalefish and Seagulls" (letter from Pehr Osbeck to Linnaeus, 26 February 1751, LSL). In later letters to his teacher he stressed the difficulties of botanizing in Canton—the European graveyard was one of the few places he was allowed to visit.

If they returned alive from their travels, Linnaeus's students typically withdrew to the respectable obscurity of country parsonages, where they wrote letters to learned academies and married the daughters of neighboring parsons. But half of Linnaeus's traveling students died: in Smyrna, in Jemen, on the coast of East Africa, in present-day Venezuela, on an island outside Vietnam, and in Kazan, for example. And the collections of those who survived went generally unused. Sierra Leone artifacts gathered dust at Uppsala; the Danish Crown locked away Arabian collections; Levant herbaria were hidden at the Swedish court. Even the unique flora from Captain Cook's first voyages was squirreled away at Soho Square. It was typical that it took a hundred years for the Swedish royal family to give in to the 1743 pleas of the Celsius family to move that family's seminal *Flora Uplandica* and its type collection to the Stockholm public library "for some more general use and its conservation in the future" (Gertz 1920, 49).

In his famous 1751 *Philosophia botanica*, Linnaeus railed against the expensive publication of natural-history collections that, even at the unlikely best of being completed, remained unavailable, because unaffordable. One example is Caroline Louise of Baden's 1770s project to engrave *Species plantarum* onto 10,000 copper plates. Some 250 plates had been completed at her death in 1783 (Broberg 1990–91). As the century aged, such publications took increasingly fanciful forms: the Flora Danica porcelain set (originally intended as a gift to Catherine the Great); empress Josephine's Sevres porcelain set supervised by Pierre-Joseph Redoute; and, also made for the empress Josephine, the 1806–8 botanic porcelain set created by the Königliche Porzellanmanufaktur. The unipatterned, single-species "Napoleon Ivy," the Wedgwood bone china designed for Napoleon's exile in St. Helena, forms an ironized close to such botanic fancies.

I now turn from Linnaeus's sciences to theoretical constructs: how he construed the relation between nature and economics. More single-mindedly than other eighteenth-century economic philosophers, Linnaeus regarded the science of economics as an applied natural history. That, vice versa, natural history was (one form of) state crafting was of course a commonplace across Europe already in the late seventeenth century. While English amateur naturalists might have stressed commerce and society over king and state, they agreed with French academicians on natural knowledge's practical beneficence. Linnaeus, though, went beyond such general sentiments to a more developed theory of the ultimate sameness of economics and the natural sciences, which he regarded as emerging within the theoretical framework of his "Oeconomy of Nature."

Proponents of this view included not only Linnaeus himself, but also his fellow founders of the 1739 Royal Swedish Academy of Science. As common to founders of minor European scientific academies, these men admired the philosophies of science expressed in the English Royal Society. Indeed, the Swedish academy was the brainchild of Mårten Triewald, an experimental machine-builder and a popularizer of Newtonian physics who had lived in England between 1716 and 1726. As the academy's early protocols witness, the academicians argued that "economics" was the main task of the academy, and by that term they meant the methodical elaboration and application of innovative technologies in farming, mining, forestry, textile production, and fishing—the labors, knowledge, and crafts that constituted the bulk of *Balticum*'s economic activities. In theory (if less in practice) they were careful to distinguish between *oeconomia publica*, which was the realm of politics and thus mostly the higher aristocracy, and their own speciality, *oeconomia privata* or *hushållning*, the management of individual farms, estates, fisheries, and manufactures (Strandell 1956–57, 131). Their self-conception of guardians of *vetenskap* and "oeconomy" also had overtones of religious orthodoxy and common sense. "Without science [*vettenskaper*]," or so Linnaeus formulated the ultimate threat in a speech to the staunchly Lutheran Swedish court in 1759, "we would recruit Priests from Rome" (Linnaeus [1759] 1939, 94).

Bettering the economy, the Swedish academicians felt, depended primarily on technological innovations (rather than, say, managerial organization or legal reforms). And this, they claimed, in turn depended on naturalists' particular knowledge. Linnaeus (1744, 24) turned to his own speciality: "The knowledge of plants is the basis of all *oeconomie*" (see also Linnaeus [1749] 1939, 190). In other words, to Linnaeus and his fellow academicians, *economics* did not mean, as it does generally today, the study of how to allocate scarce resources given infinite demand. Instead they viewed it as the discipline of how to husband the natural world and, in doing so, order society on nature's model. Most crucially, they believed that society's secular "oeconomy" was underwritten by nature's sacred "oeconomy": this view Linnaeus ([1753] 1952, 1) held as so central to his science he even put it in the preface of his seminal 1753 *Species plantarum*. In speeches at Uppsala's elaborate annual doctoral ceremonies he repeated the point: "The pillar for all economics (*hushållning*) is to know the great economy of nature" (Linnaeus [1750–59] 1954–55, 112). Linnaean oeconomy was therefore a conglomerate, applied form of natural knowledge, subdivided even into *oeconomia vegetabilium*, *oeconomia mineralium*, and *oeconomia animalum* (Frängsmyr 1971–72, 224).

The English economists—such as David Ricardo and John Stuart Mill—universalized their unique experience of the first industrializing nation. Thinkers in more backward regions, such as the Germanies and *Balticum*, sought to particularize their *Sonderwege*. While the Germans typically became organicist, emphasizing conflicts between social harmony and modernization, the Swedes mostly emphasized certain manners of rationalisms over the "invisible hand" of free competition. Perhaps their long experience of inhabiting a uniquely centralized and top-governed military state encouraged them to turn toward models of Habermasian *Gespräche* and rationalized organizational structures, just as the Germans' long experience with fragmented and irrational rule encouraged their fondness for small-scale and emotional locality writ large (somehow) onto imperialistic state structures. Viewed more broadly, Linnaeus shared the tacit assumptions governing ascetic Protestant science, as outlined by Robert K. Merton and Max Weber: his economics was supposed to establish practical proofs of his own faith, enlarge control over nature, and glorify God. It equally served the individual, society, and the deity.

Like later Max Weber, eighteenth-century Swedish improvers at once took the value of rationality as a given, *and* saw it as a historical praxis, teachable and replicable—think of Linnaeus's positioning of Lutheran parsons as mediators of experimental science. Unlike the Germans, they questioned neither the value, nor the future, nor the sustainability of modernity. But while remaining within the mindset of enlightened utilitarianism, they queried modernity's exact transplantability, that is, the replication of the English model. Rather like Friedrich List's "autarkes imperiales System," the Swedish *Wiederaufbau* of 1718 instead depended on a de facto nonaggression pact with the Atlantic Ocean empires such as England and the build-up of a local Baltic trade fortress. It was, again, a *Sonderweg*.

The Linnaean thought-complex was thus a theoretical counterpart to Sweden's *Beamtenstaat*, and it had as its predictive outcome government regulations. Viewed more philosophically, it involved rationally calibrating human action to the observable regularities of nature's plenitude, and to do this through "policing"—a mechanism Linnaeus saw as universal to nature and ideal to society. Law, order, and regulation was how "the Creator," or *Ens Entium*—Linnaeus liked this Aristotelian term for God—calibrated natural equilibria by ensuring each species kept to its station. Linnaeus at once expressed this "police of nature" in terms of human society and held it up as a natural model for human society. Linnaeus modeled both nature and society on equilibria, and in both cases equilibria enforced by "police." He understood both global nature and human society as an early modern *Ständesstaat*. Hence his frequent parallelisms between military rank, territorial order, and botanic systematics, and his many references to plants as "farmers," "nobles," "slaves," "soldiers," and the like (Linnaeus [1751] 1951, 98; [1763] 1960, 76; [1772] 1939, 112–13). What we regard as nature's checks and balances and feedback loops, Linnaeus imagined as the visible and heavy hand of the state. Linnaeus's economics was thus a mechanistic force. Its governing metaphor was that of state violence: and at every turn, the intervention of the naturalist civil servant was conceptualized as necessary.

Ultimately Linnaeus's epistemology was a matter of theology. As a student wrote in a letter of 1763, the economy of nature was knowable because its epistemology "combines Revelation and Nature's Great Works" (Sandblad 1970, 262). From Linnaeus's point of view (which he derived from seventeenth-century English physico-theology), nature was the revealed works of God in space, functioning as the geographic counterpart to God's revealed work in time, or salvation history. As he wrote of the Swedish queen's collection of shells, corals, and crystals, it mirrored the mercy and wisdom of God, "*tamquam in speculo*," as if in a mirror (Linnaeus [1754] 1939, 65). "Thus everything," he wrote, "is made to honor the Creator, not only as Witnessed by all Moralists and Theologians, but also as witnessed by Nature itself, and Man is put here to interpret this his Creator's wisdom" (57). Some twenty years later, toward the end of his life, Linnaeus still cleaved to the same view. As he wrote in the 1772 *Deliciae naturae*, the globe "is everywhere covered with a tapestry, of the most striking Miracles crocheted together . . . and this Wisdom-Light is reflected by people (as so many mirrors, turned toward the sun)" (Linnaeus [1772] 1939, 105–6).

In the Middle Ages, much theological effort went into defining the journey of the human soul. Both limbo and the dance of death were invented, and theologians elaborated upon the Second Coming and the condition of heaven and hell. Nature was seen as a disparate set of symbols of the drama of Christian salvation. While the argument from design already existed, typically nature was seen as fallen and in a state of senescence (a term that comes from Roman writers and also refers to the story of the Fall). Christian anthropocentrism made the observable patterns of living nature part of salvation history, or the movement from paradise, to Fall, to eventual redemption and beatitude (bliss), even as the study of nature also continued to operate within the confines of a scholarly genealogy dominated by Europe's ongoing reception of Aristotle.

Natural theology was developed coextensively with the "new science" of Johannes Kepler, Galileo, and Newton, and in part to ease the strains of religious conflicts—both the Anglican-Puritan civil war in Britain and the Lutheran-Catholic Thirty Years' War on the Continent. Now, nature was seen as a prelapsarian organism. It was intrinsically good and beautiful, and to investigate it was regarded at once as a source of joy (thus foreshadowing Romantic thought) and as an act of piety. By the early eighteenth century, natural theology in turn shaded into pantheism (equating God and nature) and deism (stripping God of personhood). From the outset, arguably, it was opposed to nature being endowed with a "meaning" external to itself: the phenomena of nature stood for themselves. This lack of transcendence is first noted in Benedict de Spinoza's identification of nature with God, which queries any notion of a background that is not already nature itself. It can be traced in Linnaeus's writings through the absence of Christological references and symbols and the absence of a God as a personal being who answers petitionary prayer, as well as in his uncertainty over how to name the Godhead—"the Wisdom," "the Power," "*Ens Entium*," or (rarely) "the Trinity."

As at the time of the great Aristotelian synthesis, in Linnaeus's time natural knowers were once again at the forefront of academic theology. But now, the great compromise between secular knowledge and religious thought centered on a divine "oeconomy of nature," which meant that nature was a supra-organismic being, existing in a self-regulating state of homeostasis—rather like the Gaia globe hypothesized by deep ecologists today. This refashioned teleology in turn engendered an interest in what we now consider feedback-governed equilibria: population checks, reproduction rates, predator-prey relations, food chains, species interdependence and competition, plant succession, parasitism, and hydraulic cycles. Natural theologians looked for functional interdependence between life-forms—extending even to Swammerdam's animalcules, which John Ray (1686) explained as food for insects that in turn fed birds that in turn served humans. This explanatory model of nature worked less well for investigating single life-forms, because it fell into the "functionalist fallacy" of assuming that organs or behaviors existed because they had certain functions.

In the 1766 *Usus muscorum* Linnaeus explored the limits of natural theology, as he endeavored to prove that even mosses serve humankind. They fed reindeer, bedded babies, covered straw roofs, dyed cloth, and cured rabies (Drake 1939, 218, 228). In the gloriously diverse *Flora oeconomica* he listed native wild plants that colored jellies, healed sand heaths, fed pigs, and brewed tea. Everything served humankind (Linnaeus 1749). In *Oeconomia naturae* from the same year Linnaeus restated his point: "Everything may be made subservient to his use, if not immediately, yet mediately" (Stillingfleet [1775] 1977, 123).

Linnaeus's philosophy of nature differs markedly from the modern science of ecology, which is a Darwinian discipline, and has dismantled the teleological project first set up by Aristotle. It equally differs from the modern politics of ecology, which derives from Romantic sentiments. As all early modern natural theologians, Linnaeus never questioned humankind's moral right to assert its power over nature. Ecocide, as we know it, was unthinkable to him. It was typical that Linnaeus (1913, 172) wrote that the Swedes ought to become whale-hunters, harvesting "these rich and never-ending treasures of nature." (Here he unknowingly echoed the first volume of the Royal Society's *Philosophical Transactions*, which also addresses "Attempts of mastering the Whales of those seas.")

Also, of course, natural theology was a form of Christian worship. As Linnaeus wrote in a draft of the preface of the tenth edition of *Systema naturae*: "I saw the never-ending, all-knowing, and all-powerful God's back where he walked, and I was astounded! I traced his footstep over the fields of nature and saw in each one, even in those I barely could see, an unending wisdom and power" (autograph collection, KB). Another time Linnaeus (1907, 48) remembered when he was eleven years old and first stepped outside after many months of illness: "I lay sick 1718 from the winter to Ascension, came out in the green, it seemed a paradise, not a world" (see also Linnaeus [1751] 1951, 25–26).

Linnaeus always took joy in the beauty of the everyday. "To see the light of the sun, stars, rainbows, etc. is the most wonderful thing of all, yes even just a candlelight in the darkness, if one just sees it in the right way; thus you see, how children desire the candle and would so like to put it in their mouth" (Linnaeus 1907, 231). It is a viewpoint far removed from the postlapsarian, postdiluvial world contemplated by earlier scholars—Gilbert Burnet's "dirty little planet," now decaying and disfigured.

But it was a viewpoint still animated by religiosity. If faith lacked, then, as Benjamin Stillingfleet ([1775] 1977, 129) wrote in a verse appendage to the 1775 English translation of *Oeconomia naturae*, "the golden chain / of beings melt away, and the mind's eye / sees nothing but the present. All beyond / is visionary guess—is dream—is death." Here is reversed older Christian theology, where salvation is heralded by the realization of the world's fallen state. Now, the rational contemplation of nature's perfection guarantees deliverance from death.

In 1753, writing the chancellor of Uppsala University to explain his tract *Cui Bono* ("For Whom Is It Good?"), which had been attacked by Uppsala's Lutheran theology faculty as insufficiently orthodox, Linnaeus critiques a narrowly utilitarian view of the natural world: "Let us not imagine . . . that the Creator planned the order of nature according to our private principles of oeconomy; for the Laplanders have one way of living; the European husbandman another; the Hottentots and savages a third, whereas the stupendous oeconomy of the Deity is one throughout the globe" (Stillingfleet [1775] 1977, 120–21).

Linnaeus argued for a more telescopic scale, which gauges less the immediate utility of the individual organism, but rather its role as part of a complex and benevolent whole:

> When I am demonstrating Naturalia, especially the smallest mosses, mushrooms, insects, worms &c. the question is always asked Cui bono? Because it is an assumption from old, that which isn't good enough for food, clothes, or medicine, is a fruitless curiosity. . . . But I have here argued the mediated use that people have of the smallest things, serving in the great household the creator has arranged on the earth. E. gr. Predators, a heap of insects &c. seems to us to be more a plague than a benefit, but if the world lacked them, it would be a great inconvenience. (letter to Uppsala University's chancellor, 1753, 1:1, 60, BS)

Another time, Linnaeus (1913, 212) noted how lucky we are that God had ordained insects and not bears to remove carcasses: "Then we would truly be unhappy." Linnaeus understood all life-forms as symbionts and as subordinated actors in one global teleological drama. He encouraged Swedish farmers and gardeners to use insects to destroy other insects, "like we use dogs to hunt" (239). And he considered nature itself (which he conceptualized as a superorganism) as the appropriate explanatory level for his natural philosophy. People, too, were part of this oeconomy of nature, this divinely ordained self-regulating state. Although Linnaeus granted humankind a mediatory role between God and nature, he also viewed it as a subordinate and mortal zoological part of that global equilibrium. This ties in, too, to Linnaeus's serious doubts whether humans could be distinguished from other animals. Not only might exotic variants of man shade into apes, exotic variants of apes might also shade into men (playing chess or worshipping God, for example). Human history—especially the very violent European history of the seventeenth century—also took on a new meaning, not now as a morality play but as a form of checks and balances. Wars, famines, and epidemics were no longer the three horsemen of the Apocalypse, but nature's way of rebalancing herself through "a war of all against all" (Linnaeus [1763] 1947, 85).

As Linnaeus saw it, the world was still improving itself, or being improved through human agency. "People, who themselves first came [to Scandinavia] from warm countries . . . also brought with them grains and fruit-bearing trees and plants from a warmer climate. . . . This is the reason why [north Sweden] . . . even to this day largely consists of wild forests, wide *Finnemarker*, huge deserts and commons" (letter to Uppsala University's chancellor, 13 December 1746, 1:1, 129–31, BS). *Finnmarkerna* were roadless swamps and wastelands, sparsely settled in the sixteenth century by ethnic Finns: they played the same role in Sweden as did the Pripet marshes in Poland. But even these, Linnaeus felt, would grow lusher and more fertile, as slash-and-burn rye fields gave way to crop rotations, integrated husbandry, and new cultivars.

Linnaeus's natural theology's sunny view of the material world, coupled to its radical decentering of the individual worshipper, rephrased, but did not solve, the problem of theodicy. Within its confine, people could no longer be consoled that their bodily suffering was part of a cosmic scheme with significance outside their earthly theater. Indeed to Linnaeus, the great *exempla*, Christ on the cross, disappeared as an object of theological meditation. But the extreme character of the natural theologians' optimism underlined the contrast between the world they described and the world they inhabited. Humans may still be the end of the *scala naturae*, and the only sentient being endowed with an immortal soul, but nature was no longer a set of symbols of salvation history with its principal *termini* of Creation, Fall, Flood, Redemption, and the Second Coming of Christ. Concomitant with this shifting viewpoint of nature from a mirror of salvation history to an autonomous entity of her own, for the first time, humankind was explicitly made part of nature (even if still within the framing context of a theology). This was a revolutionary perspective: while earlier people looked at nature to find themselves, natural theologians looked at ourselves to find nature.

Linnaeus's and his fellow academicians' economic concerns were typical of eighteenth-century improvers: clearing of wastelands; crop rotation;

enclosures; new crops and new forms of husbandry; new agricultural tools; veterinary medicine; countermeasures against animal pests and crop blights; and improved methods of processing agricultural products. As I have discussed in *Nature and Nation* (Koerner 1999), his economics also intimately involved voyages of discovery. Students, traveling abroad, would bring home import substitutes, and their cultivation would make economic autarky politically viable by underwriting continued consumption of colonial or tropical goods such as coffee, tea, sugar, pepper, or even bananas. For the rare product that could not thrive in *Balticum* (Linnaeus harbored high hopes of plants' adaptability to northern climes), domestic equivalences could be found—hence the vital importance of *landskapsresor*, regional travels around the Baltic Sea.

These journeys were not only intended to find luxuries. They constituted a vast and utilitarian task. In agrarian societies, and without modern metal, chemical, or petrochemical industries, plant life is the basis for most manufacturing. And with frequent crop failures, improvers urgently sought to diversify the species base of agriculture. Thus it was typical when Pehr Kalm—who later became professor of economics at Åbo, then the world's most northerly university—used his travels around *Balticum* to seek "plantarum indigenarum usu oconomico" (*sic*) "to find which of our home plants we can use to make bread, and porridge and gruel" (Hulth 1924, 47–48).

As the Linnaeans saw it, there was no theoretical distinction between travels outside and inside Europe. Both had wildernesses and savages, farming lands and city dwellers. Before leaving for America, Pehr Kalm explored many of Sweden's provinces, and especially the archipelagos, as well as Sweden's near abroad: Tavastland and Savolax, Russian and Swedish Karelia, parts of Ingria, Estonia, and even Russia and Ukraine (Odhelius 1780, 11–13). And in his writings, he discusses in similar terms all people outside his own Germano-Scandinavian world of learning. Indeed, Linnaeus and his students equalized the people of the world at all turns. Their egalitarianism did not merely extend to what Linnaeus called his "jämn-Christen och nästa"—his fellow Christian and fellow human, the peasantry of Sweden (letter to the king, undated but written in 1756, 1:1, 3, BS). Also more distant folks, such as Samoyeds and Turks, companionably mingle with the English and French on his pages (Linnaeus 1757, 10). Of course this sameness of tone was a matter of theory more than practice: one of Linnaeus's student travelers complacently reported from a ship journey in the Arabian Gulf that he had fed sugar crystals to female slaves through the bars of their cages. And the de facto slavery of South Baltic serfs—dramatically contrasted to the free Swedish yeomanry, represented in the Estates—occasioned only the stray comment as students crisscrossed these provinces, often enough as guests of the descendents of the Teutonic Knights.

But it is noteworthy that one of Linnaeus's last students, who had picked up on later Continental thought, strove in vain to convince his teacher of a hierarchy of races: "In vain we took the example of his own great genius, compared to the wild concepts of the Iriqui and the stupid thoughts of the Greenlanders; in vain we argued that they were lower below him, than the Orang-Outan below them." Linnaeus responded that all peoples of the world had "free moral will" and "powers of understanding and distinctions that can be trained" (Hedin 1808, 90–91). In a speech of 1759 to the Swedish royal family, he similarly argued that "Wild Peoples, Barbarians, and Hottentots, differ from us only because of Sciences; just like a thorny Sour-Apple differ from a tasty Renette, only through cultivation" (Linnaeus [1759] 1939, 42). And in his lectures at Uppsala he repeated: "There is only one species of man." He rejected any thought that Africans might belong to a "distinct Genus." They "are still the same Species." Nor did tall nations differ from shorter peoples: "*Majus* and *Minus* has nothing to do with this" (Linnaeus 1913, 11). Linnaeus also denied that the different orders of society differed in their inherent ability. He clamored for boys who assisted army surgeons or worked as crafts trainees to be admitted to university; he agitated for university scholarships; and he treated with an uncomplicated sense of equality those of his students—such as Pehr Osbeck—who were the sons of landless laborers (memorial on medical students, 1:1, 14, BS). Linnaeus's far-reaching naturalization of the world and her people, which was inherent to his natural theology, also involved a far-reaching—I would argue near complete—social universalism.

Linnaean economics was that of a naturalized nation. It was a border construction technology, a Berlin wall of everyday labors, and in some sense it turned on Linnaeus's essential provinciality—that part of him that was content to taxonomize breeds of horses into those from Norrland, Skåne, Öland, and Turkey (Linnaeus 1913, 55). But it also involved a globality of mind, an extraordinarily universalist thought-world. Again, that is true not only by way of his belief in the replicability of self-enclosed yet complete national communities, a belief that turned on the universalist belief in a global natural plenitude. Also, and more intriguingly for us moderns, it derived from Linnaeus's faith in humanity's essential uniformity—a uniformity that extended not only to our *jämn-Christen*, but to all peoples of the world and was based on Linnaeus's belief that all peoples were equally endowed with rational understanding and a moral sense (a belief that in turn looped back into, and extended out of, his Christian faith, as it interwove with Enlightenment thought more generally).

This is nicely illustrated in Linnaeus's correspondence with Carl Gustaf Dahlberg. Dahlberg (d. 1775) began his career as a Swedish army officer. But during Scandinavia's last large peasant rebellion, the 1743 Dalacarlia uprising, he was captured by the rioting mob and forced to shoot at his fellow officers. At his court trial he could prove that he had deliberately aimed above their heads and so escaped being beheaded. Nonetheless he had to leave Sweden under a cloud, and he joined instead the Dutch merchant marine. He then became a Surinam planter by marrying a wealthy Dutch widow. In 1762, the homesick Dahlberg, visiting his home country, gave Linnaeus a Surinam tree bark that he claimed was as powerful as quinine bark in curing fevers. In *Lignum qvassiae*, a 1763 dissertation, Linnaeus named the tree species after Qvassi, a slave of African descent owned by Dahlberg's mother-in-law. As Linnaeus told the story, "an unknown Negro slave named Qvassi discovered a medicine that he began using for his fellow slaves' severe fevers, and that with such success, that even the masters sought his help. But he was so completely against disclosing this cure that he rather sought to keep it secret as the most holy *arcanum*" (Linnaeus [1763] 1971, 5).

However, because of—or so Linnaeus and through him Dahlberg claimed—Qvassi's "veneration and love" for Dahlberg, Qvassi did show him the healing tree and explained his complex preparations of its medically active part, the roots. Dahlberg in turn planted it in his gardens and brought to Sweden its flowers, fruits, and leaves ("all conserved in wine spirits") (6). Linnaeus then entered it into the system, giving it a species name that is also a floral honorific, *Lignum quassiae*. This upset Dahlberg, who wanted himself, and not the person who, as he saw it, was his family's property, to be given the discoverer's glory and the species name. Linnaeus in turn could not understand Dahlberg's objections. As far as he was concerned, "an insignificant Negro slave" was self-evidently partner in his edifice of knowledge. Qvassi was the discoverer: he deserved the accolade of having the tree named in his honor. As Linnaeus wrote to his closest friend: "Why is Dalberg not pleased with the dissertation? Everything was after all what that fool said. He wanted to be great, but wasn't" (cited in Drake 1939, 45).

Qvassi was a lucky encounter—Daniel Rolander, Linnaeus's student of whom Dahlberg was the patron, was mentally ill and could not systematically engage with locals. But other students of Linnaeus made such dialogues a centerpiece of their research. Johan Petter Falck, who traveled in the Caucasus, Kazan, and southern Siberia between 1768 and 1774 as a member of the Orenburg expeditions, reported in detail on local botanical, medical, and economic knowledge: on Bashkirs', Ostyaks', and Cossacks' textile fibers; on Tara Tartars', Bokharans', Votyaks', Mordvins', and Kalmyks' dyestuff; and on Sayans' and other southern Siberian people's wild foodstuffs. He even noted that Kalmyks and Kazakhs offered him tea made from licorice (with butter stirred into the steaming brew), but that the Cossacks served him tea boiled from marijuana. Wild dromedaries and wild sheep Falck classified only from native collaborators' descriptions. The yak, similarly, he learned about from two old Bokharans, who in their youth had seen the yak herds owned by the khan of the Oirat khanate in Urga. Falck records the names of his informants, even: Kembache and Titow (Svanberg 1986–87).

Native informants—or what Malinowski (1948) in 1925 famously termed his "savage colleagues"—did not limit their discussions with traveling naturalists to the natural world only. They also shared their production technologies. Kalm built a bark canoe, "in that way that Professor KALM saw by the American Savages," and rowed the Swedish king about at sea (Odhelius 1780, 20). And Johan Gerhard Koenig, another of Linnaeus's students and later physician to the Danish trade mission in Tranquebar, investigated the production of Indian textiles, which at the time equaled or surpassed Europe's in complexity and skill. In 1777, he visited a native indigo dye factory "under the open sky by a little river." He, too, typically acquired knowledge from local people and wrote respectfully about *Herr Directeuren*. "The Herr Director himself was an old man, who quite politely answered our questions" (letter to Linnaeus from Koenig, 15 February 1777, LSL). The honorific title is the more remarkable since *Fabriquen* had a total of three workers—a small boy, the director, and his wife.

The travel descriptions at the heart of Linnaean economics are most fruitfully conceptualized as cross-culturally produced, asymmetric artifacts, mediating little knowledge with high occidental thought (Mark 1982; Thomas 1991; Lindsay 1993; Goonatilake 1992; Pratt 1992; Prakagh 1992). This is the case both as a matter of fact and as they were theorized by the Linnaeans at the moment of their production. It is this last moment of epistemology that is most amenable to analysis, given the asymmetries of both the production and historical documentation of Linnaean fieldwork. As P. F. Stevens (1984) has nicely put it, local knowledge was ground small as it entered the Linnaean taxonomic system. It is found most typically within descriptions of individual species and in materia medica. In turn, to understand how the European naturalists conceptualized these hybrid knowledge productions we need to recover both the materiality of the knowledge formation process—that is, field cooperation—and the culturally coded intentions of these actors, or at least of the Linnaeans among them. Alas, we cannot recover the thoughts and strategies of Qvassi, Tembache, Titow, the *Herr Directeur*, or the many other local knowers glimpsed in these faunal and floral edifices.

By the 1990s, many intellectuals had came to argue both that cultural selves are constructed most typically by means of an imaginary inversion, or "other," and that personhood was explained best by way of group identity. The self grew out of a series of misrepresentations about others. This strong program of incommensurability (an example is Tzvetan Todorov's [1999] work on the Aztec-Spanish encounter) in turn led younger scholars to reexplore commensurability across cultural boundaries. The Linnaeans arguably are part of the philosophical history of that exploration, for they illustrate a pre-Romantic history of assumed commensurability.

When analyzing the mechanisms of syncretic knowledge production, anthropologists and historians typically transpose a linguistics vocabulary (this cross-disciplinary borrowing nicely mirrors its own epistemological point). It is inflected as mediation: its most important theorist, Peter Galison (1997), draws on theories of pidgins, Creoles, and "foreigner languages" (regional trade argots). Other fruitful vocabularies, I feel, might be those of location theory (geography), trade theory (economics), and post-Marxist theories of imperialism. All these fields offer "intercalated" models—to use Galison's phrase—of how knowledge is negotiated between knowledge communities. They thus deftly solve the problems of Kuhn's step outside Kantian phenomenology toward that *Ding an sich*, the anomaly, while abandoning the unifying and unitary aspects of Kuhn's *Gestalt* switch. In Kuhn, a multiplicity of viewpoints is classed as the limit of knowledge: in Galison, it is classed as its precondition.

Nicely, this notion is already elaborated in Edwardian literature. Thus the small hero of Rudyard Kipling's *Kim* (1901) single-handedly holds together the multicultural British raj because he, an Irish mongrel bred up by locals, is a cross-cultural mediator and therefore able to gather local knowledge. Compare Kim also with Kipling's cruel parodies of the Western-educated Bengali as the Macaulian imperial mediator who cannot function, because he has rejected and no longer understands native cultures. And Agatha Christie's master detective, the Belgian policeman Hercule Poirot, can interpret the social significance of natural facts (crime-scene clues) and is given confidences otherwise not vouchsafed, because as a foreigner he is a social outsider. Compare Poirot to his stooge, the Eton-educated Captain Hasting, who conceptualizes a suspect as innocent if he is "pukka sahib" (and relish the irony of this cross-culturally produced expression), or, as Poirot mocks, "went to the same school as your uncle."

The Linnaeans provide a historical framing for this notion that multiple voices constitute the foundation of natural knowledge, rather than measure its incompleteness. For in the cross-cultural encounter of Linnaean fieldwork, knowledge is, and understands itself to be, a philosophical pidgin, while actual pidgins arose from those same knowledge sites (protocolonial trading stations, and South and East Baltic slave economies with their ethnically different lords and city folks). For Linnaeus's circles believed that new natural knowledge could form by way of a cross-cultural mediation between high and folk knowledge, and they believed that this syncretic new science was both an epistemology and a technology, that is, both a way to know and a material tool. Hence the Linnaeans' emphasis on vernacular names for flora and fauna, which they argued indicated salient characteristics and local uses (as did John Ray in his manuscript "Collection of English Words" of the 1660s). From the very start of his career, Linnaeus stressed the importance of local names: his 1736 Dutch vanity print on the banana lists—apart from five Latin synonyms and many European designations—names in Japanese, Chinese, "Bengalese," "Bramanese," "American," "Brazilian," "Malabarian," "Ethiopian," and so on (Linnaeus 1736). While this was a construct—no native informants were involved—already those of Linnaeus's students who worked in Sweden's near abroad, south *Balticum*, encountered linguistic cornucopias. Apart from the many still-flourishing languages, eighteenth-century travelers could encounter now dead or near-extinct tongues such as Sorb, Liv, Old Prussian, *platdeutsch*, and Yiddish. Further afield, Linnaean field studies sometimes importantly contributed to linguistics. Thus Linnaeus's student Johan Petter Falck's work on the flora of the Caucasus Mountains is remembered today mainly by linguists, because he recorded so many names in now-extinct languages.

Consider, too, the "orders," "instructions," "memorials," and spoken "directions" that Linnaeus gave to his traveling students. As I discuss in my book (Koerner 1999), these memorials on *observanda* did not only emanate from a scientific curiosity: they were in the main lists of life-forms, material samples, and production technologies students were expected to bring home. Linnaeus ranked utility before curiosity, and non-European cultures, in the sense of economies, over non-European nature, in the sense of wildernesses. But for our purposes, what is important is that here, Linnaeus admonished his students to study local knowledge of the natural world and particularly local economic practices. To give only one example, in 1746 the Swedish Academy of Science followed Linnaeus's recommendations in asking Pehr Kalm to find a North American "kind of Rice, tastes rather pleasant, and by one Nation, called Ilinois, is used as food instead of grains" (protocols of the Swedish Academy of Science, 20 July 1745, 1:2, 57, BS). And it asked for a "wild ox, big-bodied but short-legged, they have a rather fine and long shaggy hair. . . . The Colonies there have found ways to tame this kind of creature, employ them for everyday haulage and use their milk as food."

Linnaeus's travel instructions to Kalm echoed those requests he had inspired the academy to make. Besides economic flora like mulberries, oaks, and sugar maples, he asked for indigenous medicinal herbs and again that intriguing *vildoxe*. Kalm was thus asked to learn from Native Americans how to harvest a wild crop, and from European settlers how to handle a recently domesticated mammal. Already at the stage of projection, the Linnaeus voyage of discovery was a meeting of cultures and not a confrontation with nature. Only at the very end of Linnaeus's long "memorial" did he suggest that Kalm might also make "observations on Birds and Fishes, on Snakes and Insects, on Plants and Trees, on Stones and Minerals," which seems to be a gesture more toward foreigners: thus "the Academy and the entire Nation will become famous . . . over the whole of Europe" (letter to the Swedish Academy of Science, 10 January 1746, 1:2, 61, BS).

Linnaeus and his students intensively studied the plant lore and materia medica of both tribal people and the Baltic peasantry, particularly its "wise women" and midwives. Indeed, as Linnaeus argued in the 1752 *Obstacula medicinae* and other tracts, they regarded it as crucial for reforming academic medicine (Linnaeus [1752] 1948). Linnaeus wrote in *Vires plantarum*, a 1747 dissertation, that "empirical knowledge, or simply long experience that mostly has been learned from the wild Nations of this world, has given us knowledge of our most excellent Medicines" (quoted in Drake 1939, 141). The Linnaean project was thus similar in its impulse to Denis Diderot's *Encyclopédie*, with its investigations of button makers, lace makers, wig makers, makers of leaded windows, and other vernacular crafts. In *Obstacula medicinae*, Linnaeus ([1752] 1948, 10) warned against "failing to go on voyages of discovery . . . for it can be useful to learn about these matters even from savages." He went on to enumerate indigenous American plant cures against wounds, snakebites, and colic (cures Linnaeus had learned from his student Kalm, who by then had returned from America). Linnaeus and his students also used ethnobotany to expand the register of botanical samples in *Flora svecica* (1745), *Materia medica* (1749), and *Censura medicamentorum simplicum vegetablium* (1753). In addition, a wealth of material on folk medicines made from minerals or animals is found in *Materia medica in regna animali* (1750) and *Materia medica in regno lapideo* (1752). The Linnaeans admittedly also interested themselves in foreign high civilizations: Linnaeus especially liked the Chinese pharmacopoeia because it had, as he thought, no compound medicines (letter to Abraham Bäck, 25 November 1754, 1:4, 317–19, BS). But his central hope was to garner the knowledge of "our farmers" and "wild Nations" (Linnaeus [1763] 1960). "It is the common people," he wrote in 1752, "that we must thank for the most efficacious medicines, which they . . . even keep secret" from naturalists such as himself (Linnaeus [1752] 1948, 10).

But if the Linnaeans studied floral and faunal ethnography during their voyages, their "travel books" still acknowledge only fragmentarily how mediated their interactive model of knowledge was, how much both in fact and by intent it relied on the cross-cultural cooperation with producers of ethnic knowledge. The complexities of their mediated model of knowledge were largely lost on them (they were not philosophers). While they were aware that cross-cultural dialogues were a key means through which they accessed their "observations," they considered neither how much their travel books reflected the feature of the traveler himself, nor what they took for granted (and what we take as problematic): that other, more humbling, reverse process of mediation, whereby the cultural "other" really does inform the seemingly omniscient, fully "formed" observer.

Indeed, Linnaeus invented complicated means of "othering" himself (which involved a series of unstable mimicries where he masqueraded as an Arctic nomadic reindeer herder on frontispieces, in portraits, and during social gatherings). True, Linnaeus's notion of the moral virtues of "wild nations" was more complex than later orientalizing notions of the other. But his benign reflective exoticism, as much as his later racialisms, was essentially solipsistic. In both, the other functioned as mirror for the self.

Thus we must rely on smaller clues to reconstruct Linnaeus and his students' universalizing practices. We saw already that they encouraged the use of their botanic systems by allowing every user a possible place (by means of the honorific name) within their scientific edifice. And in *Lignum qvassiae* Linnaeus credited an indigenous or "folk" discoverer, one of those local knowers of nature and of manufacture whom the Linnaeans typically met on their travels and who acted as scouts, collectors, interpreters, and herbalists. And while the Linnaean epistemology prefigured our own notions of commensurability, their sites of research recapitulated what we now see as the material conditions of that interactivity: both mediated local and global economic spheres. And that in turn accounts for the eventual decline of this particular model for knowledge. I do not refer here to the Linnaean impulse toward a protomodern police state, which I detail in *Nature and Nation*. Rather, I mean that the Linnaeans typically worked for centers of imperialism, such as the Dutch East India Company, the British navy, the Teutonic *Ritterschaft*, and the Russian Crown. And unwittingly or not, these institutions often worked to destroy those local life worlds that enabled the syncretic knowledge formation outlined here. The project of collecting knowledge destroyed the conditions of that knowledge. It was a self-consuming artifact.

References

Abbreviations

BS: *Bref och skrifvelser af och till Carl von Linné*
KB: Royal Swedish Library, Stockholm

LSL: Linnean Society, London
SLÅ: *Svenska Linnesällskapets Årsbok*
VA: *Valda Avhandlingar*

Ambjörnsson, Ronny. 1975–76. "Guds Republique": En utopi från 1789. *Lychnos*, 1–56.

Arndt, Erst Moritz. [1804] 1806. *Reise durch Schweden im Jahr*. Part 1. Berlin: G.A. Lange.

Bref och skrifvelser af och till Carl von Linné. 1907–43. Edited by T. M. Fries, J. M. Hulth, and Arvid Hj. Uggla. Stockholm: Ljus.

Broberg, Gunnar. 1990–91. Fruntimmersbotaniken. In vol. 30 of SLÅ.

Callmer, Christian. 1956. Svenska studenter i Göttingen under 1700–talet. *Lychnos*, 1–30.

Drake, Gustaf af Hagelsrum. 1939. *Linnes disputationer: En översikt*. Nässjö: Nässjö-Tryckeriet.

Ehnmark, Elof. 1931. Linnetraditionen och naturskildringen. In vol. 14 of SLÅ, 41–71.

Frängsmyr, Tore. 1971–72. Den gudomliga ekonomin: Religion och hushållning i 1700 talets Sverige. *Lychnos*, 217–44.

———, ed. 1989. *Science in Sweden: The Royal Swedish Academy of Sciences 1739–1989*. Canton, Mass.: Science History Publications.

Galison, Peter. 1997. *Image and Logic: A Material Culture of Microphysics*. Chicago: University of Chicago Press.

Gertz, Otto. 1920. Olof Celsius D.Ä. och Flora Uplandica. In vol. 3 of SLÅ, 36–56.

Goonatilake, Susantha. 1992. The Voyages of Discovery and the Loss and Re-Discovery of "Other's" Knowledge. *Impact of Science on Society* 167:241–64.

Hedin, Sven. 1808. *Minne af von Linne Fader och Son*. Stockholm: Nordström.

Hulth, J. M. 1924. Kalm som student i Uppsala och lärjunge till Linne åren 1741–1747. In vol. 7 of SLÅ, 39–49.

Koerner, Lisbet. 1999. *Linnaeus: Nature and Nation*. Cambridge: Harvard University Press.

Kuhn, Thomas. 1962. *Structure of Scientific Revolutions*. Chicago: University of Chicago Press.

Lindsay, Debra. 1993. *Science in the Subarctic: Trappers, Traders, and the Smithsonian Institution*. Washington, D.C.: Smithsonian Institution Press.

Linnaeus, Carl. 1736. *Musa Cliffortiana florens Hartecampi*. Leyden.

———. 1744. Wäxternas kunskap, som är grunden til all oeconomie (memorandum to Riksens Ständers Utskott och Deputationer, 2 May). In BS, 1:1, 23–26.

———. 1749. *Flora oeconomica*. Received and translated by Elias Aspelin. Stockholm: Lars Salvii.

———. 1751. *Philosophia botanica*. Stockholm: Godofr. Kiesewetter.

———. 1757. *Berättelse om The Inhemska wäxter, som i brist af Säd kunne användas till Bröd- och Matredning*. Stockholm: Collegio Medico.

———. [1728] 1888. Catalogus plantarum rariorum Scaniae . . . a Carolo Linnaeo, Smolando, botanophilo. In *Carl von Linnes ungdomsskrifter*, edited by Ewald Ährling. Stockholm: Norstedt.

———. 1907. *Linnes dietetik* . . . . Edited by A. O. Lindfors. Uppsala: Akademiska Boktryckeriet.

———. 1913. *Linnes föreläsningar öfver djurriket*. Edited by Einar Lönnberg. Uppsala: Akademiska bokhandeln.

———. [1754] 1939. Naturaliesamlingars ändamål och nytta. Preface to *Museum Regis Adolphi Friderici*. In Uggla 1939.

———. [1759] 1939. Tal, vid deras Kongl: Majesteters höga närvaro. In Uggla 1939.

———. [1772] 1939. *Deliciae naturae*. In Uggla 1939.

———. [1763] 1947. Skaparens avsikt med naturens verk. Edited by Arvid Hj. Uggla. In vol. 30 of SLÅ, 71–96.

———. [1752] 1948. *Obstacula medicinae*. Received by Johan Georg Beyersten, translated by Sven-Olof Thulin, and edited by Telemak Fredbärj. In VA.

———. [1751] 1951. *Skånska resa*. Edited by Carl Otto von Sydow. Stockholm: Wahlström & Widstrand.

———. [1753] 1952. *Linnés Företal till Species Plantarum*. In vol. 35 of SLÅ.

———. [1750–59] 1954–55. Två svenska akademiprogram av Linné. Edited by Telemak Fredbärj. In vols. 37–38 of SLÅ.

———. [1763] 1960. *De raphania*. Edited and translated by Ejnar Haglund. In VA.

———. 1961. *Promotionsprogram*. In vol. 38 of VA.

———. [1763] 1971. *Lignum qvassiae*. Edited by Albert Boerman and Telemak Fredbärj. In VA.

Malinowski, Bronislaw. 1948. *Magic, Science, and Religion, and Other Essays*. New York: Doubleday Anchor.

Mark, Joan. 1982. Francis La Flesche: The American Indian as Anthropologist. *Isis* 73:497–510.

Odhelius, Johan Lorentz. 1780. *Åminnelse-Tal, Öfver Kongl. Vetensk. Acad. Ledamot Herr Pehr Kalm, Theologiae Doctor, Oecon. Professor . . . 15 Novemb. 1780*. Stockholm: Joh. Georg Lange.

Posten. 1769. No. 76, 12 April.

Prakagh, Gyan. 1992. Science "Gone Native" in Colonial India. *Representations* 40:153–78.

Pratt, Mary Louise. 1992. *Imperial Eyes: Travel Writing and Transculturation*. London: Routledge.

Ray, John. 1686. *The Wisdom of God Manifested in the Works of Creation*. London: Smith and Walford.

Rydberg, Sven. 1951. *Svenska studieresor till England under frihetstiden*. Uppsala: Almqvist & Wiksell.

Sandblad, Henrik. 1970. Bjerkander, J-P. Falck och Tessin. Några brev till och om Kinnekulle. *Lychnos*, 260–68.

Schulzenheim, David von. 1773. *Åminnelse-Tal, Öfver Kongl Vetenskaps Academiens Framledne Ledamot . . . Nils Rosen von Rosenstein . . . Den 17 November 1773*. Stockholm: Lars Salvi.

Stevens, P. F. 1984. Metaphors and Typology in the Development of Botanical Systematics 1690–1960. *Taxon* 33.2:169–211.

Stillingfleet, Benjamin. [1775] 1977. *Miscellaneous Tracts*. New York: Arno.

Strandell, Birger. 1956–57. Patriotiska Sällskapet och Linne. In vols. 39–40 of SLÅ, 130–37.

Svanberg, Ingvar. 1986–87. Turkic Ethnobotany and Ethnozoology as Recorded by Johan Peter Falck. In SLÅ.

Svenska Linnesällskapets Årsbok. 1918–. 57 vols. Uppsala: Almqvist & Wiksell.

Thomas, Nicholas. 1991. *Entangled Objects: Exchange, Material Culture, and Colonialism in the Pacific*. Cambridge: Harvard University Press.

Todorov, Tzvetan. 1999. *The Conquest of America: The Question of the Other*. Translated by Richard Howard. Norman: University of Oklahoma Press.

Uggla, Arvid Hj, ed. 1939. *Fyra skrifter*. Stockholm: Nordiska bibliofilsällskapet.

Valda Avhandlingar. 1921–. Uppsala: Svenska Linnesällskapet.

Medical Metaphors and Monetary Strategies in the Political Economy of Locke and Berkeley

C. George Caffentzis

Biographical Introduction: Between Medicine and Money

The intersection of medical and economic discourses can be traced to the beginning of the "autonomy of the economic" in the seventeenth and eighteenth centuries. It has been the subject of much recent scholarly interest (e.g., Groenewegen 2001). This intersection took many forms, from the use of medical metaphors for rhetorical effect to the direct application of medical knowledge to devise economic strategies. John Locke and George Berkeley were early contributors to this conceptual commerce between medicine and economic thought. In this essay I will show how their specific medical doctrines and practices helped determine the monetary strategies both thinkers proposed for their respective clients: the governments of England and Ireland.

The complex curricula vitae of these two philosophers certainly prepared them for a refined exploration of the territory between money and medicine.[1] Locke, besides being the consummate bureaucrat of a growing world empire, was a physician by training and wrote extensively on medical theory. He had a medical practice for a time, and the ingenious prosthetic device he implanted in his patient the Earl of Shaftesbury not only gave him entrée to the path of power, it also sealed his fame as a physician.[2]

1. A recent contribution to the investigation of the medical-economic nexus in Locke's thought is Coleman 2000.

2. An interesting account of the famous silver "tap" or pipe Locke inserted into the earl's liver can be found in Osler [1900] 1990.

Locke also, with the Earl of Shaftesbury's help, became secretary of the Council for Trade and Foreign Plantations in 1673 and began his first serious involvement with economic issues (Kelly 1990, 5). He wrote the "Fundamental Constitution of the Carolinas" at the earl's bidding in 1669. This experience of imperial economic administration and colonial political planning was crucial in his transformation from an academic to a man of affairs. It also provided the experiential humus for the writing of his famous economic texts of the 1690s: *Some consideration of the consequences of lowering the Interest, and raising the value of money* (1692) and *Further considerations concerning raising the value of money* (1695). Both texts were published as interventions in important political economic controversies, and Locke's views had weight in King William's government, since he had been such a wily (and successful) revolutionary conspirator who helped seat the Dutchman on the English throne.

Similarly, George Berkeley frequently traversed the space between medicine and money. Indeed, in the popular imagination of the eighteenth century, Berkeley was better known as the Irish bishop "shaman" of the tar-water cure for a wide variety of ailments than as the philosophical critic of matter. The medicophilosophical book he wrote in his last decade to justify his drug therapy, *Siris* ([1744] 1953), was, by far, the book of all his oeuvre most widely read by his contemporaries. But his medical research began almost three decades before in his travels in Italy as "bear leader" to a young English gentleman; he had been asked by a well-known London physician, Dr. Freind, to investigate the effectiveness of the tarantella cure for hysteria. Some of the results of his studies are included in his *Journals* on his travels in Bari, Lecce, and Taranto (Berkeley 1955; Caffentzis 2000, 329–32).

Berkeley was also well known in the eighteenth century as a projector of new monetary schemes. His most important work on political economy, *The Querist* ([1735–37] 1953), was written when he first became bishop of Cloyne in a deeply depressed and politically divided Ireland. He proposed a new form of paper currency to be issued and regulated by a national bank that would not represent or incorporate specie. This bank and currency were designed to solve the socioeconomic malaise he encountered on his return to Ireland after attempting to found a multiracial college in the Americas.

Consequently, money and medicine were often adjacent concerns in both Locke's and Berkeley's individual careers. They were brought together by an overarching political trope of their time: the body politic and the human body shared a similar structure (Kelly 1990, 69). This trope has its roots, of course, in the Platonic and Galenic tradition, but the anti-Galenic revolution in medicine was instigating a revision of many hackneyed formulations. Francis Bacon's work is full of throwaway examples of this trope, like "No body can be healthful without exercise, neither natural body nor politic; and certainly to a kingdom or estate, a just and honorable war is a true exercise" (Bacon 1955, 83), while the frontispiece of Thomas Hobbes's *Leviathan* is a locus classicus of a metonymic bond between bodies "natural" and "politic." More specifically, by the mid-seventeenth century the notion of the circular flow of economic life paralleling the circulation of the blood à la William Harvey was becoming a commonplace in political literature, while the Cartesian animal spirits were soon to be evoked in this metaphoric field (Descartes 1985, 100–101). These physiological developments led to the observation that the body politic had money as its circulating medium; consequently, there were inevitable metaphors associating monetary phenomena with the body's and person's fluids, material and mental. Hobbes employed it throughout *Leviathan*, for example, "Mony the Bloud of a Commonwealth" is a section heading. Hobbes (1985, 300) writes there:

> By Concoction, I understand the reducing of all commodities, which are not presently consumed, but reserved for Nourishment in time to come, to something of equall value, and withall so portable as not to hinder the motion of men from place to place; to the end a man may have in what place soever, such Nourishment as the place affordeth. And this is nothing else but Gold, and Silver, and Mony . . . and the same passeth from Man to Man, within the Common-wealth; and goes round about, Nourishing (as it passeth) every part thereof; in so much as this Concoction, is as it were the Sanguification of the Common-wealth: For naturall Bloud is in like manner made of the fruits of the Earth; and circulating, nourisheth by the way every Member of the Body of Man.

This metaphor is not only Hobbes's, his rival James Harrington employed it as well.[3]

3. Harrington often employed the body natural-body politic metaphor. For example, he concludes his *A System of Politics* with the following observation: "Corruption in Government is to be read and considered in Machiavel as diseases in a man's body are to read and considered in

William Petty, whose work Locke and Berkeley read, developed the "body natural and politick" metaphor in his *Political Anatomy of Ireland*, published posthumously in 1691.[4] He presented this metaphor with the cruel humor of a conqueror. He begins the book's preface by attributing "a judicious Parallel in many particulars, between the Body Natural, and Body Politick" to Francis Bacon. He points out, however, that metaphors are not enough; anatomy is needed, otherwise "to practice upon the Politick, without knowing the Symmmetry, Fabrick, and Proportion of it, is as casual as the practice of Old-women and Empyricks." He then adds a supplementary dismissal of the corpus delicti, Ireland: "As Students in Medicine, practice their inquires upon cheap and common animals, and such whose actions they are best acquainted with and where there is the least confusion and perplexure of Parts; I have chose Ireland as such a Political Animal" (Petty [1691] 1963, 129).

Innumerable tracts and pamphlets from the mid-seventeenth through the eighteenth century attest to the metaphorical link of money and blood as well as other body-state metaphors.[5] Consequently, there was an immediate metaphorical tie between the illnesses of the natural person and the illnesses of the artificial person, the commonwealth. However, this microcosm-macrocosm metaphorical link was being rapidly overwritten in this period by the increasing commodification and monetization of economic life that gave a new dimension to the medical-economic nexus. This overwriting led to confusion in its early stage, as in the case

Hippocrates" (Harrington 1977, 854). For a discussion of these metaphors in René Descartes, Benedict de Spinoza, Hobbes, and beyond, see Saccaro-Battisti 1983.

4. Petty was known to Locke both intellectually and politically. Karen I. Vaughn (1980, 88) writes on this connection: "While it is impossible to say for certain that Locke was influenced by Petty, he did possess all of Petty's major economic works, including the all-important *A Treatise of Taxes and Contributions*, which he acquired in 1667, in time for it to have an effect on his [economic] writing." Politically, of course, Petty and Locke's employer, the Earl of Shaftesbury, faced the same problem: how were those who were implicated in the Cromwellian period to keep power during the Restoration? They undoubtedly crossed paths many times in London between the early 1660s and the early 1680s. Berkeley's connection to Petty was not as direct, since he was born two years before Petty's death. But Petty had a profound impact on the Anglo-Irish ascendancy through the Down Survey he conducted in the 1650s, which became the basis of the land claims of many Anglo-Irish families in the eighteenth century. Berkeley ([1735–37] 1953, 2:199) certainly paid his respects to Petty in *The Querist* by using one of Petty's signature phrases in the following query: "Whether we are apprized of all the uses that may be made of political arithmetic?"

5. This was not the only metaphoric link between "the Body Natural, and the Body Politic" relevant to the money-commodity-money flow during this period. William Petty concluded in *Verbum Sapienti* (1665), "For money is but the fat of the body-politic, whereof too much doth as often hinder its agility, as too little makes it sick" (Hutchison 1988, 36).

of Hobbes, where the micro-macro metaphor of the circulation of blood with the circulation of money in the commonwealth is prefaced by a deduction of the commonwealth from the disciplining of the mechanical powers of bodies by a collective counter-power capable of terrorizing them into rational immobility. Moreover, by the late seventeenth century there was a sense of inevitability about the metaphor of monetary circulation, for as J. S. Peters (1995, 377) wrote: "Humans were bound to that process of continual motion which could prevent the representational systems from collapsing, bound to the continual translation of representations (money into goods into money, words into things into words). But that continual motion and translation could nevertheless reconstitute an idea of nature. Circulation was all."

As it became clear in the course of the late seventeenth and early eighteenth centuries that the thoughts, wills, and bodies of millions of economic agents were crucial for the understanding and planning of social reproduction, then any widespread "diseases" of thought, will, and body could directly lead to profound economic crises. As, for example, consumption of luxury commodities became an essential element of economic life, then the "Gouts, Stones, Cancers, Fevers, high Hysterics, Lunacy and Madness" caused by such consumption (according to the premier London physician of the first half of the eighteenth century, George Cheyne) could have direct economic impact (Turner 1992, 186). The period in question "discovered the body as object and target of power," as Foucault (1979, 136) has taught us. The physician could directly multiply his or her knowledge of individual illness to diagnose and cure economic breakdowns and thus "medicalize" the economy and legitimate a claim to a portion of this power.

Berkeley and Locke, who frequently traversed the nexus between medicine and political economy in thought and practice, were inevitably implicated in its more traditional metaphorical as well as contemporary causal dimensions.

Medicine, Money, and the Imagination in Locke's and Berkeley's Work

These biographical facts intersect with an important new feature of the field between medicine and political economy: the increasing importance of the imagination for both medicine and money. The new therapies directed toward the illnesses of the imagination offered a way of legitimizing the "medicalization" of the economy and the adaptation of particular monetary strategies.

The rapidly changing developments concerning the imagination in late-seventeenth- and early-eighteenth-century medicine paralleled the actual changes in the monetary field (especially the use of non-specie-based monetary instruments) in this period that projected the imagination (and its cognates, like fancy) as a central faculty of political economy. Once a set of therapies for illness of the imagination had become hegemonic, a simultaneous extension of these therapies to the body politic inevitably followed.

We can see this new feature at play in Locke's work. One of his most important innovations in medicine was his rejection of the attribution of the cause of madness to the passions, a belief that was shared by as varied a group of thinkers as Bacon, René Descartes, and Hobbes (James 1997, 180–81). In book 2 of the *Essay*, Locke (1975) segued to a discussion of madness after confronting the central question of an essay concerning "*human* understanding": what differentiated humans from brutes? He refused Descartes's categorical answer: brutes are machines and humans are rational.[6] There are many gradations between animals and human understanding, and on these steps one can find many bizarre creatures including talking birds, idiots, criminals, and the mad. Locke differentiated between "naturals" and "mad Men" in the following way:

> In fine, the defect in Naturals seems to proceed from want of quickness, activity, and motion in the intellectual Faculties, whereby they are deprived of Reason: Whereas mad Men, on the other side, seem to suffer by the other Extreme. For they do not appear to me to have lost the Faculty of Reasoning: but having joined together some Ideas very wrongly, they mistake them for Truths; and they err as Men do, that argue right from wrong Principles. For by the violence of their Imaginations, having taken their fancies for Realities, they make right deductions from them. (2:11:13)

This constitutes a major shift in the history of madness, taking it from the axis of reason versus passion to the realm of the imagination and fancy. The source of madness is not passion's suppression of reason, according to Locke, but an inappropriate input to the faculty of reasoning.

6. For further discussion of the social context underlying Locke's differences with Descartes on the definition of *human*, see Caffentzis 2000, 237.

In effect, Locke placed madness at the center of human creativity, making it treatable and universal at the same time. For Locke observed that madness is an amplification of a significant commonplace: one condemns another's extravagant "Opinions, reasonings, and Actions" while never perceiving the much "greater Unreasonableness" in one's own. What is the root of this madness, according to Locke? It is to be found in the essence of thought: the association of ideas. Ideas are extraordinarily plastic and polymorphous in their connections, some have a "natural Correspondence and Connexion one with another," but there is "another Connexion of Ideas wholly owning to Chance or Custom; Ideas that in themselves are not at all of kin, come to be so united in some Mens Minds, that 'tis very hard to separate them, they always keep in company, and the one no sooner at any time comes into the Understanding but its Associate appears with it; and if they are more than two which are thus united, the whole gang always inseparable show themselves together" (2:33:5). Consequently, there is a potential madness in everyone: "There is scarce a man so free from [madness], but that if he should always on all occasions argue or do as in some cases he constantly does, would not be thought fitter for Bedlam, than Civil Conversation. I do not mean when he is under the power of an unruly Passion, but in the steady calm of his Life" (2:33:4).

Locke came to these views on madness long before he published the *Essay*. They were clearly expressed in his medical journal entries in 1677–78, where he developed a formulation of madness that is simply reiterated in the *Essay*, for example, "Madnesse seemes to be noething but a disorder in the imagination, and not in the discursive faculty" (Romanell 1984, 130), or "in [the mind taking its own imagination for realities] (it seems to me) madnesse consists and not in the want of reason" (Dewhurst 1963, 101).

In these entries Locke was writing as a physician with an eye to therapy as well as to explanation. On the level of explanation, of course, it would be helpful to have an answer to the question: If the cause of madness is the imagination's ability to associate ideas, then how does it "userp the dominion over all the other facultys of the mind"? But even without such an explanation, Locke already had a rudimentary cure available: "This I thinke that haveing often recourse to ones memory and tieing downe the minde strictly to the recollecting things past precisely as they were may be a means to check those extravagant or turning [?] flights of the imagination" (quoted in Romanell 1984, 131).

This approach gave Locke a preventative program for mental health as well. For we are very careful not to put our hands in fires and teach our children to do likewise, but we are less careful about putting our ideas and those of our children in even more dangerous situations. "This wrong Connexion in our Minds of Ideas in themselves, loose and independent one of another, has such an influence, and is of so great force to set us awry in our Actions, as well Moral as Natural, Passions, Reasonings, and Notions themselves, that, perhaps, there is not any one thing that deserves more to be looked after" (Locke 1975, 2:33:9). This mental care is especially important when dealing with young children, who are "most susceptible of lasting impressions." Thus Locke warns the reader about phobiagenic "foolish Maids": "The Ideas of Goblines and Sprights have really no more to do with Darkness than Light; yet let but a foolish Maid inculcate these often in the Mind of a Child, and raise there together, possibly he shall never be able to separate them again so long as he lives, but Darkness shall ever afterwards bring with it those frightful Ideas, and they shall be so joined that he can no more bear the one than the other" (2:33:10).

The transformation of medical diagnoses and therapies into the economic realm, in Berkeley's case, was done in the context of a new understanding of hysteria and hypochondria that took place in the half century before the publication of *The Querist*. Traditionally, hysteria and hypochondria were assigned to different organs, genders, and behaviors. Hysteria was standardly rooted in the womb. Hence, it was invariably a woman's disease and involved fits, convulsions, and violently fluctuating emotional states. Hypochondria was rooted in the organic *hypochondrium*—the liver, gallbladder, and spleen. It was a man's disease, characterized by general depression, melancholy, and low spirits. Both were "insurrectionary diseases," since they involved the lower organs' invasion of the higher mental spaces associated with the head. Hysteria was literally attributed to the "wandering womb," or the movement of the womb up into the chest and throat, while hypochondria was attributed to vapors rising from the *hypochondrium* into the head.

This neat picture was radically questioned in the late seventeenth century. Thomas Willis and Thomas Sydenham rejected the womb as the etiological site of hysteria and transferred the cause to the nervous system. This called into question the identification of hysteria with women and contributed to the conceptualization of a more modulated, intergender version of the disease. Thus, though hysteria—with its characteristic fits and out-of-control frenzies—was still considered largely a woman's disease, men could succumb to it. Hysteria was more a matter of degree than kind, as Sir Richard Blackmore put it: "The convulsive Disorders and Agitations in the various parts of the Body . . . are more conspicuous and violent in the Female Sex, than in Men; the Reason of which is, a more volatile, dissipable, and weak Constitution of the Spirits, and a more soft, tender, and delicate Texture of the Nerves" (quoted in Porter 1987, 49).

The same transformation occurred for hypochondria and other splenetic conditions. The idea that somehow a vapor could rise up from the epigastric region into the head was dismissed as mechanically impossible. The true culprits in the case of hypochondria were taken to be the nerves and spirits. As Blackmore explained: "The Spasms, Twitches, jumping of the Tendons, and conclusive Motions, with which these patients are often afflicted, being occasioned by the acrimonious and acid Fluids separated from the Blood in a disproportionate Measure, irritating and urging the Extremities of the Nerves and the animal spirits, must be owing to the too wide and enlarged Orifices of the Strainers, that suffered an exorbitant Quantity of Humours to pass through" (50). With the collapse of the dichotomies that typified hysteria and hypochondria in Galenic medicine, the very differentia between them became problematic. Was hysteria due to too much acid and hypochondria to too much alkaline in the blood, or vice versa? Was hysteria hot and dry and hypochondria wet and cold, or neither (Foucault 1965, 139–41)? Their insurrectional character did not change in this transformation, however. What Michel Foucault famously pointed out in the case of hysteria applied to hypochondria as well: "For Sydenham, for the disciples of Descartes, the moral intuition [concerning hysteria] is identical to [Hippocrates' and Plato's]; but the spatial landscape in which it is expressed has changed; Plato's vertical and hieratic order is replaced by a volume which is traversed by incessant motion whose disorder is no longer a revolution of the depths to the heights but a lawless whirlwind in a chaotic space" (150).

The causes and consequences of this whirlwind became increasingly important in the eighteenth century when these two diseases were in the midst of their trajectory from the category of "serious" organic disorders to being labeled "mere" maladies of the imagination. Hysteria and hypochondria were included in the range of "nervous" disorders (often referred to as the "English malady") that were the specialty of physicians catering to a very sophisticated and wealthy clientele. The physicians often satisfied their literate patients' demand for medical information about their disorders by penning popular books on these maladies. These books included Bernard Mandeville's *A Treatise of the Hypochondriac and Hysterick Diseases* (1713), Sir Richard Blackmore's *Treatise of the spleen and vapours* ([1723] 1963), and George Cheyne's *The English Malady: A Treatise of Nervous Diseases of All Kinds* ([1733] 1990).[7] The latter transvalued the "nervous disorders" into symptoms of capitalistic success, answering the question, "why did the spleen become identified with England?" in the following way:

> The moisture of our air, the Variableness of our Weather (from our situation amidst the Ocean) the rankness and Fertility of our Soil, the Richness and Heaviness of our Food, the Wealth and Abundance of Inhabitants (from their universal Trade), the Inactivity and Sedentary Occupations of the better Sort (among whom this Evil mostly rages) and the Humour of living in great, populous and consequently unhealthy Towns, have brought forth a Class and Set of Distempers, with atrocious and frightful Symptoms, scarce known to our Ancestors and never rising to such fatal Heights, nor afflicting such numbers in any other known Nation. (quoted in Porter 1987, 83)

As Roy Porter nicely pointed out, Cheyne's book was "a Georgian precursor of *Civilization and Its Discontents*," since "being ill could be a symptomatic of well-being" (83). This was not a uniquely Cheynean insight. Physicians like Mandeville observed that the spleen was a disease of the "comfortable, those free to indulge their imaginations" (84). Consequently, these diseases were intimately identified with the central facts of economic life—Britain had become a leading commercial nation—with a concomitant rise in cultural activities, ranging from the visual to the performing arts. The very society that was rapidly learning "the pleasures of the imagination" was also sharply feeling its pains.[8]

7. There have been a number of important new contributions on the work of Mandeville and Cheyne recently; see Guerrini 2000 on Cheyne, and Hundert 1995 and De Marchi 2001 on Mandeville. For a general discussion of the medical literature genre of eighteenth-century Britain, see Porter and Porter 1989, 197–207.

8. "The Pleasures of the Imagination" is a phrase Joseph Addison popularized in a series of eleven papers comprising issues 411–21 (1712) of the *Spectator*. Addison's development of the positive aspects of the imagination is often credited as constituting a revolution in aesthetics and literary criticism (e.g., Brann 1991, 499). John Brewer (1997, 88–106) pointed out that Addison's "velvet" conceptual revolution was so successful because it was on the cusp

This metamorphosis of the classification of hysteria and hypochondria from organic diseases of the womb and *hypochondrium* into nervous diseases put them in a central position in the philosophical terrain. They acted in that intermediate zone between mind and body that was a region inhabited by the imagination in Cartesian and post-Cartesian philosophy. Descartes, for example, lodged the imagination in the crossroads of the mind and body: the pineal gland (Descartes 1985, 106). It is the faculty that transmits information about the body to the mind and vice versa: "[The] imagination . . . is nothing but a certain application of the faculty of knowledge to the body which is immediately present to it" (quoted in Brann 1991, 74). Clearly then, any defect in a person's faculty of the imagination will subvert his or her ontological balance.

Locke simultaneously ended and universalized the Cartesian centrality of the imagination. On the one side, since Locke eschewed any unique organ of connection between mind and body like the pineal gland, the imagination lost its lock on the transmission between mind and body. But Locke (1975, 2:10:8) attributed to the imagination an important role in memory (in its appearance as "fancy"): "'Tis the business therefore of the Memory to furnish to the Mind those dormant Ideas, which it has present occasion for, and in that having them ready at hand on all occasions, consists that which we call Invention, Fancy, and quickness of Parts." This hermeneutic role of fancy also involves a transmission between mind and body. Though Locke was cautious in his use of the "animal spirits traversing through the nerves" hypothesis (Yolton 1983, 157), he ventured to suggest it in the explanation of different capacities of memory:

> How much the constitution of our bodies and the make of our animal spirits are concerned in this [the "fading colors" of the "pictures drawn in our minds"]; and whether the Temper of the Brain make this difference, that in some it retains the Characters drawn on it like Marble, in others like Free-stone, and in others little better than Sand, I shall not here enquire, though it may seem probable, that the Constitution of the Body does sometimes influence the Memory; since we oftentimes find a Disease quite strip the Mind of all its Ideas, and the flames of a

of a major economic development: the expansion of the commercialized cultural commodity market, which included papers like the *Spectator*, music halls, the stage, and the "art market." Cultivated consumers must be trained in way of the pleasures of the imagination, as must those who produce for them. For a further discussion of how changes in eighteenth-century English "material culture transformed pleasure taking," see Porter 1996.

> Fever, in a few days, calcine all those Images to dust and confusion, which seem'd to be as lasting, as if graved in Marble. (Locke 1975, 2:10:5)

Consequently, the fancy would be involved in transmitting from "the Characters drawn" on the brain to the mind. The functioning of fancy qua the Hermes of the mind would be deeply affected by diseases of the body and of the nerves especially.

On the other side, the imagination in Locke's *Essay* had acquired a more comprehensive role than in Descartes's thought. In Descartes the imagination's function was to transmit corporeal images to the mind via the pineal gland, but in Locke the fantastical imagination operates throughout the margins of the mental realm. It involved the very basis of complex thought: the liberty of associating ideas. Some ideas cannot be fantastical, since they are simple and are produced by real beings. But all other kinds of ideas can go beyond the real and become fantastical. For example, some substance ideas "are fantastical, which are made up of such Collections of simple Ideas, as were really never united, never were found together in any Substance," while some mixed-mode ideas are fantastical when there is no "possibility of existing conformable to them" (2:30:5). Thus the imagination qua the source of fantastical ideas is always haunting the real world of ideas while the imagination qua the agent of memory moves between the mental and the physical realm. Clearly, breakdowns in either realm can be mirrored in calamities in the other, as can be seen in the case of madness.

Locke's Solution to Money Madness

In essence then, Locke's therapy is to "tie down" the patient's mind and continually have him or her repeat the "natural Correspondence and Connexion" of ideas in lieu of the "wrong connections" that have become the basis of his or her madness. Not surprisingly, Locke's prescription for monetary ills was similar, because money was at its root as open to the play of the imagination as was the mind. Money, as a result, was always under threat of being taken away by extravagant flights of fancy and by arbitrary, inadequate, and false connections with other ideas in the world of commerce and desire.

Locke emphasized this vulnerability of money to flights of fancy because his view of the origin of money is completely indifferent to the rationalistic "inconvenience of Barter" explanation of its origin that has been so popular from J. S. Mill and W. S. Jevons to the "transaction costs" enthusiasts of today. He was certainly aware of these inconveniences, but they play no role in the account of the original "cause of money." According to Locke, the first exchanges pertinent to money were based on fancy, not upon real need or convenience.[9] First, as Locke (1975, 3:6:46) points out in the *Essay*, people were initially attracted to "picking up" bits of gold, silver, and diamonds not for real need, but simply because it pleased them. Second, as he points out in the *Second Treatise*, the original exchanger was a person in the state of nature who was also pleased with the color of the gold or silver or the sparkling of the diamond the first person picked up. The second person exchanged something of real use (e.g., nuts or deer meat) for the fancied item that, though it was not necessary, satisfied his or her freely roving fancy (Locke 1982, sec. 46). Thus the exchange of precious metals arose from what were later called "aesthetic" or "ornamental" desires, or what Locke called imagination, fancy, and wit, that is, on the basis of (often perverse) human freedom.

Not only was the creation of money problematic, but so, too, was its dissemination. Money existed in the period before the social contract, when there were only two kinds of law: natural law and "tacit agreement." Clearly, money exchanges were not the purview of natural law, for money was not universal, nor was its use divinely dictated. But since monetary exchanges were originally based on "tacit agreements," they were founded on "nothing else but the consent of private men, who have not authority enough to make a law" (Locke 1975, 2:28:12). Yet though apparently lawless, its net of consent created a self-reinforcing, self-sustaining, informal system that was durable, though ungrounded either in "real use" or "natural law."

Finally, and again idiosyncratically, money gave rise to class division and the need for a social contract to protect the accumulators from those accumulated as servants. The *durability* of gold, silver, and diamonds exempted them from the biblical injunction that required those with a surplus that might spoil to share it with others. Thus the "rational and industrious" could exchange their surplus goods for money that will never spoil. Many did so, and they began to accumulate wealth "beyond real use." This accumulation led, of course, to the class division that presaged the grand convention of owners who contracted away their natural rights

9. A thorough reconstruction of Locke's genealogy of money can be found in Caffentzis 1989, 125–64.

for the protection banding together would bring (Locke 1982, sec. 46–50).

Notice that at each juncture in his story of money, Locke chooses the most "fanciful desire," "unnatural law," and "idiosyncratic property" reading. The anxious reader could not help but conclude that money is a very precarious human construct . . . just like human understanding. Indeed, when it came time for Locke to diagnose and cure the major monetary disease of his day, he took the path outlined by his therapy for the understanding.

The main monetary crisis Locke faced was the deterioration of the English coinage by clipping, bagging, and counterfeiting (Laslett 1969). By the early 1690s, "An experiment was made which showed that £57, 200 sterling in silver coin, which should have contained 220,000 ounces of pure silver, contained only 141,000 ounces. It was calculated that at least 4,000,000 out of 5,600,000 sovereigns in circulation had deteriorated in this way" (Vilar 1976, 218). This condition constituted for Locke a form of monetary madness, for it meant that in about 70 percent of all market transactions English men and women were, according to the experiment, falsely associating a particular idea, say, a shilling, with a particular amount of silver. This collective delusion, like all madness, had real consequences. For example, many believed that they were much wealthier than they were, but they would be economically embarrassed when the truth was revealed. Moreover, those who were outside the circle of delusion, especially the money-market traders abroad, were treating English coin as worth much less than the English evaluated it at home. As a result, the funds required to resupply English troops on the Continent (in the midst of major war) were much more than budgeted, since the value of English coins on the world market had dramatically fallen to take into account the diminished silver content in the coins.[10]

What was to be done? According to Locke, if the madness had become total, it would be foolish to deal with the situation in a gradual way. But it *had* been totalized, because, since the Civil War and Restoration, the English monetary system had slowly driven itself into a sort of collective madness. Clippers, counterfeiters, and other rogues had started it, but the royal treasury and other state offices had begun to accept clipped currency in their accounts. This practice was emulated by the landlords, common traders, and shopkeepers until the very formal distinction

10. For a detailed account of the context of the "recoinage debate" of 1696, see Laslett 1969; Caffentzis 1989; 17–44; and Kelly 1990.

between clipped and unclipped coin disappeared (Caffentzis 1989, 38). The monetary system had all but collapsed in practice. The result of clipping was the destruction in the exchanger's mind of a standard of a "full-weight" coin. Therefore, coin clipping was a semantic crime against the state (even if the clippers were merely interested in private gain). Theft is a one-time affair. The clipper's work, however, introduces a continuously deepening obscurity into our reality and ideas. What is a coin's signification, according to Locke, but the association of the idea of silver with the ideas of specific weight and purity, plus the idea of universal exchange? But we cannot hope to fix this complex of ideas and be sure of community-wide agreement concerning them without continuous testing with an external, substantial standard. Confusion, uncertainty, and abuse slowly ooze from the clipped coin and seep into the mind of every exchanger, so that universal equivalents turn into universal chaos (Caffentzis 1989, 28).

Locke's solution to this catastrophe was a direct application of his therapeutic strategy to madness: "tie down" the patients' minds and continually have them repeat mentally the "natural Correspondence and Connexion" of ideas in lieu of the "wrong connections" that have become the basis of their madness. In effect, the long experience with clipped and deteriorated coin had deprived the English of the sensations required to have clear, distinct, real, adequate, and true monetary ideas. Locke argued, "It is no wonder, if the price and value of things be confounded and uncertain, when the measure itself is lost. For we have no lawful silver money current amongst us; and therefore cannot talk or judge right, by our present, uncertain, clipped money, of the value and price of things, in reference to our lawful regular coin, adjusted and kept to the unvarying standard of the mint" (quoted in Caffentzis 1989, 27). He proposed that the mint should take in from the public the clipped coin at weight and return new coin to the public at the same weight, where crowns and shillings would keep their old silver content. In effect, this would be something of a "shock therapy" that was meant to give to every money handler a "natural Correspondence and Connexion" in the association of the idea of silver with the ideas of specific weight and purity, plus the idea of universal exchange. Each newly minted coin would be a therapeutic device to retrain the maddened public in the proper use of money.[11]

11. Locke has been charged with inconsistency in his advice concerning recoinage by a number of commentators. The nub of the charge is that since Locke was one of the formulators

My "medical" approach to Locke's solution of the recoinage crisis is at odds with Joyce Appleby's now classic explanation of Locke's position. For Appleby, Locke's premises were factually flawed. By the late seventeenth century, the most acute economic observers knew that money's value was not purely intrinsic and determined by its metallic content, as Locke claimed. Locke was ideologically the victor, according to Appleby (1976, 68–69), because he defended the primacy of property against "arbitrary, unlimited power" and gave money a natural status. "His triumph at the practical level lay in the harmony between his ideas and the vested interests of the parliamentary magnates who decided that the clipped silver coin would be called in and reminted at the old standard" (56).

Appleby's explanation of the success of Locke's view can easily become a tautology. One cannot become a "spokesperson" simply by voicing the bourgeoisie's prejudices, because often there were no such fixed prejudices to begin with. In the recoinage case there were many "decision makers" who were genuinely perplexed as to what to do with the clipped coins, otherwise there would not have been a parliamentary debate at all. Locke could not simply mouth platitudes in a time of crisis to win his case; he had to have something to say to the "bourgeoisie."

This is where the medical context is relevant. Locke was convinced that money, though originating before civil government, was not "natural" in Appleby's sense of being controlled by "inexorable regularities that derived their power beyond the reach of thought or will" (43). On the contrary, money was a human construct whose preconditions were precarious and vulnerable to many diseases of "thought or will." In the recoinage case, the perverse will of the clippers and the confused thought of those who let clipped coins pass were crucial. Monetary systems can sicken *and die* due to the action of monetary agents. Consequently, the

---

of the quantity theory of money, he should have predicted that a dramatic shrinkage of the money supply in the wake of a full-weight recoinage would lead to economic distress. For a defense of Locke against these charges, see Caffentzis 1989, 17–44. For a brief description of the consequences of the full-weight recoinage undertaken with Locke's inspiration, see Kelly 1990, 63–67. We must also recognize the impact of war on the recoinage debate. As Niall Ferguson (2001, 23–50) has recently pointed out, war is not only important to the health of the state, it is crucial for "the development of the state as a fiscal institution." There is no doubt that Locke was conscious of the impact of the outcome of the recoinage debate on governmental borrowing during King William's War. If the Lowndes approach won out, Locke suggested, the creditworthiness of the British government would be reduced. After such an episode of devaluation, creditors (who were not only English citizens) would suspect that they might be repaid in a devalued coinage in the future.

diagnosis and cure of monetary ills, like the widespread passing of clipped coinage, are not a matter of uttering bedside platitudes. Locke not only posed a medical solution to the diseases of thought and will among clippers and exchangers who precipitated the monetary crisis, he also spoke to the sense of social and political catastrophe experienced by the parliamentary decision makers who were conscious of the dangers of his prescription. *That* is why Locke became the physician for Britain's monetary woes.

Berkeley's Monetary *Pharmakon*

Berkeley and Locke shared a combined interest in medicine and monetary theory as well as a practice of transferring therapeutic methods appropriate to the diseases of the mind into cures of monetary problems. But there were many differences between their methods and cures due to their philosophical antagonism as well as to their different social contexts:

First, Locke was an ontological metallist, that is, he argued that money is a complex idea that must compound a metallic substance idea with a mixed-mode idea, while Berkeley rejected the need for the presence of any metallic substance idea in the notion of money.

Second, Locke had a unitary conception of madness, while Berkeley had a more complex notion of mental illness rooted in a spectrum of "nervous diseases" from hysteria to hypochondria.

Third, Locke saw the monetary disease caused by coin clipping as affecting nearly the whole English money-using population, whereas Berkeley saw that the economic problems of Ireland were caused by two different classes, the "native" Irish poor and the Anglo-Irish gentry. The Irish poor were gripped "by that cynical content in dirt and beggary which they possess to a degree beyond any other people of Christendom" and ridden by splenetic and hypochondriacal *economic* symptoms (Berkeley [1735–37] 1953, 1:19).[12] The Anglo-Irish gentry hysterically scattered money in buying sprees in London and Paris, returning to Ireland to engage in an endless round of drunken parties, being "absentee" to their productive responsibilities, even when they were at home (Caffentzis 2000, 328). That is, the economic behavior of these two classes

12. References to *The Querist* (Berkeley [1735–37] 1953; hereafter *Q*) are to the original version published in three parts between 1735 and 1737. A reference that reads, say, "*Q*, 3:130" means the 130th query in part 3 of *The Querist*.

mimicked the behavior of hysterics and hypochondriacs who frequented the medical offices of the most sophisticated physicians of eighteenth-century London.

As a consequence of these differences, Berkeley opposed Locke's "hard money" solution to the ills of the Irish economy, which would have called for the imposition of almost slavelike work conditions on the poor and the establishment of a full-weight, internationally recognized gold and silver coinage. Berkeley argued that the Irish poor could hardly be more repressed than they had been in the decades after the defeat of the pro-Stuart rebellion in 1690, while a full-weight, internationally recognized coinage would further stimulate the Anglo-Irish gentry in their frenzy for imported goods and absentee landholdings. Besides, the metallic substance idea Locke touted as providing an objective standard in the idea of money was as vulnerable to controversy as any other idea. According to Berkeley, gold and silver ideas are no more mind-independent than are secondary quality ideas like "red" or mixed-mode ideas like "democracy." Locke's reliance on metals to provide an autonomous control on the monetary system was a fool's paradise.

Berkeley was also an innovator in the study of the imagination. His *Treatise Concerning the Principles of Human Knowledge* (1710) shifted the imagination's locus from the intersection of the mind and body (which would have been literally nowhere in his early immaterialist doctrine) into the active dimension of the mind. He noted: "I find I can excite ideas in my mind at pleasure, and vary and shift the scene as oft as I think fit. It is no more than willing, and straightway this or that idea arises in my fancy: and by the same power it is obliterated, and makes way for another. This making and unmaking of ideas doth very properly denominate the mind active" (Berkeley [1710] 1948, sec. 29). In effect, Berkeley identified the imagination with "the mind active," which, though provoking ideas that are less strong, lively, distinct, and orderly than those sensory ideas excited in us by God, has something of a divine Promethean character. This self-exciting, creative capacity is rooted in the will. Consequently, the problems of the imagination can be attributed not to one's "unnatural" association of ideas (as Locke argued), but to the will that produced the ideas and their association. In this model, then, the problem of mental illness cannot simply be dealt with by inserting real, true, and adequate ideas into a patient's mental universe. If the will is wicked, perverse, or weak, then the ideational results will be wicked, perverse, or weak as well. As Berkeley ([1721] 1953, 337) pointed out at the end of the *Essay on the Ruin of Great Britain*, "other nations have been wicked, but we are the first who have been wicked upon principle," that is, British wickedness is willed. Almost thirty years later, in *A Word to the Wise* ([1749] 1953, 242), he notes that "our poor Irish are wedded to dirt on principle," that is, the poor people's dirtiness is willed. The difficulty with Berkeley's will-model of the imagination, however, is that the will is so difficult to discuss in the philosophical terminology provided by the early Berkeley. Since it is pure spirit, it is not an idea and generally does not qualify as discourse. Thus the source of the imagination is itself unimaginable!

This intellectual result was an embarrassment to Berkeley when he matured into a man of affairs and a social physician. As a dean in the Church of Ireland and leader of the Bermuda Project in the 1720s, he had to preserve old institutions and conceive of new ones, like his multiracial college. At this juncture, his early philosophy failed him. It was only between 1729 and 1738 that he was able to provide a rudimentary anatomy and mechanics of the social will as well as a way of examining its institutional embodiments and problematics through his development of the realm of "notions," "prejudices," and "rules and opinions" (Caffentzis 2000, 241–79).

By the mid-1730s Berkeley was quite knowledgeable about the etiology of hysteria and hypochondria, the new dominance of the "animal spirits in the nerves" in physiology, as well as the increasing philosophical and social centrality of the imagination. He displayed this knowledge seven years after he finished *The Querist* in *Siris: A Chain of Philosophical Reflexions and Inquiries concerning the Virtues of Tar-water and divers other subjects connected together and arising from one another* ([1744] 1953), his most serious exploration of medicine and therapy. It was the product of decades of personal medical investigations: for example, Berkeley first came across the use of tar-water as a medicine during his sojourn in America (1728–31) (Berman 1994, 177).

Siris was also the product of much medical erudition. Though Berkeley was self-consciously in opposition to "Newtonian medicine," as Marina Benjamin (1990) pointed out, he recognized in the pages of *Siris* all the major intellectual trends in medicine and physiology. For example, in a passage reminiscent of Richard Blackmore's *Treatise of the spleen and vapours* two decades before, he wrote:

> As the body is said to clothe the soul, so the nerves may be said to constitute her inner garment. And as the soul animates the whole,

> what nearly touches the soul relates to all. Therefore the asperity of tartarous salts, and the fiery acrimony of alkaline salts, irritating and wounding the nerves, produce nascent passions and anxieties in the soul; which both aggravate distempers and render men's lives restless and wretched, even when they are afflicted with no apparent distemper. This is the latent spring of much woe, spleen, and taedium vitae. (Berkeley [1744] 1953, 60)

Berkeley also showed a knowledge of the contemporary professional attitudes toward hysteria and hypochondria discussed above. His epidemiology was quite *courant*—"hysterical or hypochondriacal persons, who make a great part, perhaps the greatest, of those who lead sedentary lives in these islands [Britain and Ireland]" (54)—as was his symptomology—the hysteric had "bad appetite, low spirits, restless nights, wasting pains and anxieties," while the splenetic and hypochondriacal patient was "prey to imaginary woes" living in a "gloomy empire" (65, 66).

Berkeley, of course, touted the effectiveness of tar-water as a cure of hysteria and hypochondria, due to its virtue of "purifying the blood," which then will have a healthy impact on the nerves and animal spirits. But this was not the first time he studied specific cures for hysteria and hypochondria. In the spring of 1717 he traveled from Naples to Lecce and Taranto and back via Venosa to Naples with his charge, George Ashe. This was not a typical part of the grand tour that Berkeley was supposedly leading Ashe through, for that part of Italy was reputed to be filled with Turks and bandits (Berkeley 1955, 235). It apparently was undertaken in order to do medical research into tarantism and the "tarantella" cure for hysterical and hypochondriacal diseases. He apparently had discussed his trip with Dr. John Freind, a physician with Tory politics and Newtonian methods, who was deeply concerned with therapeutics (Hall 1972). Berkeley sent back to Freind "an accurate and entertaining account of the tarantula" (which has never been found).

It is not surprising that a fashionable London physician like Dr. Freind, who had previously visited Italy, should be interested in the southern Italian "dancing cure."[13] The illness the tarantella was to cure was similar to the "English malady" neuroses exhibited by many of his patients, as a standard description of the tarantistic disease like the following will

13. Undoubtedly Freind's visit with Georges Baglivi on his Italian journey in 1707 further interested him in the phenomenon of tarantism, for Baglivi was the author of "De Anatomia, Morsu et Effectibus Tarantulae" (1696), which contained the first published drawing of the tarantula spider (Hall 1972; Savory 1977, 290).

reveal: "falling on the ground, the feeling of exhaustion, the agony, the state of psychomotor agitation accompanied by occluding of the sensorium, the difficulty of standing upright, the stomach pains, nausea, and vomiting, the various ticklings and muscular aches, the excitation of the sexual appetite" (Oughourlian 1991, 133). The cause of this disease was taken to be the bite of a tarantula, and the cure was music and dance, but not just any music and dance. The patients were to dance for hours before an orchestra that would try to find "the 'right' music . . . of the tarantula in question; the 'right' music will be that which will set the tarantula in motion [*scazzicare*]" (134). Once the right music was found, the poisonous effects of the bite would be literally danced out their bodies.

Berkeley interviewed people from all classes in southern Italy to determine the range of opinion concerning the causes and cures of tarantism. He also witnessed a number of tarantella sessions, which he recorded with a remarkable phenomenological vivacity. Though his notes, which probably were the basis of his report to Dr. Freind, recorded inconclusive results with respect to causes, cures, or even the existence of the disease, the dance evidently made a striking impression on him. His journey into the land of the tarantella provided him with his first serious medical reflections, which would later flower into his diagnoses and prescriptions for an ill nation, Ireland.

Certainly, the tarantella cure was not far from the general eighteenth-century medical consensus that exercise, music, and dance were crucial components in therapy. George Cheyne in his *English Malady* ([1733] 1990, 21) noted: "There is not any one Thing, more approv'd and recommended by all Physicians, and the Experience of all those who have suffer'd under Nervous Distempers (since the distinction has been made) than Exercise, of one Kind or another." Moreover, there was an increased appreciation of music and dance in medicine during that period (Rousseau 1993, 36–40). The first English book on the medicinal use of music and dance was Richard Browne's *A mechanical essay on singing, musick and dancing . . . demonstrating . . . the alterations they produce in the human body*, published in 1727 (second edition entitled *Medicina music*, 1729). Five years after the publication of *Siris*, Richard Brocklesby published *Reflections on antient and modern musick, with the application to the cure of diseases* ([1749] 1963, 377), where "it is here submitted to the judgment of the philosophical physician, how far the power of musick, judiciously exerted, may be of service in maniacal cases."

This emphasis on bodily motion as an essential element in therapy would have struck a chord in the young immaterialist philosopher of vision who, paradoxically, argued in his *New Theory of Vision* ([1707] 1948) that we could not learn the most elementary visual ideas without having a body that had the will to move itself and to touch other bodies. Indeed, Berkeley used a pure "intelligence, or unbodied spirit" in that book as a counter-example to any alternative view. Since such a bodiless being would have no sense of touch, "He would not, therefore, judge as we do, nor have any idea of distance, outness, or profundity, nor consequently of space or body, either immediately or by suggestion" (sec. 153). Since bodily action is necessary in order to have the full panoply of visual ideas, it should not be surprising that the inducements to action in general like music and dance would be useful in dealing with medical problems involving animal spirits and failures of the will.

What kind of therapy was appropriate for illnesses of economic action? The splenetic Irish poor and the hysterical Anglo-Irish gentry manifested two different kinds of economic diseases in early-eighteenth-century Ireland. Berkeley (*Q*, 2:183) rhetorically asked whether or not the Irish poor were "the most indolent and supine People in Christendom?" Certainly this indolence is the source of spleen, a variety of hypochondria, which had been the preserve of the rich in England. Berkeley ironically suggested that the Irish poor's idleness and refusal of work made them as prone to spleen as England's gentry.[14] He summarizes the problem posed by this class and the possible way to solve it using the classic natural/political body trope toward the end of *The Querist*: "Whether the remotest Parts from the Metropolis, and the lowest of the People, are not to be regarded as the Extremities and Limbs of the political Body?" (*Q*, 3:305); "Whether, although the Capilary Vessels are small, yet Obstructions in them do not produce great Chronical Diseases?" (*Q*, 3:306); "Whether Faculties are not enlarged and improved by Exercise?" (*Q*, 3:307).[15]

The Anglo-Irish gentry, however, were not "supine." On the contrary, they were too excitable, being continually on buying sprees and drunken

14. Berkeley ([1749] 1953, 241) returned to this theme of the poor Irish's willful refusal to work in *A Word to the Wise*, a farewell address to the Irish Catholic clergy. He urged them to preach the virtues of labor. He assured them, "Was there but will to work, there are not wanting in this island either opportunities or encouragements."

15. According to Berkeley in *Siris* ([1744] 1953, 60), "all hysteric and hypochondriac cases, which, together with the maladies from indigestion, comprise almost the whole tribe of chronical diseases."

binges. They were hysterical hedonists typified by extravagant women who were only content with the most expensive foreign dresses and by extravagant men who were content only with the most expensive French wines.[16] As Berkeley asks of the gentry-women:

> Whether it be not even certain, that the Matrons of this forlorn Country send out a greater Proportion of its Wealth, for fine Apparell than any other Females on the whole surface of this terraqueous Globe? (*Q*, 3:115)

> Whether the Expence, great as it is, be the greatest Evil; but whether this Folly may not produce many other Follies, an entire Derangement of Domestic Life, absurd Manners, neglect of Duties, bad Mothers, a General Corruption in both Sexes? (*Q*, 3:116)

Berkeley was convinced that the Irish political economy was ill because its components were ill, and he explicitly invoked a medical metaphor when referring to his monetary system of paper notes issued and regulated by a state-controlled national bank. He queried, "Whether of all the Helps to Industry that ever were invented, there be any more secure, more easy, and more effectual than a National Bank?" (*Q*, 3:106); "Whether Medicines do not recommend themselves by Experience, even though their Reasons be obscure? But whether Reason and Fact are not equally clear, in Favour of this political Medicine?" (*Q*, 3:107). How would this "political Medicine" work? Gold and silver coinage should be phased out of circulation because specie made it too easy for the rich to buy foreign commodities; hence, valuable currency was drained from the country. Further, the precious metals made small change quite rare, thus crippling the petty trade that is the microscopic health of the economy and the stimulator of the poor's work effort. The old coinage would be replaced by a new monetary system. With the printing of paper notes by the national bank and the minting of small change coins by the national mint, the Irish economy would become much more monetarized internally, but at the same time its ties to the international economy would be curtailed dramatically.

Once in this new monetary system, the Irish poor would finally begin to break out of their cynical splenetic gloom. Their wages would

16. *The* classic literary representation of the vain, overdressed, and hysterical Anglo-Irish gentry-woman is Lady Isabella Rackrent in Maria Edgeworth's *Castle Rackrent: An Hiberian Tale, Taken from the Facts and from the Manners of the Irish Squires of Former Times, Before the year 1782* (1964).

increase, and they would be able to sell their small produce for cash on the local markets. Soon they would begin to move purposefully in an economic sense, because they would be integrated into the national monetary system. They would be able to buy consumer items, which ability would generate wants, and they could begin to plan for the future. To create wants, especially those leading to industry, the Irish poor must have new experiences denied to them by the economy of the day. One cannot want to eat beef (instead of potatoes) unless one has tasted beef. Wanting implies imagination, that is, an active mind, but imagination implies prior sensation. So if one expects the poor Irish to work for wages, their wants—for eating beef and wearing shoes—must be stimulated; but this can only be done if they actually have had some experience with beef and shoes.

This shift in the direction of thought from beggary to active engagement with the future, if massively multiplied, would stimulate industry and release Irish capital from the curse of "the lazy worker." Thus there would be a monetary *pharmakon* for the social hypochondria of the Irish poor.

The same "political medicine" of paper money and national bank would block the hysterical behavior of the Anglo-Irish gentry and direct it to more productive uses. Since the domestically issued paper notes would not be convertible in the international money market, they could not be used for imports of claret or for buying sprees of the latest fashions in London or Paris. Foreign exporters would not accept the inconvertible paper money of Berkeley's bank, while the gentry would have to accept rent payments in this currency. Absentee landlords would automatically return home. Once their hysterical appetite for emulating their consumerist English cousins is checked, the Anglo-Irish gentry, both men and women, would begin to invest their inconvertible money to stimulate industry in Ireland itself.

Berkeley put the productive imagination at the center of his quizzical political economy in *The Querist*. He suggested that the cause of Ireland's economic ills was rooted in the improper excitation of the will: the imaginative will of the Irish poor was depressed, while that of the Anglo-Irish gentry was excessive. The pharmacological power of the monetary system Berkeley prescribed for Ireland was duplicitous: it could simultaneously excite the will of the poor and dampen and redirect the will of the gentry.

Conclusion

The Age of Newton saw a major shift in the relation between the body (and its ills) and the economy and its "ills" (Foucault 1970). The period when an almost magical similitude between the object of medicine, the body-mind microcosm, and the object of political economy, the macroscopic field of monetary exchanges, was the basis of an extended discourse came to an end. This end, however, is not clearly marked, because the era of similitude left behind it a profusion of metaphorical vestiges that are found down to this day.

But the medicine-money nexus did not end with the demise of belief in micro-macrocosm correspondences. In its place came a new interest in multiplying the power of medicine over individual bodies and minds as a way of creating large-scale effects on the body politic. Just as the anatomical-metaphysical study of the ideal "docile body" of the soldier and prisoner led to the regulations of the army and prison that would impose docility on actual soldiers and prisoners (Foucault 1979, 136), so, too, the medical study of the ideal "economic agent" led to economic strategies and regimens that in turn were meant to create rational monetary exchangers. This direct, nonanalogic impact of medicine on the economy was noted long ago by Karl Marx and has been recently confirmed by Peter Groenewegen's (2001) edited volume.

Locke and Berkeley reacted quite differently to this shift. Although Locke did employ medical metaphors and analogies in his economic texts (Coleman 2000, 717), he did so cautiously. For example, in his *Further considerations concerning raising the value of money*, Locke employed almost no medical metaphors. Indeed, he was exceptionally miserly with metaphors in all his work. This is due to Locke's general suspicion and devaluation of the generative faculty of metaphor and analogy, the imagination and fancy, and his approval of judgment: "Judgement . . . lies quite on the other side [of fancy], in separating carefully, one from the other, ideas wherein can be found the least difference, thereby to avoid being mislead by similitude, and by affinity to take one thing for another. This is a way of proceeding quite contrary to metaphor and allusion" (Locke 1975, 2:11:2; quoted in Caffentzis 1989, 130). Consequently, Locke's medical knowledge concerning the causation of madness and its cure was not used to justify metaphorically certain economic policies, but was meant to be employed to directly affect the behavior of money exchangers to cure their monetary madness.

Berkeley's work, on the contrary, straddled both ends of this shift in the medical-money nexus. *The Querist* is filled with medical metaphors for economic processes, as illustrated above. But Berkeley also crafted a monetary reform directed at the behavior of Anglo-Irish gentry and Irish "natives" that was informed by his medical analysis of the typical members of these two classes. Why does Berkeley, who is writing forty years after Locke's *Further considerations*, apparently revert to the language of similitude in his work on money?

I argue that Berkeley's revaluation of the medical metaphor does not signify a return to the era of similitude. His use of medical metaphors arises, rather, from the ingenious "divine language" argument that he developed first in his *New Theory of Vision* ([1707] 1948) and deployed in its final form in *Alciphron* (1732).[17] The key point of the argument is that our sensory experiences of nature are not necessarily connected. For example, the elliptical visual image of a cup's rim I now see does not necessitate the circular tactile feeling I experience when tracing the rim with my finger. Our sensory ideas are like the words of a human language in that they are not necessarily connected. But, according to Berkeley, it is this very nonnecessary grammar of human language that indicates the existence of another human will that is ordering these tokens to communicate. Similarly, the nonnecessary order of sensory experience is determined by another communicator, God. Consequently, there is a semantic, communicative aspect to sensory experience that constitutes a "divine language" indicating the presence of a divine other.

It is the very arbitrariness of the interconnections between words, between monetary units, and between sensations, not their similitude, that validates metaphorical and analogical connections between different orderers of experience: the mind, the legislature, and God.[18] This applies to Berkeley's paper money as well. After all, according to *The Querist*, the

17. For a full account of the "divine language" argument, see Turbayne 1962 and Berman 1993.

18. Benjamin (1990, 192) notices a "disanalogy" between the early and the late Berkeley: "In the *Principles* Berkeley allowed for the existence of spirits—God and wills—and ideas, serving as 'marks or signs' for God's creatures. Now in *Siris* Berkeley introduced the aether as God's instrument, not to serve for the benefit of mankind as a signifier, but to aid God in his maintenance of the natural order." But there is a compelling homology between *The Querist* and *Siris* that testifies to the former's role in the gradual transformation of Berkeley's later thought. Berkeley introduced the cosmic ether in *Siris* as an intermediary. The animal spirits mediated between the mind and the limbs, and the ether, between God and nature (Caffentzis 2000, 246–47). Thus from the perspective of *Siris*, money was to become the ether of the body politic.

legislature was to be the godlike creator of the grammar and meanings of the language of money that would train the money exchanger into its proper usage (Caffentzis 2000, 172–73).[19] It is not surprising then that Berkeley, who introduced money as an intermediary between the legislature and economic agents in *The Querist*, would avail himself of the intermediaries between the mind and bodily action—which, according to contemporary medicine, included animal spirits as well as blood—to describe the functioning of the whole community: "Whether the immediate Mover, the Blood and Spirits, be not Money, Paper or Metal, and whether the Soul or Will of the Community, which is the prime Mover that governs and directs the Whole, be not the Legislature?" (*Q*, 3:318).

Berkeley in *The Querist* broke the spell of similitude between sign and referent and between money and value, he did not revive it.

References

Appleby, Joyce Oldham. 1976. Locke, Liberalism, and the Natural Law of Money. *Past and Present* 71:43–69.

Bacon, Francis. 1955. *Essays or Counsels Civil or Moral*. In *Selected Writings of Francis Bacon*, edited by Hugh G. Dick. New York: Random House.

Benjamin, Marina. 1990. Medicine, Morality, and the Politics of Berkeley's Tar-Water. In *The Medical Enlightenment of the Eighteenth Century*, edited by Andrew Cunningham and Roger French. Cambridge: Cambridge University Press.

Berkeley, George. [1707] 1948. *An Essay Towards a New Theory of Vision*. In vol. 1 of Luce and Jessop 1948–57.

———. [1710] 1948. *Principles of Human Knowledge*. In vol. 1 of Luce and Jessop 1948–57.

———. [1710] 1949. *A Treatise Concerning the Principles of Human Knowledge*. In vol. 2 of Luce and Jessop 1948–57.

———. [1744] 1953. *Siris: A Chain of Philosophical Reflexions and Inquiries concerning the Virtues of Tar-water and divers other subjects connected together and arising from one another*. In vol. 5 of Luce and Jessop 1948–57.

———. [1721] 1953. *Essay on the Ruin of Great Britain*. In vol. 6 of Luce and Jessop 1948–57.

———. [1735–37] 1953. *The Querist*. In vol. 6 of Luce and Jessop 1948–57.

———. [1749] 1953. *A Word to the Wise*. In vol. 6 of Luce and Jessop 1948–57.

———. 1955. *Journals of Travels in Italy*. In vol. 7 of Luce and Jessop 1948–57.

Berman, David, ed. 1993. *George Berkeley: Alciphron in Focus*. London: Routledge.

19. Berkeley's "divine language" argument is a subtle inversion of the much more common "argument by design" classically expressed in Alexander Pope's couplets. For a discussion of the analogies between natural and divine order developed in the English physiotheological poetry of the eighteenth century, see Jones 1966.

———. 1994. *George Berkeley: Idealism and the Man*. Oxford: Clarendon Press.

Blackmore, Sir Richard. [1723] 1963. Excerpts from *A treatise of the spleen and vapours; or, Hypocondriacal and hysterical affections*. In *Three Hundred Years of Psychiatry: 1535–1860*, edited by Richard Hunter and Ida Macalpine. London: Oxford University Press.

Brann, Eva T. H. 1991. *The World of the Imagination: Sum and Substance*. Savage, Md.: Rowman & Littlefield.

Brewer, John. 1997. *The Pleasures of the Imagination: English Culture in the 18th Century*. New York: Farrar Straus Giroux.

Brocklesby, Richard. [1749] 1963. *Reflections on antient and modern musick, with the application to the cure of diseases*. In *Three Hundred Years of Psychiatry, 1535–1860*, edited by Richard Hunter and Ida Macalpine. London: Oxford University Press.

Caffentzis, C. G. 1989. *Clipped Coins, Abused Words, and Civil Government: John Locke's Philosophy of Money*. New York: Autonomedia.

———. 2000. *Exciting the Industry of Mankind: George Berkeley's Philosophy of Money*. Dordrecht: Kluwer Academic Press.

Cheyne, George. [1733] 1990. *The English Malady: A Treatise of Nervous Diseases of All Kinds*. Edited by Roy Porter. New York: Routledge.

Coleman, William. 2000. The Significance of John Locke's Medical Studies for His Economic Thought. *HOPE* 32.4:711–30.

De Marchi, Neil. 2001. Exposure to Strangers and Superfluities: Mandeville's Regimen for Great Wealth and Foreign Treasure. In Groenewegen 2001.

Descartes, René. 1985. *A Treatise on Man*. In vol. 1 of *The Philosophical Writings of Descartes*, translated by John Cottingham et al. Cambridge: Cambridge University Press.

Dewhurst, Kenneth. 1963. *John Locke (1632–1704), Physician and Philosopher: A Medical Biography with an Edition of the Medical Notes in His Journals*. London: Wellcome Historical Medical Library.

Edgeworth, Maria. 1964. *Castle Rackrent: An Hiberian Tale, Taken from the Facts and from the Manners of the Irish Squires of Former Times, Before the year 1782*. Edited with an introduction by George Watson. London: Oxford University Press.

Ferguson, Niall. 2001. *The Cash Nexus: Money and Power in the Modern World, 1700–2000*. New York: Basic Books.

Foucault, Michel. 1965. *Madness and Civilization: A History of Insanity in the Age of Reason*. New York: Vintage Books.

———. 1970. *The Order of Things: An Archeology of the Human Sciences*. New York: Vintage Press.

———. 1979. *Discipline and Punish: The Birth of the Prison*. New York: Vintage Books.

Groenewegen, Peter, ed. 2001. *Physicians and Political Economy: Six Studies of the Work of Doctor-Economists*. London: Routledge.

Guerrini, Anita. 2000. *Obesity and Depression in the Enlightenment: The Life and Times of George Cheyne*. Norman, Okla.: University of Oklahoma Press.

Hall, Marie Boas. 1972. John Freind. In vol. 5 of *Dictionary of Scientific Biography*, edited by Charles Coulston Gillispie. New York: Charles Scribner's Sons.

Harrington, James. 1977. *A System of Politics*. In *The Political Works of James Harrington*, edited by J. G. A. Pocock. Cambridge: Cambridge University Press.

Hobbes, Thomas. 1985. *Leviathan*. Edited by C. B. Macpherson. London: Penguin.

Hundert, E. J. 1995. Bernard Mandeville and the Enlightenment's Maxims of Modernity. *Journal of the History of Ideas* 56.4:577–93.

Hutchison, Terence. 1988. *Before Adam Smith: The Emergence of Political Economy, 1662–1776*. Oxford: Blackwell.

James, Susan. 1997. *Passion and Action: The Emotions in Seventeenth-Century Philosophy*. Oxford: Oxford University Press.

Jones, William Powell. 1966. *The Rhetoric of Science: A Study of Scientific Ideas and Imagery in Eighteenth-Century English Poetry*. London: Routledge & Kegan Paul.

Kelly, Patrick Hyde. 1990. General Introduction. In vol. 1 of *Locke on Money*, edited by Patrick Hyde Kelly. Oxford: Clarendon Press.

Laslett, Peter. 1969. John Locke, the Great Recoinage, and the Origins of the Board of Trade, 1695–1698. In *John Locke: Problems and Perspectives*, edited by John W. Yolton. Cambridge: Cambridge University Press.

Locke, John. 1975. *An Essay Concerning Human Understanding*. Edited by Peter Nidditch. New York: Oxford University Press.

———. 1982. *Second Treatise on Government*. Wheeling, Ill.: Harlan Davidson.

Luce, A. A., and T. E. Jessop, eds. 1948–57. *The Works of George Berkeley, Bishop of Cloyne*. 9 vols. London: Thomas Nelson.

Osler, Sir William. [1900] 1990. John Locke as a Physician. In *A Locke Miscellany: Locke Biography and Criticism for All*, edited by Jean S. Yolton. Bristol: Thoemmes.

Oughourlian, Jean-Michel. 1991. *The Puppet of Desire: The Psychology of Hysteria, Possession, and Hypnosis*. Stanford, Calif.: Stanford University Press.

Peters, J. S. 1995. The Bank, the Press, and the "Return of Nature": On Currency, Credit, and Literary Property. In *Early Modern Conceptions of Property*, edited by John Brewer and Susan Staves. London: Routledge.

Petty, William. [1691] 1963. *The Political Anatomy of Ireland*. In vol. 1 of *The Economic Writings of Sir William Petty*, edited by Charles Henry Hull. New York: Augustus M. Kelley.

Porter, Dorothy, and Roy Porter. 1989. *Patient's Progress: Doctors and Doctoring in Eighteenth-Century England*. Stanford, Calif.: Stanford University Press.

Porter, Roy. 1987. *Mind-Forg'd Manacles: A History of Madness in England from the Restoration to the Regency*. Cambridge: Harvard University Press.

———. 1996. Material Pleasures in the Consumer Society. In *Pleasure in the Eighteenth Century*, edited by Roy Porter and Marie Mulvey Roberts. London: Macmillan.

Romanell, Patrick. 1984. *John Locke and Medicine: A New Key to Locke*. Buffalo, N.Y.: Prometheus Books.

Rousseau, G. S. 1993. Medicine and the Muses: An Approach to Literature and Medicine. In *Literature and Medicine during the Eighteenth Century*, edited by Marie Mulvey Roberts and Roy Porter. London: Routledge.

Saccaro-Battisti, Giuseppa. 1983. Changing Metaphors of Political Structures. *Journal of the History of Ideas* 44.1:31–54.

Savory, J. 1977. *Arachnida*. 2d ed. London: Academic Press.

Turbayne, C. M. 1962. *The Myth of Metaphor*. New Haven, Conn.: Yale University Press.

Turner, Bryan S. 1992. *Regulating Bodies: Essays in Medical Sociology*. London: Routledge.

Vaughn, Karen Iversen. 1980. *John Locke: Economist and Social Scientist*. Chicago: University of Chicago Press.

Vilar, P. 1976. *A History of Gold and Money, 1450–1920*. London: New Left Books.

Yolton, John W. 1983. *Thinking Matter: Materialism in Eighteenth-Century Britain*. Minneapolis: University of Minnesota Press.

Credit-Money as the Philosopher's Stone: Alchemy and the Coinage Problem in Seventeenth-Century England

Carl Wennerlind

In Goethe's *Faust*, Mephistopheles proposes that the emperor solve his financial problems by implementing a system of paper money, backed by his royal land and the gold hidden therein. His advocate, the astrologer, favorably compares this scheme to the transmutation of base metals into gold, while the skeptics exclaim: "Oh, let us off, All warmed-up stuff / It's number mystic, Alchymistic" (Goethe [1808] 1976, 4973–74). Mephistopheles ultimately prevails, and after the credit-money system is established and great prosperity ensues, the emperor's treasurer marvels: "There shall not be the faintest breath of trouble / I cherish a magician for my double" (6141–42). In this, *Faust*'s so-called paper-money scene,[1] Goethe metaphorically connects credit-money to alchemy; however, he does so in a way that only hints at the complexity of the actual link between alchemy and credit-money in the seventeenth-century.

The idea that alchemy could be used to expand the money stock and thus stimulate the economy was rather well established during the seventeenth century, as witnessed by the writings of various social reformers and by the number of European regents who patronized alchemists. However, as experiments to transmute base metals into gold repeatedly failed, the search for a new money-creation mechanism continued,

I would like to thank the participants of the 2002 *HOPE* conference and an anonymous referee, as well as the following scholars: Tony Aspromourgos, Andre Burgstaller, Neil De Marchi, Joel Kaye, Monica Miller, Laurence Moss, Margaret Schabas, Pamela Smith, and Lisa Tiersten.

1. Shell (1982) and Binswanger (1994) have analyzed the "paper-money scene" in great detail.

resulting in the conceptualization of a credit-money system. The Hartlib Circle in England, having already pursued alchemy, offered one of the earliest proposals for credit-money. While their particular proposition was not implemented, it helped define the pool of ideas available to later reformers. Eventually, once the Bank of England showed in 1694 how credit-money could function, there was a rapid falloff in the patronage of alchemists, and credit-money was elevated to the position of the best available system for money creation. Hence, at a minimum, alchemy and credit-money were linked both metaphorically and as strategies to address the same problem. I suggest, however, that the ties between alchemy and credit-money ran deeper and were more profound than has been thought previously. This is particularly true in the English context, for which I hope to show that just as alchemy served as an important theoretical and empirical framework for the development of the Scientific Revolution (Dobbs 1975; Westfall 1980; Henry 1990, 1997), so, too, did it serve as a conceptual and discursive system that helped frame the debate about the shortage of money and how to overcome that problem.

Alchemy in the Seventeenth Century

While serious financial strains affected most emerging nation-states in seventeenth-century Europe, England was particularly hard hit. In the 1620s an outflow of money and a rapid decline in England's traditional export trades exacerbated an already precarious fiscal situation (Supple 1959; De Vries 1976; Appleby 1978; Braddick 2000). Numerous attempts were made to ameliorate the fiscal and economic problems, but all measures proved inadequate. Reduced flows of gold and silver from the Americas (Vilar 1976, 197) coupled with the rapid falloff in output from central European silver mines (Bonny 1991, 420) kept coin scarce, while debasements, though sporadically used on the Continent, had been effectively eliminated as an option in England by the failure of the Great Tudor Debasement of 1544–51 (Davies 1994, 206).

Desperate for a solution to the economic and fiscal crisis, European rulers looked to alchemy as an alternative to debasement; in fact, most of the European courts patronized alchemists throughout the seventeenth century.[2] While the reasons for coveting the magic tincture were many—agricultural improvements, medicines, perfumes, and so forth—the idea

2. As William Eamon (1994, 225) points out, alchemy was a "courtly science par excellence."

of turning base metals into gold and thus gaining the ability to relieve the pressure on the state's finances and revive commerce was a strong incentive. The list of regents known to have employed alchemists includes Cardinal Richelieu (Briggs 1991, 40–41); Queen Christina (Åkerman 1991); Christian IV (Coudert 1980, 200); Gustav Adolphus (Coudert 1980, 199); Rudolph II (Holmyard [1957] 1990, 15; Evans 1973); Ferdinand III; and Leopold I (Smith 1994, 17, 179–78). In Britain, the support of alchemists dates back at least to the reign of Edward IV (1461–83), who was the dedicatee of one of the period's most famous alchemical tracts by George Ripley.[3] Edward VI (1547–53) and Elizabeth I (1558–1603) continued the support of alchemists, the latter by patronizing John Dee, who contributed greatly to the spread of alchemical studies in England (Yates 1979). Dee's successor, Kenelm Digby, gained the support of James I (1603–25) and Charles I (1625–49) (Holmyard [1957] 1990, 210). James II (1685–88) and Charles II (1660–85) not only patronized alchemists, but were also known to have personally pursued alchemical experiments, the latter building a clandestine alchemical lab under his bedroom with exclusive access via a private staircase (Allen 2001, 4; Holmyard [1957] 1990, 15).

Although the efforts to find the philosopher's stone were *mostly* unsuccessful,[4] regents continued to patronize alchemists until the end of the seventeenth century and, in France, even beyond that time (Debus 1988). Royal support thereafter declined, even though some leading scientists such as Isaac Newton and Robert Boyle continued to believe in the possibility of transmutation. I will argue that the loss of interest by crowned heads was due in part to the emergence of plausible credit-money schemes. Credit-money is paper secured by an asset such as land or, as in the case of the Bank of England, designated tax and customs receipts. Previous credit instruments, such as bills of exchange and promissory notes, had served as *means of exchange*, which meant that they mediated transactions, but a subsequent transaction was required to clear the credit extended. These instruments required a great deal of trust

3. George Ripley dedicated *The Compound of Alchemy; or the Twelve Gates Leading to the Discovery of the Philosopher's Stone* to Edward IV (White 1997, 115).

4. Numerous accounts of successful transmutations circulated during the seventeenth century. The most famous and well-respected account was reported by J. F. Helvetius, physician to the Prince of Orange (Holmyard [1957] 1990, 259–67). Benedict de Spinoza was one of the many who visited Helvetius to hear about the reported event (Gabbey 1996, 151). Another famous "success story" was Robert Boyle's destruction of gold—an accomplishment equaling that of the creation of gold ("As the saying goes, *Facilius est aurum construere quam destruere*, it is easer to make gold than to destroy it" [Doberer 1948, 167]).

and confidence to be functional, and therefore they could only circulate within close-knit groups, such as a merchant community. Credit-money, on the other hand, served as *means of payment* and had the capacity to circulate widely. These paper notes were wholly or partially convertible into assets or income streams designated as security. As such, they could fully complete a transaction and serve as a store of value, and not just as a temporary credit. Nevertheless, even though credit-money was backed by a security, uncertainties remained. For example, promised tax streams might be diverted, or, as in John Law's scheme, the public's notion of the value of the security might become unrealistically high (or low). Although suggestions for a public bank and credit-money began circulating in England as early as the 1650s, it was not until the 1690s, during the financial revolution, that the first developed system of credit-money became operational (Horsefield 1960). This system was based on the idea that the newly formed Bank of England would take over state debt on advantageous terms and issue new notes against promised interest payments from parliament. The scheme was limited but worked well—a success, I suggest, that may go far toward accounting for the rapid decline in the support for alchemy in European courts. This transition from alchemy to credit was swift and complete, perhaps nowhere more dramatically evidenced than in the Duke of Orleans's dismissal of his court alchemists in favor of John Law's land-backed paper currency (Kerschagl 1973, 64).[5]

What we observe here might be interpreted as a temporal displacement: paper money superseded the search for alchemical gold. Whether this was a necessary switch is not my concern here. What I do wish to explore is whether the alchemical tradition conditioned the way early credit-money proposals were viewed and discussed. My topic therefore is the way this particular economic notion was situated amid alchemical practice and thinking.

The possible connections between alchemical concerns and interest in credit-money have not been explored by either economic historians or historians of science, despite excellent studies on credit-money alone and a recent spate of interest in alchemy.[6] While the intellectual influences

5. For an analysis of John Law and his system, see Murphy 1997.

6. To date, all important accounts of the financial revolution have left the connection between alchemy and credit-money untapped. This may be attributed to the fact that few major studies of the financial revolution focus on the general intellectual and philosophical context or to the fact that most scholars (e.g., Peter Dickson [1967]) describe an abrupt revolution

alchemy (and more broadly, Renaissance hermeticism and mysticism) had on the seventeenth-century Scientific Revolution have been well documented,[7] the possible links between alchemy and economic ideas remain largely unexplored.[8] Toward closing this gap I shall present an overview of alchemical ideas (next section), then show by example, in the work of Johann Becher and Gerard de Malynes, how alchemy and reflections on the inadequacy of the coinage were intertwined. A more general, but also more telling context for exploring possible interactions is supplied by the Hartlib Circle. I will devote a whole section to it, following which I outline the replacement of alchemy by land banks and related schemes for credit-money, suggested by Samuel Hartlib and members of his circle. In a brief conclusion, I reconsider the nature of the connection between alchemy and credit-money in the seventeenth century.

Neo-Platonism and Baconianism

While legend suggests that alchemy originated with Hermes Trismegistus, the dominant strand of alchemical theory during the seventeenth century was influenced more directly by neo-Platonic thinkers such as Pico della Mirandola (1463–94), Cornelius Agrippa (1486–1535), and Paracelsus (1490–1541) (Rattansi 1972, 10; Henry 1990, 585). The neo-Platonic writers viewed the world as an incomplete creation, still in the process of evolving toward the perfection God had intended. This meant that nature and everything therein was alive and constantly growing, striving to attain the perfect form—acorns seeking to become oak trees and children trying to become adults. This vitalistic, organic, and animistic conceptualization of nature was combined with the idea that all parts of nature are interconnected and in harmony with the celestial

---

occurring in the 1690s, a Genesis-like beginning to a new era. Some scholars, such as Keith Horsefield (1960) and Henry Roseveare (1991), suggest that the financial revolution was less of a discontinuity and that the seeds of the transition were planted as early as the 1650s. However, while the latter two studies take a longer historical perspective, their focus is exclusively on earlier attempts to establish credit-money in England and not on the greater intellectual and philosophical climate within which credit-money developed.

7. The influence of alchemy on the development of Boyle's and Newton's scientific work has been well documented in, for example, Dobbs 1975, Westfall 1980, and Principe 1998.

8. A partial exception is Pamela Smith's (1994) analysis of how Johann Becher's interest in alchemy influenced his economic doctrines. Levin (2000) and Nummedal (2002) have also discussed the relationship between alchemy and the world of commerce.

sphere. Changes in the macrocosm (universe) were consequently believed to influence changes in the microcosm (humankind and nature), implying that "knowledge about, or control of, one thing could be gleaned by study and manipulation of other things even though they might be as remote as a flower or a star" (Henry 1990, 584).

The neo-Platonic tradition inherited the Aristotelian notion that all substances in nature are comprised of varying proportions of the four primary matters—fire, air, water, and earth. This meant that any substance could be transmuted into any other substance by altering the proportion of these matters. Minerals and metals were also comprised of the four matters, but their immediate constituents were two exhalations—earthly smoke and watery vapor—formed within the earthly womb. As Allison Coudert (1980, 21) puts it, "The earthly smoke consisted of small particles of earth on their way to becoming fire, while the watery vapour was made up of particles of water in the process of turning into air." The two exhalations were considered "philosophical sulphur and mercury," the relative proportions of which determined whether a metal obtained perfection—gold—or became a base metal—silver, copper, mercury, tin, iron, or lead.[9] Since all substances strove for perfection, the life cycle of metals—birth, maturity, marriage, copulation, reproduction, and death—was dictated by a teleological evolution toward purity. These transformations took place within the womb of the earth as a result of heat and pressure and the celestial influence of the stars.[10] As evidence and proof of life and regeneration in the mineral kingdom, the neo-Platonic writers pointed to the treelike growth patterns of metal ores (the so-called Tree of Diana) and to the reports of new silver discoveries in previously depleted mines (Debus 1988, 234).

The search for the secret source-code of the nature-universe complex was pursued through the art of alchemy. Once in possession of the philosopher's stone, the alchemist would not only command an understanding of nature's deepest secrets, but would also be able to turn base metals into gold and have access to eternal youth. The alchemists utilized their neo-Platonic understanding of nature and the universe to "harness the powers inherent in nature" (Henry 1990, 584) and to mimic nature's own processes and thus increase the pace of its natural transformations. Alchemists interested in obtaining gold sought to hasten the

9. Sulfur was the masculine and mercury the female force, their union leading to a more noble offspring (Merchant 1980, 26–28).

10. Considering that the sun and the moon symbolized sulfur and mercury respectively, their positions were of particular importance.

combination and birth of the living metals in the artificial womb of the furnace and speed up the ripening of base metals into gold. They tried to duplicate nature's own mechanisms and therefore paid close attention to the proper proportion between "philosophical sulphur and mercury," the appropriate heat of the furnace, and the most favorable alignment of the stars. Thus alchemists had to possess both technical and experimental proficiency, as well as a spiritual understanding, to be able to enter into the nature-universe relationship and expedite its natural transformations.

The alchemical understanding of the nature-universe relationship and man's role therein was an important stage in the development of the modern scientific tradition. Charles Webster (1982, 58) points out that the neo-Platonists played an important role in transcending fatalism and investing humans with the capacity to alter and manipulate the nature-universe relationship for their own benefit. Within this framework, the understanding of the natural and cosmic forces "could be turned to operative effect, opening up for man the possibility of achieving by natural means what had hitherto been regarded as miraculous. . . . All of this was to be attained by the skillful assistance, imitation, or direction of nature." Francis Bacon later formalized this idea that nature should be controlled and instrumentalized for the benefit of mankind. Refusing to work within the parameters set by the neo-Platonic nature-universe complex, Bacon advocated that humans should emancipate themselves from nature so that they may restore their dominion over creation and ensure that nature takes orders from humans and works under their authority.[11] This was the idea of the "Great Instauration" and had a profound influence upon seventeenth-century English science (Eamon 1994, 321).

While the alchemical tradition served as an important inspiration to Bacon (Rossi 1978; Henry 1997, 47), the influence also ran in the opposite direction. Whereas many of the sixteenth-century alchemists clouded their experiments in secrecy and sought the philosopher's stone for their own personal enrichment or salvation, the seventeenth-century alchemical tradition looked to establish a collaborative project in hopes of finding a new mechanism that could contribute to the transmutation of nature and society. Bacon's aim was to usher in a new era of social

11. Christopher Hill (1972, 288) points out that Bacon "had been inspired by the Hermetic religio-social ideal of controlling nature. Although he rejected the superstitious claims of magic and astrology . . . he thought they contained a core of knowledge about the physical universe which could be used."

progress through improvements in husbandry, medicine, metallurgy, education, industry, and trade. Although largely ignored during his lifetime, the Baconian research agenda was popularized during the 1640s, as a spirit of Puritan reformism enveloped England.[12] The most prominent and extensive application of Bacon's methodology was undertaken by the Hartlib Circle—the immediate precursor to the Royal Society. However, before I inquire into how the Hartlib Circle combined alchemy with Baconianism in pursuit of social and economic improvement, I consider two instances of linkages between the alchemical tradition and the discourse and policy concerns of political economists.

Alchemy and the Economy

Let us first consider Johann Becher, an alchemist, physician, and economic advisor to Leopold I who wrote several treatises on both alchemical theory and political economy. As an economic consultant, Becher promoted numerous ambitious projects such as the colonization of Guyana, industrialization of Austria, construction of a Rhine-Danube canal, and establishment of a state-funded chemistry/alchemy laboratory (Magnusson 1994, 193–95; Hutchison 1988, 91–93).[13] In his scientific pursuits, he was well regarded throughout Europe, enjoying the respect of Robert Boyle, Henry Oldenburg, Samuel Hartlib, and Gottfried Leibniz, among others.[14]

12. Eamon (1994, 324) points out that "since Bacon had developed his philosophy within the context of speculation about humanity's Fall, the Puritans found his views to be particularly congenial to their reform program."

13. Becher firmly believed in the social utility of alchemy, and while serving as an advisor to Leopold I, he designed and managed an alchemical laboratory. He argued that alchemy, if used wisely, had the capacity of achieving numerous political and social ends. Not only would it solidify the regent's domestic authority, but it would also facilitate the "extension of Christianity, suppression of traditional enemies . . . , relief of the subjects from heavy head and ground taxes, assistance of the poor, of the widowed, of orphaned and unmarried women, protection of the land and its people, and preservation of peace" (Becher quoted in Smith 1994, 213).

14. After Becher moved to England in 1679, he "had considerable alchemical interactions" with Boyle. In fact, Becher's posthumous *Alphabetum Minerale* was dedicated to Boyle (Principe 1998, 112–13). Oldenburg, later secretary to the Royal Society, met Becher during his travels on the Continent. In letters to Hartlib, Oldenburg praises Becher for his ingenuity and his inventions, in particular a perpetual motion clock and an underwater ship (Smith 1994, 60–61). Leibniz and Becher had a long-standing relationship in which they exchanged ideas on numerous topics. According to Smith, "Leibniz was fascinated, even obsessed, by Becher's activities, and saw no boundary between his own sphere and that of Becher" (247).

Becher set out to transform the negative attitudes in the Holy Roman Empire toward commerce and merchants as unproductive and a drain on society's resources (Smith 1991, 202). In his social theory, he reconceptualized the body politic as centered on the merchant, who functions as a catalyst for wealth creation. Becher proclaimed that commerce had the capacity to enrich both the sovereign and people, transcending the cameralist zero-sum relationship between the regent and the tax-paying subjects. Commerce was considered a "new source of income that would not constitute a tax on anyone but, instead, would be part of a natural, productive cycle that resulted in material increase in the form of money" (Smith 1994, 128). In his economic theory, Becher proposed something else that was distinctive, namely, that consumption is a stimulus to production. In order for this circuit to function smoothly, however, sufficient money had to be in circulation. Becher (quoted in Magnusson 1994, 195) viewed money as "the soul and nerve of the country" and thought that an increase in the quantity of money had the capacity to further expand expenditures and thus production.[15] An increase in demand would make peasants more industrious, and the presence of merchants would provide them with an outlet for their expanded output, thus bringing even more money into the country. Supplementing this idea of a net inward transfer through positive trade balances, Becher also suggested that the regent should pursue alchemy in order to directly increase his treasure and add to the money in circulation.[16] Becher did not perceive a Midas problem associated with alchemical success, such as hyperinflation from the circulation of too much gold. Instead, he suggested that "great lords can never have too much money, and if they had too much, they have a hundred opportunities to use it" (Becher quoted in Smith 1994, 241).

Becher also hints at a link between alchemy and paper money on more than one occasion. Referring to the seventeenth-century Dutch financial system, Becher noted that "credit, banknotes and hard cash [gold] are transmuted into each other every hour" (133). When elaborating on the advantages of knowing the secret of transmuting base metals into gold, he remarks that the regent "needs no letters of exchange because a little powder is enough to tincture a large amount" (Smith 1994, 216). As such, alchemy "is securer and richer than mines or exchange banks, and

15. This theoretical position earned him scorn from Joseph Schumpeter (1954, 283), who included Becher in a group of thinkers who "would as soon have doubted that they got wet when it rained as that more money spelled more profit and more employment."

16. Becher also proposed the creation of workhouses and the support of new manufactures to encourage exports and thus attract more money from abroad (Smith 1994, 190–92).

it alone will return the cost of the project" (Smith 1994, 216). Though these may be no more than hints that alchemical and paper-money means of expanding the circulation are substitutes, the example of Becher does show that the concept of paper money appears within a discourse that also embraced alchemy.

Gerard de Malynes was another social reformer inspired by neo-Platonic and Baconian themes who conceived of money within an alchemical framework.[17] A merchant, autodidact, part-time spy, assay-master, and an author of six books on political economy (Finkelstein 2000, 26), Malynes wrote on numerous topics, including the ruinous effects of usury on the poor and the money exchangers' role in precipitating the disastrous economic depression of the 1620s (Supple 1959, 94–95; Appleby 1978, 70, 42). Malynes's writings are infused with a progressive ethos, advocating policies that he thought would benefit the poor while at the same time contributing to national prowess (Johnson [1937] 1965, 53).

Malynes's concern with the employment of the poor was an interest he shared with most of the early-seventeenth-century British "mercantilist" writers.[18] Malynes supported a number of policies that he thought would stimulate England's trade[19] and, like Becher, believed that an inflow of money would increase demand, lead to higher incomes, and generate more employment.[20] And, like many of his contemporaries, Malynes did not believe that an inflow of money would be nullified by a price increase and consequent outflow of money, but rather thought that the new money would be used as liquid capital for additional investments and therefore would increase employment.[21] He argued that money "containeth the Soule which infuseth life; for if Money be wanting, Trafficke doth decrease, although commodities be aboundant and

17. Becher claimed Paracelsus and Francis Bacon as his primary intellectual influences (Smith 1994, 39).

18. Whereas Gustav Schmoller (1896) and Eli Hecksher (1955) suggested that the core of mercantilist doctrine concerned nation-building and state empowerment, Furniss ([1920] 1965), Johnson (1932), and Vickers ([1959] 1968) opined that the most salient common denominator, at least among the British "mercantilists," was the attempt to solve the so-called employment problem.

19. Malynes was in favor of the Cockayne-project; he argued for state-sponsored mining improvements, low-interest loans to the poor, new plantations, fisheries, and navigation improvements (Finkelstein 2000, 33).

20. Malynes ([1622] 1686, 37) assigned most of the blame for the 1620s economic crisis to the outflow of money: "The want of money . . . is the first cause of the decay of trade, for without money commodities are out of request."

21. J. D. Gould (1955, 125) has shown that there were compelling reasons for political economists during the first half of the seventeenth century to question the idea that "the volume

good cheape. . . . [However] if Moneys be plentifull, Commerce increaseth" (Malynes [1622] 1686, 177). While his primary policy suggestion was to reestablish the Royal Exchange in prevention of a continued outflow of money (Supple 1959, 94), his neo-Platonic understanding of metals and gold also favorably disposed him toward alchemy as a means to increase the quantity of money.

In his *Lex Mercatoria* ([1622] 1686, 181), Malynes posits an analysis of the essence of metals based on the alchemical theories of Paracelsus—"I have read all the Books of *Paracelsus*, that I could find hitherto."[22] In the spirit of the alchemical tradition, Malynes proposes that all "vegitable things" are constituted by a mix of the four elements, and all metals "have their beginning from Sulphur and Mercury" (179). The relative magnitude of sulfur and mercury and the conditions of its "birth" determine whether a base metal "grows" into gold. Malynes suggests that these two components,

> meeting and concurring together in the veines of the earth, doe ingender through the heat and qualitie of the Climate by an assiduall concoction, according to the nature of the earth wherein they meet, which produceth the diversitie of the mettalls of Gold, Silver, Copper, Tin, Lead, and Yron, in their several natures: and hereupon they have assigned them under their distinct Planets, to bee benevolent or malevolent; as Lead under *Saturne*, Tinne under *Jupiter*, Yron under *Mars*, Gold under *Sol*, Copper under *Venus*, Quicksilver under *Mercury*, and Silver under *Luna*. (179)

Since nature is continually working to "produce perfect things, but is hindered therein by accidentall causes" (178), it is therefore the philosopher's task to "perform that wherein Nature was hindered" (179) and produce that most perfect metal, gold. This requires the help of the "elixir or Quintescense. Hence proceedeth the studie of all the Philosophers to make their miraculous Stone, which I confesse is very pleasant, and full of expectations, when a man seeth the true and perfect transmutation of

---

of transactions of the country receiving the influx of bullion remained unchanged. This is precisely what did not happen in the case of the country whose success in attracting bullion it was the aim of the English Mercantilists to emulate. The Dutch contrived, in the very period in which they were regarded as the whirlpool into which the bullion of all nations was sucked, to maintain a stable or even falling level of prices."

22. Malynes had also studied the works of some later Paracelsian alchemists, such as George Ripley and Edward Kelley.

metals" (179). Malynes then gives an account (of which he has "been informed by a friend") of a German physician who successfully produced gold and became a very wealthy man, owning more than "one hundreth houses in that Citie before hee died" (180). Considering Malynes's views on transmutation in conjunction with his conviction that an increased circulation of gold has the capacity to expand trade and thus alleviate the underemployment situation, it seems plausible that he, like Becher, viewed alchemy as a possible solution to the shortage-of-money problem.

There were additional political economists during the first decades of the seventeenth century who, even though negatively disposed toward alchemy, nevertheless were influenced by the neo-Platonic worldview and addressed the issue of alchemy in their writings. For example, in his famous polemic with Malynes, Edward Misselden (1623) displayed a familiarity with neo-Platonic philosophy. In 1626, Robert Cotton ([1651] 1856) argued that British regents, in their patronage of alchemists, had corrupted the true measure and purity of money required to accurately express the wealth of the kingdom. Additionally, Rice Vaughan's *A Discourse of Coin and Coinage* (1675), written in the early 1630s, contains an attack on alchemists. To Vaughan, money was seen as useful because it has the capacity to translate all things to one. For this reason, he claimed that money "is not ill compared to the *Materia Prima*, because, though it serves actually to no use almost, it serves potentially to all uses" (10). The functionality of money was threatened by two related inconveniences, "*Rarity* and *Confusion*" (35). Confusion regarding the monetary standard arose from manipulation and abuse; those, in turn, generated outflows of money and thus a shortage of circulating coin. To Vaughan, even if the alchemists had only managed to show "that it is harder to destroy Gold than to make it" (11), they still constituted a possible threat to the solidity of money. Furthermore, the fact that they served as "foster Fathers" to the counterfeiters (55) made them guilty of contributing to the undermining of the monetary standard.[23]

23. This sentiment was echoed later during the coinage crisis of the 1690s by Joseph Aickin (1696, 4), who proclaimed that "the chief Cause of the prevailing of this Vice [counterfeiting], is the Study of *Experimental Philosophy, Alchimy*, and *Chymistry*, to which this Age is so much addicted, that almost all other Learning is despised; and when our *Chymist* has spent all his Estate in endeavouring to find out the *Philosophers Stone*, but instead thereof, finds little else but broken Pots and Glasses, with the consumption of a good Estate; afterwards, for a Livelyhood, he falls to Counterfeiting the Coin of the Nation."

The examples of Becher and Malynes show that prominent thinkers of the seventeenth century considered alchemy as a possible way to expand the money stock and thus stimulate economic development. And the very fact that Cotton and Vaughan addressed alchemy in their writings adds further weight to my view that alchemy was important to the mid-seventeenth-century discourse about the circulation of money. It was within this intellectual context that the Hartlib Circle set out to combine their neo-Platonic worldview with the Baconian scientific methodology in a search for new ways to ameliorate the currency crisis.

The Hartlib Circle

Arguably the most influential disseminator of the Baconian research project was the Hartlib Circle. With an emphasis on the operative aspects of Paracelsian alchemy and the Baconian instrumentalization of nature, the Hartlib Circle initiated a massive collaborative effort to apply scientific knowledge to the improvement of social and economic conditions.[24] The reform projects of the Hartlibians were indeed ambitious, much in the spirit of the radical reform movement that spread throughout England during the 1640s (Jacob 1997, 53–55). As Charles Webster (1974, 379) observes, "by the intelligent cultivation of science the nation was offered a solution for unemployment, prosperity in its colonies, even wealth based on mining precious metals and the transmutation of base metals into gold." In addition to the Prussian émigré Samuel Hartlib, the circle consisted of a variety of alchemists/chemists, physicians, and political economists, including Robert Boyle, Kenelm Digby, John Dury, Henry Oldenburg, William Petty, Gabriel Plattes, Henry Robinson, George Starkey, and Benjamin Worsley. The Hartlib circle, or the "invisible college," as it was also known, served as a link between Gresham College—the first systematic effort in England to apply scientific lessons to the practical affairs of the state and the demands of commercial expansion[25]—and the Royal Society, which, at its inception, emphasized

24. Webster (1970, 3) suggests that Hartlib "shared Bacon's confidence that a great co-operative effort to marshal empirical knowledge would lead to an intellectual regeneration, a return of man's dominion over nature which had been sacrificed at the Fall." Hill (1972, 288) suggests similarly that "Bacon's influence was spread wide in England after 1640, thanks especially to the exertions of Samuel Hartlib. . . . The fusion of Baconianism and Hermetic natural philosophy laid great emphasis on the social and democratic possibilities of the new science."

25. Gresham College was founded with money from Sir Thomas Gresham and received funds from merchants in the Muscovy and East India Companies (Kearney [1964] 1974, 231).

the practical application of science to problems encountered in industry, commerce, and colonization.[26] The notion of transmutation played a prominent role, both practically and metaphorically, in the Hartlib Circle's project to solve the problem of underemployment. Their vision of social change was guided by the goal of increasing society's productivity by mobilizing and activating hidden or underutilized resources.

In the 1641 pamphlet *A Description of the Famous Kingdome of Macaria*, long attributed to Hartlib,[27] Gabriel Plattes proposed a plan to the Long Parliament, "whereby the Kingdome may maintain double the number of people, which it doth now, and in more plenty and prosperity, than now they enjoy" (11). The cornerstone of this plan was to "shew the transmutation of sublunary bodies, in such manner, that any man may be rich that will be industrious" (11). The Hartlibian social reform program was based on the precocious idea that the poor were capable of improvement through education[28] and hard work.[29] Only then would the idlers become "serviceable to the Common-wealth, by reforming their ungodly life" (Hartlib 1650, 10).[30] But perhaps the greatest concern of the Hartlib Circle was the improvement of agricultural productivity through the application of science to seed refinement, fertilizers, plowing, planting, and livestock management, and through the enclosures of the commons, wastes, fens, and forests (Hartlib 1653a, 1655). These improvements, it was argued, would not only increase the yield of the land, but would also go a long way toward the amelioration of the underemployment problem—"where all hands are at work, there the

26. Webster (1982, 63) points out that initially "every effort was made to identify the Royal Society with the nation's economic interests, defence and imperial aspirations," though 'Espinasse ([1958] 1974, 350) informs us that the link between the Royal Society and industrial practices weakened toward the end of the century.

27. Webster ([1972] 1974) showed that the *Kingdome of Macaria* was in fact written by Gabriel Plattes. Nonetheless, Hartlib seems to have played a significant role in the development of the ideas proposed therein.

28. John Dury, Hartlib (1650), and William Petty (1648) made numerous proposals for the improvement and expansion of education, ranging from reforms in the teaching of languages and mathematics, to the mandatory education of poor children, emphasizing practical skills that would serve them (and the nation) as working adults.

29. Hartlib wanted to expand the role of workhouses in removing beggars, vagabonds, and idlers from the streets. In *London's Charity Inlarged*, Hartlib (1650, 9–10) suggests that all idle persons capable of working—the "sturdy-poor" —should be arrested and brought to workhouses, where they would be instructed in the Puritan gospel, taught rudimentary trade skills, and have the proper work ethic instilled.

30. The "incouragable" would be sent to the North American colonies, providing cheap labor to the settlers and relieving England of the burden of having to support them (Hartlib 1655).

whole strength of a Nation, doth put forth its endeavours, for its own advantage" (Hartlib 1653a, ii).[31]

Influenced by the French Paracelsian physician Theophraste Renaudot's *Bureau d'adress*—designed to communicate information regarding trade, manufacture, and employment—the Hartlib Circle organized their own Office of Address in 1647. The office was to serve as a clearinghouse for new ideas and information regarding "all things which are Usefull and profitable in a Common-wealth for Publick and Private Accomodation" (Hartlib [1647] 1970, 37–38). Hartlib hoped that the office would function according to the same principles as a merchant exchange, providing a formalized space for the dissemination and sharing of ideas and inventions with the capacity to improve society.[32]

The feasibility of the Hartlib Circle's programs ultimately depended upon the structure of the economy and the availability of funds to finance them. Hartlib (1655, 291) suggested that in order to expand trade, colonization, and fishing and to quicken land improvements, it was necessary "that people may know where to be furnished with stock at low interest, and that a sufficient quantity of currant money be disperced amongst them." For Hartlib, a shortage of circulating money was a major obstacle to the development of trade and employment. Like Becher and Malynes,[33] he suggested that an increase in the quantity of money would provide a stimulus to economic activity: "The more there is of money in any Nation, the quicker also must all those wayes be, wherein money is ordinarily imployed" (Hartlib 1653b, 28). Since the sole reason to hold money was as a means of exchange and as a store of value between sale and purchase, Hartlib (1655, 192) thought that an increase in the quantity of money would necessarily lead to an increase in the circulation of commodities. In turn, this would produce a domino effect, whereby "those who receive [the money] would be laying it out again upon others, and

31. For further elaboration on this facet of the Hartlib Circle, see Todd Lowry's article in this volume.

32. Hartlib ([1647] 1970, 41) writes, "The Advantages which Posthouses and Exchange-places since they have been in Use have brought unto those that trade, and to all Mens private dispatches are almost innumerable; but the Advantages, which such an Office [of Address] as this is, will bring to the Society of Mankind, will bee altogether innumerable; for all that which is good and desirable in a whole Kingdome may be by this means Communicated unto any one that stands in need thereof."

33. Malynes's *Lex Mercatoria* was reprinted numerous times during the seventeenth century, and it is clear that Hartlib read it, as he reprinted a segment from it in his *Reformed Commonwealth of the Bees* (1655) (Finkelstein 2000, 28).

those upon others, and so on, which would beget a constant return, or quick vent for commodities proportionable to the quantity of money so perpetually revolving amongst them." However, considering that England was operating under the discipline of a metallic standard and limited, if any, commodity surpluses, it was unable to attract a sufficient amount of money through positive trade balances. Yet more basic was the constraint that "there hath not bin (at least not yet) a sufficient quantity of either [gold or silver], to supply all Nations towards that increase of Trade, which a greater quantity of money (if it could be had) would produce" (Hartlib 1653b, 28).

The Hartlib Circle's search for an alternative source of money led them to undertake a large-scale alchemical project to transmute tin into gold. Benjamin Worsley, a social reformer who subscribed to the Hartlibian line regarding the link between the money supply and trade, was responsible for managing this project.[34] With the aid of Hartlib, he enlisted the support of the Dutch chemist Johann Morian and consulted the American alchemist George Starkey—one of the most influential alchemists of the middle decades of the seventeenth century[35] —and secured a £1,200-grant from an anonymous donor (Dobbs 1975, 73). Although Starkey had reportedly discovered a method of transmuting iron into gold, Worsley was unable to convince him to divulge his secret, and the gold-making venture consequently failed.[36] In 1653, Worsley wrote in a letter to Hartlib, "I have laid all considerations in chemistry aside, as things not reaching much above laborants, or strong-water distillers, unless we can arrive at this key" (quoted in Principe 1998, 33). And so the Hartlib Circle's most ambitious project to use alchemical knowledge for the purpose of producing gold to stimulate trade and employment came to an end.

34. Worsley "emerged as one of the leading proponents of Baconian experimental philosophy and of mercantilist economic policy of the mid-seventeenth century" (Webster 1994, 234). He claimed that his pamphlet *The Advocate* provided the analytical foundation for the Navigation Act (Letwin 1964, 17).

35. Starkey, also known as Eirenaeus Philalethes, was an intimate member of the Hartlib Circle from 1650 to 1653 and later had an important influence on both Boyle and Newton. For more on Starkey, see Wilkinson 1970.

36. Worsley tried to convince Starkey to actively join the project, but he refused. In a letter to Boyle, Starkey mentions that "some Gentlemen sollicite me to follow extractions of gold and silver out of antimony and iron, among whom Mr Worsley an ingenious Gentleman did much perswade" (quoted in Newman 1994, 201). Yet he refused to share the key secret to transmutation, saying that never "would I in such a way of lucre prostrate so great a secret as I judged the mercury of antimony to be" (202).

As the attempt to use alchemy to expand the money supply began to seem a hopeless enterprise, the Hartlib Circle developed an alternative strategy that seemed capable of generating the desired results. They proposed that the quantity of circulating money could be augmented by transmuting land into money—that is, by setting up a land bank that would issue credit-money on the security of land. "Credit grounded upon the best security is the same thing with Money," according to Hartlib (1655, 194). He continues, "that such Credit is as good as Money will appear if it be observed that Money it self is nothing else but a kind of securitie which men receive upon parting with their commodities, as a ground of hope or assurance that they shall be repayed in some other commoditie." As land is the most concrete and stable of commodities, there can be no better security than land to induce a person to part with their commodity in exchange. And, as opposed to alchemy, the goal of which was the transmutation of nature, credit-money required only the passive security of nature to generate additional money. Hence, for Hartlib, the organization of domestic trade around credit-money seemed perfectly sensible and practical.

The banking sector was the most appropriate institution for the development of this kind of credit-money scheme. However, Hartlib argued that the contemporary banking system had to be fundamentally restructured in order to issue credit-money. He pointed out that "banks, as they are now practiced, are nothing else in effect but places where men pawn or deposite their moneys for obtaining currant credit, as that which they may keep with lesse danger, and assign to another with lesse trouble" (295). Hence, while these deposit banks contributed to economic activity by facilitating and securing transactions, they fell short of adding to the circulation. For there to be a radical improvement in the economic well-being of the population, credit had to be available to all honest industrious men. In 1650 William Potter had proposed a scheme urging banks to add bills of exchange to the circulation. However, since the practice of honoring endorsed bills was well established only in the merchant community, this measure was incapable of providing a general relief. A further drawback of the existing setup was that the banks kept large deposits of gold and silver in their vaults, which, on the one hand, served as a constant temptation to the king, while, on the other hand, invested the owners of banks with the power to exercise undue authority over the commonwealth.[37] The most compelling reason for Hartlib's (1653b, 29)

37. Hartlib (1653b, 29) writes, "The money (deposited (as above mentioned) in any one place) proves, not onely a temptation to the sword (as lately in *Holland*) but . . . an invincible

criticism of deposit banks, however, was their inability to create "any new *Medium* of Commerce." Only if banks began issuing credit-money would the banking system be able to significantly contribute to a more elastic money supply and thus provide people with the requisite funds to undertake desired transactions. In particular, the establishment of a land bank would ensure that money

> 1. Shall be (at least) of as true intrinsick value, as Gold and Silver.
> 2. May be raised by this Common-wealth, within it self, without any parting with our Staple-Commodities for it. . . .
> 3. May be extended, to ten times more, then ever this Nation was owner of in money; to the incredible increase of in-land Commerce, and (consequently) of exportation and foreign Trade. (30)

Hartlib concludes, "It plainly appears that the way to remove Poverty, Taxes, and most publique grievances, and to make this Nation abound in Wealth, Trade, Cities, Shipping, People, and Renown" is to establish a land bank that would manage a system of credit-money (30). Significant here is the commonality between the alleged benefits of Hartlib's credit-money scheme and those of Becher's alchemy project.

We see in the Hartlib Circle an instance of credit-money superseding alchemy as the preferred mechanism for artificially expanding the money stock. Conceptual links between the two, however, remain elusive. It is conceivable, especially during a period when the shortage of money was viewed as the cause of most economic ills, that social reformers considering alchemy as a way to expand the money supply became more cognizant of the benefits of autonomous control over the monetary mechanism. Perhaps this thinking motivated members of the Hartlib Circle and others to search for alternatives to alchemy when it seemed as if transmutation was unobtainable. It is also plausible that the idea of a credit-money system was influenced by the alchemical tradition's concern with activating the hidden or passive powers and energies of nature, which, when combined with the Baconian quest to gain operational control over nature, provided a framework within which to conceive of monetary schemes of various sorts. By monetizing land and other assets,

---

opportunity, (in the hand of the possessor) against the State or Common-wealth in which such Banks are kept."

the mid-seventeenth-century reformers believed that they could activate and mobilize society's available resources and idle labor power, and thus contribute to increased employment and prosperity. Hence, there are numerous possible links between alchemy and credit-money, ranging from a common metaphor to a shared conceptual structure. The latter link is certainly a distinct possibility, particularly since the disciplinary boundaries between science and political economy had not yet been formed and philosophers and social reformers often shared approaches, models, and insights. However, it is also possible that there were no links between alchemy and credit-money schemes, each being just a distinct solution to a common problem.

Nonetheless, Hartlib Circle member Henry Robinson takes us a step closer to concluding that there was indeed a conceptual link. In a 1652 pamphlet he advocated for the creation of a merchant bank that would issue promissory notes for domestic circulation. In making the case, Robinson explicitly linked credit-money to alchemy. Although his proposed merchant bank did not have the capacity to expand the money supply to the same extent as did Hartlib's land bank, its credit-money would nevertheless add a dimension of elasticity to the monetary system. It was this self-generating capacity of credit-money that led Robinson (1652, 19) to compare it to an alchemical transmutation and suggest that credit-money is "capable of multiplying the stock of the nation, for as much as concerns trading in infinitum [*sic*]." Then, in no uncertain words, he proclaims that credit-money "is the Elixir or Philosopher's Stone." Robinson was by no means the first person to make this conceptual connection—Marco Polo had done so some four centuries earlier.[38] But what makes this comment remarkable is the fact that Robinson was a close friend of Hartlib and the manager of Hartlib's Office of Address. Moreover, he made this comparison in 1652, the very year in which Benjamin Worsley was involved in his gold-making project and Hartlib was working out his own proposal for a credit-money system. The timing and Robinson's intellectual associations argue strongly for his having been fully aware of the circle's physical experiments with alchemy and of their conceptual investigations of credit-money. In this light, Robinson's comparison of his credit-money scheme to the transmutation of base metals into gold takes on a particularly suggestive character, implying that the

38. In describing the Great Kahn's paper-money system, Marco Polo (1982, 125) suggested "that you might well say that he has mastered the art of alchemy."

Hartlib Circle indeed perceived of a conceptual proximity and functional similarity between alchemy and credit-money.

The Continued Influence of the Hartlib Circle

The Hartlib Circle gradually disintegrated toward the end of the 1650s and then ceased to exist after the Restoration when Hartlib's writings—associated with Civil War radicalism–fell out of favor with the political establishment.[39] In subsequent years, the still-active members of the circle joined the newly founded Royal Society.[40] Although no banking system with circulating credit-money was established until the 1690s, there was no shortage of creative bank proposals from the 1660s onward (Horsefield 1960, 93–103). Hartlib's own land-bank proposal survived through the work of William Petty—a longtime member of the Hartlib Circle—who shared the Hartlibian concern with finding a solution to the underemployment problem. Seeking to establish a mechanism whereby the money supply could be expanded, Petty ([1682] 1856, 165) proclaimed that "we must erect a Bank, which well computed, doth almost double the Effect of our coined Money: And we have in *England* Materials for a Bank which shall furnish Stock enough to drive the Trade of the whole Commercial World." So-called Lombard banks would issue credit-money, based on the security of "Metals, Cloth, Linnen, Leather, and other Usefuls," which would mediate medium-sized transactions, while credit-money from land banks would mediate the higher-valued transactions (Petty 1662, 18). Petty's argumentation for why a land bank provides a more secure currency than gold and silver closely resembles that of Hartlib. For example, Petty (1927, 78) suggests that land "shall not only become as money, but as a Bank of money, which is farr more safe and commodious than coynes."

Hartlib also had an indirect influence, through Petty, on the principal architect of the first land bank in England—Nicholas Barbon.[41] Barbon collaborated with John Asgill to set up a land bank in 1695 that issued

39. Webster (1970, 64) points out that Hartlib's writings were discredited along with "other reform movements, such as the Leveller tracts and the works of Winstanley."

40. The Hartlib Circle members who joined the Royal Society were Robert Boyle, Kenelm Digby, Henry Oldenburg, and William Petty (Mulligan [1973] 1974, 342–46).

41. Finkelstein (2000, 211–15) asserts that the link between Hartlib and Barbon was more direct than here indicated. Although she has no specific evidence, she argues persuasively that Barbon was influenced by the neo-Platonic philosophy that Hartlib was so instrumental in spreading throughout the intellectual circles of England.

notes backed by the security of land. For a moment it seemed as if the land bank would be elevated to a national bank, similar to the recently established Bank of England, but the credit crunch generated by William's war on France, the rampant clipping, coupled with the destabilizing recoinage of 1695,[42] prevented the land bank from materializing (Letwin 1964, 58–59). Barbon, like Malynes, Hartlib, and Petty before him, subscribed to the notion that an increase in the quantity of circulating money had the capacity to stimulate trade and employment. In addition, he argued that money could consist of more or less any material: "It is not absolutely necessary, Mony should be made of Gold or Silver; for having its sole Value from the Law, it is not Material upon what Metal the Stamp be set. Mony hath the same Value, and performs the same Uses, if it be made of Brass, Copper, Tin, or any thing else" (Barbon [1690], 6). While it was immaterial whether money consisted of metal or paper, the proper management of the quantity of it in circulation was of paramount importance. Of course the benefit of using credit-money was to gain the power to expand the money supply when appropriate; but success depended on the issuing authority maintaining the strictest discipline. For this reason, it was therefore seen as important that the quantity of money was anchored in land—the most "real" security available. In elaborating on this notion, Barbon suggests that an undisciplined issuance of credit-money is tantamount to alchemical secrets falling into the wrong hands:

> How greatly would those Gentlemen be disappointed, that are searching after the Philosopher's Stone, if they should at last happen to find it? For, if they should make but so great a Quantity of Gold and Silver, as they, and their Predecessors have spent in search after it, it would so alter, and bring down the Price of those Metals, that it might be a Question, whether they would get so much Over-plus by it, as would pay for the Metal they change into Gold and Silver. It is only the Scarcity that keeps up the Value, and not any Intrinsick Vertue or Quality in the Metals. (7)

Here, Barbon reflects the contemporary perspective on alchemy as he ponders runaway credit. Although the scientific community was still selectively willing to believe in the possibility of transmutation, most had come to deemphasize the capacity of alchemy to solve the shortage of

42. For a discussion of clipping and counterfeiting in the 1690s, see Wennerlind 2004.

money problem.[43] Perhaps due to the Hartlib Circle's arguments that credit-money was a far more expedient system than alchemy for expanding the money stock, alchemical research came to focus more on the capacity of alchemy to generate new medicines and reveal insights into the relationship between matter and spirit (Dobbs 1975; Westfall 1980; Hunter 1990; Principe 1998). While the need for an elastic money supply had now fully entered the mainstream discussion, credit-money, not alchemy, was considered the only appropriate solution. The introduction of credit-money mirrored the transition toward a mechanical worldview, in which humans had claimed center stage. The economy had now been emancipated from the neo-Platonic nature-universe complex, and humankind had acquired the power to manage and control its own affairs. However, this Faustian bargain was not without risks or temptations. Although credit-money had the capacity to increase trade and thus ameliorate the underemployment problem, if misused, it was capable of undermining the basis of the entire society. While the link between alchemy and credit-money became more tenuous after the early success of the financial revolution, the credit crisis associated with the South Sea bubble later reaffirmed the connection. Let the following street ballad about the South Sea crisis serve as a brief exemplification:

> Tis said that Alchemists of old,
> Could turn a brazen kettle,
> Or leaden Cistern into Gold,
> That noble, tempting Mettle:
> But, if it here may be allowed
> To bring in great with small things
> Our cunning South Sea, like a God,
> Turns nothing into all things.
> (Ashton [1898] 1969, 252; also quoted in Caffentzis 2000, 39)

Conclusion

Seventeenth-century alchemists were convinced that they had the capacity to operate on the organic world and hasten its natural tendency toward perfection. In the realm of metallurgy, this meant transmuting base

43. John Locke exemplifies this divide. While he believed in the feasibility of transmutation, at least until 1692 (Cranston 1957, 361), he referred sarcastically to those who "intend to set up for the Philosophers Stone" to expand the money stock (Locke 1691, 128).

metals into gold. The promise of alchemy appealed to many of the period's political economists, who theorized that an increase in the money stock would translate into expanded commerce and thus provide a solution to the underemployment problem. On direct or indirect advice from these political economists, most European regents continued their patronage of alchemists. However, as the practice of transmutation proved insurmountably difficult, an interest developed in credit-money as an alternative method of expanding the money stock. The Hartlib Circle exemplified this transition. Having already tried alchemy, but without noteworthy success, they began advocating for a system of credit-money backed by the security of land. Although the circle's proposal was not implemented, the ideas appear to have encouraged later thinkers to continue to explore and advocate for a system of credit-money. In the 1690s, the Bank of England finally engineered a system of credit-money. The success of this system coincided with (or caused) a rapid decline in royal support for alchemy, elevating credit-money to the status of sole tried and reasonably successful mechanism for the expansion of the money stock. Hence, while the prospect of expanding the money stock at will might have been conceived initially in alchemical terms, it only materialized in the form of credit-money. While the precise connection between alchemy and credit-money is difficult to establish with any exactitude, I have argued that the link transcends coincidence and that the alchemical tradition in fact influenced and framed the conceptual development of credit-money.

Francis Bacon ([1620] 2000, 71) descriptively and prophetically suggested that the primary utility of the alchemical tradition was that it sparked numerous useful inventions. He writes, "It must not be denied that alchemists have discovered quite a few things, and given men useful discoveries. They fit quite well in the story of the old man who left his daughters some gold buried in a vineyard and pretended not to know the exact spot; as a result of which they set themselves to dig diligently in that vineyard; and no gold was found, but the harvest was richer for the cultivation." In a similar vein, we may think of credit-money as an unintended consequence of the alchemical tradition. Considering that the credit-money system greatly contributed to England's transmutation from weak nation-state to an empire and industrial center, this by-product of alchemy is particularly noteworthy. As such, this essay has suggested that just as alchemy contributed importantly to the Scientific

Revolution, the alchemical tradition also contributed, in a meaningful manner, to the financial revolution.

References

Aickin, Joseph. 1696. *The Mysteries of the Counterfeiting of the Coin of the Nation, Fully Detected and Methods Humbly Offered to Both Houses of Parliament.* London: William Downing.

Åkerman, Susanna. 1991. *Queen Christina of Sweden and Her Circle: The Transformation of a Philosophical Libertine.* Leiden: Brill.

Allen, Larry. 2001. *Encyclopedia of Money.* New York: Checkmark Books.

Appleby, Joyce. 1978. *Economic Thought and Ideology in Seventeenth-Century England.* Princeton, N.J.: Princeton University Press.

Ashton, John. [1898] 1969. *The History of Gambling in England.* Montclair, N.J.: Patterson Smith.

Bacon, Francis. [1620] 2000. *The New Organon.* Cambridge: Cambridge University Press.

Barbon, Nicholas. [1690]. *A Discourse on Trade.* London: Milbourn.

Binswanger, Hans Christoph. 1994. *Money and Magic: A Critique of the Modern Economy in the Light of Goethe's* Faust. Chicago: University of Chicago Press.

Bonny, Richard. 1991. *The European Dynastic States, 1494–1660.* Oxford: Oxford University Press.

Braddick, Michael. 2000. *State Formation in Early Modern England: c. 1550–1700.* Cambridge: Cambridge University Press.

Brewer, John. 1989. *The Sinews of Power: War, Money, and the English State, 1688–1783.* New York: Knopf.

Briggs, Robin. 1991. The Académie Royale des Sciences and the Pursuit of Utility. *Past and Present* 131:38–87.

Caffentzis, George. 2000. *Exciting the Industry of Mankind: George Berkeley's Philosophy of Money.* Dordrecht: Kluwer.

Cotton, Robert. [1651] 1856. *A Speech Made by Sir Robert Cotton, Before the Lords of His Majesty's most Honourable Privy Council.* In McCulloch 1856.

Coudert, Allison. 1980. *Alchemy: The Philosopher's Stone.* Boulder, Colo.: Shambala.

Cranston, Maurice. 1957. *John Locke: A Biography.* New York: Macmillan.

Davies, Glyn. 1994. *A History of Money: From Ancient Times to the Present Day.* Cardiff: University of Wales Press.

Debus, Allan. 1988. Alchemy in an Age of Reason: The Chimical Philosophers in Early Eighteenth-Century France. In *Hermeticism and the Renaissance: Intellectual History and the Occult in Early Modern Europe*, edited by I. Merkel and A. Debus. Cranbury: Associated University Presses.

De Vries, Jan. 1976. *The Economy of Europe in an Age of Crisis: 1600–1750.* Cambridge: Cambridge University Press.

Dickson, P. G. M. 1967. *The Financial Revolution in England: A Study in the Development of Public Credit, 1688–1756*. London: Macmillan.

Dobbs, Betty Jo Teeter. 1975. *The Foundations of Newton's Alchemy or "The Hunting of the Greene Lyon."* Cambridge: Cambridge University Press.

Doberer, K. K. 1948. *The Goldmakers: Ten Thousand Years of Alchemy*. London: Nicholson & Watson.

Eamon, William. 1994. *Science and the Secrets of Nature: Books of Secrets in Medieval and Early Modern Culture*. Princeton, N.J.: Princeton University Press.

'Espinasse, Margaret. [1958] 1974. The Decline and Fall of Restoration Science. In Webster 1974.

Evans, R. J. W. 1973. *Rudolf II and His World: A Study in Intellectual History, 1576–1612*. Oxford: Clarendon Press.

Finkelstein, Andrea. 2000. *Harmony and the Balance: An Intellectual History of Seventeenth-Century English Economic Thought*. Ann Arbor, Mich.: University of Michigan Press.

Furniss, Edgar. [1920] 1965. *The Position of the Laborer in a System of Nationalism: A Study in the Labor Theories of the Later English Mercantilists*. New York: Kelley.

Gabbey, Alan. 1996. Spinoza's Natural Science and Methodology. In *The Cambridge Companion to Spinoza*, edited by D. Garrett. Cambridge: Cambridge University Press.

Goethe, Johann Wolfgang Von. [1808] 1976. *Faust: A Tragedy*. Translated by W. Arndt. New York: Norton.

Gould, J. D. 1955. The Trade Crisis of the Early 1620s and English Economic Thought. *Journal of Economic History* 15:121–33.

Hartlib, Samuel. 1650. *London's Charity Inlarged, Stilling the Orphans Cry*. London: Symmons and Ibbintson.

———. 1653a. *A Discoverie For Division or Setting out of Land, as to the best Form*. London: Richard Wodenothe.

———. 1653b. *An Essay upon Master W. Potters Designe: Concerning a Bank of Lands to be erected throughout this Common-Wealth*. London: Richard Wodenothe.

———. 1655. *Legacy of Husbandry*. London: Richard Wodenothe.

———. [1647] 1970. Considerations Tending to the Happy Accomplishment of England's Reformation. In Webster 1970.

Hecksher, Eli. 1955. *Mercantilism*. London: Allen and Unwin.

Henry, John. 1990. Magic and Science in the Sixteenth and Seventeenth Centuries. In *Companion to the History of Modern Science*, edited by R. C. Olby et al. London: Routledge.

———. 1997. *The Scientific Revolution and the Origins of Modern Science*. New York: St. Martin's Press.

Hill, Christopher. 1972. *The World Turned Upside Down: Radical Ideas during the English Revolution*. London: Penguin.

Holmyard, E. J. [1957] 1990. *Alchemy*. New York: Dover.

Horsefield, Keith. 1960. *British Monetary Experiments: 1650–1710*. London: Bell.

Hunter, Michael. 1990. Alchemy, Magic, and Moralism in the Thought of Robert Boyle. *British Journal for the History of Science* 23:387–410.

Hutchison, Terence. 1988. *Before Adam Smith: The Emergence of Political Economy, 1662–1776*. Oxford: Basil Blackwell.

Jacob, Margaret. 1997. *Scientific Culture and the Making of the Industrial West*. Oxford: Oxford University Press.

Johnson, E. A. J. 1932. Unemployment and Consumption: The Mercantilist View. *Quarterly Journal of Economics* 46:698–719.

———. [1937] 1965. *Predecessors of Adam Smith: The Growth of British Economic Thought*. New York: Kelley.

Kearney, H. F. [1964] 1974. Puritanism, Capitalism, and the Scientific Revolution. In Webster 1974.

Kerschagl, Richard. 1973. *Die Jagd Nach dem Künstlichen Gold: Der Weg der Alchemie*. Berlin: Duncher.

Letwin, William. 1964. *The Origins of Scientific Economics*. Garden City, N.Y.: Doubleday.

Levin, John. 2000. The Meanings of Gold: Alchemy and Economy in Seventeenth-Century England. Unpublished paper.

Locke, John. 1691. *Some Considerations of the Consequences of the Lowering of Interest and Raising the Value of Money*. London: Churchill.

Magnusson, Lars. 1994. *Mercantilism: The Shaping of an Economic Language*. London: Routledge.

Malynes, Gerard de. [1622] 1686. *Lex Mercatoria: or, the Ancient Law-Merchant*. London: Basset.

McCulloch, J. R., ed. 1856. *A Select Collection of Scarce and Valuable Tracts on Money*. London: Political Economy Club.

Merchant, Carolyn. 1980. *The Death of Nature: Women, Ecology, and the Scientific Revolution*. San Francisco: Harper.

Misselden, Edward. 1623. *The Circle of Commerce, or The Balance of Trade, in defence of free Trade*. London: Dawson.

Mulligan, Lotte. [1973] 1974. Civil War Politics, Religion, and the Royal Society. In Webster 1974.

Murphy, Antoine. 1997. *John Law: Economic Theorist and Policy-Maker*. Oxford: Oxford University Press.

Newman, William. 1994. George Starkey and the Selling of Secrets. In *Samuel Hartlib and Universal Reformation: Studies in Intellectual Communication*, edited by M. Greengrass, M. Leslie, and T. Raylor. Cambridge: Cambridge University Press.

Nummedal, Tara. 2002. Practical Alchemy and Commercial Exchange in the Holy Roman Empire. In *Merchants and Marvels: Commerce, Science, and Art in Early Modern Europe*, edited by P. Smith and P. Findlen. New York: Routledge.

Petty, William. 1648. *The Advice of W. P. to Mr. Samuel Hartlib for the Advancement of some particular Parts of Learning*. London.

———. 1662. *A Treatise of Taxes and Contributions*. London: Brooke.

———. [1682] 1856. Sir William Petty's Quantulumcunque Concerning Money. In McCulloch 1856.

———. 1927. *The Petty Papers*. 2 vols. Edited by the Marquis of Lansdowne. London: Constable.

Plattes, Gabriel. 1641. *A Description of the Famous Kingdome of Macaria*. London: Francis Constable.

Polo, Marco. 1982. *Travels of Marco Polo*. Translated by R. Latham. New York: Abaris Books.

Principe, Lawrence. 1998. *The Aspiring Adept: Robert Boyle and His Alchemical Quest*. Princeton, N.J.: Princeton University Press.

Rattansi, P. M. 1972. The Social Interpretation of Science in the Seventeenth Century. In *Science and Society, 1600–1900*, edited by P. Mathis. Cambridge: Cambridge University Press.

Robinson, Henry. 1652. *Certain Proposals in Order to the People's Freedom and Accomodation in some Particulars with the Advancement of Trade and Navigation of this Commonwealth in General*. London: M. Simmons.

Roseveare, Henry. 1991. *The Financial Revolution: 1660–1760*. London: Longman.

Rossi, Paolo. 1978. *Francis Bacon: From Magic to Science*. Chicago: University of Chicago Press.

Schmoller, Gustav. 1896. *The Mercantile System and Its Historical Significance*. New York: Macmillan.

Schumpeter, Joseph. 1954. *History of Economic Analysis*. New York: Oxford University Press.

Shell, Marc. 1982. *Money, Language, and Thought: Literary and Philosophical Economies from the Medieval to the Modern Era*. Berkeley, Calif.: University of California Press.

Smith, Pamela. 1991. Curing the Body Politic: Chemistry and Commerce at Court, 1664–70. In *Patronage and Institutions: Science, Technology, and Medicine at the European Court, 1500–1750*, edited by B. Moran. Rochester, N.Y.: Boydell Press.

———. 1994. *The Business of Alchemy: Science and Culture in the Holy Roman Empire*. Princeton, N.J.: Princeton University Press.

Supple, Barry. 1959. *Commercial Crisis and Change in England: 1600–1642*. Cambridge: Cambridge University Press.

Vaughan, Rice. [1675] 1856. A Discourse of Coin and Coinage. In McCulloch 1856.

Vickers, Douglas. [1959] 1968. *Studies in the Theory of Money: 1690–1776*. New York: Kelley.

Vilar, Pierre. 1976. *A History of Gold and Money: 1450–1920*. New York: Verso.

Webster, Charles, ed. 1970. *Samuel Hartlib and the Advancement of Learning*. Cambridge: Cambridge University Press.

———. [1972] 1974. The Authorship and Significance of Macaria. In Webster 1974.

———, ed. 1974. *The Intellectual Revolution of the Seventeenth Century*. London: Routledge & Kegan.

———. 1982. *From Paracelsus to Newton: Magic and the Making of Modern Science*. Cambridge: Cambridge University Press.

———. 1994. Benjamin Worsley: Engineering for Universal Reform from the Invisible College to the Navigation Act. In *Samuel Hartlib and Universal Reformation: Studies in Intellectual Communication*, edited by M. Greengrass, M. Leslie, and T. Raylor. Cambridge: Cambridge University Press.

Wennerlind, Carl. 2004. The Death Penalty as Monetary Policy: The Practice and Punishment of Monetary Crime, 1690–1830. *HOPE* 36.1.

Westfall, Richard. 1980. *Never at Rest: A Biography of Isaac Newton*. Cambridge: Cambridge University Press.

White, Michael. 1997. *Isaac Newton: The Last Sorcerer*. Reading, Pa.: Helix Books.

Wilkinson, Ronald. 1970. The Hartlib Papers and Seventeenth-Century Chemistry, Part II. *Isis* 17:85–110.

Yates, Frances. 1979. *The Occult Philosophy in the Elizabethan Age*. London: Routledge.

Adam Smith's Debts to Nature

Margaret Schabas

Adam Smith (1723–90) was *the* towering figure of Enlightenment political economy, a stature he attained in his own lifetime much as Sir Isaac Newton had in his. The secondary literature on Smith is enough to sink a small boat; there are more than 1,000 books and journal articles.[1] Unfortunately, or perhaps fortunately, most of these are Whiggish efforts to show just how modern Smith was in his economic analysis. As Jacob Viner (1991, 92) once remarked, "An economist must have peculiar theories indeed who cannot quote from the *Wealth of Nations* to support his special purposes." Such versatility has lent itself to considerable abuse among modern economists in search of venerable ancestry.

Smith, however, did not view himself as an economist. Indeed, the English term was not in common usage at the time.[2] Smith was a

I would like to thank the following scholars for their comments and criticisms: Neil De Marchi, Simon Schaffer, Leon Montes, Ian Simpson Ross, Roger Hahn, Paul Wood, Vivienne Brown, Mary Terrall, and Jay Foster. The usual disclaimer holds true. In addition to the workshop at Duke University, I have also benefited from presentations at the University of British Columbia, the 2002 History of Science Society Meetings in Milwaukee, and the York/Toronto workshop in the history of economics.

1. On some recent literature, see Brown 1997 and Tribe 1999. Smith was most popular with the French, judging from the obituary notices (see Teichgraeber 1986 and Rothschild 2001).

2. The term *oeconomist* was common currency in the eighteenth century, but it meant a good manager of household resources, or one who practices or advocates saving. The *Oxford English Dictionary* gives 1804 as the first time the term is used to mean a teacher or student of the subject of political economy, in the Earl of Lauderdale's *Inquiry into the Nature and Origin of Public Wealth*. The physiocrats called themselves "les économistes," and both Hume and Smith referred to them as such.

professor of logic and moral philosophy, with a wide range of interests, including jurisprudence, natural philosophy, rhetoric, and belles lettres. Although we have reason to believe that he wrote voluminously, he only shepherded two books into print, the *Theory of Moral Sentiments* (1759) and the *Wealth of Nations* (1776).[3] Both were revised substantially throughout his remaining years. Smith lived to see the sixth edition of his first book appear just weeks before he died, and the sixth edition of the second was published in the following year. For Smith, the *Theory of Moral Sentiments* was the more significant of the two, but it waned from the philosophical firmament after Immanuel Kant and, while increasingly appreciated, has yet to regain canonical standing.[4]

As numerous scholars have argued, natural and moral philosophy were closely joined by philosophers of the Scottish Enlightenment, arguably more so than in France or northern Europe.[5] Smith, needless to say, was a shining example of this felicitous union. He took up Newton's challenge to extend his rules of reasoning into uncharted land and was regarded by others, such as John Millar and Thomas Pownall, as "the Newton of the moral sciences" (see Redman 1997, 208–15). My objective here is to adumbrate Smith's indebtedness to concepts rather than methods of early modern natural philosophy. Some of the many topics in Smith's economics where nature rears its head are labor, markets, and the pursuit of wealth.

1. Smith's Knowledge of Natural Philosophy

We know that Adam Smith was well versed in classics, mathematics, and natural philosophy, a grounding he received first in Scotland, at his local school and at the University of Glasgow (1737–40), and then, to a lesser degree, at Oxford (1740–46). His most influential teacher was Francis Hutcheson, who served as professor of moral philosophy at Glasgow but who also had a solid grounding in logic and natural philosophy, including Newtonian physics. Hutcheson was known for promoting the methods

3. Smith had sixteen manuscript volumes burned right before his death. In keeping with his pared-down published record, there are only 179 extant letters by Smith. We know that more than fifty are still missing, but even including those it averages out to only four letters per year. Smith clearly kept his cards close to his chest. See Smith 1987 and Tribe 1999.

4. The scholarship of Knud Haakonssen (1981), Vivienne Brown (1994), and Charles Griswold Jr. (1999) has rekindled an interest in Smith's moral philosophy.

5. See, for example, the articles by Roger Emerson (1990) and Paul Wood (1990b), as well as the collection in Rousseau and Porter 1980.

of Newton in other fields and is credited with inspiring Smith for doing just that in moral philosophy. One of the more memorable courses Smith took from Hutcheson was on the subject of "Pneumaticks," by which was meant the "science of spirits or spiritual beings" (Ross 1995, 43). What little evidence we have of the course suggests that Hutcheson treated the subject as speculative physics (see Moore and Silverthorne 1983). It covered metaphysical questions about ethereal beings as well as the new physics of airs and other elastic fluids.

Smith also took courses from Robert Dick on experimental physics, a subject that was much emphasized in the Glasgow curriculum. According to Ian Simpson Ross (1995), the Scottish universities were keen to be "modern" and thus keep abreast of recent innovations in experimental natural philosophy, unlike the more traditional curriculum at Oxford.[6] An additional fee of three shillings per session was levied on each student to fund the purchase of equipment. While some equipment had been acquired in the late seventeenth century, the collection was mostly developed in the early to mid-eighteenth century. In 1726, the University of Glasgow purchased twenty-eight pounds worth of scientific apparatus built by the well-known instrument maker for the Royal Society, Francis Hauksbee. Following this, annual expenditures on laboratory equipment ranged as high as 350 pounds in 1763, when Smith, as vice rector at the University of Glasgow, authorized a new laboratory for Joseph Black (see Swinback 1982).

After his student days, Smith forged friendships with the leading savants of Scotland. The most intense and enduring friendship was with David Hume, whom Smith met circa 1750 in Edinburgh, and which lasted right up until Hume's death in 1776. Another friendship forged at this point in time was with William Cullen, who found in Smith "a like-minded ally" (Donovan 1975, 72). Cullen was appointed as professor of chemistry to the University of Glasgow in 1751, the same year as Smith, and then moved to the University of Edinburgh in 1755, where he is largely credited for turning the medical school into the most prestigious in Europe. He found the school run by disciples of Hermann Boerhaave, the great Leiden physician, treating the body as a hydraulic machine completely severed from the soul. Cullen, along with Robert Whytt and Alexander Monro, transformed the study of medicine by treating the

6. To become modern was costly, and Glasgow did not always have the financial resources. Ross (1995, 55) infers that Smith had Oxford and Glasgow in mind when he drew a comparison between rich and poor universities in the *Wealth of Nations* (see Smith 1976a, 2:772–73).

body as essentially neurological. While this may have had no greater therapeutic value, it meshed well with the associationist psychology of Locke and Hume, as well as with the drift toward vitalism and away from mechanistic thinking. There was also, as we will see, a reciprocal influence between Cullen and Smith. Cullen emphasized the nervous system in part because Smith convinced him that sympathy was the most fundamental of human sentiments. Likewise, Smith drew upon Cullen's neurology when he depicted sympathy as essentially a physiological reaction to the plight of others (see Lawrence 1979; Forget, this volume).

Cullen was a Newtonian when it came to method, but not when it came to metaphysics (see Schofield 1970, 206–9, 218). He found his teacher, John Desaguliers, too rigid and faithful to the great Sir Isaac. Moreover, Cullen cultivated a strong fascination for the concept of the ether as the seat of natural powers. According to J. R. R. Christie (1981, 86), "eighteenth-century Scotland's most committed ethereal scientist was the chemist and physiologist William Cullen." Cullen's absorption with the ether in turn led him to endorse Stephen Hales's doctrine of subtle fluids, as an improvement over the mechanical philosophy of the seventeenth century. Cullen appears to have shared Hales's suspicions, noting that the mechanical philosophy "never could, nor ever can be applied to any great extent in explaining the animal economy" (quoted in Schofield 1970, 206). René Descartes's vision to subsume everything but the human mind under a mechanical philosophy did not bear enough fruit by the early 1700s. Numerous phenomena that were linked to vitalism, namely heat, light, magnetism, and electricity, were gaining preferential treatment as subtle or imponderable fluids (see Schofield 1970; Olson 1975; and Hankins 1985, chap. 3).

The idea that solid bodies such as amber or beeswax could absorb and hold air was first broached by Hales in the 1720s. Although Smith did not know Hales personally, we know that he much admired his work and would thus, presumably, have followed the development of these ideas in the hands of Cullen and Joseph Black, who succeeded Cullen in the chair at Glasgow (see Donovan 1976). In 1754, Black was the first to isolate a new "fixed air" and communicated his results in correspondence with Cullen. The official publication came two years later and constituted a major step toward unraveling the ancient doctrine of four elements. Fixed air, or carbon dioxide, as we now know it, was released upon heating magnesia alba and found to be highly soluble in water (seltzer water). The air is thus "fixed" in both solids and liquids, and subsequent experiments showed that the amounts could be quite substantial. Cullen used Hales's ideas to investigate the properties of evaporation, and both Cullen and Black extended this process in their respective theories of heat as a substance, a caloric fluid. Black also developed the concept of latent heat that, along with fixed air, ushered in the so-called Chemical Revolution of the late eighteenth century (see Lawrence 1982 and Golinski 1992).

Both Black and James Hutton, the leading geologist of his age, became good friends with Smith in the middle decades of the eighteenth century. After Hume died in 1776, they accepted Smith's invitation to serve as his literary executors and were present when Smith expired. From Hutton, Smith would have garnered a greater appreciation of the earth's fertility and become acquainted firsthand with experimental agriculture.[7] The mid-eighteenth century was a period when the emerging industrial order forced comparisons with agriculture as the locus of nature's gifts. Hutton had deemed agriculture the most virtuous of activities insofar as it gave humans, like God, dominion over their natural kingdom. It does not seem that Smith was so persuaded, since mercantile trades tended to breed better the virtues that he ranked most highly, namely, honesty, probity, prudence, and self-command (Smith 1976b, 63, 146; see also Rosenberg 1990). Nevertheless, Smith maintained that agriculture was the most productive sector, per unit of capital invested, because of the added assistance of nature (De Marchi 1999, 27; Smith 1976a, 1:363–64; Smith 1978, 522). In this respect, the windfall gains of nature trumped human agency, and hence economic growth was still conceived of as closely wedded to the agrarian sector.

In 1759, Smith befriended Benjamin Franklin. While the extant record indicates a shared concern for political unrest in America, there is reason to believe that Smith also appreciated Franklin's scientific work. In his essay "Of the External Senses," Smith (1980e, 147) cites Franklin's experiments on the propagation of sound.[8] Smith's library contained a wide selection of books on natural philosophy, including Franklin's famous

7. Simon Schaffer (1997, 138–41) sees Hutton as the spearhead of a movement of rational agriculture in eighteenth-century Britain. Cullen, too, had pursued experimental agriculture in 1752, after the encouragement of Lord Kames. Cullen and Black's analyses of the properties of lime also had direct applications for the use of fertilizers in agriculture, as Hutton recognized. Also, one of Smith's early patrons, Henry Home, was associated with improvements in agriculture. See Lowry, this volume, for a different viewpoint.

8. Kevin Brown (1992, 334) has argued that Smith wrote the essay later than has been commonly supposed, probably in 1758 rather than prior to 1752. This would support the view that

letters on electricity (see Mizuta 2000). On mathematics and mechanics, he had the oeuvre of Francis Bacon, Galileo, Christian Huygens, Robert Hooke, Pierre Gassendi, Newton, Colin Maclaurin, and John Keill. On chemistry he had Pierre-Joseph Macquer and Joseph Priestley, and on natural history the works of Marcello Malpighi, Lazzaro Spallanzani, Carl Linnaeus, Charles Bonnet, and Georges-Louis Leclerc de Buffon. He also had an extensive set of volumes of the *Philosophical Transactions of the Royal Society*, one of the leading periodicals for scientific discoveries. Following his appointment to the Royal Society in 1773, Smith would have rubbed shoulders with the leading English natural philosophers of the day, notably Henry Cavendish. In 1780 Smith wrote to a Danish friend that for the past six years he had, in addition to revising the *Wealth of Nations*, studied botany and "some other sciences to which I had never given much attention before" (Ross 1995, 227). There is ample reason to believe that Smith sustained an interest in natural philosophy over the course of his career.

Smith's juvenile essay on the "History of Astronomy" provides us with the best glimpse into his fascination for the natural sciences. Smith first sketched the essay soon after he left Oxford in the late 1740s and completed most of it by 1758, if not 1752 (see Hetherington 1983 and Cleaver 1989). Smith specifically requested that his essay be published after his death, though the last section on Newton was left unfinished and there is no corresponding conclusion to balance the rather elaborate introduction to the essay.[9] Black and Hutton, as his literary executors, note that Smith's essay was part of a larger unfinished project, which might explain why Smith never ushered it into print despite its long genesis.[10]

Oddly, Smith's essay on the history of astronomy makes deprecatory remarks about chemistry, no doubt a vestige of his earliest draft that

Smith knew Franklin's published scientific papers. Brown's argument, however, is consistent with the more likely scenario that Smith wrote and revised his essay over the entire decade.

9. In a letter to Hume in 1773, Smith (1987, 168) wrote, "As I have left the care of all my literary papers to you, I must tell you that except those which I carry along with me there are none worth the publishing, but a fragment of a great work which contains a history of the Astronomical Systems that were successively in fashion down to the time of Des Cartes. Whether that might not be published as a fragment of an intended juvenile work, I leave entirely to your judgement; tho I begin to suspect myself that there is more refinement than solidity in some parts of it."

10. Published with "The History of Astronomy" essay are two more posthumous contributions to the history of science, namely, "The History of Ancient Physics" and "The History of the Ancient Logics and Metaphysics."

preceded his acquaintance with Cullen and Black (Smith 1980c, 46). Smith also bestows much praise on Descartes, which would have been appropriate in the 1740s, but not in the mid-1750s. In his letter to the *Edinburgh Review* of 1755–56, Smith accurately observes that the French had shifted their allegiance from Cartesian to Newtonian physics: "They seem now however to be pretty generally disengaged from the enchantment of that illusive philosophy" (244). And in a later version of the essay on astronomy, Smith cites several recent findings that enabled Newton's cosmology to supersede that of Descartes, but did not delete his earlier passages on Cartesian physics.[11] All of this suggests that the essay did not undergo much revision after the early 1750s. Even in his 1773 letter to Hume, who was to serve as literary executor, Smith notes that his essay covered the history of astronomy "down to the time of Descartes." Most likely, Smith had yet to complete the section on Newtonian physics, or was all the more persuaded of its instrumentalist standing through the ongoing influence of Hume.[12]

According to Smith's essay, nature presents us with phenomena, both wondrous and mundane, and the task of the philosopher is to find the principles that connect the phenomena, guided by analogy and resemblance. That there are such chains Smith seems never to doubt, but he doubts very much that we can ever find them fully. The chains are analogous to those in machinery, such as those used to produce the scenery in opera theaters, or the fanciful automata found in many European clock towers.[13] That the machines he has in mind are for imitative purposes is all to the point, since the main message of his lengthy account is to develop what we would now call an instrumentalist position. Astronomers

11. These were an expedition by Pierre-Louis Moreau de Maupertuis and Alexis Clairaut to Lapland, in 1737, to measure the earth's curvature in the polar regions; the solution of the lunar orbit by Clairaut, announced in 1749 and published in 1752, in terms of a series of approximations of the three-body problem (Smith 1980c, 100–101); and Edmund Halley's prediction that a comet would return in 1758 or 1759, a prediction that was made much more precise by Clairaut. A footnote, added later, notes that the prediction by Halley was confirmed, and also that "the whole of this Essay was written previous to the date here mentioned" (1980c, 103).

12. There are clear indications of the influence of Hume's *Treatise*, such as references to "custom" and the significance of resemblance as the starting point for philosophical inquiry (see Smith 1980c, 37–42). Hume arrives at the central claim that "all our reasonings concerning causes and effects are deriv'd from nothing but custom" (see Hume [1739–40] 1978, 183). Resemblance for Hume is the first principle by which the mind associates one idea with another (Wightman 1980, 11).

13. Charles Griswold Jr. (1999, 65–70) observes the extensive use of theatrical metaphors in Smith's work. Simon Schaffer (1999, 129–35) explores the possible links between Smith's analysis of the division of labor and the widespread fascination for automata at the time.

over the centuries have offered different theories or systems to make sense of the phenomena of the heavens, and while one can see a gradual increase in the richness and accuracy of these systems, there is no definitive system to correspond to reality. The Tychonic system helps underscore the arbitrariness of this, and even when the Copernican theory was first broached, there was no clear empirical superiority. Moreover, Smith observes, Copernicus was forced to introduce the device of the epicycle, despite his strong desire to eliminate it from astronomical systems.

Descartes is seen as a significant improvement, in linking the terrestrial and celestial phenomena and providing a mechanical account, however fanciful. Descartes offered "a vast, an immense system, which joined together a greater number of the most discordant phaenomena of nature, than had been united by any other hypothesis" (Smith 1980c, 96). Smith (1980d, 244) elsewhere suggests that Descartes was as much an advance over Aristotle as Newton was over Descartes. Newton's theory is the most sophisticated of all, in that it partly accounts for the lunar orbit and can calculate the respective densities and distances of the planets. Newton's system is one "whose parts are all more strictly connected together than those of any other philosophical hypothesis" (Smith 1980c, 104). Smith, however, does not present the Newtonian "hypothesis" as the definitive word on the subject, only as the one to offer the most satisfactory account to date. What should be emphasized is Smith's conviction that the links that connect phenomena—the more disparate ones the better—are what give Newton's account its epistemological strength. And for Smith the reason lies in the fact that nature is indeed law-governed; there are real chains that "bind together her several operations," even if we may never know the correct chains (105).

2. Appeals to Natural Philosophy

Scholars have long identified the emphasis on concepts of nature in Smith's political economy (see Skinner 1974, Campbell 1975, and Foley 1976). Perhaps the most obvious example is Smith's figurative use of gravitational attraction in his treatment of market prices. He draws an explicit contrast between the price in the market and the "natural price" to which "the prices of all commodities are continually gravitating" (Smith 1976a, 1:75). Moreover, just as gravity connects all the bodies of the physical world, sympathy might be said to be that which connects all persons in the moral world. Several scholars have written on these parallel ascriptions between the physical and moral spheres in Smith's texts. Vernard Foley (1976), for example, traces the Stoic and Cartesian components of Smith's naturalism, while Charles Clark (1992) provides a detailed coverage of Smith's use of the natural-law tradition, of arguments from natural theology, and of Smith's appeals to human nature as the foundation for an orderly moral realm. Norris Hetherington (1983) and Deborah Redman (1997) explore the Newtonian thrust in Smith's pronouncements on methodology, while Andrew Skinner (1967) and Paul Wood (1990a) trace Smith's appreciation for natural history.

Several other facets of Smith's economic thinking reflect his insight into the heuristic value of analogical reasoning.[14] I will argue that Smith uses recent ideas in chemistry and physiology in his treatment of labor and sympathy, specifically in terms of subtle fluids. Moreover, Smith's appeals to market adjustments and the broad sweep of time may well have been shaped by his knowledge of natural history, particularly that of Linnaeus, Buffon, and Hutton. Finally, Smith's distinction between appearance and reality in the moral realm may well have been the product of his long struggle with the metaphysical aftermath of Copernicanism. I will develop these three themes here because they are relatively original, but by no means will I exhaust the ways in which Smith debited nature's bank.

Commentators have often noted the two senses in which Smith advances a labor theory of value. He speaks in places of the value of goods being determined by what labor can command, and the value of goods being determined by the amount of labor embodied in the object. It is the latter sense that was more enduring, particularly in the works of David Ricardo and Karl Marx. But what was perhaps more interesting in the case of Smith was that he depicted the stuff of labor (imagine a subtle or imponderable fluid) implanting itself in objects and being stored up for later extraction. As he notes in the *Wealth of Nations*, "the labour of the manufacturer *fixes* and realizes itself in some particular subject or vendible commodity, which lasts for some time at least after that labour is past" (my emphasis; Smith 1976a, 1:330). This image serves Smith well in drawing a distinction between productive and unproductive labor. "The labour of the menial servant, on the contrary, does not *fix* or realize itself in any particular subject or vendible commodity. His services generally perish in the very instant of their performance, and seldom leave

14. W. P. D. Wightman (1980, 13–15) directs us to Smith's emphasis on interdisciplinary analogies as a means for discovery. See also Skinner 1974.

any trace or value behind them, for which an equal quantity of service could afterwards be procured" (my emphasis). In sum, any labor that is ephemeral, that cannot fix itself in an object for a later use, is unproductive. This encompasses "the declamation of the actor, the harangue of the orator, or the tune of the musician, [because] the work of all of them perishes in the very instant of its production" (331).

This image of fluid-like substances, fixing themselves in grosser objects, would have been a process familiar to Smith firsthand from his friendships with Cullen and Black, and secondhand from his reading of Hales. Moreover, only certain bodies could permit the fixation of air, just as only certain kinds of labor could be productive. I have argued elsewhere that Hume treated money as a subtle fluid, possibly under the inspiration of experiments with the electric fluid during the 1730s and 1740s (Schabas 2001). Clearly, Smith thinks of labor as a substance, insofar as it can be transferred, be stored, be extracted, and evaporate for that matter. While we have no record of the genesis of Smith's new approach to labor (there is no trace of it in his earlier lectures at Glasgow), it seems reasonable to assume that Smith utilized the conceptual tools of close friends among contemporary chemists. That the fluids of heat and air could be stored or fixed in gross bodies and then retrieved at a later time has an important analogue in the way in which labor was conceived to be a vital fluid storable in objects and then extracted at a later point in time.[15]

Smith's treatment of labor is strikingly original and not to be found in Locke or Hume, although both broach the idea that labor creates value. For Locke (1980, 19), labor can be "mixed" or "annexed" to other objects, especially land, but he thinks of this primarily in terms of the creation of property rights. That is to say, we have property in our own persons, actualized by our labor, and this can be transferred to land to create estate.[16] Hume ([1739–40] 1978, 505–6 n) challenges this position, noting in a footnote in book 3 of the *Treatise* that "we cannot be said to

15. The verb *to fix* is of great vintage and connotes, for example, the immaterial implantation of sentiments and memories in the mind, as well as the material definition. Interestingly, Norton Wise and Crosbie Smith (1989) have shown that, in the early nineteenth century, there was a close reciprocity between the economist's concept of labor and the physicist's definition of work in protoenergetic terms.

16. Locke (1980, 20) also uses *to fix* in the context of property rights: "The labour that was mine, removing them out of that common state they were in, hath fixed my property in them," and, "As much as any one can make use of to any advantage of life before it spoils, so much he may by his labour fix a property in." But in both sentences, it is the property that is being fixed, not the labor. Still, this may have been sufficient to prompt Smith to his own articulation of the concept of fixed labor.

join our labour to any thing but in a figurative sense. Properly speaking, we only make an alteration on it by our labour." The physiocratic method, likewise, was to emphasize the view that labor can alter but not create anything, and certainly does not embed itself in objects or generate value. Smith, it appears, was the first to consider labor an alienable stuff that could, in the case of productive labor, be packed into other objects.

This might all sound somewhat strange if we did not have good reason to believe that Smith also thought of human sympathy in terms of a vital fluid. As Chris Lawrence (1979, 27) has suggested, Edinburgh physicians such as Alexander Monro Primus (a good friend of Hume, Smith, and Cullen) developed in the early 1750s, along with John Gregory, "a model of the body in which sensibility, a property of the nervous system, predominated. . . . This they did by using the notion of 'sympathy'—which was no more than the communication of feeling between different bodily organs." But even more fascinating is the effort to conceptualize the nervous fluid as an electric one.[17] This was used to explain why feelings were communicated, not only within a body, but between different persons. As Gregory observed, "people subject to hysteric fits will often by sympathy fall into a fit by seeing another person fall into the same" (quoted in Lawrence 1979, 28).

Lawrence then links this to Adam Smith's work on sympathy and emphasizes that these communications of the nervous system transpire without consciousness (28–31). He maintains that feeling rather than reason was the predominant basis for moral philosophy in Hume and Smith, and that they viewed sympathy as a sentiment, something felt as a sensation (see also Rothschild 2001 and Forget, this volume). Smith underscores the rapidity by which sympathy springs into action. Even the most hardened criminal is not exempt from such sentiments, suggesting again that sympathy is physiological and not a function of one's stock of virtue.

Lawrence (1979, 33) believes that the analogy between the body and society was deeply entrenched in Scottish philosophy at the time, and

17. Roderick Home traces the evolution of the efforts to understand the nervous fluid as a form of the electric fluid. The two were often identified in the late 1740s and helped inspire medical usages of electricity, for example, the work of P. J. C. Mauduyt, N.-P. Le Dru, and the celebrated Anton Mesmer of mesmerism (see Sutton 1981). Albrecht von Haller was the pivotal figure in attempting to sever the two fluids, circa 1760, although Luigi Galvani's famous dissection of a frog brought them back together. Nevertheless, the nervous fluid was always grouped with the collection of subtle fluids (see Home 1970).

that this is particularly evident in the concept of sympathy: "As society was held to depend on the mutual feeling, or sympathy, between the parts, so, too, was the body. In the same way that the Edinburgh elite perceived itself, so the nervous system was seen as a structure of interacting sensibilities, binding together and controlling the whole." Smith's attention to sympathy was thus undergirded by his appreciation for Cullen's physiology. Likewise, his concept of labor may have fed on his appreciation for subtle fluid theory and more specifically the doctrine of fixed air.

Paul Wood (1990a, 89) has argued that one of the most prominent pursuits of the Scottish Enlightenment was natural history. Smith (1980d, 248–49) was instrumental in importing the ideas of René-Antoine Réaumur and Buffon, noting in his 1756 letter to the *Edinburgh Review* that "none of the sciences indeed seem to be cultivated in France with more eagerness than natural history." This and what we know about the contents of Smith's library point to a keen and sustained interest in the subject. We know that he much admired Linnaeus, who had promoted the scientific standing of cameralism in Sweden and cultivated a distinctive argument for national autarky (see Koerner 1999 and Rausing, this volume). Smith had read Linnaeus's most famous work, the *Systema Natura*, for he makes use of it in his essay "Of the External Senses" (most likely written before 1752).[18] He also had in his library Benjamin Stillingfleet's 1759 translation of Linnaeus's *Oeconomy of Nature* and may well have read the original 1749 Latin version. Smith (1980c, 38) also notes the adaptiveness of species and makes an oblique reference to classification by genera and species in his essay on the history of astronomy.

In his *Theory of Moral Sentiments*, Smith (1976b, 2:77) inserts a lengthy passage on the oeconomy of nature, which recognizes that "self-preservation and the propagation of the species, are the great ends which Nature seems to have proposed in the formation of all animals." We are bestowed with various instincts that motivate actions with unintended consequences. "Hunger, thirst, the passion which unites the two sexes, the love of pleasure, and the dread of pain, prompt us to apply those means for their own sakes, and without any consideration of their tendency to those beneficent ends which the great Director of nature intended to produce by them" (2:78). It is language and our propensity to "truck, barter, and exchange" that set us apart from all other species and

18. Wightman (1980, 15, 133–34) makes this argument, based on the presence of Berkeley's and the absence of Hume's ideas in the essay.

give rise to commerce and trade (Smith 1976a, 1:30). But in every other respect, we are seamlessly joined to the richer oeconomy of nature.

Linnaeus ([1749] 1977, 95) had noted "the wonderful disposition of the Creator, in assigning to each species certain kinds of food, and in putting limits to their appetites." Smith (1976a, 1:181) possibly echoes these sentiments in his own ascription of a circumscribed stomach: "The desire of food is limited in every man by the narrow capacity of the human stomach." But much more may have been drawn from the Linnaean concept of an oeconomy of nature. Presumably his economic processes, such as the geometric rate of reproduction, the supply and demand for food, and the mechanisms by which equilibria are restored, were not lost on Smith (see Müller-Wille, this volume). For example, in Smith's (1976a, 1:76–77) analysis of the adjustment process that is unleashed by a sudden increase in the demand for black cloth due to a public mourning, we see many of the same supply-and-demand adjustments that Linnaeus identified in the case of a sudden fluctuation in the population of a given species. Resources are shifted in response to the disturbance, and equilibrium is once again restored. In this sense, Linnaeus had the most developed conception of an economy, albeit an oeconomy of nature, for the mid-eighteenth century (see Koerner 1999; Schabas 1990; and Müller-Wille, this volume).

Smith's 1756 letter to the *Edinburgh Review* also comments on Buffon's early volumes of his monumental *Histoire naturelle*, "one of the most widely read scientific works of the eighteenth century" (Wood 1990a, 89). Going beyond the sheer fascination many had for natural history, Buffon proposed nascent theories of biological evolution and ascribed substantial antiquity to the earth. Needless to say, this caused quite a stir, for both its scientific and theological implications. Smith's letter was noncommittal. Buffon's system, he wrote, "is almost entirely hypothetical," though "supported or connected . . . with many singular and curious observations and experiments" (Smith 1980d, 248). While we do not know Smith's true beliefs on the matter, it is well demonstrated that he, along with other members of the so-called Scottish historical school, such as Adam Ferguson and Lord Kames, sought to cultivate a natural history of humankind in the tradition of Linnaeus and Buffon (Bryson 1945; Skinner 1967; Wood 1990a). This entailed a study of human nature by tracing us back to earlier stages of development. Smith's letter also acknowledged Rousseau's appeals to the "noble savage" (Smith 1980d, 251), and there are a number of similar petitions in his own two texts, to the dignity of African slaves or the courage of aboriginal Americans (Smith 1976b, 205–9).[19]

There is also a strong predilection in Smith to view the economy developmentally and to think in large chunks of time, as do Buffon and Hutton. Such an approach was relatively novel in the history of economic thought—not the reference to historical events per se, but the effort to think of the flow of wealth from nation to nation at the rate of a few if not several centuries. Hume had already observed, albeit in his correspondence, that no country could sustain its economic hegemony forever (Rotwein 1970, 200). Smith (1976a, 1:377) emphasized the extent to which human institutions could thwart if not reverse "the natural progress of opulence," which he envisioned in terms of hundreds of years. Moreover, Smith pointed to the ascendancy of the American economy and admonished Britain to grant independence to its colonies and thus "to accommodate her future views and designs to the real mediocrity of her circumstances" (2:947). In sum, Smith's work was resonant with Enlightenment natural history at numerous levels.[20]

J. Ronnie Davis (1990) has argued persuasively that Smith was committed to the role of deception in driving the moral universe. The invisible hand is also a "sleight of hand." The poor toil hard because they believe, falsely, that riches are worth the effort, when in fact they are apt to lose the serenity that they now possess. "It is this deception which rouses and keeps in continual motion the industry of mankind" (Smith 1976b, 183). This in itself strongly suggests that for Smith the moral world was carefully designed such as to bring about the most benevolence. And of course it also had built into it all sorts of tendencies toward greater general prosperity over time, through the division of labor and trade.

Interestingly, the first acknowledgment of the invisible hand is in Smith's astronomy essay, and it is the hand of Jupiter (see Ahmad 1990). Smith would have gathered from the triumph of the Copernican system over the Ptolemaic that the heavens themselves are so construed as to be one grand deception. After all, the sun does not really rise and set every day, as the common people might think. The new astronomy implied that the world was designed in a more complex fashion, so as to create certain illusions of self-centeredness (the earth as if it were the center of the

19. As Lisbet Koerner (1999, chap. 3) has noted, Linnaeus also cultivated these sentiments in tribute to the Sami of Lapland, to the point of frequently donning their costumes for his European lectures.

20. Stefano Fiori (2001) has recently argued this with respect to Smith's favored distinction between the visible and the invisible, noting the influence of Maupertuis and Buffon.

universe) and certain illusions of stability (the earth seemingly at rest). All of this had been threshed out among natural philosophers of the seventeenth century. Galileo and Descartes, with their distinction between primary and secondary qualities, established the immense gulf between the physical world and the internal world of the mind.

George Berkeley attempted to restore a commonsense metaphysics by proclaiming that only that which is perceived can exist. His famous motto, "esse est percipii" (to be is to be perceived), entailed that the material substratum, the swirl of atoms, simply did not exist.[21] Hume in certain respects shared Berkeley's aversion to the mechanical philosophy and also sought to restore a reality that matches that of our experience.[22] But Hume was less emphatic about denying the existence of the material substratum. He was not an immaterialist like Berkeley, merely a skeptic about how much we could discern about the microscopic world. And he did not share Berkeley's (1979, 67–69) wish to reduce metaphysics to the view of a common gardener. Quite the contrary, he deplored "the vulgar, who take things according to their first appearance" (Hume [1739–40] 1978, 132). Philosophers, on the other hand, recognize that "in every part of nature there is contain'd a vast variety of springs and principles, which are hid, by reason of their minuteness or remoteness."

When Smith first read Descartes, Berkeley, and Hume, whether at Oxford or after his return to Scotland, remains a matter for conjecture, but their influence on his ideas is unmistakable, not least because he cites them explicitly. It seems difficult to believe, then, that Smith's rich insight that the moral world is full of deception did not owe something to these philosophers and their own struggles with the implications of the heliocentric theory.[23] True, the idea of unintended consequences was already developed in Bernard de Mandeville's *Fable of the Bees*, but for

21. Given what little was known of the atomic substratum, not to mention the fanciful accounts by Descartes or Robert Boyle, Berkeley was on solid ground to question such knowledge.

22. Barry Stroud's influential study (1977) redeemed Hume from a position of deep skepticism and emphasized his naturalism. As Hume ([1748] 2000, 44) observed in his section titled "Sceptical Solution of These Doubts," there is a "pre-established harmony between the course of nature and the succession of our ideas; and though the powers and forces, by which the former is governed, be wholly unknown to us; yet our thoughts and conceptions have still, we find, gone on in the same train with the other works of nature."

23. Gordon Wood (1982, 425), drawing upon Bernard de Mandeville and others, argues that "the idea of deception became the means by which the Augustan Age closed the gaps that often seemed to exist between causes and effects. . . . This problem of deception was a source of continuing fascination in eighteenth-century Anglo-American culture." See also Oswald 1995.

Mandeville vice and malevolence were much more evident. Smith saw the world in more benign terms, yet at the same time he recognized that the virtues of industry and prudence, coupled with our pursuit of self-interest, would induce a harmonious if not beneficent world.

Even more profound was Smith's realization that all the "bustle of the world" was for naught. In *The Theory of Moral Sentiments*, there is a passage depicting a man of little means, whom "heaven in its anger had visited with ambition." The man works incessantly to move up the ladder of social rank and income, to endear himself to "those whom he hates," and to be "obsequious to those whom he despises," only to discover "in the last dregs of life, his body wasted with toil and diseases, his mind galled and ruffled by the memory of a thousand injuries and disappointments which he imagines he has met with from the injustice of his enemies, or from the perfidy and ingratitude of his friends, that he begins at last to find that wealth and greatness are mere trinkets of frivolous utility" (Smith 1976b, 181). What really matters, "ease of body, or tranquillity of mind," is as elusive as wisdom. Berkeley had made a concerted effort to demonstrate that God could not be a deceiver. For Smith, it could not be otherwise. His message on the meaning, or meaninglessness, of life owes much to the metaphysical debates of the early modern period.

3. Conclusion

For Smith, economic phenomena were closely wedded to physical and biological nature, and his construal of these phenomena reflects their links to nature. Moreover, he retained the physiocratic predilection for agriculture over manufacturing. Locke's *Second Treatise* had deemed the cultivation of the land to be our mission in the state of nature; agriculture was natural in a way that manufacturing was not. The physiocrats buttressed the case even more by granting nature the exclusive right of creating wealth. It seems that Smith shared many of these sentiments. For all his appreciation of the division of labor in his pin factory, our ties to the land run deeper. On the accumulation of capital, for example, he argues that new wealth is first invested in the land, since it can be kept securely in view. But more than that, the ownership of land brings visible esteem, the recognition from others we so dearly crave. The display of wealth is best done with estate homes, equipage, and carriages. And in the natural development of economic wealth, it is agriculture that must form the right and true foundation to subsequent extensions into trade and commerce (see McNally 1988).

Most importantly, Smith believed that the economy had a natural order, that it was self-governed in much the same way that the physical world was self-governed. I have suggested here that there are manifestations in Smith's writings of the scientific ideas put forth by Hales, Cullen, Black, Linnaeus, Buffon, and even, indirectly, Copernicus. This is hardly surprising, given Smith's deeply rooted belief that the world is designed and providential (see Viner 1991 and Hill 2001). Our human oeconomy would necessarily sit upon the oeconomy of nature and resonate with it. The invisible hand is not so hidden.

References

Ahmad, Syed. 1990. Adam Smith's Four Invisible Hands. *HOPE* 22.1:137–44.

Berkeley, George. 1979. *Three Dialogues between Hylas and Philonous*. Edited by Robert Merrihew Adams. Indianapolis, Ind.: Hackett.

Brown, Kevin L. 1992. Dating Adam Smith's Essay "Of the External Senses." *Journal of the History of Ideas* 53:333–37.

Brown, Vivienne. 1994. *Adam Smith's Discourse: Canonicity, Commerce, and Conscience*. London: Routledge.

———. 1997. "Mere Inventions of the Imagination": A Survey of Recent Literature on Adam Smith. *Economics and Philosophy* 13:281–312.

Bryson, Gladys. 1945. *Man and Society: The Scottish Inquiry of the Eighteenth Century*. Princeton, N.J.: Princeton University Press.

Campbell, T. D. 1975. Scientific Explanation and Ethical Justification in the *Moral Sentiments*. In *Essays on Adam Smith*, edited by Andrew Skinner and T. Wilson. Oxford: Clarendon Press.

Christie, J. R. R. 1981. Ether and the Science of Chemistry: 1740–1790. In *Conceptions of Ether*, edited by G. N. Cantor and M. J. S. Hodge. Cambridge: Cambridge University Press.

Clark, Charles. 1992. *Economic Theory and Natural Philosophy*. Aldershot: Edward Elgar.

Cleaver, K. C. 1989. Adam Smith on Astronomy. *History of Science* 27:211–18.

Davis, J. Ronnie. 1990. Adam Smith on the Providential Reconciliation of Individual and Social Interests: Is Man Led by an Invisible Hand or Misled by a Sleight of Hand? *HOPE* 22.2:341–52.

De Marchi, Neil. 1999. Adam Smith's Accommodation of "Altogether Endless" Desires. In *Consumers and Luxury: Consumer Culture in Europe, 1650–1850*, edited by Maxine Berg and Helen Clifford. Manchester: Manchester University Press.

Donovan, Arthur. 1975. *Philosophical Chemistry in the Scottish Enlightenment: The Doctrines and Discoveries of William Cullen and Joseph Black*. Edinburgh: University of Edinburgh Press.

———. 1976. Pneumatic Chemistry and Newtonian Natural Philosophy in the Eighteenth Century: William Cullen and Joseph Black. *Isis* 67:217–28.

Emerson, Roger. 1990. Science and Moral Philosophy in the Scottish Enlightenment. In Stewart 1990, 11–36.

Fiori, Stefano. 2001. Visible and Invisible Order: The Theoretical Duality of Smith's Political Economy. *European Journal of the History of Economic Thought* 8:429–48.

Foley, Vernard. 1976. *The Social Physics of Adam Smith*. West Lafayette, Ind.: Purdue University Press.

Golinski, Jan. 1992. *Science as Public Culture*. Cambridge: Cambridge University Press.

Griswold, Charles L., Jr. 1999. *Adam Smith and the Virtues of Enlightenment*. Cambridge: Cambridge University Press.

Haakonssen, Knud. 1981. *The Science of a Legislator: The Natural Jurisprudence of David Hume and Adam Smith*. Cambridge: Cambridge University Press.

Hankins, Thomas L. 1985. *Science and the Enlightenment*. Cambridge: Cambridge University Press.

Hetherington, Norriss S. 1983. Isaac Newton's Influence on Adam Smith's Natural Laws in Economics. *Journal of the History of Ideas* 44:497–505.

Hill, Lisa. 2001. The Hidden Theology of Adam Smith. *The European Journal of the History of Economic Thought* 8:1–29.

Home, Roderick W. 1970. Electricity and the Nervous Fluid. *Journal of the History of Biology* 3:235–51.

Hume, David. [1739–40] 1978. *A Treatise of Human Nature*. Edited by A. Selby-Bigge. Oxford: Oxford University Press.

———. [1748] 2000. *An Enquiry Concerning Human Understanding*. Edited by Tom L. Beauchamp. Oxford: Clarendon Press.

Koerner, Lisbet. 1999. *Linnaeus: Nature and Nation*. Cambridge: Harvard University Press.

Lawrence, Christopher. 1979. The Nervous System and Society in the Scottish Enlightenment. In *Natural Order, Historical Studies of Scientific Culture*, edited by Barry Barnes and Steven Shapin. Beverly Hills, Calif.: Sage.

———. 1982. Joseph Black: The Natural Philosophical Background. In Simpson 1982, 1–5.

Linnaeus, Carl. [1749] 1977. The Oeconomy of Nature. In *Miscellaneous Tracts Relating to Natural History, Husbandy, and Physick*, translated by Benjamin Stillingfleet. 3d ed. New York: Arno Press.

Locke, John. 1980. *Second Treatise of Government*. Edited by C. B. Macpherson. Indianapolis, Ind.: Hackett.

McNally, David. 1988. *Political Economy and the Rise of Capitalism: A Reinterpretation*. Berkeley, Calif.: University of California Press.

Mizuta, Hiroshi. 2000. *Adam Smith's Library*. 2d ed. Cambridge: Cambridge University Press.

Moore, James, and Michael Silverthorne. 1983. Gershom Carmichael and the Natural Jurisprudence Tradition in Eighteenth-Century Scotland. In *Wealth and Virtue*, edited by Istvan Hont and Michael Ignatieff, 73–87. Cambridge: Cambridge University Press.

Olson, Richard. 1975. *Scottish Philosophy and British Physics, 1750–1880*. Princeton, N.J.: Princeton University Press.

Oswald, Donald J. 1995. Metaphysical Beliefs and the Foundations of Smithian Political Economy. *HOPE* 27.3:449–76.

Redman, Deborah A. 1997. *The Rise of Political Economy as a Science*. Cambridge: MIT Press.

Rosenberg, Nathan. 1990. Adam Smith and the Stock of Moral Capital. *HOPE* 22.1:1–17.

Ross, Ian Simpson. 1995. *The Life of Adam Smith*. Oxford: Clarendon Press.

Rothschild, Emma. 2001. *Economic Sentiments: Adam Smith, Condorcet, and the Enlightenment*. Cambridge: Harvard University Press.

Rotwein, Eugene, ed. 1970. *David Hume: Writings on Economics*. Madison, Wisc.: University of Wisconsin Press.

Rousseau, G. S., and Roy Porter, eds. 1980. *The Ferment of Knowledge: Studies in the Historiography of Eighteenth-Century Science*. Cambridge: Cambridge University Press.

Schabas, Margaret. 1990. Ricardo Naturalized: Lyell and Darwin on the Economy of Nature. In *Perspectives on the History of Economic Thought*, edited by Donald E. Moggridge. Aldershot: Edward Elgar.

———. 2001. David Hume on Experimental Natural Philosophy, Money, and Fluids. *HOPE* 33.3:411–35.

Schaffer, Simon. 1997. The Earth's Fertility as a Social Fact in Early Modern Britain. In *Nature and Society in Historical Context*, edited by Mikulás Teich, Roy Porter, and Bo Gustafsson. Cambridge: Cambridge University Press.

———. 1999. Enlightened Automata. In *The Sciences in Enlightened Europe*, edited by William Clark, Joan Golinski, and Simon Schaffer. Chicago: University of Chicago Press.

Schofield, Robert E. 1970. *Mechanism and Materialism: British Natural Philosophy in an Age of Reason*. Princeton, N.J.: Princeton University Press.

Simpson, A. D. C., ed. 1982. *Joseph Black 1728–1799: A Commemorative Symposium*. Edinburgh: Royal Scottish Museum.

Skinner, Andrew S. 1967. Natural History in the Age of Adam Smith. *Political Studies* 15:32–48.

———. 1974. Adam Smith, Science, and the Role of the Imagination. In *Hume and the Enlightenment*, edited by William B. Todd. Edinburgh: University of Edinburgh Press.

Smith, Adam. 1976a. *An Inquiry into the Nature and Causes of the Wealth of Nations*, 2 vols. Edited by R. H. Campbell and A. S. Skinner. Oxford: Clarendon Press.

———. 1976b. *The Theory of Moral Sentiments*. Edited by D. D. Raphael and A. L. McFie. Oxford: Clarendon Press.

———. 1978. *Lectures on Jurisprudence*. Edited by R. L. Meek, D. D. Raphael, and P. G. Stein. Oxford: Clarendon Press.

———. 1980a. The History of the Ancient Logics and Metaphysics. In *Essays on Philosophical Subjects*, edited by W. P. D. Wightman. Oxford: Clarendon Press.

———. 1980b. The History of Ancient Physics. In *Essays on Philosophical Subjects*, edited by W. P. D. Wightman. Oxford: Clarendon Press.

———. 1980c. The History of Astronomy. In *Essays on Philosophical Subjects*, edited by W. P. D. Wightman. Oxford: Clarendon Press.

———. 1980d. A Letter to the Authors of the *Edinburgh Review*. In *Essays on Philosophical Subjects*, edited by W. P. D. Wightman. Oxford: Clarendon Press.

———. 1980e. Of the External Senses. In *Essays on Philosophical Subjects*, edited by W. P. D. Wightman. Oxford: Clarendon Press.

———. 1987. *Correspondence of Adam Smith*. Edited by E. C. Mossner and I. S. Ross. Oxford: Clarendon Press.

Stewart, M. A., ed. 1990. *Studies in the Philosophy of the Scottish Enlightenment*. Oxford: Clarendon Press.

Stroud, Barry. 1977. *Hume*. London: Routledge.

Sutton, Geoffrey. 1981. Electric Medicine and Mesmerism. *Isis* 72:375–92.

Swinback, Peter. 1982. Experimental Science in the University of Glasgow at the Time of Joseph Black. In Simpson 1982, 23–35.

Teichgraeber, Richard F. 1986. *"Free Trade" and Moral Philosophy: Rethinking the Sources of Adam Smith's* Wealth of Nations. Durham, N.C.: Duke University Press.

Tribe, Keith. 1999. Adam Smith: Critical Theorist. *Journal of Economic Literature* 37:609–32.

Viner, Jacob. 1991. *Essays on the Intellectual History of Economics*. Princeton, N.J.: Princeton University Press.

Wightman, W. P. D. 1980. Introduction to *Essays on Philosophical Subjects*. Oxford: Clarendon Press.

Wise, M. Norton, and Crosbie Smith. 1989. Work and Waste: Political Economy in Britain, 1750–1834. *History of Science* 27:263–301.

Wood, Gordon S. 1982. Conspiracy and the Paranoid Style: Causality and Deceit in the Eighteenth Century. *William and Mary Quarterly* 39:401–41.

Wood, Paul B. 1990a. The Natural History of Man in the Scottish Enlightenment. *History of Science* 28:89–123.

———. 1990b. Science and the Pursuit of Virtue in the Aberdeen Enlightenment. In Stewart 1990, 127–49.

Evocations of Sympathy: Sympathetic Imagery in Eighteenth-Century Social Theory and Physiology

Evelyn L. Forget

Sympathy drove Adam Smith's theory of moral sentiments and was used by many others in the eighteenth century to explain aspects, if not the whole, of human behavior. Smith himself supplied numerous examples of sympathy at work, without positing that it is a force like the passions, far less that it is inborn. At the same time, physicians made use of the term to conceptualize a rapidly expanding body of physiological knowledge. The phenomena that eighteenth-century philosophers and physicians attempted to explain by means of sympathy were quite real. Physicians used the term to characterize the unconscious communication between different organs in the human body. Organs within the human body did seem, somehow, to coordinate their actions. The health of a mother did influence a developing fetus (Blondel 1729; Boucé 1987; Kirkland 1774). Animal magnetizers did have an effect on their subjects. The mood of one individual did, sometimes, infect others. Theater did entrance its patrons. When the word *sympathy* disappeared from use in medicine, there was a need for something to replace it. Edward Shorter (1992, 12–24) has shown how terms such as *consensus* took over, in nineteenth-century medical discourse, the job that *sympathy* did in the eighteenth century. Alison Winter (1999) has traced this insight in the

I conducted the research for this essay while visiting the Wellcome Institute. I am grateful to the late Roy Porter and his colleagues for their support and encouragement. I would also like to thank the Social Sciences and Humanities Research Council of Canada for financial support, and the editors and referees of this journal for very helpful advice. Unless otherwise indicated, all translations are mine.

context of nineteenth-century mesmerism. Oliver Sacks ([1992] 1999, 3–6) goes so far as to argue that contemporary explanations of such neurologically complex conditions as migraine and epilepsy owe a great deal to, and are often indistinguishable from, eighteenth-century sympathetic explanations, although the word no longer appears. Perhaps there is among economists a similar felt need to find a cognate term, and this drives them periodically to resuscitate *sympathy*.

Be that as it may, tracing the various meanings attached to the term provides a window into an era when ideas were not constrained by disciplinary boundaries. Indeed, there was no clear distinction between medicine and what was to become social theory. Ideas developed in medicine enriched social discourse, and poetry engaged philosophical debate. Knowledge, developing more quickly than the vocabulary in which new discoveries could be expressed, borrowed terms still carrying the freight of alchemy and astrology. Scholars adapted existing words to new uses by playing upon the metaphorical implications of existing terms.[1]

The use of the same word for similar ideas in analyses of the human body and the social body is more than an analogy. There is a logical continuity between physiological and sociological investigations. The same physiological communication that was imagined to account for somatic sympathy was used to explain the effects of the "passions of the mind" on the sensations and impressions of the body. And the "passions of the mind," these physicians noted, are very often infectious, illustrating one form of the unconscious communication between different people that is captured by the concept of "social sympathy."[2]

Section 1 of my article examines the highly ambiguous use of the word *sympathy* in eighteenth-century social discourse. Section 2 examines the use of the term in medicine. Behind both bodies of literature, however, was another, much older, set of ideas that still appeared in popular medical writing as well as in poetry and literature. An ancient system of sympathies and antipathies between all bodies in the universe, detailed in section 3, pervaded the popular imagination. Physicians of the eighteenth century explicitly dissociated their work from such "superstition," yet they drew upon it freely for imagery and even for scientific content. Social thought was also subject to these older associations. Finally, section 4 notes that these archaic associations disappeared from

1. In Samuel Johnson's (1755, preface) words, "the tropes of poetry make hourly encroachments, and the metaphorical will become the current sense."

2. See Macfarquhar and Gleig 1788–97 (cited hereafter as *Britannica*), 18:250–51.

social analysis, as they did from medicine, by the nineteenth century. *Sympathy* was an idea too tainted by political events, and too much a product of a worldview that encouraged metaphorical associations rather than the analytical precision that came to dominate the scientific aspirations of the nineteenth century, to survive intact.

1. Ambiguity among the Social Theorists

Eighteenth-century Scotland generated a wealth of social theorists who made sympathy, characterized by Lord Kames (1751, 17) as "the great cement of human society," the center of their work. Francis Hutcheson, professor of moral philosophy at Glasgow from 1730 to 1740, based his social theory on sympathy in *An Inquiry into the original of our ideas of beauty and virtue* (1725). David Hume developed these ideas in the second part of *A Treatise of Human Nature* (1739). Adam Smith's sympathetic analysis, which became the basis for his social and ethical theory, appeared in *The Theory of Moral Sentiments* ([1759] 1976).[3] Sympathy characterizes the writing of Adam Ferguson ([1767] 1966, xxvii), as well as that of John Gregory, who from 1766 was chair of medicine at Edinburgh, where, along with his cousin Thomas Reid, he helped to develop the "philosophy of common sense" (Gregory 1772).

Despite the pervasiveness of the concept, these social theorists used sympathy in anything but an unambiguous way. Sometimes, sympathy was conceived as a social instinct "which prompts the individuals of our species to congregate, and form themselves into tribes,"[4] a phenomenon referred to by the physician and philosopher John Gregory (1772, 86) as a "distinguishing principle of mankind . . . that which unites them into societies and attaches them to one another by sympathy and affection." Sometimes, *sympathy* referred to an imaginative exchange with another human being, such that one might experience another's circumstances as if one were that individual. That is, the imagination would allow one to compare one's own circumstances in a given social state with the circumstances of another human being with a unique character and history, in a

3. While economists and scholars of Adam Smith are apt to think of sympathy and the impartial spectator as inseparable, sympathy is much broader than the system of ethics founded upon it by Smith.

4. "We can trace the same congregating quality in the bee, in the beaver, and even in the ferocious wolf. It is, however, less frequent in those of ferocious character" (Harris [1755] 1841, 291).

very different social state. Adam Smith ([1759] 1976, 317), for example, wrote:

> When I sympathize with your sorrow or your indignation. . . . When I condole with you for the loss of your only son, in order to enter into your grief I do not consider what I, a person of such a character and profession should suffer, if I had a son, and if that son was unfortunately to die: but I consider what I should suffer if I was really you, and I not only change circumstances with you, but I change persons and characters.

And this passage draws to mind the marginally different popular use of *sympathy* meaning the state of commiserating with the sorrow of another.

Sometimes, *sympathy* referred to a more limited act of imagination. For David Hume ([1751] 1983, 51), for example, imagination facilitates fellow-feeling, but "No force of imagination can convert us into another person, and make us fancy, that we, being that person, reap benefit from those valuable qualities which belong to him. Or, if it did, no celerity of imagination could immediately transport us back into ourselves, and make us love and esteem the person, as different from us." *Sympathy* could also refer to not only understanding what another person must feel in his or her circumstances, but also caring about the outcome in such a way that one's own well-being is enhanced when another gains, and one is distressed by the distress of another. Adam Smith ([1759] 1976, 9–10) sometimes evokes this interdependence: "His agonies, when they are thus brought to ourselves, when we have thus adopted and made them our own, begin at last to affect us. . . . Persons of delicate fibres and a weak constitution of body complain, that in looking on the sores and ulcers which are exposed by beggars in the streets they are apt to feel an itching or uneasy sensation in the corresponding parts of their own bodies." Understanding how another feels, understanding how we should feel if we were in another's circumstances, and caring about how another feels are quite different ideas, all captured under the label *sympathy*.

Sympathy was used sometimes in ways that called to mind other more specialized meanings. Smith's reference to the "sores of beggars," as Christopher Lawrence (1979, 32) aptly remarks, could have been drawn from the medical texts of the period.[5] Physiologists, who used *sympathy*

5. The way that physiology infected various senses of sympathy is strikingly illustrated by a poem entitled *Sympathy; or, A sketch of the social passion*, by Samuel Jackson Pratt (1781, 45):

to refer to the communication between bodily organs by means of some as yet unknown process, extended the meaning to include sympathy between different individuals. The 1797 *Britannica* (18:250) entry on sympathy, which draws freely upon the work of Edinburgh medical graduate Seguin Henry Jackson, notes: "Sympathy . . . denotes the quality of being affected by the affection of another; and may subsist either between different persons or bodies, or between different parts of the same body. . . . Sympathy . . . is often an imitative faculty, sometimes involuntary, frequently without consciousness: thus we yawn when we see others yawn, and are made to laugh by the laughing of another." That is, sometimes sympathy requires no voluntary act of imagination at all.

At other times, *sympathy* was used to invoke not only the facility of understanding or feeling with another, but also that perfect harmony between two individuals upon which could be founded romantic love or friendship. Sophie Condorcet (1798, 99), for example, the French translator of the sixth edition of Smith's *Theory of Moral Sentiments*, writes in 1798, "Only hearts that are generous and capable of attending to the happiness of others, know how to love. The conformity of opinions, of tastes, of characters, all the signs of individual sympathy can unite people and draw together their hearts."[6] Such love requires, she claims, "une connaissance mutuelle et parfaite des âmes" (102). But it is not the *salonnière* alone who draws this connection. The *Britannica* (18:250) entry that goes on to detail recent developments in physiology begins by defining "sympathy [as] an agreement of affections and inclinations, or a conformity of natural qualities, humours, temperaments, which make two persons delighted and pleased with each other." Similarly, the chevalier de Jaucourt, writing for the *Encyclopédie*, begins his discussion of the physiological meaning of sympathy with these words:

> Sympathy, (Physiolog.) that conformity of affection and inclination, that lively intelligence of hearts, communicated, shared, felt with

---

"Hail, sacred source of sympathies divine, / Thine ev'ry social pulse, each fibre thine; / Hail, symbols of the God to whom we owe / The nerves that vibrate, and the hearts that glow." Mr. Pratt, of courses, uses sympathy in all kinds of ways. Among other allusions is this striking reference to the great chain of being: "This then is clear, while human kind exist, / The social principle must still subsist, / In strict dependency of one on all, / As run the binding links from great to small" (41).

6. "Il n'y a que les coeurs généreux et capables de s'attendrir au bonheur d'autrui, qui sachent aimer. La convenance des opinions, des goûts, des caractères, tous les motifs de la sympathie individuelle peuvent rapprocher les hommes et unir en apparence leurs coeurs."

> an inexplicable rapidity; that conformity of natural qualities, ideas, moods, and temperaments, by means of which two matched souls seek out, love, and attach themselves to one another, blend together, is called *sympathy*. . . . but it is not at all this happy intimacy of which I must inform the reader. Here I write about the communication between the parts of the body. . . . It is true, nonetheless, that this communication also produces sometimes, by the same mechanism, a transport, a series of pleasurable sensations.[7]

Jaucourt, too, was writing primarily about physiology yet felt the need to allude to the more commonly accepted meaning of *sympathy*.

Sometimes, *sympathy* carries with it a faintly pejorative tone, particularly when it refers to the extreme (and fashionable) sensibility of women of a refined station. Seguin Henry Jackson (1781, 111–12), who published much on maternal influence, pregnancy, and midwifery, writes:

> The falling into epileptic and hysteric convulsions on any slight alarm, or at the relation of an affecting story, appear to me to be inconsistent with *natural sympathy*, and an affront to the dignity of human nature; when the same takes place at the sight of a distressed and suffering object, I view them as those inordinate actions, which arise from the weakness of human nature, at a time when she ought to command ability and strength of reason, to have assisted in the distress she has just been witness to, and not have exposed herself to the necessity of receiving the same, if not greater assistance, from others. I am inclined to place under the same head of sympathy, as an *irregular imitative faculty*, those inordinate convulsive actions which arise . . . on seeing another in the agony of an epileptic paroxysm. Frequent instances occur.

The debilitating effects of sentimental novels on the extremely reactive sympathies of "weak minds and spirits, and therefore . . . women" (112)

7. "Sympathie, (Physiolog.) cette convenance d'afection & d'inclination; cette vive intelligence des coeurs, communiquée, répandue, sentie avec une rapidité inexplicable; cette conformité de qualités naturelles, d'idées, d'humeurs & de tempéramens, par laquelle deux ames assorties se cherchent, s'aiment, s'attachent l'une à l'autre, se confondent ensemble, est ce qu'on nomme *sympathie*. . . . mais ce n'est point de cette heureuse liason, dont je dois entretenir le lecteur. Il s'agit ici de cette communication qu'ont les parties du corps. . . . Il est vrai pourtant que cette communication produisoit aussi quelquefois par le même mécanisme un transport, un enchaînement de sensations agréables" (Diderot and d'Alembert 1751–80, 15:736).

is a common theme (cf. Wollstonecraft 1792, 414–52). That is, sometimes sympathy is not a symmetric relationship between the minds of two equals but suggests rather the influence of those of greater mental powers over weaker individuals.

The suggestion of inequality, so apparent in references to gender, also extended to relations between relatively weak human beings and an omnipotent divinity. Francis Hutcheson, for example, refers to "the *universal Benevolence* [of the Creator] toward all Men, we may compare to that principle of *Gravitation*, which perhaps extends to all Bodys in the Universe" (quoted in Solkin 1993, 233). The same suggestion of inequality between individuals sharing a sympathetic relationship also appears in literature. William Godwin ([1794] 1982, 112), in *Caleb Williams*, describes the persecuted man as tied by "magnetical sympathy" to his patron. Similarly, Mary Shelley's *Frankenstein* ([1818] 1992) describes a creature that is "invisibly bonded" to his creator, surely echoing the sympathetic ties between human beings and a deity.

It is no wonder that eighteenth-century characterizations of social sympathy have been called ambiguous (cf. Mercer 1972 and Fontaine 1997). A more sympathetic (that is, kinder) reading would lead to Jackson's (1781, 114) conclusion: "The attraction or cohesion of bodies in general amount to the same general principle and point out to us, that through all nature sympathy is the universal bond." But despite its apparent universality, the definition of sympathy varied among writers and within the body of work of any single social theorist.

The eighteenth century, however, is the period when social theory and physiology are just beginning to emerge from natural philosophy and to distinguish themselves from one another. Yet sympathy was a concept common to all of the still-indistinct realms of intellectual and popular discourse. The idea belonged to a group of terms and principles whose meanings and uses were not yet clearly isolated from one another. Recent works, such as those by G. J. Barker-Benfield (1992), John Mullan (1988), and, especially, Constance Classen (1998), trace the links among imagination, feeling, gender, and public culture in the period. But there were intellectual forces within both social theory and physiology that required greater clarity, and terms whose meanings could be defined and fixed. The idea of sympathy allowed one to appreciate the subtle nuances of complex and related ideas, but it did not allow either body of thought to begin to define its boundaries and develop its theoretical apparatus.

The frustration of attempting to found theory on what was essentially a premodern concept can still be seen in economic analysis. Many economists, though attracted to the concept of sympathy, find it too slippery a signifier to work with easily. Philippe Fontaine (1997), for example, relying on the *Oxford English Dictionary* to tame a language rich in associations, proposes a new taxonomy to guide contemporary analysis: he distinguishes between *empathetic identification*,[8] which may be "partial" or "full," and *sympathetic identification*. Partial empathetic identification refers to an imaginative exchange of circumstances with another so that one might, for example, imagine how one would feel upon the death of a child. Full empathetic identification refers to an exchange of circumstances and persons with another. That is, one not only imagines the circumstances that another faces, but also imaginatively shares another's reactions as if one were that individual, with that individual's unique history and character. And sympathetic identification refers to what economists often call "interdependent utility functions"—the idea that one person's well-being affects another's. This clarity is not only useful to a social scientist who wants to reinforce the concept of sympathy in contemporary social theory. It is absolutely consistent with the spirit of eighteenth-century theorists of language, including Adam Smith, who pleaded for clarity and precision of terminology as an aid to scientific development.

The eighteenth century, however, was an arena that saw a complex interplay between learned discourse and popular imagination, and the language of social philosophy retained the traces of broader associations. In particular, the social theorists who used the term *sympathy* never defined it in a clear and unambiguous way. And it was this very ambiguity that allowed traces of older meanings to infect and enrich theory, as we shall see in section 3 below.

2. The Sympathy of the Nerves

Scientific discovery forces practitioners to adapt existing terminology to describe new ideas and previously unrecognized, or unnamed, phenomena. It is frequently the case that the terminology of one scientific field will be adapted to serve in another. For example, the eighteenth-century

8. Fontaine is aware that *empathy* is a word not available to eighteenth-century commentators. He notes that E. B. Titchener introduced it into English in 1909 as a translation of the German *Einfühlung*.

French physiologist Xavier Bichat (1852, 57–59) recognized the historical contingency of scientific discourse. He noted that the language of physics had been used in physiology simply because scientific advances in physics had preceded developments in physiology. If physiology rather than modern physics had developed first, he argued, one would expect to find physical phenomena explained in terms more appropriate to living matter. Crystals would attract one another by means of the "excitation" they exerted on each other's sensibilities, and planets would move because they "irritate" one another across great distances. This, he noted, is no more, and certainly no less, exact than talking about "doses," "quantities," "sums," or "gravitation," "attraction" and "repulsion" in physiology. Similarly, Seguin Henry Jackson (1781, 173) asks pardon for "using the old language" of sympathy in a scientific discussion of the communication of bodily organs.[9]

Metaphor is the language of scientific discovery. Those eighteenth-century scientists who endorsed Locke and "plain writing," designed to render language transparent and precise, nevertheless used figurative language because they had no alternative. But their metaphors did not unambiguously compare distinct phenomena with stable definitions. Metaphors rely on constantly shifting associations, and meaning is negotiated as one particular use shades into another. And, indeed, some authors deliberately sought the rich associations of a figurative language. This was at least as true of the physiologists as of the social theorists.

In this literature, sympathy is a special case of sensibility, and the terms are often used interchangeably. As sensibility accounts for the reaction of a particular organ receiving data from contact with the environment, sympathy is the communication of different bodily organs. It is often but not always unconscious and manifests itself by disturbances in one organ when another is stimulated (Macilwain 1836). The notion built, in a rather unclear way, upon the century-old work of Thomas Willis (1684), who argued that the intercostal nerve mediated sympathy.

In 1747, the role of the nervous system and nervous sympathy first began to make inroads into the Edinburgh medical establishment with

9. "Before I proceed, I think it proper to observe, that these terms, *sympathy and consent*, in the sense here used, seem liable to some objections and restrictions. . . . At present I shall use the old language, that I may not be misunderstood" (Jackson 1781, 173). "These terms have however been found useful to explain, or account for, occult causes, and are sometimes the last resource, the *ne plus ultra* of a deficient comprehension" (226). *Occult*, in the eighteenth century, referred simply to causes not understood, rather than unknowable causes (cf. Fara 1996, 176).

the appointment of Robert Whytt as professor of medicine. According to Christopher Lawrence (1979, 27), he was the first to "give the term [*sympathy*] a clearly defined structural and functional significance" in about 1744, and subsequent Edinburgh physiologists—William Cullen, John Gregory, and Alexander Monro—developed the idea. Until Whytt's appointment, the school had been run by men trained at Leiden by Hermann Boerhaave (1743), whose model of the human body as a hydraulic machine dominated European physiology until the midcentury. But the growing influence of Lockean psychology, with its basis in sensation, led to an intellectual distancing from the mechanistic models of an earlier period. Whytt's main contribution was to introduce a "sentient principle" into his model of human beings. This principle could receive stimuli and direct the various organs of the body to make the appropriate response. Behavior, that is, was purposive, even if it was not necessarily conscious. And the nervous system, and nervous function, became the mechanism that coordinated the actions of the human body; nervous sympathy was its tool of communication (Lawrence 1979, 25).

William Cullen, an intimate of Smith and Hume, joined the medical school in 1755 (Donovan 1975, 34–76; cf. Lawrence 1979, 26). Cullen was uncomfortable with the notion of an exogenous "sentient principle," which resembled too closely the idea of a soul. But he was equally uncomfortable with a mechanistic model of the body. His solution was to replace Whytt's "sentient principle" with a "vital principle," which he characterized as an etheric fluid in the nervous system. In an excited state, this fluid served all the purposes of Whytt's "sentient principle"—it coordinated bodily function and transmitted sensation to the appropriate organs—but it did so without introducing an outside principle. Subsequent contributors to Edinburgh physiology built upon the ideas of Whytt and Cullen. John Gregory and Alexander Monro, for example, both adopted the notion of a sentient principle but also accepted the idea of an electric nervous energy (Lawrence 1979, 27; Cullen 1789).

All of these physiologists imagined sympathy as an extension of sensibility. The 1797 *Britannica* (18:251) begins its description of somatic sympathy by linking it to the ways in which a human being derives data from the environment through the senses: "The five senses, *hearing, tasting, smelling, feeling, and seeing*, are conscious of a sympathetic impression from odious objects. . . . The most agreeable as well as odious objects operate in a secondary way, in producing those sympathetic impressions and actions which they commonly give rise to. An increased secretion of saliva often takes place at the sight of a favourite dish." The article goes on to explain the coordination of bodily function by means of sympathy. For example, "There is a very apparent reason why a sympathy should take place between the eyes. Hence their motions are synchronous" (251).

There is a logical continuity between somatic sympathy (or communication between various organs in a single body) and the effects of the "passions of the mind" on the sensations and impressions of the body: "The passions and affections of the mind produce in the body different sensations and impressions, and, as sympathies of consciousness, determine in general the spirits to those parts which labour most, or are most apt to be affected. Thus fear and anger determine to the heart. . . . It may also be further observed, that those tender sympathetic affections which lay hold of the mind, at the representation of theatrical performances, originate from the same principle" (250–51). Moreover, the sympathetic communication between two different people is explained by the same principle: "The affections of the mind of one person will often work upon the spirits of the many. . . . It has been said, that the passions of the mind are occasionally infectious, particularly, some of them. Thus *fear* and *shame* are sometimes very suddenly so" (251). The epistemological continuity between the physiological theories of the Edinburgh medical school and the social theories of Smith and Hume seems apparent. The same principle explains the action of sensation, the coordination of the organs of the body, and the "social principle" that allows "fellow-feeling" to emerge in a society.

Physiologists, however, were very aware that sympathetic connections between individuals are not entirely benign. Particularly in France, and particularly after the Revolution, the effect an especially charismatic speaker might have on the minds of a crowd was attributed to sympathy (see Condorcet 1798, 426–28). Echoing the common understanding that "the depravity and force of the imagination in the production of sympathies . . . always operate most upon weak minds and spirits," the *Britannica* (18:251) nevertheless contends that these effects can be controlled by reason: "Such effects are obviated upon the same principle which establishes the prevention of bodily disease: for an infection and contagion from body to body (as, for example, during the plague), the miasma may be received, but from the strength and good disposition of the body, it is expelled and wrought out before it has had sufficient time to form the disease." Jackson (1781, 101) acknowledges the special susceptibility of "weak minds and spirits, and therefore . . . women, superstitious and fearful persons, sick people, children, and young creatures," but claims that "the serious passions may surely be so under the control of reason, as to resist infection, whatever may be the case of *temporary muscular or nervous attraction*" (99).

Moreover, the recognition that imagination clearly had some role to play in the generation of sympathy was uncomfortably close to "superstition," a charge the physiologists were keen to dispute. Jackson, for example, writes:

> There is not a doubt, but the *force of imagination* often gives energy to our actions. It may however, unless we are much on our guard, easily delude us aside from reason. It has been the *tree* which has yielded the fruits of superstition in former times, and which has often fed the human mind with the most extravagant notions of sympathy. Sympathy of this kind, *such as the power of charms, and the like*, are now pretty generally exploded. (102–3)

But Jackson and the editors of the *Britannica* and the *Encyclopédie* were a little too swift to condemn such beliefs as the superstition of times past, as we shall see below.

Moreover, even seemingly serious scientific discourse frequently slid into a retelling of stories from the past. For example, Jackson claims, "There is much reason to suspect that a connection between the affections and sensations of the female mind and uterus is very materially concerned in the process of generation" (100). Recognizing that sympathy is "one of the most extensive principles in the animal œconomy" (chap. 2, sec. 1), Jackson is also aware that the effects of maternal actions on the developing fetus had been a matter of speculation for some time. He quotes Francis Bacon at length on the effects of diet, alcohol, and tobacco consumption, too much thinking, beans and onions (which were imagined to cause vapors to rise to the head and create lunatics), and coriander (the vapors of which were thought to induce ingenuity) on fetal development (206–10). He also claims that science supports some of these contentions, but Jackson gives far greater weight to the potential harm caused a developing fetus by maternal ignorance. But how far from this is an old tale, often cited in this literature, that he attributes to the priest and philosopher Nicolas Malebranche? It purports to relate the story of a woman, two months pregnant, who went to see a criminal broken on the wheel. Seven months later, the baby was born with every limb broken. The cause? Sympathy. Or Jackson's own claim that pregnant women are particularly susceptible to "tender and sympathetic feelings" and frequently go into labor when they witness another in labor (112–13).

By the third quarter of the eighteenth century, there was a remarkable agreement among physicians as they delineated the various sympathies operative in the human body. What they disagreed about profoundly, however, was the process by means of which sympathy occurred. Jackson, for example, claims that "sympathy could only properly arise from nervous connection" (227) but writes:

> I have delivered it as my opinion in several parts of this treatise, that the *extreme arterious vessels*, forming a part of the capillary system, are most likely to become the channels of *medical sympathy*, through the medium of the sympathizing heart. I cannot therefore close the subject, without informing my reader, that some very eminent men are of a different opinion. The sympathy of an animal body has been explained by the unison of sound produced on the strings of a musical instrument. . . . Such sympathy has been referred by Mr. J. Hunter to the system of *lymphatic vessels*. Mr. Cruickshanks is of opinion, that it takes place by consent of the *nerves*. And Dr. Cullen is an advocate, in *pyrexia*, *arthritis*, and *dyspepsia*, at least, for sympathy between *muscular fibres*. The reader is left to judge. (231–32)

The *Britannica* (18:251), nevertheless, chastised these scientific speculators in 1797: "Many have attempted to account for the remarkable sympathy which takes place between parts of the body seemingly unconnected with each other; but as these attempts are merely conjectures, without any solid principles to rest on, we pass them over as the dreams of ingenious men. It would be fortunate for science, if men would confine themselves to those subjects which can be known, and never draw conclusions till they have established the principles." Thirty years earlier, Whytt (1765, vi-vii) had defended the theoretical speculation condemned by the *Britannica*:

> If it should be said, that to account for diseases from the sensibility of sympathy of nerves, while we know not wherein these powers consist, is no better than referring them to a *facultas incognita*, or the hypothetical *motions* and *countermotions* of the animal spirits; I shall

> only answer, that altho' we cannot explain why grief or joy should, by means of the nerves, excite a greater motion than usual, in the vessels of the lachrymal glands, yet it is leading us to the truth, and advancing one step further in our knowledge, to shew that the increased secretion of tears, occasioned by those passions of mind, proceeds from this cause, and not from any compression of the lachrymal glands or their ducts, by the neighbouring muscles, as has been commonly imagined.

Clearly, physiologists believed that some sort of bodily communication existed, and they captured its effects under the label of *sympathy*. Moreover, they seemed convinced that this somatic communication was allied to the social sympathy that philosophers used to explain the fellow-feeling between human beings that allowed a society to cohere. But uncertainty about the process by means of which somatic communication occurred allowed scientists to entertain sometimes fantastic speculations, and it was through these speculations that the broader associations of sympathy infected scientific discourse.

3. The Shadow of the Occult

Even though physiologists tended to dismiss the occult associations of sympathy as "superstition," they drew upon them in the creation of their own texts. Jackson (1781, 113), again, provides an example: "I cannot conclude the subject without observing that the influence of sympathy even extends itself to the inanimate part of nature. Plants, metals, &c sympathize with each other. The whole world was formerly supposed by the ancients to sympathize in all its parts. Their doctrines were, however, carried too far, and built upon superstitious principles, though they were occasionally supported by many [observations]." Sympathy, until well into the eighteenth century, was part of an ancient system of sympathies and antipathies. John Trenchard, in *The Natural History of Superstition* (1709, 26–27, 30), illustrates the position of which Jackson was critical: "There is a certain Sympathy and Antypathy in Nature. . . . The Loadstone draws Iron to it, Gold Quicksilver; The Sensitive Plant shrinks from your Touch; Some sorts of Vegitables, though set at a distance, attract one another . . .; A Ratlesnake fixing his Eyes upon a Squeril, will make him run into his Mouth. . . . Some of the Quakers have arrived to a great proficiency in this natural Magnetism, or Magick" (see also Fara 1996, 149). Sympathy was not clearly distinguished from magnetism until well into the eighteenth century. Early-eighteenth-century dictionaries tend to discuss sympathy in terms of loadstones and iron (cf. Bailey 1731, "sympathetic").

A seventeenth-century German medical text by the eminent Jesuit natural philosopher Athanasius Kircher offers an illuminating illustration (Joscelyn Godwin [1979] provides a thorough discussion of his work). Kircher's *Magneticum Naturae Regnum sive Disceptatio Physiologica* (1667) has as its frontispiece an image that captures many of the associations referred to by later writers (see figure 1). The picture shows Platonic rings extending from God's hand to unite all the parts of the harmonious universe—"the binding links from great to small." Magnetic imagery is apparent in the compass. "Sympathy" is depicted between the sunflower and the sun and between the moon and the moonflower. The rooster and deer represent the sympathetic relationship between animals. The phases of the moon, the seasons, and the mirroring of celestial relations on and beneath the earth are also depicted, as is the balance of nature and eternal judgment (represented by the scale in the angel's hand).

This imagery was still very common throughout the eighteenth century, not only in early encyclopedia accounts, but also in poetry, literature, and popular medical texts. Sympathetic medicine, based on similar principles, appealed to the popular imagination, even though the medical establishment was wont to declare it outgrown superstition. Samuel Johnson's *Dictionary* (1755) defines "sympathetick" as "having mutual sensation; being affected . . . by what happens to the other; feeling in consequence of what the other feels," and quotes Thomas Brown's *Vulgar Errors*: "Hereupon are grounded the gross mistakes, in the cure of diseases, not only from the last medicine and sympathetick receipts, but amulets, charms, and all incantatory applications." Yet sympathetic medicine still had enough of a following to occasion the publication and reprinting of key texts (Irvine 1756).

Kenelm Digby, in 1644,[10] first published *Of Bodies and of mans soul. To discover the immortality of reasonable souls. With two discourses of the powder of sympathy, and of the vegetation of plants*. This extremely popular work was reprinted many times, in English, Latin, and French (at least), over the next century and attracted many notices and

10. Sorting out the publication history of Digby's opus extends far beyond the scope of this essay. He was a very prolific writer and an even more prolific publisher, with multiple editions of the same work appearing under different titles, very often in the same year.

Figure 1 Frontispiece to *Magneticum Naturae Regnum sive Disceptatio Physiologica* (1667), by Athanasius Kircher. The Latin motto reads "the world is tied by secret knots." Reprinted courtesy of the British Library.

comments. The powder of sympathy purported to heal at a distance, in very much the same way that Paracelsian weapon salves of an earlier period claimed to heal a wound by applying ointment to the knife that caused it. Later, Digby (1668, 45) offered a sympathetic cure for toothache, in *Receipts in Physick*, which gives some flavor of the technique: "With an Iron-nail raise and cut the Gum from about the Teeth, till it bleed, and that some of the blood stick upon the nail; then drive it into a woodden beam up to the head: After this is done, you never shall have the toth-ach in all your life." Despite the assurances of the enlightened encyclopedias and scientific writers of the late-eighteenth century, sympathetic medicine was still seriously credited. Indeed, late-eighteenth-century medics and practitioners such as Ebenezer Sibley, John B. de Mainauduc, and Franz Anton Mesmer deliberately sought out precedents in these earlier works, exacerbating relations with the medical establishments.

Ebenezer Sibley's extremely popular astrological and medical text, *A Key to Physic, and the Occult Sciences*, was published in 1794 and drew very explicitly on Kircher's imagery. The interwoven nature of sympathetic imagery is particularly apparent in this text. Sibley (1794, 256–76) details a complex system of sympathies bonding plants and animals throughout a harmonious nature. Then his medical text veers into a related field. Sibley endorses animal magnetism (which was assumed to rely on the manipulation of sympathy) and combines a tale of magnetic effluvia with allusions to contemporary French theories of "vital fluids" (reminiscent of Cullen's etheric fluid): "Animal magnetism is a sympathy which exists between the magnet and the insensible perspiration of the human body, whereby an æther, or universal effluvia, is made to pass and repass through the pores of the cuticle" (256) (see figure 2).

One of the best known and successful of the London animal magnetizers was John B. de Mainauduc, who disassociated himself from Mesmer and the Parisian influence.[11] He argued that sensations were conducted along nerves in the human body, which he envisioned as chains of linked atoms, just as atmospheric nerves conduct sound. In accord with God's will, human volition could direct this atomic activity through the agency of animal magnetism (Mainauduc 1798). Animal magnetism,

11. The reception of animal magnetism in London, after it had been discredited in Paris by the commission made up of Benjamin Franklin and others, is traced by Fara (1996, 195–207), Porter (1985, 1987, 1988, 1989), and Winter (1999).

Dodd del.
ANIMAL MAGNETISM — The Operator putting his Patient into a Crisis.

Figure 2 Illustration from *A Key to Physic, and the Occult Sciences* (1794), by Ebenezer Sibley. This figure illustrates the sympathetic ties between the magnetizer and the female client. Women were deemed particularly susceptible to mesmerism, just as Jackson and his colleagues deemed them particularly susceptible to "tender and sympathetic feelings." Reprinted courtesy of the Wellcome Institute Library, London.

despite being ridiculed in Paris, attracted the attention of the serious medical establishment (Godwin 1785). John Hunter (1835–37, 1:317–37) included the topic in his long discussion of sympathy and referred sensations. While boasting of his ability to resist the effects of mesmerism, Hunter allowed that others felt its power.

These developments in physiology did have implications for social theory. Patricia Fara (1996, 199) has argued convincingly that de Mainauduc developed a model of a harmonious universe in which animate and inanimate matter were linked through the circulation of atoms. The health of the human being relied upon the free circulation of these atoms, and disease and ill health were the result of a blockage or disequilibrium. In de Mainauduc's view, the appropriate role of the physician was to assist nature to reestablish a healthy circulation. John Hunter shared this vision of a universe based upon freely circulating atoms. Both he and de Mainauduc saw the human body as a mirror of a commercial society, whose health depended on "the free movement of self-motivated entities contributing towards the larger well-being" (Fara 1996, 199; cf. Rosenberg 1983, Sennett 1994, Marcovich 1982, and Lawrence 1979). That is, the image of the body or animal oeconomy shared by establishment physicians and by quacks created a model for a commercial economy in which the actions of the individual agents are spontaneously ordered. This similarity between nascent ideas in social theory and the model of the human body emerging in this literature would lead one to expect the continued harmonious development of these two sciences.

There were, however, other forces at work. A strong loathing of French materialism animated many Scottish intellectuals in the later eighteenth century. Jack Morelly (1971) surveys the terrain and provides many crucial details. This intellectual distaste, however, was inextricably bound up with political events. By the end of the eighteenth century, animal magnetism was associated with French ideas, and French ideas—inexorably—with revolution. Sympathy, now taking on the slightly mocking or pejorative sense of being "weak-minded" and thus susceptible to hypnotic influence, was similarly associated with dangerous and radical French notions. Robert Southey linked his criticism of animal magnetism to the revolutionary threat of popular leaders in his *Letters from England* (1951). John Robison (1797) tied animal magnetism to revolution and to the English revolutionary visionary Richard Brothers, in an amazing conspiracy theory—Rosicrucians, natural philosophers, and animal magnetizers were all in on an organized attempt to spread the atheist ideals of revolution. Robison (1801, 1:iv) was responsible for the articles on natural philosophy in the 1801 supplement to the third edition of the *Britannica*. The purpose of the supplement was to counteract "the seeds of Anarchy and Atheism" sown by "that pestiferous work"—the *Encyclopédie* (cf. Fara 1996, 130).[12]

The British political campaign against scientific innovation, and especially scientific innovation by foreigners, is most apparent in a little pamphlet attributed to "The Sceptic" (1800) and directed, in the first event, against Humphry Davy, and entitled *The Birth of Wonders!* The tale opens with the French Revolution, the first wonder, soon followed by his little sister—"Mesmeria." Her "eye fascinated and charmed to the spot," and her "mysterious power of inchantment, subverted the laws of nature":

> The next which came to light of the same gender, was invisible, and only known to be a female by the noise she made.—She vanished instantaneously: fled into Italy, and entered the body of a Frog, which professor Galvani was dressing for his Wife's supper.—As she has never condescended to render herself visible, or useful; I think proper to treat her as beneath my notice. Were I a frog, indeed, I should think myself justifiable in cursing the moment of her birth, and execrating the fools who, dead to all the feelings of humanity, heap aggravated tortures on the race—harmless as doves!—to see them—shake a leg! (6)[13]

The last of the wonders—brothers Antiphlogiston and little Caloric—heaped mischief upon the world. The literature is fascinating—from pulpits (cf. Hole 1989), to pamphlets, to political cartoons, to apparently serious political commentary—women, French people, indeed foreigners of all persuasions, animal magnetizers, natural philosophers,

12. For Robison's own views on the *Encyclopédie*, see Robison 1797, 519–20. His extreme hostility toward all things French is quite striking. I note that Robison suffered an extreme opium addiction, particularly toward the end of his life, which may have played some role in the etiology of his particular paranoia.

13. In 1786, Luigi Galvani obtained muscular contraction in a frog when he touched its nerves with a pair of scissors during an electrical storm. He built on this result and published an essay in 1791 that argued that animal tissue contained an unknown vital force, which he labeled "animal electricity," and concluded that the brain is the organ from which this "electric fluid" is secreted while the nerves act as conductors (see Galvani 1954). Physiologists attempting to explain the mechanism of nervous sympathy often cited this work.

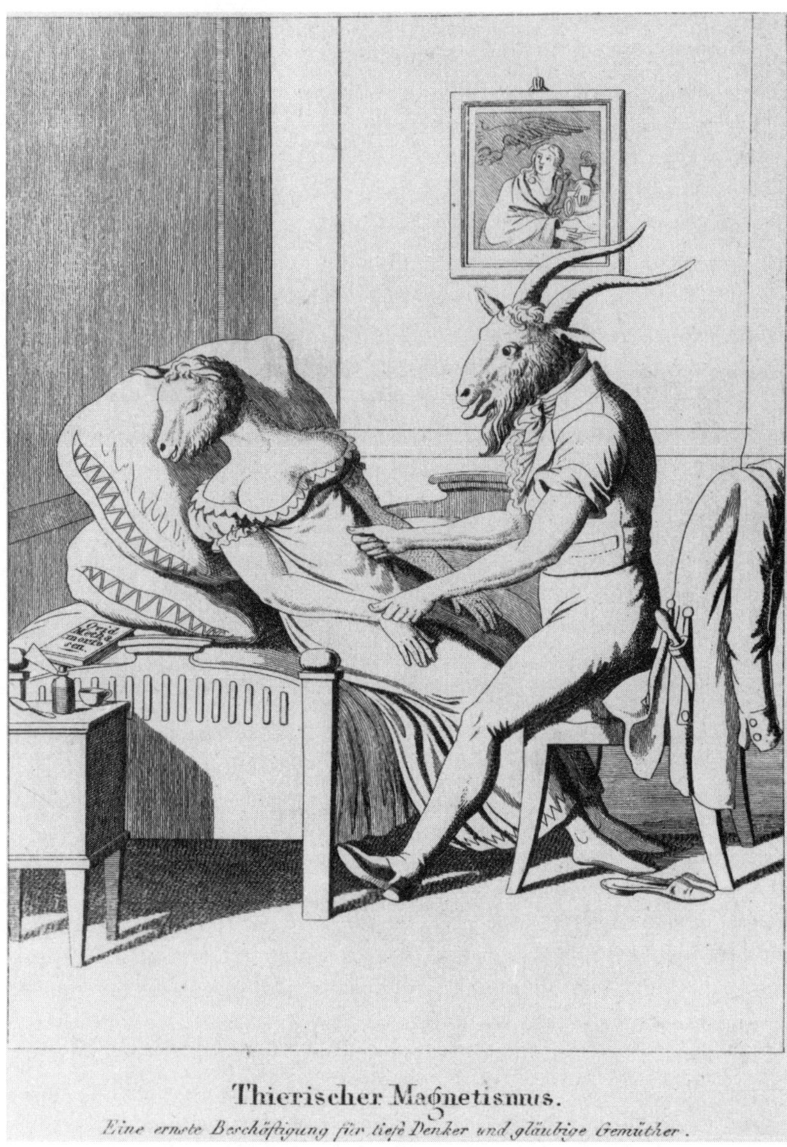

Thierischer Magnetismus.
Eine ernste Beschäftigung für tiefe Denker und gläubige Gemüther.

Figure 3 Etching after M. Voltz (1815). The goat-headed man caressing a sleeping, ewe-headed woman in this figure satirizes the notion of animal magnetism, its applications by physicians, and its gender implications. Reprinted courtesy of the Wellcome Institute Library, London.

Rosicrucians, Jesuits, Catholics, non-Catholics, Quakers, Swedenborgians, and even Methodists came under attack. The real fear was of insurrection, a repeat of the French Revolution on British soil, but the apparent target was animal magnetism (see figure 3).

Animal magnetism was often justified in the language of contemporary science. Its practitioners spoke of etheric fluids and explained its efficacy in terms of human physiology and the operation of sympathy. But its true antecedent is the much older set of associations called to mind by the term *sympathy* and, in particular, the alchemical ideas that had found expression in Kenelm Digby's powder of sympathy and Kircher's medical text. Superimposed on these associations was the historical pairing of animal magnetism with French ideas at a time when all French ideas were suspect because of potential implications of regicide and revolution.

The extreme disrepute that was associated with animal magnetism spilled over into more sober areas of scientific discourse. Social theory, in particular, was already promulgating such novel ideas as free markets that were linked, in the minds of some, with republicanism. It could not afford the taint of association with dangerous and revolutionary French ideas. For whatever reason, this evocative form of sympathy virtually disappeared from British social theory with the turn of the nineteenth century.

4. The Much Diminished Sympathy of the Nineteenth Century

Sympathy was used to explain many apparently similar, but subtly different, phenomena in the eighteenth century. Those who used it had no very clear understanding of how sympathy was supposed to work, either in society or in the body. Sympathy was not observable, either in its social aspects or in its bodily operation. It was visible only in its presumed effects. Speculation about its nature was grounded more in the imagination of scientists than in their experimental observations. As philosophers and scientists grew more and more convinced of the legitimacy of their knowledge, a word that alluded to a mystical alchemical past became less attractive. Those who wanted medical or social explanations running only in terms of the observable, the measurable, the unambiguous, and the strongly causative found unacceptable a term that did not lend itself to stable definition. And the union in the popular imagination of animal magnetism, *sympathy*, and France, at a time when British intellectuals were disinclined toward Gallic ideas, did little to salvage its reputation. All of this would seem enough to doom the idea of sympathy.

Despite vestiges of sympathetic analysis in such places as Charles Fourier's utopian socialism and John Stuart Mill's politics, the language of sympathy was transformed in the social discourse in the nineteenth century (Silberling 1911, 422; Mill 1973–74, 8:899). In physiology, the language of sympathy gradually gave way to the language of consensus, irritation, nervous connection, electricity, vibrating fibers, and the like. The same rich associations, stemming from an earlier worldview of interlocking sympathies and antipathies throughout a harmonious universe, that allowed eighteenth-century philosophers to grapple with big ideas and new discoveries, ultimately doomed the exercise. The connotations of the term made it very difficult for the would-be scientific writing of the period to distinguish itself from superstition. And because the idea of sympathy was never corralled and tamed, never limited and confined within a tight body of thought, it proved equally useful to those operating at the edges of science as it did to those at the medical school in Edinburgh. These less reputable scholars included the animal magnetizers. And an accident of history, a revolution that convulsed the staid world of British science even as it reshaped the French political scene, ensured that a word that already had some significant limitations would now be saddled with political connotations as well.

Sympathy could not survive intact.

References

Bailey, Nathan. 1731. *An Universal Etymological Dictionary*. 5th ed. London: J & J Knapton.

Barker-Benfield, G. J. 1992. *The Culture of Sensibility: Sex and Society in Eighteenth-Century Britain*. Chicago: University of Chicago Press.

Bichat, Xavier. 1852. *Recherches physiologiques sur la vie et la mort*. Edited by Dr. Cerise. Paris: V. Masson.

Blondel, James A. 1729. *The Power of the Mother's Imagination over the Foetus Examin'd*. London.

[Boerhaave, Hermann]. 1743. *An Essay on the Virtue and Efficient Cause of Magnetical Cures*. London.

Boucé, Paul-Gabriel. 1987. Imagination, Pregnant Women, and Monsters, in Eighteenth-Century England and France. In *Sexual Underworlds of the Enlightenment*, edited by George S. Rousseau and Roy Porter, 86–100. Manchester: Manchester University Press.

Classen, Constance. 1998. *The Color of Angels: Cosmology, Gender, and the Aesthetic Imagination*. London: Routledge.

Condorcet, Sophie de Grouchy, marquise de. 1798. *Lettres à C[abanis], sur la théorie des sentimens moraux*. In *Théorie des sentimens moraux*, by Adam Smith. Translated by Condorcet. Paris: F. Buisson.

———. 1994. *Lettres sur la sympathie suivies des letters d'amour*. Edited by Jean-Paul de Lagrave. Montreal: L'Étincelle Éditeur.

Cullen, William. 1789. *A Treatise of the Materia Medica*. 2 vols. Edinburgh.

Diderot, D., and J. D'Alembert. 1751–80. *Encyclopédie, ou, Dictionnaire raisonné des sciences, des arts et des métiers*. 35 vols. Stuttgart-Bad Cannstatt.

Digby, Kenelm. 1644. *Of bodies and of mans soul. To discover the immortality of reasonable souls. With two discourses of the powder of sympathy, and of the vegetation of plants*. London: S. G. and B. G. for John Williams.

———. 1668. *Receipts in Physick*. London.

Donovan, A. 1975. *Philosophical Chemistry in the Scottish Enlightenment*. Edinburgh: Edinburgh University Press.

Fara, Patricia. 1996. *Sympathetic Attractions: Magnetic Practices, Beliefs, and Symbolism in Eighteenth-Century England*. Princeton, N.J.: Princeton University Press.

Ferguson, Adam. [1767] 1966. *An Essay on the History of Civil Society*. Edinburgh: Edinburgh University Press.

Fontaine, Philippe. 1997. Identification and Economic Behavior: Sympathy and Empathy in Historical Perspective. *Economics and Philosophy* 13:261–80.

Galvani, Luigi. 1954. *Commentary on the Effect of Electricity on Muscular Motion*. Translated by Margaret Glover. Norwood, Conn.: Burndy Library.

Godwin, Joscelyn. 1979. *Athanasius Kircher: A Renaissance Man and the Quest for Lost Knowledge*. London: Thames and Hudson.

Godwin, William. 1785. *Report of Dr. Benjamin Franklin, and Other Commissioners, Charged by the King of France, with the Examination of the Animal Magnetism as Now Practised at Paris*. London.

———. [1794] 1982. *Caleb Williams*. Edited by David McCracken. Oxford: Oxford University Press.

Gregory, John. 1772. *A Comparative View of the State and Faculties of Man compared with the Animal World*. 5th ed. London.

Harris, James. [1755] 1841. *The Works of James Harris, esq. With an account of his life and character, by his son, the Earl of Malmesbury*. Oxford.

Hole, Robert. 1989. *Pulpits, Politics, and Public Order in England, 1760–1832*. Cambridge: Cambridge University Press.

Hume, David. 1739. *A Treatise of Human Nature: being an attempt to introduce the experimental method of reasoning into moral subjects, etc*. London: John Noon.

———. [1751] 1983. *Philosophical Essays concerning Human Understanding*. Edinburgh: Edinburgh University Press.

Hunter, John. 1835–37. *The Works of John Hunter, FRS with Notes*. Edited by J. Palmer. 5 vols. London: Longman et al.

Hutcheson, Francis. 1725. *An Inquiry into the original of our ideas of beauty and virtue, in two treatises, in which the principles of the Earl of Shaftesbury are explain'd and defended against the author of the Fable of the Bees [B. De Mandeville] . . . With an attempt to introduce a mathematical calculation in subjects of morality*. London.

Irvine, Christopher. 1756. *Medicina Magnetica: or, the rare and wonderful art of curing by sympathy; laid open by aphorismes; proved in conclusions; and digested into an easy method, etc.* London.

Jackson, Seguin Henry. 1781. *A Treatise on Sympathy*. London: Printed for the author and sold by J. Murray.

Johnson, Samuel. 1755. *A Dictionary of the English Language: In which the words are deduced from their originals, and illustrated in their different significations by examples from the best writers*. London.

Kames, Lord Henry Homes. 1751. *Essays on the Principles of Morality and Natural Religion*. Edinburgh.

Kircher, Athanasius. 1667. *Magneticum Naturae Regnum sive Disceptatio Physiologica*. Rome.

Kirkland, Thomas. 1774. *A Treatise on Child-bed Fevers and on the methods of preventing them: being a supplement to the books lately written on the subject. To which are prefixed two dissertations, the one on the brain and nerves, the other on the sympathy of the nerves, and on different kinds of irritability*. London.

Lawrence, Christopher. 1979. The Nervous System and Society in the Scottish Enlightenment. *Natural Order: Historical Studies of Scientific Culture*, edited by Barry Barnes and Steven Shapin, 19–40. Beverly Hills, Calif.: Sage.

Macfarquhar, C., and G. Gleig, eds. 1788–97. *Encyclopædia Britannica; or, A Dictionary of the Arts and Sciences, and Miscellaneous Literature*. 3d ed. 18 vols. Edinburgh: Bell and Macfarquhar.

Macilwain, George. 1836. *Remarks on the unity of the body, as illustrated by some of the more striking phenomena of sympathy, both mental and corporeal, with a view of . . . improving the application of the constitutional treatment of local diseases*. London.

Mainauduc, John B. de. 1798. *The Lectures of J. B. de Mainauduc*. London.

Marcovich, Anne. 1982. Concerning the Continuity between the Image of Society and the Image of the Human Body: An examination of the Work of the English Physician, J. C. Lettsom (1746–1815). In *The Problem of Medical Knowledge*, edited by Peter Wright and Andrew Treacher, 69–86. Edinburgh: Edinburgh University Press.

Mercer, Philip. 1972. *Sympathy and Ethics: A Study of the Relationship between Sympathy and Morality with Special Reference to Hume's "Treatise."* Oxford: Clarendon Press.

Mill, John Stuart. 1973–74. *A System of Logic*. In vols. 7 and 8 of *Collected Works of John Stuart Mill*, edited by J. M. Robson. Toronto: University of Toronto Press.

Morelly, Jack. 1971. Professors Robison and Playfair, and the *Theophobia Gallica*: Natural Philosophy, Religion, and Politics in Edinburgh, 1789–1815. *Notes and Records of the Royal Society* 26:43–63.

Mullan, John. 1988. *Sentiment and Sociability: The Language of Feeling in the Eighteenth Century*. Oxford: Oxford University Press.

Porter, Roy. 1985. *"Coming under the French Influence": The Early History of Mesmerism in England*. London: Wellcome Institute for the History of Medicine.

———. 1987. The Language of Quackery in England, 1660–1800. In *The Social History of Language*, edited by Peter Burke and Roy Porter, 73–103. Cambridge: Cambridge University Press.

———. 1988. Before the Fringe: "Quackery" in the Eighteenth-Century Medical Market. In *Studies in the History of Alternative Medicine*, edited by Roger Cooter, 1–27. London: Macmillan.

———. 1989. *Health for Sale: Quackery in England, 1660–1850*. Manchester: Manchester University Press.

Pratt, Samuel Jackson. 1781. *Sympathy; or, a sketch of the social passion*. 2d ed. London.

Robison, John. 1797. *Proofs of a Conspiracy against all the Religions and Governments of Europe, Carried on in Secret Meetings of Free Masons, Illuminati, and Reading Societies*. London.

———. 1801. Magnetism. In supplement to vol. 2 of *Encyclopædia Britannica*, 3d ed., edited by G. Gleig, 112–56. Edinburgh.

Rosenberg, Charles E. 1983. Medical Text and Social Context: Explaining William Buchan's *Domestic Medicine*. *Bulletin of the History of Medicine* 57:22–42.

Sacks, Oliver. [1992] 1999. *Migraine*. New York: Vintage Books.

Sceptic, The. 1800. *The Birth of Wonders!* Retford: Printed by E. Peart and sold by West and Hughes.

Sennett, Richard. 1994. *Flesh and Stone: The Body and the City in Western Civilization*. London: Faber & Faber.

Shelley, Mary. [1818] 1992. *Frankenstein, or the Modern Prometheus*. Edited by Maurice Hindle. London: Penguin.

Shorter, Edward. 1992. *From Paralysis to Fatigue: A History of Psychosomatic Illness in the Modern Era*. New York: Free Press.

Sibley, Ebenezer. 1794. *A Key to Physic, and the Occult Sciences*. London.

Silberling, E. 1911. *Dictionnaire de sociologie phalanstérienne: Guide des œuvres complètes de Charles Fourier*. New York: Burt Franklin.

Smith, Adam. [1759] 1976. *The Theory of Moral Sentiments*. Oxford: Oxford University Press.

Solkin, David H. 1993. *Painting for Money: The Visual Arts and the Public Sphere in Eighteenth-Century England*. New Haven, Conn.: Yale University Press.

Southey, Robert. 1951. *Letters from England*. Edited by J. Simmons. London: Cresset Press.

Trenchard, John. 1709. *The Natural History of Superstition*. London.

Whytt, Robert. 1765. *Observations on the nature, causes and cure of those diseases which are commonly called Nervous, Hyperchondriac or Hysteric; to which are prefixed some remarks on the sympathy of nerves*. Edinburgh: T. Beckett, P. du Hondt, and J. Balfour.

Willis, Thomas. 1684. *The Practice of Physick*. London: T. Dring, C. Harper, and J. Leigh.

Winter, Alison. 1999. *Mesmerized*. Chicago: University of Chicago Press.

Wollstonecraft, Mary. 1792. *A Vindication of the Rights of Woman: With Strictures on Moral and Political Subjects*. London.

Business Ethics, Commercial Mathematics, and the Origins of Mathematical Probability

Edith Dudley Sylla

The origins of mathematical probability are usually traced to the 1654 correspondence of Blaise Pascal and Pierre de Fermat about games of luck, and then to Christiaan Huygens's 1657 *On Reckoning in Games of Luck*, which was motivated by the work of Pascal and Fermat. This essay argues rather that the conceptual context within which Huygens developed probability mathematics was, ultimately, that of ethical business practice as it was embodied in commercial mathematics.

In choosing to use Huygens's work on games of luck, along with his own comments, as part 1 of his *The Art of Conjecturing* (published posthumously in 1713, but largely completed in the 1680s), Jacob Bernoulli also operated within the framework of ethics and commercial mathematics. When in part 4 of his book Bernoulli extended the art of conjecturing from games to civil, moral, and economic decision making, he applied the mathematics of games of luck to epistemic probability, bringing games of luck into conjunction with the preexisting concept of probable opinion, something Pascal, Fermat, and Huygens had not done.[1] In this way the conceptual context of probability came full circle, from ethical business practice to prudent decision making, all within the

I would like to thank Joel Kaye and Neil De Marchi for reading the original version of this article and offering new references and suggestions for revision. I would also like to thank the librarians of the Triangle Research Libraries Network (North Carolina) and especially those of North Carolina State University for the many resources they provided through interlibrary loan.

1. For lack of space here, I will not consider the conceptual frameworks within which Pascal and Fermat proposed their solutions, but their attention to the division problem, or "problem of points," connects them, I would argue, to traditional problems of commercial arithmetic.

compass of concepts of the moral oeconomy (cf. Daston 1983 on the relationship of classical mathematical probability and the moral sciences).

In his 1711 "De mensura sortis, seu, de Probabilitate Eventuum in Ludis a Casu Fortuito Pendentibus" [On the measure of chance, or, on the probability of outcomes in games depending on contingency] and his 1718 *The Doctrine of Chances; or A Method of Calculating the Probability of Events in Play*, Abraham De Moivre, like Bernoulli, brought the word *probability* into conjunction with games of luck, but, at the same time, he shifted the foundations of mathematical probability from ethical business partnerships to relative frequencies. Thus almost at the moment when mathematical probability was first developed, it received a new foundation.[2] This has encouraged historians of probability to read De Moivre's frequentist conceptual framework into their interpretations of Huygens and Bernoulli and to overlook its origins in concepts of the moral oeconomy.

This article results from my wish to understand in its historical particularity the conceptual framework within which Jacob Bernoulli proposed to develop an art of conjecture, a wish that arose in the process of my trying to choose the best English words for translating the key technical terms of Bernoulli's *Ars Conjectandi* from Latin into English.[3] Clearly, there is no reasonable alternative to translating the Latin *probabilitas* by the English *probability*, even though *probabilitas* in Bernoulli's Latin did not have the strong connotations of relative frequency that *probability* now inevitably has. But problems of translation also arose for the words *alea*, *sors*, and *casus*. Should all three of these words be translated *chance*, and, if so, why were three words used for a single meaning? Moreover, why, as became obvious to me in the course of my translation, did Huygens and Bernoulli often use *sors* and *expectatio* interchangeably?[4] It was in trying to resolve my translation problems that

2. Cf. Schneider 1980. Ivo Schneider (1981, 8–10) sees in the Port-Royal logic, shortly after Huygens, a "translation of ratios of chances in random decisions into a ratio of degrees of probability." The text does not speak of ratios of chances as such but only of degrees of probability (Arnauld and Nicole [1662] 1981, 353): "Il ne faut pas seulement considerer le bien & le mal en soi, mais aussi la probabilité qu'il arrive ou n'arrive pas." In a game where each of ten players puts in a coin and the winner takes all, "il est aussi neuf fois plus probable à l'égard de chacun qu'il perdra son écu. . . . Ainsi chacun a pour soi . . . neuf degrés de probabilité de perdre un écu."

3. I completed an English translation of the *Ars Conjectandi* ten years ago and hope to publish it soon.

4. Interestingly, in his notes on Huygens's *De ratiociniis in ludo aleae*, Isaac Newton ([1665?] 1967, 60) favored the translation *lot* for *sors*, for instance, "If I bargaine with one or two more to cast lots in order untill one of us by an assigned lott shall win the stake *a*: Since

I was led to see the connection of Huygens's and Bernoulli's work to business ethics and the related commercial arithmetic.

The background of early mathematical probability theory in the mathematics of ethical business practice has been obscured by histories of economics that overemphasize the Catholic Church's condemnation of usury while failing to recognize that the same theologians and lawyers who frowned on usury could smile on profit-making business relationships based on just contracts pursued in an ethical way (cf. Noonan 1957 and Munro 2001–3). There are a number of excellent recent books and articles that attempt to construct a different and more diverse narrative of medieval economic ethics.[5] What I want to do here is to link this recent scholarship to the work of Huygens and Bernoulli.[6]

Jacob Bernoulli was the son and grandson of merchants. He was trained as a theologian and began the sort of work that might be expected of a Protestant pastor but gave it up to teach mathematics and physics at the University of Basel. More than anything else, *The Art of Conjecturing* is a mathematics book. The "missing link" in most histories of mathematical probability, which connects the ethics of business relationships to the work of Huygens and Bernoulli, is commercial mathematics. Before I discuss commercial mathematics, however, let me review the evidence that the context of Huygens's and Bernoulli's work on games of luck is business partnerships and economic justice rather than relative frequencies.

The Evidence of the Earliest Texts of Mathematical Probability

In Christian Huygens's *On Reckoning in Games of Luck* [*De ratiociniis in ludo aleae*] and in Jacob Bernoulli's notes on it published in part 1 of *The Art of Conjecturing* [*Ars Conjectandi*], expectation is defined in

---

y[e] chances may succede infinitely I onely consider y[e] first revolution of them. The valor of each mans whole expectation being in such proportion to one another as y[e] valors of their lots in one revolution. . . . If our bargaine bee soe y[t] there is some lott at y[e] beginning of our play w[ch] returnes not in y[e] after revolutions, detract y[e] valor of those irregular lotts from y[e] stake & y[e] rest shall bee y[e] stake of ye lots w[ch] follow & revolve successively."

5. See, for example, Baeck 1999, Kantola 1994, Kaye 1998, Langholm 1979, 1992, 1998, and Todeschini 1980.

6. Recent authors have done much to trace the conceptual background of mathematical probability. I have found particularly helpful Coumet 1970, Garber and Zabell 1979, Schneider 1981, Schneider 1988, Daston 1988a, Hauser 1997, Poitras 2000, and Franklin 2001.

a way that seems "suspiciously circular" or "somewhat obscure" from the point of view of modern mathematical probability theory.[7] Huygens wrote:

> I use the fundamental principle that a person's chance or expectation to obtain something in a game of luck should be judged to be worth as much as an amount such that, if he had it, he could arrive again at a like chance or expectation contending under equitable conditions. So, for example, if someone hides three similar coins in one hand and seven in the other, without my knowing which hand has which amount, and he offers to let me have the money in whichever hand I choose, then this offer is worth as much to me as if he gave me five coins. This is because, if I had five coins, then I could arrive again at a situation in which I had an equal expectation of getting three or seven coins, contending on equal terms [*aequo lusu*]. (Bernoulli [1713] 1968, 3–4)[8]

Jacob Bernoulli accepted this principle but tried to make it clearer, saying: "Here the author of this treatise is explaining the fundamental principle of the whole art. . . . Since it is very important that this principle be correctly understood, I will try to demonstrate it by reasoning which is more popular than the foregoing and more adapted to common comprehension. I posit only this as an axiom or definition: *Anyone may expect, or should be said to expect, just as much as he will obtain without fail*" (5).[9] From today's point of view, this choice of a foundational principle for expectation—and, in Bernoulli's case, for mathematical probability—seems counterintuitive. Where we would expect Huygens and Bernoulli to begin by considerations of probabilities of chance events, instead they begin with the amount adequate to buy a given position in a game or what a person will obtain without fail ("infallibiliter obtinebit").[10]

7. Cf. Daston 1988a, 24–26; Freudenthal 1980; and Hald 1990, 69.

8. Here and elsewhere I use my translation of the *Ars Conjectandi*.

9. Just before Bernoulli's note, Huygens had said, "If I have an equal chance of winning 3 or 7, then by Proposition I my expectation is worth 5. And it is certain that if I had 5, then I could again obtain the same expectation. For if I and another player both put up 5, with the provision that the winner will give the loser 3, then our game will be altogether just, and I will obviously have an equal chance of losing and getting 3 or of winning and getting 7 (since if I win, I get 10, but I give 3 of this to the other player)" (Bernoulli [1713] 1968, 4–5).

10. Ernest Coumet (1970, 576) points out that in Pascal's approach to the problem of points everything is also necessary.

But how does a player in a game of chance obtain something without fail? If we examine the situations that Huygens and Bernoulli describe, it emerges that the infallibility involved is that of a fair business contract: when the players of a game take a Rawlsian approach to equity or justice and when they assume a veil of ignorance (Rawls 1971, 11–12, 136–37)—none of the players knows who will win or lose the game—then they have equal claims to the stake, and this is what they will obtain without fail. In Bernoulli's ([1713] 1968, 212) terms, this is *contractual* or *institutional* necessity, as opposed to physical or hypothetical necessity:

> Something is *necessary* if it cannot not exist, now, in the future, or in the past. This necessity may be physical, hypothetical, or contractual. It is *physically necessary* that fire burn, that a triangle have three angles equal to two right angles, and that a full moon occurring when the moon is at a node be eclipsed. It is *hypothetically necessary* that something, while it exists or has existed, or while it is assumed to exist or to have existed, cannot not exist or not have existed. It is necessary in this sense that Peter, whom I know and posit to be writing, is writing. Finally, there is the *contractual* or *institutional necessity* by which a gambler who has thrown a six is said to win necessarily if the players have agreed beforehand that a throw of a six wins.

It is this contractual or institutional necessity that explains Bernoulli's identification of expectation with what one may obtain without fail.[11] If there were not a market in the sense of other players willing to engage in a fair game, a player could not infallibly arrange to be in the same position.

In following Huygens's path, Jan De Witt, in his *The Value of Life Annuities in Proportion to Redeemable Annuities*, explicitly used fair or equitable contracts to define expectation: "I presuppose that the real value [*rechte waerdye*] of certain expectations or chances [*expectativen of kanssen*] of objects, of different value, should be estimated by that which we can obtain from as many like expectations or chances [*tot ghelijcke expectativen of kanssen*] dependent on one or several equitable contracts [*by een of meer esgale Contracten*]."[12] In *The Doctrine of*

11. Cf. Bernoulli 1975, 46, and Schneider 1981, 16–17, 23, for related texts.

12. As quoted in Daston 1988a, 28. I have modified the translation slightly by comparison to the Dutch in Bernoulli 1975, 329.

Chances, Abraham De Moivre ([1756] 1967, 3) explained the reasoning behind this approach as follows:

> For supposing that an Event may equally happen to any one of 5 different Persons, and that the Person to whom it happens should in consequence of it obtain the sum of 100 L. it is plain that the right which each of them in particular has upon the Sum expected is ⅕ of 100 L. which right is founded in this, that if the five Persons concerned in the happening of the Event, should agree not to stand the Chance of it, but to divide the Sum expected among themselves, then each of them must have ⅕ of 100 L. for his pretension. Now whether they agree to divide that sum equally among themselves, or rather chuse to stand the Chance of the Event, no one has thereby any advantage or disadvantage, since they are all upon an equal foot, and consequently each person's expectation is worth ⅕ of 100 L.

In the preface to his *Of the Laws of Chance; or, A Method of Calculation of the Hazards of Game*—which was more or less an English translation of Huygens's *On Reckoning in Games of Luck*—John Arbuthnot (1692, f. A11r) likewise wrote:

> Since Gaming is become a Trade, I think it fit the Adventurers should be upon the Square; and therefore in the Contrivance of Games there ought to be a strict Calculation made use of, that they mayn't put one Part in more probability to gain than another; and likewise, if a Man has a considerable Venture, he ought to be allow'd to withdraw his Money when he pleases, paying according to the Circumstances he is then in: and it were easie in most Games to make Tables, by the inspection of which, a Man might know what he was either to pay or receive, in any Circumstances you can imagin, it being convenient to save part of ones Money, rather than venture the loss of it all.

Thus equity among associates or partners rather than probabilities in the sense of relative frequencies provided the foundation of the earliest mathematical probability theory. This was already true in Jerome Cardan's ([1663] 1961, 5) *Book on Games of Chance*: "The most fundamental principle of all in gambling is simply equal conditions, e.g. of opponents, of bystanders, of money, of situation, of the dice box, and of the die itself. To the extent to which you depart from that equality, if it is in your opponent's favor, you are a fool, and if in your own, you are unjust." In sum, the basis for judgments of fairness among players of games of chance in the seventeenth century was their concept of equity among business partners (cf. Hauser 1997, 28). The sense of what was fair or equitable in business had, in turn, been worked out in scholastic works on usury and on business contracts.[13] Moreover, when, during the seventeenth century, the solutions offered to what became known as the "problem of points"—how to divide the prize if a game is interrupted—evolved from those that, on the one hand, took account of what had happened in a game up to the point when it was broken off to those that, on the other hand, paid attention to what might happen in the rest of the game, we may see this evolution as the result of thinking, not about what is justly due to the person dropping out, but instead about the just or equitable price to be paid by a new person willing to buy a player's place in a partially completed game.

In the rest of the essay, then, I first examine practical mathematics as it was applied to business. I then argue that it was the simple algebra of business mathematics applied to partnerships and other medieval and early modern business contracts that lay behind the work of Huygens and Bernoulli on the mathematics of games of luck, which, in turn, formed the starting point for mathematical probability.

Commercial Mathematics

Whatever the theologians and lawyers may have said, pro or con, regarding profits on loans (*usura*) or on business investments (*interesse*, justified by *lucrum cessans*, *damnum emergens*, *periculum sortis*, and so on—cf. Brodrick 1934, 123), from an early date mathematical textbooks explained how to calculate what is owed to business partners in various cases, where the assumption is that profit ought to be distributed in proportion to the capital or labor invested. A very obvious reason for this is that, as the Europeans learned the new techniques of algebra from the Arabs, the "story problems" of the algebra books included such questions. Already in the *Algebra* of al-Khwarizmi (1986, 86), many of the problems concerned distribution of inheritances according to the applicable laws together with the special facts of a case, as, for instance, if, when a man died, one of two sons who would otherwise have inherited equally owed him money, while the man had, at the same time, willed

13. Cf. De Roover 1967, 14, with regard to Bernardino da Siena; Daston 1988a, 18–26; and Parmentier 1993, 449–50. Schneider (2000, 591) remarks with some surprise that Leibniz in his writings on insurance does not use probability (in the sense of relative frequencies).

some part of his estate to a non–family member.[14] According to Islamic inheritance law, an individual's estate did not go to the oldest son but was distributed among many family members in a complex way depending on the order in which people were born or died (Kuran 2002, 22–27). No more than a third of an individual's property could be included in special bequests, a daughter was to receive half as much as a son, and so forth. Many Muslims took part in contractual business partnerships and *commenda*, which legally had to be dissolved when a partner died, with the property of the partnership converted into cash and distributed to the partners or their heirs according to the partnership contract (Udovitch 1970). In this context, when mathematicians proposed methods for calculating how inheritances were to be divided among heirs, they had, simultaneously, to address problems of calculating the value of the decedent's share in the business partnerships that were to be broken off in midstream because of the death. In addition to being legally intertwined, moreover, the problems of dividing inheritances could be formally or mathematically analogous to problems of dividing the capital or profits of a company in the sense that similar algebraic expressions resulted (see Ore 1960, 414).

Did mathematics problems concerning business partnerships migrate from Islamic to Christian lands with no question of the relevance of such problems in the European context? We know that Leonardo Pisano, or Fibonacci, learned much of his mathematics from the Arabs. Did he include problems of business partnerships in his writings simply because he found them in his sources, or did he include them because he expected them to be relevant to his European readers? Mathematics has sometimes been treated as morally neutral, so that the mathematician may explore topics that the moralist would put out of bounds (see Davis 1960, 20, 25). Historians of mathematics have usually neglected the mercantile formulation of the mathematics problems they study to concentrate on the mathematical forms of the resulting equations. It is at least possible, however, that the existence and transmission of these commercial mathematics problems had an impact on conceptions of business ethics: if everyone can agree on how to calculate the fair distribution of the profit and risk of a business partnership, then that form of business partnership may be considered ethically permissible.

14. Bernoulli (1975, 42–48), in his journal *Meditationes*, has a related case about the distribution of a dowry.

A few examples of relevant commercial mathematics problems should suffice to make my point.[15] In the 1202 *Liber Abbaci* of Leonardo of Pisa (Fibonacci), there are long series of problems of business partnerships, voyages, and so forth. For example, the section on societies begins with the problem: "Suppose that there are two men who have made a society, of which one paid 18 pounds of some money into the society and the other 25 pounds. And suppose that they have made a profit of 7 pounds. How much of the 7 pounds should each one of them receive?" (Leonardo Pisano [1202] 1857, 135). The succeeding problems increase in difficulty by assuming that the investment of the partners and the profit involves fractions as well as whole numbers and by assuming that the society has three or four members, but the basic principle of distributing the profit in proportion to the investment holds. Nearly every business mathematics book had problems of this sort, often under the heading of the "rule of fellowship" or double rule of fellowship, taking account of time (Daston 1988a, 20).

In a later section, Leonardo ([1202] 1857, 258) then considers "voyages," problems that assume that the business conducted between various partners can be segmented into voyages in the course of each of which there is a certain ratio of profit and certain costs. According to the first problem in this section, someone goes to Lucca, where he doubles his money and spends twelve denarii; then he goes to Florence and again doubles his money and spends twelve denarii; finally, he comes back to Pisa, where he doubles his money and spends twelve denarii. It is supposed that at the end he has nothing. What did he begin with? The answer, as Leonardo shows, is ten and a half denarii. At Lucca, the merchant doubles his money to twenty-one but spends twelve, leaving him with nine. At Florence he doubles his money to eighteen but spends twelve, leaving six. Returning home, he doubles his money to twelve and spends twelve, leaving nothing.

A later problem concerns two men who have a society in Constantinople. One takes from the common capital a certain amount and goes to Alexandria to do business, remaining there five years and seventy days. There he earns a profit of one-fifth of his capital for each year he is there and spends twenty-five *byzants*. The partner who remains at home earns a profit each year of one-seventh of his capital and spends thirty-seven *byzants*. At the end of the five years and seventy days when the partner

15. For a thorough and thought-provoking exposition of the relevant business mathematics, see Schneider 1980, 1981, 1985, 1988, 2000.

returns from Alexandria, the partner at home is left with nothing, while the partner returning has as much as the Constantinople partner began with. How much did each partner begin with? In this problem, Leonardo explains, you can assume there are two voyages, one for the partner who travels and one for the partner who stays in Constantinople. He first calculates the financial picture for the man who stays at home. If he had nothing at the end, what did he have seventy days earlier, at the end of the five years? This he calculates prorating the profit and expenditure, assuming that seventy days is seven-thirty-sixths of a year, and concludes that at the end of the five years the stay-at-home partner had seven *byzants*. Calculating back through the five years, he first adds the expenses of thirty-seven *byzants* and then takes seven-eighths of the result to get the capital at the beginning of the year. Doing this five times, which requires an incredibly labored calculation with fractions, gives the result that the partner in Constantinople had at the start fractionally more than one hundred twenty-nine *byzants*.[16] Then the partner who went to Alexandria must end up with this amount. Following the rules for his profits and expenditures over five years and seventy days leads to the conclusion that he initially took fractionally more than two hundred six *byzants* (Leonardo Pisano [1202] 1857, 274–76). In these problems, the author's attention seems to be on the problems of calculating with fractions, with no attention to particular problems of business ethics or whether a given partnership arrangement is licit or not. Nevertheless, if the graduates of a commercial school could, following their training using Leonardo's book, so exactly keep track of which partners deserve what, would that not serve to increase confidence in the propriety of such partnerships?

In later business mathematics textbooks, there are not only problems of dividing profits according to the various partners' investments, but also problems that take into consideration that one or more of the partners joins the company late or leaves it early (see, e.g., Castellani [c. 1400] 1984). Often the share of a partner in an enterprise is prorated by the percentage of the time he or she is part of the company, irrespective of when, during the course of the business, profits were received or losses incurred. This makes sense, since profits received early in an enterprise might later be lost and losses made up before the books were closed at the end of the undertaking. In *Behende und hubsche Rechnung*

16. Leonardo often used unit fractions, as found in Egyptian mathematics, writing $\frac{98}{100}$ as $\frac{1}{100} + \frac{1}{50} + \frac{1}{5} + \frac{1}{4} + \frac{1}{2}$. See Boyer and Merzbach 1991, 255.

auff allen Kauffmanschaft (1489, 179–80), J. Widman includes a problem concerning a society in which several partners join and leave over the course of several weeks. In a complicated calculation, he pays no attention to whether the partners took part in the early weeks of the business or the later ones.[17]

But in certain circumstances the timing of participation in a business was assumed to make a difference. Notably, in his 1494 *Summa de arithmetica, geometria, proportioni et proportionalità*, distinction 9, treatise 1 on "All kinds of companies and their division" ["Compagnie in tutti modi e lor partire"], Luca Pacioli assumed that in such problems it is necessary to look at the pacts and contracts the partners made with each other, whether by faith, by testimony, by writing, or by other instrument ("si deve attendere ali pacti e conventioni che infra loro fanno per fede o per testimonio o per scripto o altro instrumento"). According to these, he says, the profit or loss should be divided (Pacioli 1494, 150). Case 60, for example, poses the following problem. Two people form a company for a year. One puts in seven hundred florins and the other five hundred. They agree that at the end of the year they will divide the capital and earnings in half. It happens that, at the end of the tenth month, they dissolve the company and find that the earnings are two hundred florins. How should they divide the company ("commo si dovera partire ditta compagnia"), and what should each take? Answer: if the company had lasted twelve months, the second would take one hundred florins of capital from the first. How much then should he take for ten months? If in twelve months he gets one hundred, then in ten months he should get $^{10}/_{12}$ of one hundred or 83 $^{1}/_{3}$. So with regard to the capital, the first should take 616 $^{2}/_{3}$ and the second 583 $^{1}/_{3}$. Then the profit should be divided, following commercial law ("per le compagnie dritte dicendo"), on the assumption that the first provided 616 $^{2}/_{3}$ in capital and the second 583 $^{1}/_{3}$, and the two-hundred-florin profits should be divided in this ratio. Pacioli (1494, 156, para. 65) thus finds that the first should take 102 $^{7}/_{9}$ of the profit and the second 97 $^{2}/_{9}$.

I cite this case because it shows clearly that Pacioli's computation assumes that in calculating the distribution of capital and profits when a company ends, it is the contract between the partners and commercial law that provide the basis for calculating the desired result. In the

17. In contrast to Widman, Nicolas Chuquet (Flegg, Hay, and Moss 1985, 307) complains that this sort of calculation ignores the fact that a profit may be made on a profit received in an earlier period, as well as on the initial investment.

example given, which must have seemed to Pacioli's readers to correspond to at least occasional practice, the first partner has agreed to transfer one hundred florins of his invested capital to the other during the course of the business. This would amount to the first partner paying the second partner a guaranteed 20 percent return on his investment of five hundred florins beyond a half share of any profits. Nothing is said about the morality of this sort of contract, but the obvious implication is that such a contract is a possibility. Neither is anything said about why the company is dissolved before its planned end. Perhaps if one partner had initiated the dissolution against the wishes of the other, he would have been assessed a penalty for early withdrawal (along the lines of what was called *damnum emergens*). For my purposes here, the main point to be made is simply that Pacioli's mathematics assumes that the partners' expectations depend upon the contract that they made initially. In this particular case, the contract stipulates a transfer of capital as well as a division of profits.

Commercial Mathematics and Games

In light of this business mathematics background, then, it is hardly surprising that Pacioli solved the division problem for an interrupted game (the so-called problem of points) by looking to what had been accomplished of the original agreement up to that point.[18] Niccolo Tartaglia criticized this answer but gave an alternate one also based on how much more, proportionally, of the contracted number of wins one player had completed than the other (Kendall [1956] 1970, 27). For his part, Pacioli said that he had found several different approaches to the problem, but that he was going to give the correct one (Schneider 1985, 239).

About the same time as Pacioli, Filippo Calandri, author of a printed arithmetic published at Florence in 1491, in a manuscript work titled *Varie ragioni tratte da vari luogi* (held at the Biblioteca Communale of Siena), also said that alternative approaches are possible. In problem 12 of Calandri's work, two players who had planned to play until one had won six times, break off their game when one has won four games and

18. Pacioli is often set aside in discussions of the history of the problem of points because his answer is thought to be false. See David 1962, 37, which notes that Pacioli based much of the contents of his work on Leonardo's *Liber Abbaci*, although David did not find the source of this problem. For the analogy of games and business, cf. Schneider 1985, 242–43. Incidentally, there is a new translation of Leonardo's work, by L. E. Sigler, published by Springer (New York, 2002).

the other three. How much should each receive? Calandri says: "There are two methods of determining the ratio of division: one is to determine the ratio by what has been done and the other is to consider what remains to be done" (Toti Rigatelli 1985, 231). Whereas Pacioli had preferred the first method, Calandri favors the second. He reasons that since the first player needs two to win, and the second player needs three more, the first should receive, inversely, three-fifths of the deposit, while the second receives two-fifths. Calandri is not sure that this is the correct solution, however, since a game of fortune is involved. In problem 43, Calandri again says that there are two methods of solving a division problem (in this case one for three players) and concludes that it is undetermined which is better (231).

Ivo Schneider has pointed out that the games discussed by Pacioli and other mathematical authors include chess and other games that are not primarily games of luck. Perhaps this helps explain why mathematicians consider what has been accomplished up until the game is broken off, rather than what might happen afterward. Schneider argues that what is important in this history is that Pacioli, like the businessmen who formed *commenda*, thought that there was only one correct solution to the problem, as in the traditional *commenda* contract, where the ship captain received a set fraction of the earnings after the voyage, whatever might have occurred. By the sixteenth century, however, thanks to the commercial revolution, other sorts of business arrangements were possible (Schneider 1985, 239–40). When Jerome Cardan rejected Pacioli's solution to the division problem, his arguments, in Schneider's view, were no more objective than Pacioli's. What seemed fair to Pacioli seemed grossly unfair to Cardan: in a nineteen-point game, where one player had won eighteen and the other nine, Pacioli's method would divide the stake in a ratio of 2 to 1 because one player had won twice as many games as the other up to that point. Cardan argued, to the contrary, that the expectation of the player with only one more point to go was as much as 20 to 1 better than that of the player with ten more points to go. Indeed, Cardan's own formula for the division problem gave the ratio 55 to 1 for this case (243–44). Tartaglia, on the other hand, considering the real-world situation, concluded that such a problem was better solved legally than rationally—no matter how it is solved, he said, there will always be grounds for complaint (244).[19]

19. Schneider quoting Tartaglia, *La Prima Parte del General Trattato di Numeri et Misure* (1556).

What should be noticed here, I believe, is that *if the issue is the expectation of a new player buying the place in a game* of a person who has been playing up to that point, then, naturally, that buyer will only care what his or her future expectations are. In his *Practica Arithmetica* of 1539, after arguing that what counts is not what has happened up to a certain point in a game, but rather what still needs to be done to win, Jerome Cardan wrote: "For the demonstrative reason for this is that if, after the division, the game were begun again, the players would have to stake the same as they received at the time of stopping" (as quoted in Franklin 2001, 298). Why should a buyer wish to reward a seller for what he or she has accomplished up to a given point in a game? The past is not the buyer's concern. Thus the secondary market for positions in partly completed games would reasonably lead mathematicians to look at the expectations in the rest of the game rather than at what has come before. If players on quitting a game partway through were only intending to divide the stake fairly given the rules of the game, they might conceivably look to the history of the game up to that point; but if a new partner is entering and buying the position, the past becomes irrelevant to the just or equitable price to be paid.[20]

Uncertainty and Contracts

Lorraine Daston has suggested that mathematical probability emerged at a time when life in Europe became more predictable, when it became possible to assume that the future on average would be similar to be past (cf. Daston 1987; 1988a, 113, 164, 183–87; 1988b, 232–35; and 1992, 45). In the case of business, one might ask, for instance, when the danger of sending a merchant ship to the East became fairly predictable, so that merchants might consider what percentage of ships are typically attacked by pirates or what percentage encounter storms so severe as to result in the loss of the entire cargo. In the case of selling annuities, one might ask what the average life expectancy might be for individuals who have already achieved a given age.

Historians have noticed that when governments first sold annuities as a means of raising government revenue, little or no attention was paid to the age of the person who bought the annuity, so that the expected value

20. We know there were secondary markets for the forced loans in Florence and elsewhere; see Ceccarelli 2001, 619. For more on commercial mathematics, see Benoit 1988, Swetz 1987, and Flegg, Hay, and Moss 1985.

of an annuity sold for a given price might vary considerably depending upon whether the annuity was for a young or an old person.[21] They have also noticed that little effort was expended in collecting statistics concerning losses at sea or other shipping disasters (cf. Daston 1988a, 120). They did not take averages.[22]

In his 1921 book, *Risk, Uncertainty, and Profit*, Frank Knight distinguished "risk," where the probabilities of various outcomes are known, from true "uncertainty," where what might happen is unpredictable by any known method. The seventeenth-century founders of mathematical probability, such as Jacob Bernoulli, Abraham De Moivre, and Pierre Remond de Montmort, all used games of chance as models for calculations of mathematical probability. Some of the games for which they calculated probabilities were not pure games of luck, but involved skill as well, while others involved risk in Knight's terms, rather than true uncertainty. In the case of business partnerships or insurance, on the other hand, it was not known risks, in Knight's sense, that encouraged mathematicians to calculate probabilities, but rather the implicit or explicit contracts between players or business partners and, further, the existence of markets in which a player or a business investor could, for a just price, sell his or her position to someone else in case he or she wanted to withdraw before the anticipated end of the game or business enterprise. The disciplinary context for thinking about these issues was business ethics, and the relevant characteristic of ethical business practice was equity or justice. In cases where prudent businesspeople bought or sold things subject to doubt or uncertainty, they were expected to use their good judgment to adjust the price accordingly.[23]

21. Cf. Veraja 1960, 176. In practice annuities were often sold at a price such that the entire investment would be returned in five or six years. In the selling of modern annuities, one assumes that the money paid in will be invested and may be expected to earn on average at least a certain percentage rate of return. Then the life annuitant may receive each year both the profit or interest earned and a part of the capital. In early modern discussions of annuities, only the return of the capital seems to be considered, and not the profit that might be earned by investing it. Perhaps this was true because the money paid for annuities was used to pay for current government (military) expenses and so was not available to invest in business.

22. Cf. Franklin 2001, 339, "To set a premium for an insurance one must, at least unconsciously, have observed a relative frequency. Yet there was no serious numerical study of such things until 1660, despite the apparently obvious commercial advantages. The reasons for this remain obscure."

23. Admittedly, some authors came close to a frequency approach when they wrote about the "ease" or facility with which an event may occur. See, for instance, Conrad Summenhart, who writes in *De contractibus* (1500), "What occurs more easily is more likely to occur" (quoted in Veraja 1960, 176). Ease or facility is not the same, however, as statistical frequency.

Understanding that it was the contract between business partners or between governments and the purchasers of annuities—rather than statistical estimates of life expectancies or dangers to shipping, or other actuarial knowledge—that underlay business practices, helps us to comprehend the behavior of governments and individuals in the seventeenth and early eighteenth centuries. Often one finds mutual insurance agreements rather than third-party insurance. For instance, at the end of the seventeenth century, we find groups of 2,000 or so individuals agreeing that if one of them died, each of the others would pay a certain amount to the heirs of the deceased. This does not require estimating how many people are likely to die, since there are no set premiums paid in advance to be used for paying survivors a promised amount. On an alternative scheme, set premiums were paid, but then the resulting sum was divided equally between the survivors of all who died in that year, with a smaller amount paid if a larger number died (Poitras 2000, 460–62). In another sort of plan, a number of men joined together to assure that their daughters would have the necessary dowries when the time came—and this, perhaps, before their daughters were even born. What made these contracts legitimate was the parity of knowledge or ignorance among the men.[24]

A different situation arose when individuals wanted to create a secondary market for buying and selling contracts of various types.[25] Then the uncertainty could not be managed simply by the agreement to share costs equally or proportionally; a value or price had to be attached to the ongoing contract, whether for a life annuity, a business partnership, a forced loan, and so forth. Within a latitude or range of possibilities, the

24. See Daston 1988a, 22, quoting Jean Domat, *Les lois civiles dans leur ordre naturel* (Paris, 1777). Trustees of funds reserved for the dowries of orphan girls might be expected to invest the funds wisely, so that they would grow and not shrink over time, to be worth something when they were needed. To invest these funds in a way that might in a different context be considered usurious could be justified on the grounds that trustees were expected to avoid risking money they had in trust. Sometimes the guaranteed rate of return on the investment might be set to what was judged to be the "normal profit rate" or "probable profit" at that place and time. Cf. Mormando 1999, 185, concerning *monte delle doti* in Florence; and McLaughlin 1939, 105, 139. See also Daston 1988a, 120–21.

25. One of the most common topics of business ethics concerned the question of whether it was moral to buy or sell forced loans (*monte commune*) that governments exacted and for which they paid interest. If it was immoral to engage in usury, but if the citizens who were forced to make interest-paying loans had no choice in the matter, what about a person who assumed such a loan with its accompanying interest payments (see Ceccarelli 2001, 618–19)? According to one analysis, the interest that was paid on the *monte commune* was like an insurance payment, compensating the person who received it for the risk that he would never get his capital back.

price might be set by negotiation between the buyer and seller, assuming that if a contract is entered into freely by two parties who are equal in their knowledge or ignorance, it must be fair (cf. Langholm 1998). In games, mathematics could be used to estimate a just price for a game position, which the prudent buyer or seller could then use in determining the price to offer or to accept—the individual's conception of a fair price varying depending upon his or her attitude toward risk or chance.[26] The switch, then, in discussions of the "problem of points," from considering what each player has achieved up to the point in the game at which it is ended to considering how close each player is to winning, would naturally arise from the need or desire to sell one's position in the game to someone else.

Historians of probability are accustomed to judging that only the probabilistic calculation that looks to the future is correct, while one that looks to the past is erroneous, but it makes more sense to consider the actual business situation of players of games of luck: looking to the past is reasonable if only the original players are involved. Looking to the future is appropriate if a new player is expected to buy into the game. Considerations of this sort governed the mathematics of business partnerships before they were applied to the "problem of points" in games.

Commercial Mathematics in Early Works of Mathematical Probability

In general, then, the terminology of early works on games of luck reflects their analogy to business partnerships with the added feature of looking forward from any given point in the middle of a game at which one player might sell his or her position to another (cf. Schneider 1988). When Huygens first wrote *On Calculations in Games of Luck* in Dutch, the word he used for what a player might expect was *kans* (chance) or *kansse* (chances). The Latin word that one would have expected to be correlated with *kans* was *sors*. But when Huygens suggested to Franz van Schooten what words to use in the Latin translation, he proposed *expectatio*. Van Schooten followed Huygens's suggestions, except that at the beginning of the treatise he used the alternative *sors seu expectatio*—allowing the reader to understand that *expectatio* meant the same thing as *sors* in the usual mercantile use, before going on to use the

26. Cf. Coumet 1970, 591, quoting Jean Domat, *Les lois civiles dans leur ordre naturel* (1689–94).

word *expectatio* on its own.[27] In his notes on proposition 1 of Huygens's book, Bernoulli ([1713] 1968, 5) noticed that *expectatio* was being used in something other than its common meaning:

> It can be seen from what we have said that the word "expectation" is not used here in its ordinary sense, according to which we are commonly said to expect or to hope for what is best of all, though worse things can happen to us, but rather according to the extent to which our hope of getting the best is tempered and diminished by fear of getting something worse. So by its value is always meant something intermediate between the best we hope for and the worst we fear. This should be understood here and throughout the following.

Where van Schooten did not have Huygens's suggestions to follow (Huygens translated only the propositions, not their justifications), he occasionally translated *kans* as *sors*, forgetting to use *expectatio* for this purpose, and Bernoulli, likewise, often used *sors*, when what is referred to is the expectation in the modern sense.[28] So in the derivation of proposition 1, van Schooten translated: "let x equal my expectation [*expectationi*]. This means that if I had x, I could arrive again at a similar chance [*sortem*] contending on equitable terms" (Bernoulli [1713] 1968, 4). And in his notes on proposition 3, Bernoulli wrote, "if I get a in p cases, b in q cases, and c in r cases, then my chance [*sortem*] becomes $(pa + qb + rc)/(p + q + r)$."

In using *sors* for a player's expectation, van Schooten and Bernoulli were identifying a player's chance (*sors*) with an investor's capital investment—also called *sors—and* with his or her expected receipts from a partnership. It seems odd that the same word *sors* was used for what seem to be two quite different concepts. How did this come about? In its original meaning a *sors* or "lot" was a token upon which the chance in a lottery was supposed to depend. The Romans had used lots or physical

27. So in Huygens's ([1657] 1968, 3–4) fundamental principle, where Huygens had suggested the translation, "in aleae ludo tanti aestimandam esse cujusque expectationem ad aliquid obtinendum, quantum si habeat, possit denuo ad similem expectationem pervenire, aequa conditione certans," van Schooten actually wrote, "in aleae ludo tanti aestimandam esse cujusque sortem seu expectationem ad aliquid obtinendum, quantum si habeat, possit denuo ad similem sortem sive expectationem pervenire, aequa conditione certans."

28. Already in the opening paragraph Huygens had suggested using *sors* where, for consistency's sake, he should have used *expectatio*. The question was what a person should pay if he wanted to take over my position in a game. In Dutch he had said "my game" (*mijn spel*). Van Schooten indicated his hesitation over Huygens's suggestion to translate this by *sortem meam*, by expanding to read, *locum sortemque*.

tokens to distribute government jobs, and the Jews used lots to distribute land.[29] From this likely came the idea of a person's lot in life or fortune. In business contracts, then, the capital a person invested in a partnership or loaned to another person was the *sors*—both what a person paid in and what he or she could expect back, paying a just price in a fair partnership where—apparently—there is assumed to be no net profit. Thus, when people linked a business partner's or a gamester's investment or stake with his or her expectation, both called *sors*, they seem to have assumed that they were dealing with nonusurious investments or fair zero-sum games. They assumed that gamesters were gentlemen or -women who put up a stake to play a game and who divided the resulting pot of money at the end of the game according to the previously agreed-upon rules. There was no "house" or government that skimmed part of the players' wagers off the top. The Port-Royal logic remarked that, because the house takes part of the stakes, lotteries are manifestly unfair (Arnauld and Nicole [1662] 1981, 353). When a business partnership made a net profit, this could have raised questions about fairness among those outside the company.

From the mathematicians' point of view, many conceptually disparate problems may be seen as analogous because the mathematics involved is the same (cf. Hauser 1997, 70). In an early publication, Jacob Bernoulli (1975, 91) combined a question of usury with the solution to a game problem. In the usury problem, a debtor was supposed to make installment payments on a loan, and the problem was how to allocate the payments between interest payments and repayments of the principal—affecting the interest due in the next period. In this connection Bernoulli used the word *sors* to mean the principal of the loan.[30] In turning to the game problem, then, he noted that the calculations both of amounts due

29. *Sors* meaning "lot" appears several times in the Vulgate. For instance, in Numbers 26:55 and 33:54, God instructs Moses to assign land to the different families according to the fall of the lot (this is a "sors divisoriae"). In the Book of Esther 3:7 and 9:24, the feast of Purim is said to be named after "Pur"—the Hebrew for lot (*sors*)—which Haman, the enemy of Jews, had cast with the intent of destroying the Jews, "taking the days and months one by one, and the lot fell on the thirteenth day of the twelfth month, the month of Adar" (this would be a "sors consultoria"). Then in Acts 1:26, lots are said to have been cast to choose Matthias to replace Judas as the twelfth apostle. Using lots to predict the future is a "sors divinatoria." See Aquinas 1976. For *sors* in medieval law, see, e.g., Bracton [c. 1210–68].

30. The work "J. B. Quaestiones nonnullae de usuris, cum solutione Problematis de Sorte Alearum," was published in the *Journal des Sçavans* in 1685. Typical phrases are, "sors debita initio temporis" and "posito sortem *m* tempore *n* parere usuram *p*."

on an interest-bearing loan (*sors*) and of the ratio of chances (*ratio sortium*) in the game in question involved the summing of infinite series.

As Bernoulli pointed out in *The Art of Conjecturing*, the simplest equation for calculating expectations in games was identical to the equation long used by merchants to calculate the price of a mixture. Commenting on Huygens's proposition 3, which calculates a player's expectation if he has p cases in which he receives a and q cases in which he receives b out of a total $p+q$ cases, Bernoulli ([1713] 1968, 10) noted:

> It is clear from consideration of this calculation that it has great affinity to the arithmetic rule called *Of mixtures*, according to which things of diverse prices in given quantities are mixed, and the price of the mixture is sought. In fact, the two calculations are clearly the same. Just as the sum of the products of the quantities and prices of the individual ingredients, divided by the total quantity of all the ingredients, gives the required price, which is always intermediate between the highest and lowest prices, so too the sum of the products of the numbers of cases and amount acquired in those cases, divided by the total number of cases, gives the value of the expectation, which likewise is always intermediate between the greatest and least amounts that can be acquired.

Other mathematicians recognized different analogies to the same law. Gottfried Leibniz (1981, 465–66) referred to it with the Greek term *prosthaphaeresis*, a formula used in astronomy for finding the position of a planet:

> The foundations they built on involved *prosthaphaeresis*, i.e. arriving at an arithmetic mean between several equally admissible hypotheses [*suppositions également recevables*]. Our peasants have used this method for a long time, guided by their natural mathematics. For instance, when some inheritance or piece of land is to be sold, they appoint three teams of assessors—these teams are called *Schurzen* in Low Saxon—and each team assesses the commodity in question. . . . This is the axiom *aequalibus aequalia*—equal hypotheses [*suppositions égales*] must receive equal consideration. (translation slightly modified)

Alternately, as Nicolaus Bernoulli pointed out, the mathematics of calculating expectations in games was the same as the mathematics of calculating centers of gravity. Thus the same mathematical relationships might correspond to very different real-world relationships that nevertheless had the same formal structure.

That the foundation of Huygens's method (and of Bernoulli's method for games, insofar as Bernoulli built upon Huygens's work) was not chance but rather the justice of contracts is evident in Huygens's repeated use of such phrases as "with equitable chance" (*aequa sorte*), "contesting on equal conditions" (*aequa conditione certans*), and "equal right" (*aequale jus*).[31] When the history of mathematical probability has been written retrospectively from the modern frequentist perspective, part 1 of Jacob Bernoulli's *Art of Conjecturing* has been understood as if he approached games in the modern probabilistic or relative frequency sense. Then part 4 of the work, applying the same mathematics to legal, moral, and economic decision making, has been understood as if it, too, were built upon this same frequentist or statistical basis. Taking this perspective, it comes as a shock when in part 4 Bernoulli describes cases in which the sum of all the probabilities in a given case is greater or less than one. If, however, it is understood that Bernoulli had in mind probability of judgments and not relative frequencies, it is not so surprising that he proposes examples in which the sum of all the probabilities is greater or less than one (see Shafer 1978).

That at the end of the seventeenth century, the word *probable* had overwhelmingly epistemic and only rarely frequentist meanings has been hidden from historians of mathematical probability in part by the association of epistemic probability with so-called probabilism, an ethical doctrine supported by many Jesuit confessors and rejected by the Jansenists, which historians of mathematical probability have considered unworthy of their attention. According to probabilism, "if an educated man considers two opinions to be probable, then, no matter which of the two he follows, he does not sin."[32] Standard histories of mathematical probability highlight the Jansenist critiques of the Jesuits, perhaps because Blaise Pascal, in addition to playing a key role in the development of mathematical probability itself, famously satirized probabilism in his *Provincial Letters*. From the strict perspective of the Jansenists, the Jesuits were to be condemned for their permissiveness or laxity. They

31. Cf. Grotius, *De jure belli et pacis* (1625), as quoted by Daston 1988a, 22: "In all contracts, natural justice required there should be an equality of terms." See also Hauser 1997, 69–70, "Huygens' Theorie liess sich ohne jeden Rekurs darauf [to the betting analogy]—im Kontext der kaufmännish-juristischen Vorstellungen, der ökonomischen Analyse vor allem der Mathematik seiner Zeit—verstehen."

32. P. Vitoria quoted in Brodrick 1934, 137. For the Jansenists, cf. Taveneaux 1977.

were accused of having adopted probabilism in order to cater to the wealthy businessmen and patrons whose confessions they heard. But as Albert Jonsen and Stephen Toulmin (1988, 20) have argued in *The Abuse of Casuistry: A History of Moral Reasoning*, casuistry does not deserve the blanket condemnation it so frequently receives.[33] To understand Jacob Bernoulli's approach to probability, it is important to pay attention to the meaning of *probable* in these contemporary discussions of casuistry.

Jacob Bernoulli himself included a "case of conscience" in his intellectual journal or *Meditationes*, asking whether a person whose culture takes it as a sign of respect to remove one's hat should do so when taking part in a sacred ritual in China, given that the Chinese think that keeping one's head covered is a sign of honor.[34] His attitude to casuistry was not that of Pascal's *Provincial Letters*. In the sense of *probable* relevant to casuistry, a "probable opinion" is one that can be reasonably supported, and a "more probable opinion" is one held by more or by more authoritative or respected thinkers, or one backed up by more and better arguments. A "probable profit" is what most prudent businesspeople think reasonable. To determine what a probable profit in a business might be, one consulted experienced businesspeople; one did not collect data. The probability of an opinion depends upon the extent of one's knowledge—what is probable to one person will not be probable to someone else who has additional information.[35] If someone sold something such as an annuity for a lifetime and if the annuitant died almost immediately, the contract might still be considered fair, and the seller not required to refund

33. "The arguments by which Blaise Pascal and his successors have brought the enterprise of casuistry into disrepute contain, in turn, their own fundamental flaw." As James Franklin (2001, 94–101), points out, Pascal was guilty of bad faith in his portrayal in the *Provincial Letters* of Jesuit moralists in that he omitted the context of the passages he excerpted. The Catholic Church contributed to a misunderstanding of the historical development in the controversies involving the Jansenists and Jesuits, in part by imposing silence on the parties at an earlier stage. Cf. Mahoney 1987, 90–91, "The disedifying spectacle of the Louvain theologians condemning the Jesuits as Pelagians for vaunting man's moral freedom, and being in turn condemned of Calvinism, with attempts to prevent Jansen's work being published, culminated in 1653 in papal condemnation of five propositions ascribed to Jansen."

34. Bernoulli 1677–80, 2 (meditation 3): "Casus cons. An in China aliisque locis (ubi mos viget signum honoris tegendo exhibere) tecto aut aperto capita sacra peragenda sint?"

35. It was a factor in judging contracts to be fair that the partners in the contract should have similar knowledge or ignorance of the future. One might hold a person responsible for finding out as much as possible about the factors involved. Ignorance of the facts or of the law could only be used in denial of guilt if it had been impossible for the person to find out about the facts or law (involving so-called invincible ignorance). Cf. Kantola 1994, 76, 161–63.

the balance of the price paid, because neither person knew ahead of time that such an unexpected death would occur. The situation was the same as when someone sells a horse. Even if the horse should die unexpectedly the next day and the buyer doesn't get any use out of the horse, the seller would not have to give a refund (see Alessandro di Alessandria 1960, 214–15). When it came to hereditary annuities, one might argue that the just price should be estimated using only the first two or three lives, and not all the lives, because there was no way to estimate how long such a period might last.[36]

In contrast to Huygens and Jacob Bernoulli, with their emphasis on expectations in partnerships, De Moivre founded his own doctrine of chances on relative frequencies or probabilities in the frequentist sense. He began his *De mensura sortis* with the proposition: "If p is the number of cases in which some event may happen, and q the number of cases in which it may not happen, both the events that happen and those that do not have their degrees of probability; if all the cases in which the event may happen or may not happen occur equally easily, then the probability of happening to the probability of not happening will be as p to q" (De Moivre 1711, 215, my translation).

Only after establishing this base did De Moivre turn to the game context in which Huygens had operated, saying:

> If two players A and B compete about outcomes, on the grounds that if p cases happen A will have won, but if q cases happen, B will have won; and if a is the sum deposited, the chance or expectation of A will be $pa/(p+q)$, while the chance or expectation of B will be $qa/(p+q)$, and therefore if A or B sell their expectations, it will be fair if they receive $pa/(p+q)$ and $qa/(p+q)$ respectively for them. (215)

And similarly, De Moivre went on, if after the game is agreed upon, the players decide not to play, the premium should be divided according to the same ratios.

In the preface to the first edition of *The Doctrine of Chances*, De Moivre (1718, ii) said that when he wrote *De mensura sortis* he had been "absolutely resolved to reject" "the Method of Huygens," "as not seeming to me to be the genuine and natural way of coming at the Solution

36. Alessandro di Alessandria (1960, 216–27) argued this way. On this approach one might solve the St. Petersburg paradox by counting only the first two or three terms of the infinite series in estimating the value of the bet.

of Problems of this kind." The first edition of *The Doctrine of Chances* begins with a more general statement corresponding to the opening of *De mensura sortis*: "The Probability of an Event is greater, or less, according to the number of Chances by which it may Happen, compar'd with the number of all the Chances, by which it may either Happen or Fail" (1). By the third edition of *The Doctrine of Chances*, De Moivre ([1756] 1967, 1–2) has added a second proposition: "Wherefore, if we constitute a Fraction whereof the Numerator be the number of Chances whereby an Event may happen, and the Denominator the number of all the Chances whereby it may either happen or fail, that Fraction will be a proper designation of the Probability of happening." While Bernoulli had probabilities that added to more than 1, De Moivre (1718, 1) states on the first page of the first edition, "Therefore, if the Probability of Happening and Failing are added together, the Sum will always be equal to Unity." And expectation is the product of the value of the thing to be obtained times the probability of obtaining it (De Moivre 1718, 2; [1756] 1967, 3). The word *probability*, he explains in the third edition, "includes a double Idea; first, of the number of Chances whereby an Event may happen; secondly, of the number of Chances whereby it may either happen or fail" (De Moivre [1756] 1967, 2).

The oeconomy of De Moivre's *Doctrine of Chances*, especially in the later editions, is thus quite different from that of Huygens and Bernoulli as far as expectation and probability are concerned. As De Moivre himself says, he was resolved to reject Huygens's approach to calculations in games of chance. While Huygens based himself on conceptions of fair games, related, as I have argued, to just business contracts, De Moivre bases himself on probability as measured by ratios of chances. Coming so soon after *The Art of Conjecturing*, De Moivre's *Doctrine of Chances* was immediately recognized by many as the natural approach to mathematical probability. Thus in histories of this subject, the origin of mathematical probability in the moral oeconomy and business mathematics has been overlooked, and the foundations of Huygens's and Bernoulli's thought in the expectations of business partners has come to seem counterintuitive or even circular. I hope to have shown that the foundations that Huygens chose for his mathematics of games of chance resulted naturally from its background in the moral oeconomy of ethical business partnerships and the related calculations of commercial mathematics textbooks.

References

Alessandro di Alessandria. 1960. *Tractatus de Usuris*. In Veraja 1960.

al-Khwarizmi. 1986. *The Algebra of Mohammed ben Musa*. Edited and translated by Frederic Rosen. Hildesheim: Olms.

Aquinas, Thomas. 1976. *Liber de sortibus*. In vol. 43 of *S. Thomae de Aquino* Opera Omnia, edited by H. F. Dondaine. Rome. Editori de San Tommaso.

Arbuthnot, John, trans. 1692. *Of the Laws of Chance; or, A Method of Calculation of the Hazards of Game, Plainly demonstrated, and applied to Games at present most in Use, which may be easily extended to the most intricate Cases of Chance imaginable*. London: Printed by Benjamin Motte and sold by Randall Taylor.

Arnauld, Antoine, and Pierre Nicole. [1662] 1981. *La logique, ou L'art de penser*. Edited by Pierre Clair and François Girbal. 2d ed. Paris: Vrin.

Baeck, Louis. 1999. The Legal and Scholastic Roots of Leonardus Lessius's Economic Thought. *Storia del pensièro economico* 37. www.cce.unifi.it/dse/spe/indici/numero37/baeck.htm.

Benoit, Paul. 1988. The Commercial Arithmetic of Nicolas Chuquet. In *Mathematics from Manuscript to Print*, edited by Cynthia Hay, 96–116. Oxford: Clarendon Press.

Bernoulli, Jacob. 1677–80. *Meditationes*. Unpublished transcription, Basel University Library, MS L I a 3.

———. [1713] 1968. *Ars Conjectandi*. Brussels: Culture et Civilisation.

———. 1975. *Die Werke von Jakob Bernoulli*. Vol. 3. Basel: Birkhauser.

Boyer, Carl, and Uta Merzbach. 1991. *A History of Mathematics*. 2d ed. New York: John Wiley.

Bracton, Henry. [c. 1210–68]. *De Legibus et Consuetudinibus Angliae*. http://bracton.law.cornell.edu/Bracton.

Brodrick, James. 1934. *The Economic Morals of the Jesuits: An Answer to Dr. H. M. Robertson*. London: Oxford University Press.

Cardan, Jerome. [1663] 1961. *The Book on Games of Chance (Liber de Ludo Aleae)*. Translated by Sydney Henry Gould. New York: Holt, Rinehart and Winston.

Castellani, Maestro Gratia de'. [c. 1400] 1984. *Chasi Sopra Chonpagnie*. Edited by Marisa Pancanti. Siena: Servizio Editoriale dell'Università di Siena.

Ceccarelli, Giovanni. 2001. Risky Business: Theological and Canonical Thought on Insurance from the Thirteenth to the Seventeenth Century. *Journal of Medieval and Early Modern Studies* 31.3:607–58.

Coumet, Ernest. 1970. La théorie du hasard est-elle née par hasard? *Annales* 25:574–98.

Daston, Lorraine. 1983. Mathematical Probability and the Reasonable Man of the Eighteenth Century. *Annals of the New York Academy of Sciences* 412:57–72.

———. 1987. The Domestication of Risk: Mathematical Probability and Insurance 1650–1830. In *Ideas in History*, vol. 1 of *The Probabilistic Revolution*, edited by Lorenz Krüger, Lorraine J. Daston, and Michael Heidelberger, 237–60. Cambridge: MIT Press.

———. 1988a. *Classical Probability in the Enlightenment*. Princeton, N.J.: Princeton University Press.

———. 1988b. Fitting Numbers to the World: The Case of Probability Theory. In *History and Philosophy of Modern Mathematics*, edited by William Aspray and Philip Kitcher, 221–37. Minnesota Studies in the Philosophy of Science, vol. 11. Minneapolis: University of Minnesota Press.

———. 1992. The Doctrine of Chances without Chance: Determinism, Mathematical Probability, and Quantification in the Seventeenth Century. In *The Invention of Physical Science*, edited by Mary Jo Nye, Joan Richards, and Roger Stuewer, 27–50. Boston Studies in the Philosophy of Science, vol. 139. Dordrecht: Kluwer.

David, F. N. 1962. *Games, Gods, and Gambling: The Origins and History of Probability and Statistical Ideas from the Earliest Times to the Newtonian Era*. London: Charles Griffin & Co.

Davis, Natalie Zemon. 1960. Sixteenth-Century French Arithmetics on the Business of Life. *Journal of the History of Ideas* 21:18–48.

De Moivre, Abraham. 1711. De mensura sortis, seu, de Probabilitate Eventuum in Ludis a Casu Fortuito Pendentibus. *Philosophical Transactions of the Royal Society* 27:213–64.

———. 1718. *The Doctrine of Chances*. London: W. Pearson.

———. [1756] 1967. *The Doctrine of Chances*. 3d ed. New York: Chelsea.

De Roover, Raymond. 1967. *San Bernardino of Siena and Saint' Antonino of Florence: The Two Great Economic Thinkers of the Middle Ages*. Boston: Baker Library, Harvard Graduate School of Business Administration.

Flegg, Graham, Cynthia Hay, and Barbara Moss, eds. 1985. *Nicolas Chuquet, Renaissance Mathematician: A Study with Extensive Translation of Chuquet's Mathematical Manuscript Completed in 1484*. Dordrecht: D. Reidel.

Franklin, James. 2001. *The Science of Conjecture: Evidence and Probability before Pascal*. Baltimore: Johns Hopkins University Press.

Freudenthal, Hans. 1980. Huygens' Foundations of Probability. *Historia Mathematica* 7:113–17.

Garber, Daniel, and Sandy Zabell. 1979. On the Emergence of Probability. *Archive for History of Exact Sciences* 21:33–53.

Hald, Anders. 1990. *A History of Probability and Statistics and Their Applications before 1750*. New York: John Wiley.

Hauser, Walter. 1997. *Die Wurzeln der Wahrscheinlichkeitsrechnung: Die Verbindung von Glücksspieltheorie und Statistischer Praxis vor Laplace*. Boethius: Texte und Abhandlungen zur Geschichte der Mathematik und der Naturwissenschaften, vol. 37. Stuttgart: Franz Steiner Verlag.

Huygens, Christiaan. [1657] 1968. *De ratiociniis in ludo aleae*. In Bernoulli [1713] 1968.

Jonson, Albert R., and Stephen Toulmin. 1988. *The Abuse of Casuistry: A History of Moral Reasoning*. Berkeley, Calif.: University of California Press.

Kantola, Ilkka. 1994. *Probability and Moral Uncertainty in Late Medieval and Early Modern Times*. Helsinki: Luther-Agricola-Society.

Kaye, Joel. 1998. *Economy and Nature in the Fourteenth Century: Money, Market Exchange, and the Emergence of Scientific Thought*. Cambridge: Cambridge University Press.

Kendell, M. G. [1956] 1970. The Beginnings of a Probability Calculus. In *Studies in the History of Statistics and Probability*, edited by E. S. Pearson and M. G. Kendell. London: Griffin.

Knight, Frank. [1921] 1965. *Risk, Uncertainty, and Profit*. New York: Harper and Row.

Kuran, T. 2002. The Islamic Commercial Crisis: Institutional Roots of Economic Underdevelopment in the Middle East. Research paper no. C01–12, University of Southern California Center for Law, Economics, and Organization. http://papers.ssrn.com/abstract_id=276377.

Langholm, Odd. 1979. *Price and Value in the Aristotelian Tradition*. Bergen: Universitetsforlaget.

———. 1992. *Economics in the Medieval Schools*. Leiden: E. J. Brill.

———. 1998. *The Legacy of Scholasticism in Economic Thought: Antecedents of Choice and Power*. Cambridge: Cambridge University Press.

Leibniz, Gottfried Wilhelm. 1981. *New Essays on Human Understanding*. Translated and edited by Peter Remnant and Jonathan Bennett. Cambridge: Cambridge University Press.

Leonardo Pisano. [1202] 1857. *Liber Abbaci*. Edited by Baldassarre Boncompagni. Rome: Tipografia delle Scienze Matematiche e Fisiche.

Mahoney, John. 1987. *The Making of Moral Theology: A Study of the Roman Catholic Tradition*. Oxford: Clarendon Press.

McLaughlin, T. P. 1939. The Teaching of the Canonists on Usury (XII, XIII, and XIV Centuries). *Mediaeval Studies* 1:81–147.

Mormando, Franco. 1999. *The Preacher's Demons: Bernardino of Siena and the Social Underworld of Early Renaissance Italy*. Chicago: University of Chicago Press.

Munro, John. 2001–3. The Late-Medieval Origins of the Modern Financial Revolution: Overcoming Impediments from Church and State. Working Paper Archive of the Department of Economics and the Institute for Policy Analysis, Department of Economics, University of Toronto. www.chass.utoronto.ca/ecipa/archive/UT-ECIPA-MUNRO-01-02.pdf.

Newton, Isaac. [1665?] 1967. Loose Annotations on Huygens' *De Ratiociniis in Ludo Aleae*. In vol. 1 of *The Mathematical Papers of Isaac Newton*, edited by D. T. Whiteside, 58–62. Cambridge: Cambridge University Press.

Noonan, John T. 1957. *The Scholastic Analysis of Usury*. Cambridge: Harvard University Press.

Ore, Oystein. 1960. Pascal and the Invention of Probability Theory. *American Mathematical Monthly* 67:409–19.

Pacioli, Luca. 1494. *Summa de arithmetica, geometria, proportioni et proportionalita*. Venice: Paganino de Paganini.

Parmentier, Marc. 1993. Concepts juridiques et probabilistes chez Leibniz. *Revue d'histoire des sciences* 46:439–85.

Poitras, Geoffrey. 2000. *The Early History of Financial Economics, 1478–1776: From Commercial Arithmetic to Life Annuities and Joint Stocks*. Cheltenham: Edward Elgar.

Rawls, John. 1971. *A Theory of Justice*. Cambridge, Mass.: Belknap Press.

Schneider, Ivo. 1980. Christiaan Huygens's Contribution to the Development of a Calculus of Probabilities. *Janus* 67:269–79.

———. 1981. Why Do We Find the Origin of a Calculus of Probabilities in the Seventeenth Century? In vol. 2 of *Probabilistic Thinking, Thermodynamics, and the Interaction of the History and Philosophy of Science: Proceedings of the 1978 Pisa Conference*, edited by Jaakko Hintikka, David Gruender, and Evandro Agazzi, 3–24. Dordrecht: Reidel.

———. 1985. Luca Pacioli und das Teilungproblem: Hintergrund und Lösungsversuche. In vol. 12 of *Mathemata: Festschrift für Helmuth Gericke*, edited by Menso Folkerts and Uta Lindgren, 237–46. Stuttgart: Franz Steiner Verlag Wiesbaden GMBH.

———. 1988. The Market Place and Games of Chance in the Fifteenth and Sixteenth Centuries. In *Mathematics from Manuscript to Print*, edited by Cynthia Hay, 220–35. Oxford: Clarendon Press.

———. 2000. Geschichtlicher Hintergrund und wissenschaftliches Umfeld der Schriften. In *Hauptschriften zur Versicherungs- und Finanzmathematik*, by Gottfried Wilhelm Leibniz, edited by Eberhard Knobloch and J.-Matthias Graf von der Schulenburg, 591–623. Berlin: Akademie Verlag.

Shafer, Glenn. 1978. Non-additive Probabilities in the Work of Bernoulli and Lambert. *Archive for History of Exact Sciences* 19:309–70.

Swetz, Frank. 1987. *Capitalism and Arithmetic: The New Math of the 15th Century, Including the Full Text of the* Treviso Arithmetic *of 1478*. Translated by David Eugene Smith. LaSalle, Ill.: Open Court.

Taveneaux, René. 1977. *Jansénism et prêt à intérêt: Introduction, choix de textes et commentaires*. Paris: J. Vrin.

Todeschini, Giacomo. 1980. *Un trattato di economia politica francescana: Il "De emptionibus et venditionibus, de usuris, de restitutionibus" di Pietro di Giovanni Olivi*. Studi Storici, fasc. 125–26. Rome: Istituto Storico Italiano per il Medio Evo.

Toti Rigatelli, Laura. 1985. Il "Problema delle Parti" in Manoscritti del XIV e XV Secolo. In vol. 12 of *Mathemata. Festschrift für Helmuth Gericke*, edited by Menso Folkerts and Uta Lindgren, 229–36. Stuttgart: Franz Steiner Verlag Wiesbaden GMBH.

Udovitch, A. 1970. *Partnership and Profit in Medieval Islam*. Princeton, N.J.: Princeton University Press.

Veraja, Fabiano. 1960. *Le Origini della Controversia Teologica sul Contratto di Censo nel XIII Secolo*. Rome: Edizioni di Storia e Letteratura.

Widman, J. 1489. *Behende und hubsche Rechnung auff allen Kauffmanschaft*. Microfilm. London: Goldsmith Library.

Where Mechanism Ends: Thomas Reid on the Moral and the Animal Oeconomy

Harro Maas

Theories of life have consequences for how the social order is conceptualized. I pursue this theme in the work of the Aberdeen philosopher of mind Thomas Reid (1710–96), or more accurately, in his reactions to others' views. Reid typically developed his own ideas into a coherent view in juxtaposition to ideas to which he took exception. This means entering into a number of apparently discrete contexts before the unifying threads can be made plain. Let me introduce my theme with a not untypical example of Reid's way of clarifying by accentuating difference.

In 1794, just two years before he died, Reid gave two lectures to the Glasgow Literary Society. The subjects were apparently unconnected. In the first lecture Reid extensively criticized and commented on Joseph Priestley's materialist philosophy. The central point of dispute was the inertness of matter and its consequences for physiology and religion: "By what force [the muscular fibers] are contracted and relaxed, either in voluntary or involuntary Motion, Philosophy has never discovered. . . . It is here that Mechanism ends, at least human wisdom has never been able to carry it farther; and some cause must operate that has the power of beginning motion" (Wood 1995, 202).

I would like to thank Margaret Schabas, Neil De Marchi, and Evelyn Forget for their encouragement and comments on an earlier version of this essay. Paul Wood and Anette Hagan provided me with valuable information on Colin Maclaurin, and Frans van Lunteren on the more general scientific context of Maclaurin's work. Aberdeen and Edinburgh University Library kindly gave permission to cite from archival materials in their holding. Lastly, I would like to thank the anonymous referees of this journal for their incisive comments. The usual disclaimer obtains, of course.

Reid dealt with the second topic, utopian political systems, in perhaps his last lecture to the Glasgow Literary Society (1794). He sketched a social order in which a heavy role was reserved for the state for the distribution of goods and the moral education of its citizens, while there was hardly any role for that most favored and theorized institution of David Hume and Adam Smith: the market. Referring favorably to the historical example of the Jesuits in Paraguay, Reid's utopian system knew "neither Money nor Property nor Traffick" (Reid 1990, 284), and there was no role for "private Interests," which in Reid's view were so often opposed to "that of the Publick" (287).

Was Reid's discussion of Priestley of purely philosophical interest? What link, if any, was there to that of his second lecture, on a utopian social order? The connection runs via eighteenth-century Scottish physiology, which was also split. Some physiologists considered the living body something governed "by the laws of mechanism," as John Allen, Edinburgh physiologist and political radical, put it (quoted in Jacyna 1994, 61–63). Others considered that the natural powers of the living body are subject to an ever-present surveying agent, which view was espoused by one of Dugald Stewart's students, Thomas Thomson, writer of the influential *System of Chemistry* (1807) and lifelong friend of James Mill.

Reid intervened in the middle of the debate, transferring the existing divisions into philosophy. He insisted that a line be drawn between natural and moral, or mental, philosophy. He felt the need for a demarcation that would enable him to clarify humankind's duties to God, nature, and society. Rather than an exercise in mechanically computing the best line of action, moral agency was, in Reid's view, a matter of human wisdom. The political consequence Reid drew from this was a social order based on the guidance of the state, rather than being left to the whims and vices of the market.

In what follows, I first discuss the limits Reid set to mechanical philosophy. I then turn to his reading in physiology and show how his resistance toward mechanism and materialism determined his approach to moral and mental philosophy. We are then in a position to examine Reid's remaining lecture notes on utopian systems.

Reid's Essay on Quantity

In 1748 Thomas Reid published a short tract, *An Essay on Quantity*, in the *Proceedings of the Royal Academy of London*, in criticism of

Francis Hutcheson's use of mathematics in his famous *Inquiry into the Original of Our Ideas of Beauty and Virtue* ([1725] 1726). In his essay Reid complained, "Those who have defined quantity to be *whatever is capable of more or less*, have given too wide a notion of it" and had been led "to apply mathematical reasoning to subjects that do not admit of it." Reid observed that "pain and pleasure admit of various degrees, but who can pretend to measure them?" (Reid 1967 [hereafter cited as *Works*], 2:715). Reid foresaw the possibility of measuring pleasures and pains only once human "affections and appetites" had been reduced to quantities. But such reduction, in his view, was inconceivable, so that he rhetorically concluded that Hutcheson's use of mathematics in the field of moral philosophy only served "to ring changes on words without advancing one step in real knowledge" (717). Reid continued his short but pointed criticism of Hutcheson with a discussion of the so-called *vis viva* controversy in mechanical philosophy, on which he sadly concluded that "much mathematical and experimental dust" had been raised for something that was essentially a matter of giving the "same name to different mathematical conceptions" (719).[1]

By family ties[2] and by interest Reid, in the first half of the eighteenth century, had pursued studies predominantly in mathematics, natural philosophy, and Newtonian mechanics as a student at Marischal College, New Aberdeen.[3] After working as librarian at the college and being appointed for fourteen years as the minister of New Machar, he became regent at King's College, Old Aberdeen, in 1751. He succeeded Adam Smith at the Glasgow chair in moral philosophy in 1764, that is, after the publication of his *Inquiry into the Human Mind* that same year, a book that established his fame as the most important contemporary critic of

1. The *vis viva* controversy was originally a dispute between Cartesians and Leibniz on the proper mathematical formula for what we now consider as two distinct concepts: momentum (mv) and kinetic energy ($1/2mv^2$). The controversy had its roots in Descartes's law of the quantity of motion and was of direct influence on how to think about God as the general cause of motion in the universe and about God's perfection. These subjects were, as we will see, far from alien to Reid's philosophical pursuits. In the end all contemporary philosophers of some importance engaged in the controversy. On the *vis viva* controversy, see Iltis 1971, and in relation to Reid, Laudan 1968.

2. As noted by Haakonssen, Reid (1990, 6) was through his mother related to the Gregorys, well-known mathematicians and scientists. James Gregory, the son of John Gregory, was his successor in the chair of medicine at Edinburgh.

3. For good biographical information on Reid, see Norton 1966, 17–20; Reid 1990, chap. 1; and Wood 1984, 1995, 2001. Also Conrad's (1987) study on the Aberdeen Wise Club and Wood's (1993) study on the Aberdeen Enlightenment are valuable sources of information on Reid. I would like to thank Stephen Conrad for sending his book to me.

Hume. Paul Wood (1984, 55–56) dates Reid's first airing of the essay on quantity to the 1730s, that is before d'Alembert's 1743 alleged settling of the so-called *vis viva* controversy as "une dispute de mots."[4]

Rarely, if ever—to paraphrase Theodore Porter (1994, 390)—are discussions about quantifying qualities merely semantic disputes. As we will see, thinking of the phenomena of the mind quantitatively led in Reid's eyes to a detrimental misapprehension of the character of moral agency. Though on the whole his contemporaries greeted Hutcheson's *Inquiry* with approval, this was not so for his use of mathematics. Some moral philosophers, like Archibald Campbell and John Gay, did not reject its mathematics in principle but argued that consideration should have been given to the intensity and duration of virtue and vice to give a proper account of their quantities.[5] But Hutcheson encountered harsher critics as well. Well-known is Laurence Sterne's comment that "Hutcheson, in his philosophical treatise on beauty, harmony and order, plus's and minus's you to heaven or hell, by algebraic equations—so that none but an expert mathematician can ever be able to settle his accounts with S. Peter" (quoted in Scott [1900] 1992, 31–32 n. 4). Bernard Mandeville, too, ridiculed Hutcheson for being "very expert at weighing and measuring Quantities of Affection, Benevolence, &c." And he challenged "that curious Metaphysician" to weigh humankind's alleged noble motives "abstracted from selfishness" and then to "shew us in his demonstrative way, what Proportion the Quantities bore to each other" (Mandeville [1714] 1924 [hereafter cited as Kaye], 2:346).[6] Even though Mandeville objected most to Hutcheson's attempt to get rid of selfishness as the prime motive for action, his comment pinpointed an obvious weakness in Hutcheson's use of mathematical ratios: do feelings have properties that afford measurement, or is such an idea just "curious metaphysics"? Weighing human passions and affections, ran the objection, seemed as hopeless an enterprise as weighing their soul.

Hutcheson had not been the first to think of the passions in terms of quantities, however, and Laurence Sterne's reference to Saint Peter

4. See, on the "myth" of d'Alembert's settling of the *vis viva* controversy, especially Laudan 1968. Larry Laudan also makes valuable comments on the reliability of the text as it was included by Sir William Hamilton in Reid's *Philosophical Works*.

5. Because of his influence on David Hartley, John Gay is historically the more important of these commentators. For a still very useful overview, see Bernard Peach's introduction to Hutcheson [1728] 1971, esp. 7.

6. All references to Mandeville's *Fable of the Bees*, including the many extensions and elucidations, are to F. B. Kaye's unsurpassed 1924 two-volume edition. On Mandeville, see Goldsmith 1988, Hundert 1994, 1995.

perhaps unknowingly referred back to Oresme, Buridan, and the so-called calculators at Merton College, Oxford, who not only used their geometrical skills to get a grip on the motion of bodies, but used geometry literally to quantify the passions of the soul so as to have a "measure" of the balance of a person's virtues and sins on the day of judgment. Motion, virtue, and vice were all comprehended in terms of intensity and duration.

Perhaps because of its little practical use this tradition had long since gone into oblivion, and in the early eighteenth century only playful use seems to have been made of geometry in the realm of the mind.[7] Francesco Algarotti's *Le Newtonianisme pour les dames*, which appeared somewhat later (1741), made an exact analogy between the intensity of the love of a man and his distance from his beloved and Newton's law of gravitation, but this was rather to keep ladies attentive to the subject than to make any substantial claims on the laws governing human passions.[8]

There had been more serious transgressions between the natural and the moral realm shortly before Hutcheson's famous *Inquiry*, however. Well known is John Locke's suggestion in his *Essays* (1967, 4:3:6) of "thinking matter," taken up by materialists like Julien Offroy de La Mettrie to argue that a human being was no more than a "thinking machine." Earlier, and following Pierre Gassendi, Mandeville had argued in a similar vein that a person's "moral anatomy" should be based on his or her physiology.[9]

Although much less outspokenly materialistic, Pierre Bayle once compared the human soul to a balance, which weighed reasons and passions, instead of physical weights. This metaphor had been taken up by Leibniz in his *Théodicée* and was referred to by him as the "Balance of Reason."[10] In Leibniz's comparison, John Yolton (1983, 132) remarks,

7. Jevons used intensity and duration as the dimensions of his calculus of pleasures and pains. In the *Theory of Political Economy* (1970, 55) he referred favorably to Hutcheson's mathematical exercises, which he considered "crude and premature" but over the whole "beyond praise." He explicitly used Jeremy Bentham's theory of circumstances to motivate his choice for intensity and duration as the dimensions of pleasure and pain. I know of no reference to or knowledge of either Bentham or Jevons from the work of the Merton school of calculators. On the adequacy of Jevons's rendering of Bentham's multidimensional view on utility, see Warke 2000 and Sigot 2002.

8. I generously thank Frans van Lunteren for bringing this literature to my attention.

9. On the influence of Gassendi in the eighteenth century, see Paul Christensen's contribution to this volume.

10. The philosopher Marcelo Dascal is currently working on an edition of minor papers of Leibniz on controversies that will include *Brief Commentaries on the Judge of Controversies,*

"Reasons, passions, even ideas tip the balance of the will one way or other, or, when equal, the balance is unmoved." The metaphor of the balance suggested that there were close similarities between the mental or moral and the natural domain, or at least close enough similarities to make comparison possible. However, as the arms of the balance cannot resist moving under the influence of the heavier weight, this metaphor implies that the will is equally unable to resist that line of action in which human appetites and passions propel us most forcefully.

Closer to Aberdeen, Colin Maclaurin had speculated at a young age on the possibilities of applying Newton's theory of fluxions to the moral realm.[11] In close parallel with Newton's centripetal forces, Maclaurin considered the existence of a "vis bonipeta" and showed how we might compute its quantities by considering its dimensions of intensity and duration by the use of fluxions. It is not quite clear whether Maclaurin considered his small exercise in moral arithmetic something serious or merely an illustration of Newton's theory of fluxions, yet a letter of Maclaurin to his uncle Daniel makes clear that his use of Newtonian physics is not to be taken lightly. Referring to his thesis on Newtonian mechanics, he wrote that

> the establishing of the universality of the law of Gravity & the necessity of referring it to a first cause . . . is of the greatest importance & use seeing it furnishes us with a most clear & mathematical proof of the existence of a god & his providence that he not only made the world but that he rules & governs it concerning himself in the affairs of it being present every where in it working that w^h^ is best for the inhabitants of it. (Colin Maclaurin Papers, Edinburgh University Library, MS 3099.15.1:2)

While Francis Hutcheson, Maclaurin's fellow student at Glasgow, seemed merely to have emphasized the usefulness and practicality of

---

or the Balance of Reason and Norm of the Text (originally in Latin, presumably written after 1669).

11. Colin Maclaurin (1698–1746) was among the first to promote Newton in Britain. He is best known for his *Account of Sir Isaac Newton's Philosophical Discoveries*, which was published posthumously in 1748. He contributed greatly to the geometrical tradition of British mathematics in an unpublished and undated manuscript entitled *De Viribus Mentium Bonipetis*, clearly referring to Newton's *De Viribus Centripetis*. Some of its geometrical illustrations look extremely modern. Even though the manuscript is undated, it seems to have been written when Colin Maclaurin was young, around 1714, which is when he wrote his thesis on Newtonian mechanics at Glasgow. The manuscript is located at Edinburgh University Library, call mark MS 3099.15.6.

his mathematical ratios in reasoning upon moral subjects, Maclaurin's extension of Newtonian mechanics to the moral realm seems to have been based on the farther-reaching assumption that where God's active power is constantly at work in the law of gravity, His hand similarly is constantly presupposed in human actions toward the good. Mathematical proof revealed the providential order in nature and society.

Providence was not at odds with Hutcheson's *Inquiry*, however. Quite to the contrary, he had been provoked to write his two essays in response to Mandeville's *Fable of the Bees* ([1714] 1924), which was rightly considered a direct attack on Lord Shaftesbury's *Inquiry concerning Virtue or Merit* (Shaftesbury [1711] 2001). Just after his own speculations on "Moral Arithmetick," Shaftesbury concluded that "the Wisdom of what rules, and is FIRST and CHIEF *in Nature*, has made it to be according to the *private Interest* and *Good* of every-one, to work towards the *general Good*," from which it further followed that "VIRTUE is *the Good*, and VICE *the Ill* of every-one" (2:100). No conclusion of course could have been more at odds with Mandeville's, as he clearly and proudly recognized. From Mandeville's *Fable* the conclusion was to be drawn either that "the Wisdom of what rules" was of wicked nature and made us act from vice to attain—unexpectedly—the public good, or that there was no providential moral order at all. In the last case humankind simply acted on its biological frame without any moral consideration, and the "clever politician" made use of human nature to move in the direction of the general good (Cook 1999; see also De Marchi 2001). In his rejection of "rational systems of ethics" Mandeville took this last route, considering men and women as only animate machines: "I believe Man (besides Skin, Flesh, Bones &c. that are obvious to the Eye) to be a compound of various Passions, that all of them, as they are provoked and come uppermost, govern him by turns, whether he will or no" (Kaye, 1:39).

Neither of these conclusions was acceptable to Hutcheson, and he took it as his task to show that a person's moral sense gave him an intuitive insight into the moral order. This insight might lead to self-interested behavior, but that was only to be considered vicious by gratuitously naming it so. For mankind did not act solely out of self-interest, but out of benevolence as well. One's moral sense preceded one's judgment, and, according to Hutcheson, one acted upon the sense, not upon the judgment. The measure of the goodness of the act was its contribution to the public good, and it was an objective property of the act whether it did or did not contribute to it (Norton 1974). Hutcheson's mathematical exercises thus find their place in the same context as those of Maclaurin; they were a veneration of the wisdom of the deity and of the inherent goodness of the social order.

Especially in Aberdeen there were strong ties between Newtonianism and providentialism, and Maclaurin's short teaching period at Marischal College, after his graduation from Glasgow, certainly contributed to this. Reid's teacher in moral philosophy, George Turnbull, propagated the use of the Newtonian method in the moral domain. Turnbull emphasized Newton's inductive method of inquiry rather than his mathematics. By the inductive method, Turnbull asserted, "it has been proved, that our mundan [*sic*] system in all its parts is governed by excellent general laws" (quoted in Norton 1975, 705). According to Turnbull, we could apply this same inductive method with as much fruit to our inner world as Newton had applied it to the external world. As David Fate Norton summarizes Turnbull's position, reflection on our "mental frame" left no doubt "that the mind of man is as ordered a part of nature as any other, and hence that there is no reason to doubt that divine providence has aptly fitted us for the successful pursuit of virtue" (708).

This firm belief in the providential order, in the natural as well as the moral domain, was central to Reid's thoughts, but this did not mean he was altogether happy with the way it was argued for by Hutcheson and his teacher Turnbull. Reid did not dispute that there was a "moral sense" that gave insight into the moral order, but he did take issue with Hutcheson's notion that this insight preceded judgment, so that we act upon instincts rather than reason. Reid feared that Hutcheson's otherwise welcome defense of the moral order was in fact indistinguishable from the selfish system, in which we acted mechanically upon our passions.

This fear joined with Reid's belief that to apply the language of geometry to the realm of the mind was stretching Newton's method too far. Any analogy between the natural and moral or mental realm should not imply that the phenomena of the mind had similar properties to those of matter. Matter was extended in space, was measurable, and therefore could be described by means of geometry, just as derived phenomena like "*velocity*, the *quantity of motion*, *density*, *elasticity*, the *vis insita* and *impressa*, the various kind of *centripetal forces*, and different orders of *fluxions*," could all "as carefully as Sir Isaac Newton appears to have done" be brought in relation to measure (*Works*, 2:716). To think similarly about the phenomena of mind was to suppose that forces act upon us just as they do upon innate matter. But life and moral agency were not to be reduced to mechanisms.

Indeed, arguing against the Cartesians, Maclaurin himself had warned in his *Account of Newton* against those who, "from their fondness to explain all things by mechanism, have been led to exclude every thing but matter and motion out of the universe" (quoted in Turco 1999, 72). This sentence might well be taken as Reid's creed. From his first acquaintance with Newtonian mechanics, Reid embraced its inductive method. But he rejected the idea, embraced by some and illegitimately associated with Newton, that persons in their moral actions were moved by forces.

Like Maclaurin and Turnbull, Reid considered Newton's discovery of the universal law of gravity evidence for the divine order in nature. As becomes clear from his later work, he distinguished between natural laws, which hold universally, and the cause of these laws, that is, the deity that makes these laws to hold. Reid derived this distinction from considerations on the inertness of matter, which he, with so many of his contemporaries, considered essential to Newtonian mechanics. Inertness, according to Reid, meant nothing more than that matter cannot move from itself but needs a force to be impressed upon it. This force, of consequence, cannot itself be material, but must be of immaterial origin. To make this force act constantly, however, an agent was needed that constantly exerted its power to guarantee the force to act.

Reid's considerations naturally led to the idea of a divinity whose constant interference was needed to make things move. According to him, the deity is the "true cause" of movement, its efficient cause, while natural laws do not state causes, but rather the rules according to which the deity exerts its power. The distinctions among active powers, the exertion of these powers, and natural laws, and the parallel distinction between natural and efficient causation, are essential to Reid's thought. In his early work Reid did not have these distinctions ready at hand, of course, but we see them emerge from his reading in natural philosophy. They find full expression only by the time he published his *Essays on the Active Powers of Man*, in 1788.

Reid on the "Sentient Principle" and Human Agency

Dugald Stewart's account of Reid's life and work characterized him as a philosopher whose dominant interests lay in moral and mental philosophy, and whose scarce essays in natural philosophy were only matters of diversion and, moreover, the product of his younger years. It is particularly due to Paul Wood's important research into Reid's unpublished materials, and into the scientific context of eighteenth-century Aberdeen, that this one-sided view has been considerably nuanced (see esp. Wood 1993, 1995; see also Wood 2000). Reid's reading in natural philosophy in the first half of the eighteenth century is rather to be taken as the period in which his own philosophical system came to fruition. From Reid's reading in physiology it becomes clear not only that he opposed mechanistic and materialist accounts of life and human agency, but that he separated the moral from the animal economy as well.

In a comment on Buffon's *Système de la nature* (1750), Reid summarized Buffon's human physiology as follows:

> The Nerves that administer to Sensation, the brain & Spinal Marrow, and the nerves that administer to voluntary Motion[,] Make one System and are the Several parts of one Animal Machine. The first are the parts to which the power is applied, the second the fulcrum or fixed point, the third that by which the weight is moved or the effect produced. But the Brain is not only capable of reacting as it is acted upon. It is itself active because it retains long the impressions made upon it by external objects by means of the Senses. (Wood 1995, 92)

The antimaterialist physiologist Robert Whytt, whom I will treat presently, published his important *Essay on the Vital and Involuntary Movements of the Muscles* in 1751, one year after Buffon's *Système*, and it is mere guessing whether Reid made his notes having read Whytt already or not. However that may be, there was certainly too much of materialism in Buffon for Reid's liking. He also rejected Buffon's assertion (directed against Carl Linnaeus) that all classification of nature was human work, nature having no order of its own. The comparison of the "animal machine" with a balance, where the brain and spinal cord have the function of a turning point that passively transmits the sensations that put the muscles into "voluntary Motion," reduces human agency to a balancing act. It is not clear where volition should be located in this train of events. That a person is more than a machine follows, however, from the addition that the fulcrum (the brain) is in fact not merely passive, but can move of itself: "it is itself active," and the possibility of this activity resides for Buffon in memory. Without memory, the animal machine would have acted "in a purely mechanical way," as Reid further exemplified with the example of the working of the eye, when separated from memory (Wood 1995, 92).

Reid clearly was intrigued by Buffon's acknowledgment that the animate creation was governed not by mechanical laws but by laws "peculiar to it" (91). In his much later comments on Joseph Priestley's materialism, he refers to Buffon's dissection of the brain of an orangutan and a man, from which Buffon felt "forced . . . to confess that there must be something else in Man than Matter and organisation" (133). Reid found even more support for distinct laws governing the animate creation in the Scottish physiology of the first half of the eighteenth century. However, his engagements with physiology brought out clearly that moral agency could not be understood without the notions of judgment and active power as essential to it. To see how Scottish physiology helped Reid in framing his views on human agency, it is useful to consider the more general background of physiological research in Scotland.

In the early eighteenth century it was common practice for Scots physiologists to study in Leiden with the famous Hermann Boerhaave (Underwood 1977). It is generally considered that Boerhaave developed a theory of the human body in accordance with the Cartesian dichotomy of mind and matter, a theory that was dominant at the beginning of the eighteenth century (and even earlier, in Leiden) and formed the benchmark for all departures from it.[12] Boerhaave conceived of the human body as a hydraulic machine that functioned according to the same laws as governed inanimate nature.[13] The regular breathing of the lungs, the pulses of the heart, all served to pump fluids through the body. Muscular contractions and relaxations were also conceived in terms of fluids being pumped into the muscles, or flowing from them. Boerhaave distinguished between feelings and sensations on the one hand, which were phenomena of the mind, and mechanical changes in our body, including the brain, on the other. Phenomena of the mind were only related to acts of thought and to self-consciousness; at no moment did they affect the actions of the body. In Boerhaave's conception, human feelings were considered an epiphenomenon; they played no causal role in moral conduct, nor in physiology.

12. There exist extensive critical studies on Boerhaave. In my view the best still is Lindeboom 1968. For the influence of Boerhaave on Edinburgh physiologists, see especially Underwood 1977, 102. See also Wright 1990.

13. See, however, Wright 1990, esp. 262, for a discussion of the validity of this generally received view of Boerhaave. See Klever 1994 on Boerhaave's alleged Spinozism, which is to be traced to his teacher and predecessor at Leiden, Burcher de Volder.

In the course of the eighteenth century, Scottish physiologists distanced themselves from the Boerhaavian mechanical image of the human body. The medical faculty in Edinburgh was particularly pivotal in this. Due to the eminence of its teachers and professors, especially Robert Whytt (1714–66), John Gregory (1724–73), and William Cullen (1710–90), this Edinburgh medical school became one of the most outstanding in Europe and contributed significantly to the flourishing of the Scottish Enlightenment.[14] It is well established that Edinburgh physicians played an important role in the circles of the Edinburgh literati (Lawrence 1979; Sher 2000). Cullen, for example, was Hume's physician and the friend of both Hume and Smith.

In contrast with Boerhaave, Edinburgh physiologists placed feelings and sentiments at center stage in their understanding of animal life. But not only did physiologists distance themselves from the Cartesian dichotomy of mind and matter that had been dominant until then. Human feelings and moral sense were equally important for Scottish Enlightenment philosophers, scientists, and literati. They thus blended moral and natural philosophy, as is seen in Hume's and Smith's moral theories.[15] Indeed, as Richard Sher (2000, 103) recently observed, the Scottish focus on the sentiments "cut across the different discourses of philosophy, medicine, history, and moral fiction."

The arguments against Boerhaave's theory of the animal body were many. One of the more obvious was that the image of the animal body as a hydraulic machine simply would not work in mechanical terms. For example, the amount of fluids needed to flow into the muscles to contract was simply too large in theory, and violated empirical observations as well. Also, there was no clear idea from where the heart got its motive force. This made the animal body something like a perpetual mobile—which obviously violated mechanical principles. But it was not such difficulties that made Edinburgh physiologists look in other directions. Recent findings, such as Abraham Trembley's famous polyp, caused vehement debates as to whether there was a notion of wholeness regarding the animal body, a unifying principle, which implied that the body functioned as a unity and not as an assemblage of parts. The polyp, a water-plant-like animal, amazed natural historians by its Hydra-like ability to regenerate into as many complex animals as it was cut into (Vartanian 1950, 259–60).

14. On the Edinburgh medical faculty, see Barfoot 1983.

15. The obvious reference here is, of course, to Lawrence 1979, but see also Barfoot 1983.

Trembley's polyp gave most support to materialist ideas, such as those of La Mettrie, but this was not the turn of ideas in Scotland.[16] There the unifying principle of the animal body was considered to be nonmaterial. It was referred to as the "sentient" or "vital" principle. William Porterfield, the first professor of medicine at the new medical school at Edinburgh, though he had been a student of Boerhaave at Leiden, spoke of a "vital Principle" working in the human body, and he conceived of this principle as an "active immaterial cause" (Wright 1990, 273). Thinking of the animal body as a machine consequently provided an incorrect image of its functioning.

In relation to Reid but, perhaps more than is commonly acknowledged, to Smith as well, Robert Whytt's work is of special importance.[17] Whytt lectured in medicine at the medical faculty of Edinburgh until his premature death in 1766. He was then succeeded by William Cullen, who would dominate Scottish physiology until the end of the century. In his most important publication, the *Essay on the Vital and Involuntary Motions of Animals* (1751), Whytt set out his own physiology in contrast to mechanical theories such as those of Boerhaave, but also in contrast to Stahlian rationalism. According to Georg Stahl, involuntary motions of the body could be explained by recourse to habit. While involuntary motions first had been conscious acts, habit made consciousness fade away. This theory ran into so many difficulties that it was totally unacceptable to Whytt. The sucking reflex of a newborn child, for example, on Stahl's account had to be explained by the child's behavior first having been a conscious act that only later turned into habit, a very unpromising route to take. It was much more natural to see reflexes like the sucking of newborns as instincts that made human and animal life to some extent alike.

Whytt was more concerned with mechanical and materialist doctrines. He focused on the nervous system. According to him all movement in (or of) the body originated from feelings. Such feelings began in their turn from stimulation of the nerves, from stimuli. Via the brain and the spinal marrow these feelings put into motion the appropriate muscles so as to get rid of these feelings. This image is close to what we saw earlier in Reid's reading of Buffon. However, to make the brain and the spinal marrow mediate between the nerves and the muscles, Whytt assumed the existence of the already mentioned "sentient principle" or "soul." This

16. On the importance of Trembley's polyp, especially in relation to materialism, see Vartanian 1950.

17. Exceptions are the already mentioned Lawrence 1979 and Barfoot 1983.

sentient principle was spread through the body and remained in its parts for a short while when a part was dismembered from the whole. This explained why a chicken that was robbed of its brain still reacted to stimuli for a considerable time. A frog robbed of both its brain and spinal cord, however, no longer reacted to stimuli, lacking any means of mediation of the feelings to the muscles.

Whytt thus broke with the Cartesian distinction between a material substance extended in space and a thinking substance that was not so extended. However, rather than implying a sort of materialism, the theory of the sentient principle blocked the route to it. The sentient principle, not the "muscles and fibres" of animals, was endowed with the "power of generating motion." In reaction to the German physiologist Albrecht von Haller, Whytt wrote: "We cannot but acknowledge that He has animated all the muscles and fibres of animals with an active SENTIENT PRINCIPLE united to their bodies, and that to the agency of this principle are owing the contractions of stimulated muscles" (quoted in French 1969, 68–69).

According to Whytt, the relation between nerves and motions of the body was one of sympathy. All sympathy consequently was mediated through the intervention of the soul or sentient principle. It is important to emphasize that no consciousness or judgment was involved in the sympathetic reaction of (parts of) our body. Sympathy between organs, or the more general sympathetic reaction of a person to a fellow human being (so famously described in the first pages of Smith's *Theory of Moral Sentiments*) was rather a reflex, to use a modern term, and Whytt is nowadays seen as a precursor of reflex theory, which was developed in the 1830s by Marshall Hall. As French (1969, 31) summarizes: "Whytt put both sympathy and the other involuntary motions of animals on the same footing—nerves communicating through a central, unconscious and necessarily acting sentient principle."

Whytt argued that feelings necessarily influence our involuntary or vital bodily functions, whereas in the moral realm these feelings are accompanied by a consciousness of freedom (Wright 1990, 283–84 n. 48). The distinction between voluntary and involuntary actions lay consequently only in this consciousness of freedom. However, as Porterfield pointed out in his criticism of Whytt, it was not clear how to reconcile the claim that feelings necessarily cause bodily actions in the one case, while this necessity is absent when it concerns moral action (288–89). Both issues, that sympathy was a reflex, rather than a conscious feeling, and the uneasy distinction between the voluntary and involuntary acting of the sentient principle, will prove to be of considerable importance with respect to Reid.

Whytt gave various arguments why the relation between nerves, brain, and muscles could not be explained mechanically. On mechanical principles the reaction of the muscles to a stimulus would always have to be the same, but this was clearly not so in the case of muscular motion. Whytt referred to experimental evidence in support. Referring to Stephen Hales's experiment on a decapitated frog, Whytt observed that this frog did not immediately react when a leg was stimulated. Only after some time did the frog move his leg. This was, according to Whytt, because the greater pain of decapitation first overshadowed the lesser uneasiness of the stimulation of the leg. The sentient principle consequently did not act in accordance with mechanical laws, yet it provided a lawlike explanation of the animal economy.

There were also strong theoretical reasons to think of the sentient principle as immaterial. If the sentient principle itself were of material origin, this would have violated the Newtonian doctrine of the inertness of matter, which as we saw earlier was considered an established fact. Clearly referring to Locke, Whytt argued that to think "that matter may, of itself, by any modification of its parts, be rendered capable of sensation, or of generating motion, seems to be as unreasonable as to ascribe to it a power of thinking" (quoted in French 1969, 69).

Whytt's physiology met with considerable approval in the Aberdeen Philosophical Society. The Wise Club was especially taken with his antimechanical explanation of life. For example, John Gregory, one of the founding members of the Wise Club, with Reid, and successor of Whytt at Edinburgh, argued against Boerhaave for having "considered Man entirely as a Machine," and thus having made "a feeble and vain attempt to explain all the Phaenomena of the Animal Oeconomy, by mechanical and chemical principles alone" (quoted in Wood 1990, 92–93). Just like Whytt and Porterfield, Gregory emphasized the importance of the "sentient principle," which placed the physiology of animals, including humans, apart from the mechanics governing inanimate nature. And in a discussion of the "involuntary motions of animals" Reid refers to Whytt's theory of the sentient principle as "the most probable Hypothesis yet advanced on this Subject & I think the onely one that deserves examination" (Wood 1995, 101).

But Reid had worries about Whytt's theory as well. The most important of these bring us back to a debate between the German physiologist Albrecht von Haller and Whytt on Whytt's use of the term *stimulus*, a debate that concerned the distinction between *irritability* and *sensibility*.[18] According to Haller, Whytt falsely imputed sensation, or feeling, to all parts of the animal body. Many of the involuntary motions of the body did not involve any feeling at all. Haller therefore argued that the notion of a stimulus should be attached to conscious sensations only, or put more precisely, there were no sensations without consciousness. Reid shared Haller's concerns: "We can affix no other Idea to the Word Stimulus but that of Pricking or the Sensation arising from pricking," but we "feel nothing of this kind in the Circulation of the Blood the Motion of the Lungs or Peristaltick Motion of the Gutts." However, to think of a "Stimulus that is not felt or perceived Seems to border upon a Contradiction" (Wood 1995, 102). Haller's solution, to think of irritability as an "inherent property" of matter, must have been as "impious and unphilosophical [a] declaration of mechanism" for Reid as it had been for Whytt (French 1969, 68). The idea that "mere inert Matter is acted upon by a Stimulus" would imply that matter itself was able to feel. Reid, on the other hand, retained the suggestion that there was perhaps a distinction to be made between the sentient principle and the mind, which he did not pursue in his reading notes.

Yet it is precisely here that Reid's departure in moral philosophy from predecessors and contemporaries such as Hutcheson, Hume, and Smith is located. Stimulus, sensations, judgment, consciousness, and mind were for Reid related concepts. What he got out of Whytt's discussion of the sentient principle was that there was some sort of active power that infused the animate creation with life. As Reid made clear in his much later comments on Priestley's materialism, this active power "preserves the Organisation of the living Being . . . while Life continues" (Wood 1995, 225; the order of the quoted passages was reversed). As in the case of Newton's law of gravitation, the sentient principle was evidence for the constant interference of a deity to sustain life. The life soul was not something just given, but something constantly enforced by the deity. The uneasy relation of the sentient principle to consciousness pointed, however, to a distinction between instincts and reason, between a "living force" and the mind. Whytt on the one hand gave evidence against materialist theories of life, but he showed on the other that moral theories

18. On this debate, see French 1969 and, recently, Wright 2000.

that treated sentiments or sensations as the basis for moral conduct were not able to distinguish between animals who acted by necessity on sensations, and humans who did so voluntarily. In Reid's view, moral theories giving prime importance to feelings like sympathy (as of course that of Smith) made humans act by necessity, thus robbing them of their power to act as agents. The very idea of moral agency was thus misrepresented from the very outset.

Judgment and Human Agency

John Wright (2000, 177) has recently argued that "it is not commonly recognized that debates about materialism in eighteenth-century Britain focus as much on the question whether matter can support life as on the question whether matter can think." As noted by Wright, Reid discusses both these questions in his lectures on Priestley to the Glasgow Literary Society, though for Reid they should be considered distinct issues. It was one thing to argue, on the basis of the new findings in physiology, that the animate creation could not be properly understood without taking into account the role of feelings, sentiments, and some active power like the "sentient principle." It was quite another to make this physiology the basis of a theory of moral agency, let alone of the moral order.

For Reid, the basis of moral conduct, and by implication of sociability, was not to be sought in a human agent who necessarily acted on his or her sentiments. For on this basis humans could not be distinguished from any other animal. Reid's criticism of moral theories of the sentiments or passions in whatever form was that it was wrongfully assumed that a moral order could emerge from agents acting merely on their biological frame. Human agency was unthinkable without taking into account the features that distinguish us from animals: our reasoning faculty and our volition. As Reid put it in his comments on Priestley's materialism: "Man is distinguished from his fellow Animals by a rational & Moral Nature, which is the Image of his Maker" (Wood 1995, 230).

Reid's emphasis on the role of humans' judging faculty for moral agency is a constant in his writing. This we see in his lecture notes, as well as in his mature texts, most notably in his *Essays on the Active Powers of Man* (1788). In a note on self-love and benevolence, likely to have been written for use in his class lectures at Glasgow, Reid emphasized that a passion that is not accompanied by judgment should be considered an "animal passion." An animal passion "is not guided by judgment but draggs the judgment after it." And in these same notes Reid considers that when Hutcheson speaks of the "cool passions" he must have in view those passions in which judgment is involved. The judgment may be true or false, but "it is still a Real Judgment," and without it, Reid argues, it is impossible to discover the "true worth" of things (Birkwood Collection, AUL 2131/7/V/1). In lecture notes of January 1765, Reid emphasizes that even self-love "requires in its operations more of Reflection . . . than men generally bestow" (Birkwood Collection, AUL 2131/8/III/3:5). The nature of our "moral faculty or conscience," therefore, consists not "barely in having certain agreeable or disagreeable sensations," but involves judgment as well: "approbation and disapprobation imply Judgment" (Birkwood Collection, AUL 2131/8/III/3:7). Elsewhere, he made clear that he did not object to Hutcheson's use of the term *moral sense*, as long as this was meant to include judgment (Reid 1990).

We find similar expressions in lecture notes on Smith's notion of sympathy. The gist of them all is that "it is evident that this Sympathy supposes a moral Judgment and consequently a moral faculty." Judgment and the moral sense are "necessarily antecedent to our Sympathy and consequently our moral Sentiments cannot be the Effect of Sympathy" (Robertson and Norton 1984, 314). In his *Essays on the Active Powers of Man* (1788) Reid reconsiders the issue of the relation of feelings and judgment to moral conduct by arguing against those philosophers who use "the word *sentiment*, to express feeling without judgment." To use it thus was for Reid in fact an "abuse of a word . . . for the word *sentiment*, in the English language, never, as I conceive, signifies mere feeling, but judgment accompanied with feeling" (*Works*, 2:674).

Reid is commonly, and rightly, seen as defending a moral system of duties, rather than of virtues. Knud Haakonssen traces this divide between Reid and moral philosophers like Hutcheson and Smith to their very different views on the nature of moral judgment (Reid 1990, 52–54). From Reid's perspective, however, neither Hutcheson nor Smith did justice to the role of judgment in moral agency at all. (For a recent nuanced assessment of the role of judgment in Smith's theory of moral agency, see Montes 2002, especially chapter 4.) For this reason, Reid lumped moral theories that penultimately based moral agency on the passions or sentiments (as Hutcheson, Hume, and Smith did) in the same class as those that conceived man as a mere animated machine (as did, for example, David Hartley and Joseph Priestley).

Reid on Utopian Political Systems

Reid drew the consequences of his view on moral agency for the social order in his discourse on utopian systems, delivered as late as 1794 before the Glasgow Literary Society. Reid gave his lecture in the aftermath of the French Revolution, when his first enthusiasm had been considerably tempered by the Terror that swept France. The two questions he addressed in his discourse were, first: "What is that Form or Order of political Society which, abstractly considered, tends most to the Improvement and Happiness of Man?" And second: "How a Form of Government which actually exists and has been long established may be changed?" (Reid 1990, 277). The second question obviously bears on the French Revolution. In treating this question Reid understandably warned against the dangers of "sudden and violent changes" in government.[19] The attention devoted in the contemporary press to this part of his lecture may well have contributed to Reid's reputation as a political conservative. This hardly does justice to him. In fact, his abstract outline of a utopian system had some quite radical traits.

Reid contrasted the utopian system with the system of private property. Of this last system he denied that it could lead to a beneficial social outcome. For anyone thinking about political economy after Smith such a denial must have been stunning. Indeed, Reid's argument against the emergence of a beneficial social order based on self-interested behavior may be rendered in a number of questions to Smith. Was it not to be observed that inequality grew in a society based on self-interest? Was self-interest not a spur to the corruption of morals of "both the poor and rich"? Was it not to be observed that interest in the "public spirit" and the "public good" diminished rather than grew under the system of private property? Finally, what evidence was there for the idea that self-interested behavior turned out for the good of all? Either one assumed that the order in society was regulated in a manner similar to the order of nature, which was to ignore human free will and the possibility of violating the moral order, or one assumes that human judgment always guides us to contribute to the public good, which was to deny that human actions are guided by self-interest.

19. As Wood (2001, 38) documents, fragments from this part of Reid's discourse were printed in the *Glasgow Courier* for 18 December 1794, apparently with the purpose to distance Reid from sympathies with the French Revolution—sympathies for which Reid had been threatened with physical assault.

If instead, humankind voluntarily adhered to a moral order, one prescribed by the deity but having no natural or necessary existence, then a heavy role fell to the state. Reid discussed three principles that outlined the scope of the government's actions. First, individual minds should be "strengthened" in the "Principles of Virtue and true Religion." Second, there should be as few temptations to wrong and criminal conduct as possible. Third, "real Merit" and "Esteem and Honour" should be ranked equally. In realizing these principles education would help, but it could not be relied on while the corrupting effects of private property were allowed to continue. As long as private property enforced the temptation to act out of self-interest, there was no guarantee that people would actually act in accordance with their knowledge of the moral good. Consequently, the system of private property should be abolished, and property should be "under the Administration of the State for the common benefit of the whole political family" (Reid 1990, 286). In Reid's utopian system, education, unopposed by private interest, would enable people to act toward the public good, and citizens would be rewarded according to their merit.

Reid outlined a meritocracy to replace the system of commerce. Only a limited role was admitted for trade, and this only via the central state, not via individual trading. The government should take care of the exchange of surpluses with foreign states. Internally, a system of distribution should provide each with his or her needs and merits. And, since the market could not establish a just distribution, this, too, fell to the state.

Conclusion

Theories of life, we have seen, did indeed have consequences for how Reid thought about the social order, although the relation is more complex than a simple parallel. In his *Fable of the Bees* Bernard Mandeville claimed to have considered "man as he really is" and based his theory of the social order on this assumption. In eighteenth-century Scotland, however, it was far from clear what exactly was meant by this simple phrase. Was it to consider humans in terms of their physiological frame? Or was it to consider them as inanimate matter, as reasoning machines? Or again, was it to see them as driven by feelings of benevolence or sympathy?

Whytt reinforced Reid's disposition and general arguments against a materialist and mechanistic understanding of the moral and animal economy. Yet Reid also sharply divided the moral from the animal kingdom.

Humans were more than mere animals; our faculty of judgment and our power to act out of free will distanced us, as moral agents, from the animals. From this stance, he criticized contemporaries who seemed to acquiesce in a social order in which humankind acted from self-interest, rather than from human wisdom. To act on the sentiments or passions and to act mechanically were equivalent expressions for Reid. He did not trust private interest to bring benefits for all, and his utopian alternative was based on the firm conviction that a just social order only begins where mechanism ends.

References

Barfoot, Michael. 1983. James Gregory (1753–1821) and Scottish Scientific Metaphysics, 1750–1800. Ph.D. diss., University of Edinburgh.

Birkwood Collection, Aberdeen University Library, Aberdeen.

Conrad, Stephen A. 1987. *Citizenship and Common Sense: The Problem of Authority in the Social Background and Social Philosophy of the Wise Club of Aberdeen*. New York: Garland Publishing.

Cook, Harold J. 1999. Bernard Mandeville and the Therapy of "The Clever Politician." *Journal of the History of Ideas* 60.1:101–24.

De Marchi, Neil B. 2001. Exposure to Strangers and Superfluities: Mandeville's Regimen for Great Wealth and Foreign Treasure. In *Physicians and Political Economy: Six Studies of the Work of Doctor-Economists*, edited by Peter Groenewegen. London: Routledge.

French, R. K. 1969. *Robert Whytt, the Soul, and Medicine*. London: The Wellcome Institute.

Goldsmith, M. M. 1988. Regulating Anew the Moral and Political Sentiments of Mankind: Bernard Mandeville and the Scottish Enlightenment. *Journal of the History of Ideas* 49.4:587–606.

Hundert, E. J. 1994. *The Enlightenment's Fable: Bernard Mandeville and the Discovery of Society*. Cambridge: Cambridge University Press.

———. 1995. Bernard Mandeville and the Enlightenment's Maxims of Modernity. *Journal of the History of Ideas* 56.4:577–93.

Hutcheson, Francis. [1725] 1726. *An Inquiry into the Original of Our Ideas of Beauty and Virtue*. London: Darby, Bettesworth.

———. [1728] 1971. *An Essay on the Nature and the Conduct of the Passions with Illustrations on the Moral Sense*. Edited by Bernard Peach. Cambridge, Mass.: Belknap Press.

Iltis, Carolyn. 1971. Leibniz and the Vis Viva Controversy. *Isis* 62.1:21–35.

Jacyna, L. S. 1994. *Philosophic Whigs: Medicine, Science, and Citizenship in Edinburgh, 1789–1848*. London: Routledge.

Jevons, William S. 1970. *The Theory of Political Economy*. Edited and introduced by R. D. Collison Black. Middlesex: Harmondsworth.

Klever, Wim. 1994. Herman Boerhaave (1668–1738) oder Spinozismus als rein mechanische Wissenschaft des Menschen. In *Spinoza in der europäischen Geistesgeschichte*, edited by Hanna Delf and Julius Hans Schoeps, 75–93. Berlin: Hentrich.

Laudan, Larry L. 1968. The *Vis Viva* Controversy, a Post-Mortem. *Isis* 59:131–43.

Lawrence, Christopher. 1979. The Nervous System and Society in the Scottish Enlightenment. In *Natural Order: Historical Studies of Scientific Culture*, edited by Steven Shapin and Barry Barnes, 19–40. Beverly Hills, Calif.: Sage Publishers.

Lindeboom, G. A. 1968. *Herman Boerhaave*. London: Methuen.

Locke, John. 1967. *An Essay Concerning Human Understanding*. Edited and with an introduction by John W. Yolton. London: Dent.

Maclaurin, Colin. Papers. Edinburgh University Library, Edinburgh.

Mandeville, Bernard. [1714] 1924. *The Fable of the Bees*. Edited and introduced by F. B. Kaye. Oxford: Clarendon Press.

Montes, Leonidas. 2002. Philosophical and Methodological Underpinnings of Adam Smith's Political Economy: A Critical Reconstruction of Some Central Components. Ph.D. diss., University of Cambridge.

Norton, David Fate. 1966. From Moral Sense to Common Sense: An Essay on the Development of Scottish Common Sense Philosophy, 1700–1765. Ph.D. diss., University of California, San Diego.

———. 1974. Hutcheson's Moral Sense Theory Reconsidered. *Dialogue* 13.1:3–23.

———. 1975. George Turnbull and the Furniture of the Mind. *Journal of the History of Ideas* 35.4:701–16.

Porter, Theodore M. 1994. Making Things Quantitative. *Science in Context* 7.3:389–407.

Reid, Thomas. 1967. *Philosophical Works*. Edited and introduced by Sir William Hamilton. Hildesheim: Georg Olms Verlag.

———. 1990. *Practical Ethics, Being Lectures and Papers on Natural Religion, Self-Government, Natural Jurisprudence, and the Law of Nations*. Edited and introduced by Knud Haakonssen. Princeton, N.J.: Princeton University Press.

Robertson, Stewart C., and David Fate Norton. 1984. Thomas Reid on Adam Smith's Theory of Morals. *Journal of the History of Ideas* 45.2:309–21.

Scott, William Robert. [1900] 1992. *Francis Hutcheson: His Life, Teaching, and Position in the History of Philosophy*. Bristol: Thoemmes Press.

Shaftesbury, Third Earl of (Anthony Ashley Cooper). [1711] 2001. *Characteristicks of Men, Manners, Opinions, Times*. Vols. 1–3. Indianapolis, Ind.: Liberty Fund.

Sher, Richard. 2000. Science and Medicine in the Scottish Enlightenment. In *The Scottish Enlightenment: Essays in Reinterpretation*, edited by Paul B. Wood, 99–156. Rochester: University of Rochester Press.

Sigot, Nathalie. 2002. Jevons's Debt to Bentham: Mathematical Economy, Morals, and Psychology. *Manchester School of Economic and Social Studies* 70.2:262–78.

Turco, Luigi. 1999. Maclaurin, Reid, and Kemp Smith on the Ancestry of Hume's Philosophy. *Reid Studies* 2.2:71–87.

Underwood, E. Ashworth. 1977. *Boerhaave's Men at Leyden and After*. Edinburgh: Edinburgh University Press.

Vartanian, Aram. 1950. Trembley's Polyp, La Mettrie, and Eighteenth-Century French Materialism. *Journal of the History of Ideas* 11.3:259–86.

Warke, Tom. 2000. Mathematical Fitness in the Evolution of the Utility Concept from Bentham to Jevons to Marshall. *Journal of the History of Economic Thought* 22.1:5–27.

Wood, Paul B. 1984. *Thomas Reid: Natural Philosopher: A Study of Science and Philosophy in the Scottish Enlightenment*. Ph.D. diss., University of Leeds.

———. 1990. The Natural History of Man in the Scottish Enlightenment. *History of Science* 28.1:89–123.

———. 1993. *The Aberdeen Enlightenment: The Arts Curriculum in the Eighteenth Century*. Aberdeen: Aberdeen University Press.

———. 1995. *Thomas Reid on the Animate Creation*. Edinburgh: Edinburgh University Press.

———. 2000. Dugald Stewart and the Invention of "The Scottish Enlightenment." In *The Scottish Enlightenment: Essays in Reinterpretation*, edited by Paul Wood, 1–37. Rochester: University of Rochester Press.

———. 2001. Who Is Thomas Reid? *Reid Studies* 5.1:35–52.

Wright, John P. 1990. Metaphysics and Physiology. In *Studies in the Philosophy of the Scottish Enlightenment*, edited by M. A. Stewart, 251–301. Oxford: Clarendon Press.

———. 2000. Materialism and the Life Soul in Eighteenth-Century Scottish Physiology. In *The Scottish Enlightenment: Essays in Reinterpretation*, edited by Paul B. Wood, 177–98. Rochester: University of Rochester Press.

Yolton, John W. 1983. *Thinking Matter: Materialism in Eighteenth-Century Britain*. Oxford: Basil Blackwell.

Economia civile and *pubblica felicità* in the Italian Enlightenment

Luigino Bruni and Pier Luigi Porta

1. The "New Science" in Italy

Happiness is the pivotal concept of Italian economic thinking during the latter half of the eighteenth century. This essay proposes to demonstrate that the two main Italian groups of political economists of the time developed the theme of happiness following rather interesting complementary patterns. The Milanese group worked along eudemonistic eighteenth-century lines, moving from a hedonistic perspective: individual happiness provides the starting point. The Neapolitan side was based, in its turn, on an original reinterpretation of the Aristotelian and Scholastic tradition; Neapolitan authors attempted to update that tradition and bring it into line with the new scientific method: civil economy is the result of that effort.

In both cases, the canons of the "new science" are naturally woven into the political and economic discourse; political economy, in particular, is indeed elaborated by making use of those canons. In fact, this has the further incidental consequence of creating a continuum between political economy and technological applications of science. The emphasis on technical matters among reformers and political economists more generally stands out as typical of Italian enlightenment.

It is, further, a special character of the Italian tradition, generally speaking, that the study of the polity in the light of the principles of the new science is not conducive to any purely mechanical view of the economy and society. It leads rather to a civic conception implying a quite sophisticated blend of institutional interactions, which is aptly described by Antonio Genovesi's term *economia civile*; it is a conception that can be traced easily through the Italian tradition in later periods well into the nineteenth century. *Pubblica felicità* and *economia civile* are the terms that best describe and qualify the system of political economy developing in Italy particularly during the latter half of the eighteenth century. As indicated above, we shall limit the discussion in this essay to the Milanese and the Neapolitan cases: the former group mainly reflects an emphasis on happiness and, more particularly, on *public happiness*; the latter is known for its peculiar use of the phrase *civil economy*. This statement, however, holds within limits, for the two terms do in fact apply in some sense to both the Milanese and the Neapolitan experience, as we shall see.

Newtonianism had a role in the development of political economy in Italy throughout the eighteenth century. At the same time, however, it would be impossible to understand the relationship between Italian political economy and the Scientific Revolution without taking the Italian tradition of physics and mechanics, and in particular the contribution of Galileo, into account. The main achievement of Galileo, as far as physics is concerned, is as much experimental as intellectual, especially as it concentrates on showing the effectiveness of mathematical reasoning in developing ideal cases. In that sense we can speak of a Galileo-Newtonian tradition.[1]

The frame of reference and the intellectual sources for the present treatment are twofold. On the one side is a large current of thinking that can be termed *moral Newtonianism*; on the other side we have the developments of *sensism* and *materialism* in eighteenth-century thought.[2]

1. See I. B. Cohen (1994, chap. 5; 1980) on the relationship of Galileo to the "Newtonian style." S. Cremaschi (1984, chap. 2) writes about the "Galileo-Newtonian way of proceeding" as an element leading into "moral Newtonianism." On "moral Newtonianism," see also Cremaschi 1992, where the concept is applied to the context of Scottish Enlightenment. Adam Smith (1976–95, vol. 3, sec. 4, para. 44) himself notes that Galileo proceeds "from reason and experience." "Moral Newtonianism," in the above sense, seems to parallel what Jessica Riskin calls "sentimental empiricism" in her contribution to the present volume.

2. *Sensism* is the doctrine that reduces all knowledge to sensation: for sensist philosophers there is no need to have recourse to the intellect or to any faculty other than *sense*. The classic text of sensism is Condillac's *Traité des sensations* ([1754] 1803–13), though Thomas Hobbes and Pierre Gassendi, for example, were also sensists. Sensism, therefore, is more radical than empiricism. Empiricism, in fact, needs something more than pure sensation. John Locke, for instance, was rather an empiricist than a sensist *stricto sensu*, because to him the source of all knowledge comes from *perception*, which presupposes intelligence and understanding (as in the title of his *Essay Concerning Human Understanding*); and the latter cannot be included under sensation. To sensists, rather, sensations are primitive (see also Cremaschi 1984).

These two currents of thinking developed their influence in Italy, and they were a driving force in the flourishing of economic thought especially during the latter half of the eighteenth century. At the same time, this essay shows that the *oeconomy* that flourishes in Italy, within that frame of reference, is largely a development of the theme of happiness, and of *public happiness* more precisely, within a "constitutional" setting.

A locus classicus of moral Newtonianism is to be found in Adam Smith's *Essays on Philosophical Subjects* and more particularly in his essay on the history of astronomy. Following Hume on the method of the new science and on the connection or association of ideas, Smith is led to emphasize the idea of *connection*, thus turning a treatment of the physical world into something of interest in the realm of morals and politics. He is, in fact, dealing with natural *philosophy*: "Philosophy is the science of the connecting principles of nature" (Smith 1976–95, vol. 3, sec. 2, para. 11). Adam Smith (1976–95, 2:769) would, in due course, go on to state the same of *moral philosophy* in the *Wealth of Nations*.[3] It is really the implications of the use of analogy, together with the application of Occam's razor, that form the bases for Smith's admiration of the Newtonian system "as the greatest discovery that ever was made by man, the discovery of an immense chain of the most important and sublime truths, all closely connected together" (Smith 1976–95, vol. 3, sec. 4, para. 76). It evidently is in that sense and in view of that use that Smith insists on such a great discovery as a product of imagination as well as an unveiling of truths.[4]

In their turn the developments of the materialistic branch of the Enlightenment can take either a mechanistic (*homme machine*) or a vitalistic (*homme sensible*) drift.[5] The use of analogy, either mechanical or biological, signals the distinction. We take such and kin offshoots to represent the French-Continental branch of Newtonianism, which links up with eighteenth-century sensism and materialism. A typical intellectual figure, whose significance also extends to highlighting the influence of

3. "The beauty of a systematical arrangement of different observations connected by a few common principles, was first seen in the rude essays of those antient times towards a system of natural philosophy. Something of the same kind was afterwards attempted in morals. The maxims of common life were arranged in some methodical order, and connected together by a few common principles, in the same manner as they had attempted to arrange and connect the phenomena of nature. The science which pretends to investigate and explain those connecting principles, is what is properly called moral philosophy" (Smith 1976–95, 2:768–69).

4. This is what Cohen (1980, esp. chap. 3) calls "Newtonian style." See also Cremaschi 1984.

5. See Giannetti da Fonseca 1991.

Newton on the moral and political sciences, is Pierre-Louis Moreau de Maupertuis (1698–1759). Other significant authors include Étienne Bonnot de Condillac, Jean d'Alembert, Paul Henri Dietrich d'Holbach, Denis Diderot, Claude-Adrien Helvétius, and Julien Offroy La Mettrie. In discussing the Italian case, we should bear in mind that the above ramifications of Newtonianism work their way through the Italian eighteenth-century context and spread their influence on rising major groups of political economists. We will focus here almost exclusively on two leading figures of the Milanese and Neapolitan schools, Pietro Verri and Antonio Genovesi, respectively.[6]

2. Political Economy in Milan

The Accademia dei Pugni and the review *Il Caffè* are the institutions through which the Milanese group of political economists came into existence during the early 1760s. Pietro Verri was the founder, leader, and active contributor to both. *Il Caffè* appeared between 1764 and 1766 in successive *fogli* made in two volumes. *Foglio* 19 of volume 1 has an article by Pietro Verri (1993b) devoted to thoughts on the spirit of Italian literature.[7] Here Verri describes Galileo-Newtonianism at the philosophical level as a force of renovation, providing a new connecting frame for scientific reasoning, in the spirit of what we have called above moral Newtonianism.

The "new science," or the Galileo-Newton tradition, provides the frame of reference to illustrate the sources and the methods of enlightened thinking. In his *Enquiries*, Hume ([1777] 1975, sec. 3, 204) mentions—as "Newton's chief rule of philosophizing"—the idea, "where any principle has been found to have a great force and energy in one instance, to ascribe to it a like energy in all similar instances." This is sometimes called the principle of the "analogy of nature," which postulates similar hidden forces behind parallel phenomena in different fields of experience.[8] Hume, for example, singles out "usefulness" as a principle of that kind as a basis for justice. The Italian thinkers, Pietro Verri among

6. Joseph Schumpeter (1954, chap. 3, sec. 4d, p. 177)—in his treatment of eighteenth-century Italian economic thought—is basically correct to say that "only two 'schools,' in the strict sense of the term, can be identified: the Neapolitan and the Milanese."

7. Unless otherwise indicated, translations from Italian texts are ours. On Verri, see Porta and Scazzieri 2002.

8. Cremaschi 1984, esp. chaps. 1 and 2, discusses the influence of Newtonianism beyond physics and astronomy.

them, were ready to make large use of the principle of usefulness in their explanations in the field of morals, political economy and political science. In the case of Verri, this line of thinking is conducive to a dynamic view of society, as a system of motions or movements that are studied to find their *equilibrium*. "Interest" takes the place of "force"; "sympathy" and "passions" act in the place of "attraction." In the British experience Hume's *Treatise* ([1739–40] 1978, bk. 1, pt. 1, sec. 4) aimed at extending the notion of *attraction* from the natural to the moral universe; Smith made use of the analogy of gravitation in the dynamics of market prices. Among the Milanese, Verri (e.g., 1964, 7) developed his own philosophy from the premise that seeking pleasure and shunning pain are the great engines of human action.[9] The mechanical analogy seems prima facie dominant; but the biological analogy is also pervasive, particularly as political systems are compared to bodies that can experience corruption and decline but also healing and recovery. It is in that connection that the *sensistic* and *materialistic* components of eighteenth-century thought acquire their significance.

Before examining Verri's works, which are the most deserving from the standpoint of the construction of a system of political economy, it is worth mentioning that a number of contributions published in the volumes of *Il Caffè* touch on one or the other of the two strands, as described in the above, of the Galileo-Newton tradition, namely, the application of the "analogy of nature" on one side and the "sensistic views" on the other. In particular Cesare Beccaria, Pietro Verri, the latter's brother Alessandro, and Paolo Frisi are among the main authors. To these men other related figures should be added, among whom Gian Rinaldo Carli and Alfonso Longo. As an example, Paolo Frisi's "Saggio sul Galileo" (1993b), which was published in 1765 in *foglio* 3 of the second volume of the journal, takes its place in the context of the scientific inspiration of the journal, which includes contributions entirely devoted to problems of applied mathematics, physics, and astronomy.[10] At the same time Frisi's essay on Galileo should be considered in conjunction with similar essays in which the author approached d'Alembert, Cavalieri, and, above all, Newton.

The works of Pietro Verri afford the best opportunity to examine the influence of the Galileo-Newtonian tradition on political economy.

9. Verri praises M. de Maupertuis (particularly his *Essai de philosophie morale* of 1749) for giving a rigorous mathematical theory and a practical measure of pleasure and pain.

10. Examples are Boscovich 1993, Frisi 1993b, and Beccaria 1993b, famous as an early example of mathematical political economy.

Particularly his works on happiness and on political economy (Verri [1773] 1781, 1964) develop his views on value, money, and market equilibrium, together with his conception of the dynamics of the system. They provide probably the most interesting analysis of the working of the economy within the Milanese school. Here we summarize Verri's view of economy, bringing into full light (1) the working of forces of attraction and repulsion, (2) his hedonistic philosophy, and (3) his constant desire to speak of measurable phenomena.

For a full understanding of Verri's views on *commercial society*, we have to turn to his formative years. As early as 1763, in his *Meditazioni sulla felicità*—usually classified as a philosophical pamphlet—Verri spells out the foundational pieces of his approach to civil life, and he argues that the excess of desires over and above possibilities or "power" is a measure of *unhappiness*.[11] The search for happiness in the form of the *removal of unhappiness* is a core issue in Pietro Verri's political philosophy. He appears from the start as one of the leading representatives of eighteenth-century eudemonistic views. *Happiness*, Verri argues, can be pursued in two ways. Happiness, in fact, consists in the reduction of the *difference* between the two elements of *desires* and *power*; that reduction can be achieved by acting upon either one or the other of the two elements. It can be said therefore that the object of happiness being reduced to a difference, it can be conquered either by "addition" (of power) or by "subtraction" (of desires). Verri declares addition to be superior. An addition in the form of the *enlargement of power* provides the main route to happiness as compared with a check on desires. Verri, however, lays a special emphasis upon *creativity* rather than mere enjoyment of what is already in our possession as a condition for happiness. Anyone who has reached the possession of a moderate fortune, Verri argues in the opening sentences of the *Meditazioni* ([1763] 1997), will tend either through lack of prudence to prefer present whims to future needs or through ill-considered distribution to postpone present needs to future whims; either way, the mistaken calculation of both the extravagant and the miser consists in preferring chimerical to real needs. When the

11. "L'eccesso de' desiderj sopra il potere è la misura della infelicità" (Verri 1964, 74). Verri's theory explicitly moves from Maupertuis, who proposed to measure pleasure and pain and argued that the total amount of pain exceeds the total amount of pleasure. See in particular his *Discorso sull'indole del piacere e del dolore*, in Verri 1964, 3–68. The first edition of that work was published by Verri only in 1773, but it contains the philosophical basis for his theory. Verri's *Meditazioni sulla felicità* are quoted in this article from the 1781 edition, published as *Discorso sulla felicità* (now in Verri 1964, 69–124).

fortunes of an individual or a family exceed the limits of subsistence, a lust for more is generated and the sum of desires is multiplied.[12]

The appropriate concept to be used to clarify Verri's point of view in this context is *ambition*, an ambivalent passion, described by him at the same time as the most ruinous and the most deserving among the passions. His own moral and jurisprudential approach leads him to attribute an algebraic sign to the content of passions. Ambition can carry both signs: there exists a positive ambition, which coincides with creativity and a person's continuous desire to better his or her condition;[13] however, much as we owe any great achievement to it, at the same time, Verri (1993c, 323) argues, ambition spawns that peculiar desire for rank and distinction that easily becomes extravagance and prodigality, a delusive drift into ruin not infrequently exciting sneering and contempt.[14] Mere enjoyment is to be distinguished from *creative enjoyment* or the *pleasure to make and create*. Virtue, Verri states, is every *useful* act. Verri's definition of *utility* is a disposition to *perform* good acts: utility is an "attitudine a far del bene" (Verri 1993a, 315).[15] Utility to him has an *active meaning* that provides the basis for his view of society in its formative steps as an industrious gathering of cooperating forces, founded upon a compact the end of which is the participants' well-being or public happiness (the greatest possible happiness distributed with the greatest possible equality).[16] Verri invites his readers to reflect on how purely human beneficence is a by-product of our love for pleasure: "la beneficenza puramente umana sia una emanazione dell'amore del piacere." Love of pleasure, in turn, operates through a secret connection—"secreta connessione"—between our own pain and the pain of others. To

12. "Le ricchezze portano seco la sete di accrescerle, —moltiplicano la somma de' nostri desiderj." See also "Sulla spensieratezza nella privata economia" (on prodigality in the private economy), Verri 1993c.

13. We purposely echo here a Smithian expression, significantly close to the wording used by Verri himself. See also, e.g., the passage on ambition in *Il Caffè* [1764–66] 1993, 1:200.

14. Much as ambition is an ambiguous force, so are riches, as Verri argues in section 2 of his *Meditazioni sulla felicità*: greater riches do not *necessarily* mean greater happiness.

15. Concerning utility, we shall see presently that Verri's thinking can be encompassed within what has been called "an accomplished rendering of the Italian utility-cum-scarcity version of the natural-law theory" within limits only (Hutchison 1988, 304). In particular the active meaning of the term *utility* should never be forgotten. That undoubtedly makes of Verri a rather more interesting animal than a mere precursor of the marginal utility theory.

16. Society, in fact, is analyzed in the *Meditazioni* of 1763 as "industriosa riunione di molte forze cospiranti" based on a "patto," the end of which is "il ben essere di ciascuno, il che si risolve nella felicità pubblica o sia la maggiore felicità possibile divisa colla maggiore uguaglianza possibile" (33).

Verri good arises from evil, sterility produces abundance, poverty generates wealth, burning needs spur ingenuity, and blunt injustice arouses courage.[17] In other words, pain is the moving principle of the whole humankind—"il dolore è il principio motore di tutto l'uman genere," Verri writes. Without it a person would turn into an inert and stupid animal—"un animale inerte e stupido." Pain excites labor, leads to the perfection of trades, teaches us to think and reflect; it creates sciences, induces us to conceive the arts and to refine them.

Let us now consider Verri's main book on political economy as such. Through the forty sections of the *Meditazioni sulla economia politica*, a work of his maturity published anonymously in 1771, Pietro Verri lays great stress on *creativity* as the source and origin of the formation of wealth and the real object of the science of political economy. An important example of this emphasis on creativity occurs in section 13 of his political economy.[18] "In a country made rich through industry," Verri (1986, 44) wrote, "machines and tools are perfected to such a degree that the workman in a single day will produce an article which in a less industrious nation would take several days to make; such are the resources available to a country which has grown rich through its industry, resources that are lacking in a country whose riches have come spontaneously from the land." Of course, "need or, in other words, the sensation of pain is the goad used by nature to arouse man from the indolent state of stagnation in which he would otherwise languish" (sec. 1, 4). "*Need*," he continued, "sometimes leads men to plunder, sometimes to trade. For trade to exist there must be both *want* and *plenty*." Concerning plenty, Verri explains, outspokenly challenging the "sect of the economists," that "reproduction applies as much to manufacture as it does to work in the fields," so that we should speak of "this highly fruitful *sterile class*," on the product of which entire cities and states survive (sec. 3, 9). This and similar concepts crop up time and again through Verri's writings. Particularly noticeable is the *unity* of three works, all of them originally drafted by him during the 1770s and later collected by

17. *Discorso sull'indole del piacere e del dolore*, in Verri [1773] 1781, §11 ("Il dolore precede ogni piacere ed è il principio motore dell'uomo"); cf. Verri 1964, 55.

18. Section 13 is often quoted by commentators. Under the title "Of the Value of Money and Its Influence on Industry," the section basically focuses on the power of industry in increasing what the author calls "annual reproduction." This provides the essential premise on which his argument on the value of money rests. It is, however, quite common to focus merely on the argument's implicit criticism of Hume on money in that section. This is unfortunate, as the criticism cannot in fact be understood without the premise.

the author himself under the heading of *Discorsi*: his work on happiness, on the nature of pleasure and pain, and on political economy.[19]

Verri's economic philosophy consists of three related elements. The first is philosophical. It finds significant expression, a few years after his book on political economy, in his *Discorso sull'indole del piacere e del dolore* ([1773] 1781). In that work Verri makes clear, as hinted above, the influence of Maupertuis on his own reflections. Without going to the extremes touched in La Mettrie's *Homme machine* or even, later during the eighteenth century, in de Sade's *Philosophie dans le boudoir*, Maupertuis had indeed proceeded sufficiently along the road of materialistic and deterministic sensism to endorse the reduction of all forms of happiness to pleasure and to think of it as measurable. At the same time, Verri takes from Maupertuis a certain pessimistic tone, which inclines him to think that, in the ordinary course of life, the sum of the evils is larger than that of the goods; thus we should try and reduce evils as much as we can.[20] The second element has to do with Verri's attitude as a civil servant. Political economy to him consists in intellectual challenges for the solution of practical problems. The third element finds expression in his bent for "political arithmetic," both in terms of logical reasoning and in terms of empirical inquiry. Since the very start of his own activity as a writer, particularly through his compilation and discussion of the balance sheets of foreign trade for the State of Milan, it is clear that political economy, to him, is an empirical science. Verri is thus representative of a circle that, along with that in Naples, best illustrates the fruits of the Galileo-Newton tradition in moral philosophy.

Public happiness, in Verri's system, must be the object of *policy*. Verri's system is based on free trade and on competitive markets; however, without an appropriate context determined by the institutional setting, there is little presumption that the effects will be progressive. Verri is perhaps the best representative of a generation that had been acutely aware of the dangers of decline in a civilized country; his own reading of Lombard history provides a signal illustration of this attitude. It would be proper here to refer more fully to Verri's works on the history of the

19. Verri [1773] 1781, [1796] 1964. The present argument has its natural sequence in Verri's theory of price, on which we refer the reader to Porta and Scazzieri 2002, where Verri's political economy of "effective supply" is discussed. See also Porta and Scazzieri 1999.

20. Maupertuis is mentioned in that *Discorso* on account of his attempts to calculate pleasures and pains (Verri [1773] 1781, sec. 6). Although we do not possess an instrument of measurement in that case, Verri observes, still in the practice of our actions we continually tacitly make that exact kind of comparison of good and evil and of pleasure and pain (sec. 14).

State of Milan, to which we have, however, chosen to make only a passing mention in the present essay. It is relatively easy then, along the line of reasoning indicated above, to understand the special kind of ambivalence he constantly stresses in most of the concepts he analyses. In that way, as a signal example of that ambivalence, Verri's insistent elaboration on the significance of intermediate bodies and on the rule of law does not contradict his lifelong struggle against those particular bodies and institutions that had come into existence and were in power in the State of Milan as a result of Spanish rule and that historically acted, in his view, as factors of decline. Verri's conception of the economy, organized along competitive principles, is intimately connected with a constitutional view of the polity.[21] What his moral Newtonianism implies is that there is no simple mechanistic or deterministic view of competitive equilibrium, as it were; his whole conception is much closer to the Scottish tradition than to the French Enlightenment.

Verri's ambivalence, in the above sense, finds its foundation at a deeper level, which must be hinted at here as an expression of his own eudemonistic science. In his *Discorso sull'indole del piacere e del dolore*, Verri (1964, 7–68) introduces the distinction between physical and moral feelings.[22] Moral feelings or sentiments are indirect or higher-order feelings, which cannot be experienced unless a reflecting faculty is sufficiently developed, that is, an attitude to consider a mirrored reality and to evaluate one's feelings in relation to it: Verri establishes a direct association between the degree of development of "moral sense" of individuals or social groups and the cultural complexity of their relational setting. However, in his view, the historical evolution of moral sense is far from being of a monotonic type; in particular, the transition from a primitive to a civilized state may either increase or decrease human unhappiness. In Verri's thought a distinction is implied between *incivilimento* (as a process) and *vita civile* (as a condition or state). It is generally maintained that the progress of civilization is *not* necessarily associated with the attainment of civility linked with wealth and well-being; for civilization expands the human capacity to develop moral sentiments and artificial needs. However, human industry and civility are only increased whenever the capacity to conceive new wants and new comforts is associated with trade and the division of labor rather than with plunder.

21. Verri's biographer Carlo Capra has duly highlighted that aspect of Verri's politico-economic view, especially in the chapters on political economy and reforms. See Capra 2002, esp. 291, 383.

22. For more on the issue, see Porta and Scazzieri 2002, 95–98.

Verri's study of the connecting principles of nature, applied to the polity, in short, is designed to show that the achievement of public happiness is a complex process, which cannot be the effect of the work of simple mechanic devices.

In bringing out the philosophical role of Newtonianism as a connecting frame throughout the development of the Milanese school and the Accademia dei Pugni, Paolo Frisi certainly is the outstanding personality.[23] As a researcher and teacher of mathematics and physics, Frisi soon acquired a strong reputation that put him at the center of an extraordinarily rich web of international connections. At the same time, he showed a unique capacity in linking his own interests as a professional scientist with wider interests encompassing politics and literature. He embodied at its best, perhaps, within the Milanese group, the ideal of the cosmopolitan scientist, and, at an early stage, in 1753, he became a member of the Académie des sciences; soon after, at Franklin's suggestion, Frisi joined the Royal Society as a fellow. He traveled extensively in Italy and Europe, and he had important and close contacts in Naples, particularly with Antonio Genovesi, whose philosophical influence on the Milanese intellectuals is, generally speaking, quite significant.

As a physicist Frisi belongs entirely to the Newtonian tradition; at the same time, in his philosophical works, he blends Newtonianism with the whole eudemonistic current, leading him to identify happiness or pleasure with virtue and to propose measures of pleasure and pain. The most relevant aspect of Frisi's personality in the present context concerns his conception of the analogy between physics and political economy. He believed that just as reciprocal and free natural impulses increase the quantity of movement in elastic bodies, so they enhance industry and wealth through competition in political bodies. The price of commodities is the arithmetical result of the quantity of commodities and the numbers of buyers and sellers. That conception forms the basis for Frisi's mathematical notes on Verri's *Meditazioni sulla economia politica* ([1771] 1964), and particularly for his notes on Verri's formula of price; these provide an example of the fruits of scientific spirit in the Milanese Enlightenment.[24]

23. Paolo Frisi came from Melegnano, a village south of Milan, where he was born in 1728, the same year as Pietro Verri. He would die in Milan in 1784.

24. Frisi's analogy is spelled out in his *Elogio a Maria Teresa*, quoted in Luini 1996, 131. Verri's (1986, sec. 4, 18) formula implies that price is in direct proportion to the number of

By far the best-known and influential personality of the Accademia dei Pugni and *Il Caffè* is Cesare Beccaria. We need only recall in the present context a few traits of Beccaria's contribution, which link up with the rise of the Italian tradition. As is well known, Beccaria, in his twenties, though a younger member of the group, already enjoyed a superior international reputation, indeed the highest of the group. This followed the appearance of his pamphlet *Dei delitti e delle pene*, of crimes and punishment, in 1764. Empress Maria Theresa took the bold step of creating a professorship of *Scienze Camerali* for him in Milan at the Scuole Palatine in 1769, a move that Verri did not particularly welcome at the time.[25] Beccaria was also a consultant administrator as a member of the Supremo Consiglio di Economia from 1771. He contributed a number of *Consulte* within the *Consiglio*. We have no space here to delve into his *Elementi di economia pubblica*, reflecting Beccaria's own teaching, which is inferior to Verri's as an achievement and would be published only posthumously in the "Collezione Custodi" (Custodi 1803–16) early in the nineteenth century.[26]

Beccaria would die in Milan in 1794. Curiously enough his travels were comparatively quite limited. It is significant in the present context that chapters 41 and 42 of his pamphlet on crimes and punishment ("Of the Means of Preventing Crimes" and "Of Sciences") were merged together in Morellet's French edition: in the resulting chapter some commentators incline to read a short history of civil society in a Fergusonian fashion (Venturi 1983). Natural laws of force and attraction are at work also in the moral domain with the opposite "attractions of pleasure and pain." A sort of stadial model of human development is sketched by him, of a kind that would be prominent also in the author's *Ricerche intorno alla natura dello stile* of 1770 and in the opening chapters of the *Elementi di economia pubblica*. In Beccaria's conception, the progress of nations is revealed through the discovery of the *unity* of *all* phenomena; accordingly, the use of *analogy* becomes more widespread and sophisticated. More particularly, a principle of "economy of action" (*minima azione*) appears to be common to the physical and the moral world.[27]

---

buyers and in inverse proportion to the numbers of sellers. On the issue, see Theocharis 1961 and Luini 1996.

25. As a professor Beccaria would be soon succeeded by Alfonso Longo, and the name of the chair would change to "Istituzioni economico politiche." Longo left an interesting *Prolusione* of 1773 under the same title.

26. See, however, Schumpeter 1954, 179–80. For a fuller treatment, see Porta 1990.

27. These ideas are developed also in Beccaria 1993a, 277–84.

An example of the above kind of moral Newtonianism is developed by Beccaria (1993a, 411–19) in an essay that opens the second volume of *Il Caffè* and that discusses the conception of the *unity of science* as the real object of the journal and as *the* way of spreading *useful* knowledge. It is here that the sensistic and materialistic sides of the Galileo-Newton tradition come to the surface. His conception was utilitarian. It was Beccaria who effectively contributed to launch the famous *dictum* that laws are to be considered—as he writes in the introduction (*A chi legge*) of his 1764 pamphlet, thus making use of a formula of Scottish origin—from the standpoint of "the greatest happiness of the greatest number." Jeremy Bentham would stress the importance of Beccaria along with Helvétius and Maupertuis in the development of utilitarianism.[28] Beccaria, in Bentham's opinion, pursued and completed in an important way Maupertuis's 1749 work on moral philosophy.

3. Civil Economy and Public Happiness in Naples

Scientific Thought in Naples

It is hard to point out a Neapolitan peculiarity during the classical period: premodern Italy was a crossroads of different cultures. Naples, as a European city, experienced a deep cross-fertilization of ideas with the whole of European culture.[29] The works of Neapolitan thinkers were often translated into the main European languages.

It seems possible, however, to single out at least *four* characteristics that can be considered typical of Neapolitan scientific culture; their discussion seems to be a necessary preliminary for an understanding of both civil economy and public happiness in the Neapolitan context. The close connection of the two concepts of *civil economy* and *public happiness* seems to be the peculiar feature of the Neapolitan school of political economy during the latter half of the eighteenth century, as it was in Milan.

A first element concerns the strong presence of Scholastic theology and philosophy. It should be recalled that Thomas Aquinas had been

28. Bentham's quotes are reported by Franco Venturi in his edition of Beccaria's work (see Beccaria [1764] 1965, 562–63).

29. Ferdinando Galiani (1728–87), for instance, after 1759 went to Paris, where he accomplished the second part of his career, all the time in close contact with Naples and its economic and philosophical schools. Antonio Genovesi (1713–69) also had profound relationships with the French philosophes and was familiar with European literature and philosophies.

active as a professor and teacher at the University of Naples (see Ferrone 1982 and Venturi 1962).

We should then mention as a second element the role of the outstanding personality of Giambattista Vico (1668–1744), the central figure in Neapolitan eighteenth-century culture. To Vico only historical analysis is true knowledge. Science is important in view of its practical applications for improving civil life and welfare. His main interest, however, lay in civic practice or social life. *Verum est factum*, the hallmark of his philosophical system, expresses the idea that true knowledge ought to be based on *facere* (as opposed to the Cartesian *cogito*), which includes both conceptual elaboration (metaphysics) and experimenting (physics; see Amerio 1947, sec. 2). Vico was essentially receptive to, though not uncritical of, the Galileo-Newtonian tradition, which also explains why mechanics acquired a central role in Naples at the time.[30] Vico's thought is based on sociality: to Vico civilization meant sociality, and he used the adjectives *uncivil* and *solitary* interchangeably (Amerio 1947). In Vico's thinking only civil life or civil society, individual and self-directed passions become social and produce "*civil* happiness." We shall see how these Vichian ideas have affected the core of Genovesi's theory.

We have then to consider, as a third point, the role and influence of Celestino Galiani (1681–1753) and Bartolomeo Intieri (1678–1757), two key figures in Neapolitan civic and economic renaissance. Both men had arrived in Naples from abroad: Galiani from Rome in 1732 and Intieri from Tuscany in 1699. The diffusion of Newton's thought in Naples dates from the 1730s, that is, the time when Galiani moved to Naples, where he became prominent as *Cappellano Maggiore del Regno* from 1732. Before then, he had been active in Rome updating the Scholastic tradition in the light of the new scientific and philosophical ideas of Galileo, Newton, and Gassendi.[31]

Bartolomeo Intieri, himself a disciple of Galileo and Torricelli and a representative of the Florentine tradition of civic humanism (Baron 1988; Garin [1947] 1994), had moved to Naples much earlier than

30. "Id curarunt in nostra Italia maximus Galilaeus et alii praeclarissimi physici, qui antequam methodus geometrica in physicam importaretur, innumera et maxima naturae phaenomena hac ratione explicarunt" (G. B. Vico, *De Antiquissima Italorum Sapientia* [1710], quoted in Amerio 1947, 58).

31. In 1727 in Florence Pierre Gassendi's *Opera omnia* was translated into Italian. Behind this translation were, among other people, Celestino Galiani and Bartolomeo Intieri. The publication of Gassendi's work was part of the larger philosophical project of spreading the Scientific Revolution of Galileo, Torricelli, and Newton. The same publisher, Stamperia granducale of Florence, also published Galileo's (1718) and Torricelli's (1715) *Opera Omnia*.

Celestino Galiani. Intieri had studied mathematics and physics; however, far more than anything else, he became prominent as an inventor of machines for agriculture. Following the vision of civic humanism, he stuck to the idea that sciences must be of practical and civil utility, rather than objects of mere intellectual speculation: "I do not appreciate those who spend their whole time in reading Geometry and Arithmetic without caring to see the fruit of their labors" (quoted in Venturi 1962, 553). Therefore in Naples he spent his whole energy and talent in inventing new machines, for example, for the cultivation and storage of grains. Science should lead to technical improvement, which in turn is conducive to social improvement through reforms and the promotion of public happiness. To Intieri, mechanics and technology were tools for public happiness.

The seat where the above intellectual and practical evolution took place was the Accademia delle Scienze,[32] founded in Naples in 1732 by Celestino Galiani and Bartolomeo Intieri.[33] The Accademia was, at the same time, the place of the diffusion of Galilean, Lockean, and Newtonian thought. It also became the workshop where technical experiments were conceived and realized for the improvement of the arts and the economy of the kingdom of Naples.

The idea of linking together in a chain of continuity civil economy and mechanics was mainly due in Naples to the Florentine Intieri, and the name of the chair he established in 1753 in Naples—"Mechanics and Civil Economy"—is an icon of Intieri's cultural approach. It is interesting that the man he chose to be the first incumbent to the new chair, Antonio Genovesi, was known as a philosopher, and he was certainly *not* the best-reputed economist in Naples: at the time Naples hosted Antonio Broggia and, above all, Ferdinando Galiani, a nephew of Celestino and prominent as the author of *Della moneta*. The choice of Genovesi was obviously in line with Intieri's vision and political philosophy.

32. The Accademia delle Scienze was methodologically and culturally a sequel to the Accademia degli Investiganti, founded in Naples in 1663 and active until 1670, when it was suppressed. The Investiganti had arisen in Naples out of the dispute between the *veteres* and the *novatores*. The latter had introduced in Naples the works of Gassendi, Cartesio, and Galileo.

33. Intieri was mainly a practical man, the manager of vast lands of Tuscan families. The knowledge of mechanic and economic laws was a tool for civil improvement of the kingdom. However, he was also a scholar, a mathematician in particular. From 1703 to 1706 he published papers on mathematics and geometry (see Genovesi 1963, 30), and few years later he wrote articles on the transportation and conservation of grains, and on the fabrication of windmills (Intieri 1733). At the same time, his country house near Naples (Massa Equana) was equipped with a very rich library, where economic books abounded (see Venturi 1962, 566).

Genovesi's *Economia civile* as "Scienza del ben vivere sociale"

The idea of *public happiness* forms the fourth, and the most relevant item in our reconstruction of the Neapolitan case, in which Achille Loria's dictum seems especially perceptive: "All our [Italian] economists, from whatever regional background, are dealing not so much, like Adam Smith, with the wealth of nations, but with public happiness" (Loria [1893] 1904, 85).

Modern political economy is sometimes supposed to have been a by-product of the desire to legitimize the quest for wealth. However, before Adam Smith published his *Wealth of Nations* in 1776, a different approach had gained ground, and it was in particular in the French and Italian traditions to characterize the direct object of research in the newly born "political economy" as "public happiness." It is hardly surprising that the term *happiness* (*felicità*, and more particularly *felicità pubblica*) appears in the title of books and pamphlets by Italian economists of the time: examples are Giuseppe Palmieri (*Reflections on the Public Happiness*), Ludovico Muratori (*On Public Happiness*), of course Pietro Verri, and others. It should also be noted that in Italy the theme of public welfare must be coupled with the idea of *ben vivere sociale* (the social weal),[34] an association that had been characteristic of the Italian humanist tradition, from Francesco Petrarca to Leon Battista Alberti and Lodovico Antonio Muratori. A special Neapolitan echo of that tradition stayed alive in Naples, thanks to Giambattista Vico, Pietro Giannone, and Paolo Mattia Doria. In particular, to the Neapolitans *pubblica felicità* meant that the *economia civile* should deal *directly* with the tools and ways of increasing the happiness of the people—mechanics being among those tools.[35]

34. The phrase was used in a well-known title by Lodovico Bianchini (1845), one of its early historians, as a hallmark of Italian economic thought. An excellent treatment of the issue is given in Parisi 1984, chap. 2.

35. That the issue of happiness is strongly connected with civil economy is very clearly a pivotal tenet in Genovesi's theory. Aristotle, G. B. Vico, Lord Shaftesbury, Francis Hutcheson, and the Platonic school of Cambridge were the sources of the philosophical works of Genovesi that focused on sociality as the key human characteristic (see Genovesi 1748, 1749). The sensist, hedonistic, and Epicurean approach to happiness, although present, did not deserve a central place to him. Both in Galiani and in Genovesi we find strong and clear statements against sensism and Epicureanism: this was surely partly due to political reasons (they were both abbots in Naples), but that was also due to the spell of other (as mentioned above) influences on Neapolitan culture. In particular, although not a follower of his philosophy of nature

Antonio Genovesi: A Chair of "Civil Economy and Mechanics"

When, in 1753, Antonio Genovesi[36] began his teaching of *economia civile* in Naples, he had already acquired a reputation as a professor of metaphysics and logic in Naples itself.[37] At the beginning of the 1750s his personal story had a turning point, passing from "*metafisico* to *mercadante*," as he himself described the passage from metaphysics to economics in his autobiography (see Pagden 1987, Venturi 1969). In the cultural environment of his time, it is easy to understand why Genovesi was strongly convinced that science should serve the improvement of society and public happiness.[38] The passage from philosophy to civil economy, the Italian version of the "Adam Smith problem," was a development of an internal intellectual research, more and more focused on the civic and social utility of sciences.[39] In this he displayed great similarity with Celestino Galiani, and even greater with Intieri:[40] "The greater part of

and his metaphysics, Genovesi after all agreed with Aristotelian ethics and politics and with the Vichian philosophy of history. On Genovesi's concept of happiness, see Bruni 2003.

36. We have adopted the following conventions for referring to Genovesi's works: for the *Lezioni di economia civile* (Genovesi [1765–67] 1824, hereafter cited as *Lezioni*), page references are to the 1824 edition (a reprint of the 1768 Milanese second edition of the work), but we have also given chapter and section numbers, which are the same in the several different editions. Page references for *Della diceosina o sia della filosofia del giusto e dell'onesto* (Genovesi [1766] 1973, hereafter cited as *Diceosina*) are to the 1973 edition. *Diceosina* is a Greek word that means "the philosophy of the right and honest." *Autobiografia* and *Lettere* both refer to Genovesi's correspondence (Genovesi 1963). For the other books cited in this section, page references are to the reprints in Genovesi 1979 (hereafter cited as *Scritti*). All English translations are ours: as far as we know, there are no English editions of Genovesi's books.

37. On the vicissitudes of this chair, see Genovesi 1963, 77–78. Bellamy 1987 gives the fullest English-language account of the intellectual milieu in Naples in which Genovesi wrote his work. See also Pii 1984.

38. Many years of Spanish domination had destroyed the networks of civil society that had existed since the pre-Roman era. It was only in 1724 that Naples became an independent kingdom under Bourbon rule. The decades following this event were an era of new hope for a civil and enlightened government. Genovesi was one in a group of thinkers who tried to understand the failures of the old regime and to find new routes to economic and social development.

39. Venturi (1969) sees the transition from philosophy to economics as a break in Genovesi's intellectual evolution; Pii (1984) and Bellamy (1987) argue for a consistent interpretation emphasizing continuity of Genovesi's whole system of thought.

40. Genovesi's *Discorso sopra il vero fine delle lettere e delle scienze* (1754), his opening lecture in his chair, is often considered to be the manifesto of Italian Enlightenment: it is in the *Discorso* that Genovesi best expressed his ideas on development, philosophy, and economic science. The purpose of letters and sciences is to improve the welfare, or the happiness, of the people. The *Discorso* also contains an appreciation of Intieri, for his "great inventions" that had enriched the kingdom of Naples (*Scritti*, 259).

the discourses, of the little but brilliant conversation of Mr. Intieri, was centered on the progress of human reason, art, commerce, of the economy of the state, of mechanics and physics: therefore Mr. Intieri was a great enemy of useless abstractions, and of pedantic questions turning on words" (*Autobiografia*, 32).[41]

The first name that comes to mind in searching for the sources of Genovesi's and the Neapolitan philosophical approach toward knowledge science and economy is Galileo. Furthermore, again thanks to Intieri, the influence of the Tuscan Accademia dei Georgofili and their commitment to the application of technology to agriculture was there, too. At the same time Newton is also a significant source for Genovesi's work.[42] If we look through the mature works of Genovesi (*Lezioni* and *Diceosina*) we find the presence of Newton's ideas both in his anthropology (or psychology) and in his political writings and his political economy. Newton is present mainly via his gravitational law, seen as a new powerful key for understanding human beings and society.[43]

In fact, Genovesi's account of human nature is based on Newtonian elements. In his *Diceosina*, he argues that some passions are manifestations of self-love (*forza concentrativa*), though others reflect "love of the species" (*forza espansiva* or *diffusiva*).[44] The whole of Genovesi's theory of action is constructed upon the idea that any phenomenon, whether human, social, or physical, can be explained as an "equilibrium" between two opposite forces, namely the *attractive* and the *repulsive*. To Genovesi the two forces are primitive, but on sympathy (as he, following

41. It is easy to find in this criticism of the "questions of words" a similarity with the criticism, present in Galileo's *Dialogue concerning the Two Chief World Systems*, of the "paper word," as opposed to the real word of facts.

42. It is interesting to note that Genovesi edited in 1754 the reprint of a work of an important "georgofilo," Ubaldo Montelatici ("Discorso sopra i mezzi più necessari per far fiorire l'agricoltura"). Genovesi was thoroughly acquainted with Newtonian philosophy and physics before his commitment to economic matters. In 1748 in Naples he had edited, together with Giuseppe Orlandi (a physicist who had a certain role in Genovesi's knowledge of Newton and the new sciences), a book of the Dutch Newtonian Peter van Musschenbroeck (1745), containing a popularization of Newtonian ideas. Already in 1746, in his letters to the scientist Antonio Conti, Genovesi had mentioned Newton and his theory of "mutual attraction of bodies" (*Lettere*, 55–57).

43. Baron Montesquieu was one of the first to apply the Newtonian notion of contrasting forces to social dynamics: it is plausible that the French author had a certain influence in Genovesi on this point (see De Mas 1971).

44. As it is well known, the concept of contrasting *force*, although present in Galileo and in other scientists at the time, would become the key element of mechanics only with Newton, whose third law claims that for every force there is an equal and opposing one.

Hutcheson, also calls the *attractive force*; see *Lezioni*, vol. 1, sec. 17) depend three-quarters of all human actions. This conception provides the logical basis for the criticism of Mandeville's and Hobbes's egoistic conceptions of man that we find throughout Genovesi's work, in the *Diceosina* in particular.[45] The language and the concepts of Newtonian mechanics are also present in Genovesi's political and economic theory. These concepts brought him to "see in political life a social machine made of centripetal and centrifugal forces" (Venturi 1969, 566).

In the *Lezioni*, "forza concentrativa" and "forza espansiva" (the expressions Genovesi used in his *Diceosina*) are also called "forza coattiva" (coercive force) and "forza direttiva" (directive force), a semantic shift emphasizing the recourse to the Newtonian idea of "force" for explaining social matters in the *Lezioni*: "It is true that as the attraction of bodies is maximal in their contacts and decreases proportionally to distances; in the same way the reciprocal attraction and love among men is very great in the family, among companions, in the homeland, etc., and decreases with greater distances" (*Diceosina*, vol. 1, chap. 1, sec. 17, pp. 42–43).[46] In this passage there is the idea (that we also find in Hume and Smith) that in small societies *sympathy* is dominant, whereas in large ones *self-interest* is the basic passion. It is interesting that in Genovesi this thesis is justified by means of an explicit reference to the Newtonian theory of mechanics. Newtonian themes appear also in a footnote to the *Lezioni* (vol. 1, chap. 10, sec. 26, p. 144): "All solitary men are wild, cruel, unforgiving, since in solitude there is no room for the diffusive force of human heart, and only the concentrative force works, which makes men hypochondriac and brutal." This passage is important because it links the Newtonian elements present in Genovesi's thought with a pivotal theme of his system, namely, *sociality*, on which his theory of happiness depends. While Galiani used Newtonian mechanics to build the fundamental principle of his economic theory (self-interest),[47]

45. It is well known that sympathy is not altruism (that is, concern for the well-being of others); it is a matter of *relations* between people.

46. A very similar thesis can be found in Hutcheson, and it is not esoteric to suppose an influence of the Scot philosopher on Genovesi—given the latter's acquaintance with Scottish moral philosophy. In fact in Hutcheson's early *Inquiry* of 1725, we read: "The universal benevolence toward all men, we may compare to that principle of gravitation, which perhaps extends to all bodies in the universe; but increases as the distance is diminished, and is stronger when bodies come to touch each other" (quoted in Silver 1990, 1489).

47. Ferdinando Galiani had explicit recourse to Newtonian gravitational theory: as in Newton's mechanics planets remain in their orbits because of the action of gravitational law, the same holds in economic transactions, where "love of money, namely the desire of living happy,

Genovesi used the same analogy—giving it a meaning closer to the Newtonian original—as a cornerstone of his civil economy based on "mutual attraction of bodies," on *reciprocal assistance*. Following the civic humanist tradition, Genovesi argues that each person has a *natural* right to the benefits of reciprocal assistance and a corresponding duty to provide them for others (*Lezioni*, vol. 1, chap. 1, sec. 18, p. 27). Thus, a person's willingness to help those who stand in relations of *reciprocity* toward him or her is a virtue in the same vein as justice and honesty. Genovesi understands economic relations as relations of reciprocal assistance: in an economic system, each agent is helping others to satisfy their wants. On this conception of civil economy, engagement in economic relations is an exercise of civic virtues.

Newtonian themes are used by Genovesi for building the core idea of his system: the implications of Genovesi's social account of economics affect his whole theoretical construction, as becomes clear in his discussion of trust, one of the most original parts of his economics. His *civil economy* expressed both the orientation of economic knowledge toward public happiness and the role of civic virtues, such as reciprocity, mutual friendship, and public trust in securing economic development: "nothing is truer: the first spring of art, opulence, happiness of every nation is the good custom and virtue" (*Lezioni*, vol. 1, chap. 14, sec. 19, p. 210).[48]

---

is in the man exactly what gravity is in physics" (Galiani [1751] 1803, 91). In Galiani's methodological approach there is the conviction that love for money is so exact and scientific as the law of gravity. In particular, love of money is the equivalent of the desire of being *happy*. Galiani did not specify which kind of happiness he had in mind, but it is very probable that he meant the hedonist happiness, as the utilitarian and hedonist economists will do later. The "public happiness" of Genovesi and the Neapolitan school was not there. Finally, as the law of gravity is the cornerstone of the new mechanics, and all the other laws can be derived from it, so can all laws of economic theory be deduced from the economic principle—as one century later the Italian marginalist economist Maffeo Pantaleoni ([1889] 1898) wrote, basing his theory on Galiani and Genovesi, among others. In fact, in *Della moneta* (Galiani [1751] 1803) we find the definition of the economic principle, what will become the first rule of neoclassical pure economics.

48. Genovesi, more than Galiani and the other Italian economists of his time, saw his activity in continuation with the classic (Thomistic and Aristotelian) tradition. His theoretical system was an attempt at fertilizing the new school with the positive elements of the classical thoughts. His emphasis on "trust" echoes Paolo Mattia Doria, his happiness is the Aristotelian *eudaimonia*, and his theory of unintended consequences is Vichian. These classical elements were conjoined with the Galileian, Gassendian, Lockean, and Newtonian ones: this synthesis makes Genovesi a very interesting and modern thinker. On the relevance of Genovesi's theory for the contemporary debates on trust and social capital, see Bruni and Sugden 2000.

Genovesi's account of happiness is strictly linked to his anthropology: "Every person has a natural obligation to be happy," we read in the first chapter of his *Lezioni* (vol. 1, chap. 1, sec. 34, p. 29). This thesis, if not immediately and properly qualified, would look very similar to that of many hedonist philosophers of his time, from Maupertius to Beccaria, from Bentham to Smith. In fact, the peculiarity of Genovesi's vision of happiness lies elsewhere. His is a theory of happiness as *public happiness* and, at the individual level, as *eudaimonia*: to Genovesi happiness means the Thomistic (and Aristotelian) *eudaimonia*. In an academic letter we find a very clear sentence which synthesizes Genovesi's (1963, 449) theory of happiness as *eudaimonia*: "Every man acts with a view to his own happiness; otherwise he would be less of a man. . . . The more one acts for interest, the more, if he is not mad, he must be virtuous. It is a universal law that it is impossible to make our own happiness without making the happiness of others." Therefore, to Genovesi it is only natural that every human being acts in pursuit of his or her own "interest"; he does not condemn self-interest; for that reason we can say that Genovesi belongs to same modern side as Niccolò Machiavelli and, more particularly, his *maestro*, Vico (see Hirschman 1982). To Genovesi, however, interest means a kind of "happiness" that is ontologically *social*, because it can only be reached through others and thanks to others: in his view, in other words, happiness can only be *public* happiness.

4. Conclusion: Lesson from the Italian Case

Newtonianism, or more specifically *moral* Newtonianism, provides the leading idea through eighteenth-century political economy in Italy. The concept does not simply convey the notion of a field of application of the methods of natural science. It embodies a special kind of science based on the interplay of physical and moral feelings, of physical sensation and a certain kind of reflecting faculty. The result of this is an antimechanistic view both of man and of the polity.[49]

As argued in this essay, happiness, and *public happiness* more particularly, is the great object of policy for the Italian economic thinkers during the latter half of the eighteenth century. Milanese authors took up the issue along eudemonistic eighteenth-century lines, making use of the canons of the "new science." The Neapolitan group, on the other

49. This notion is akin to Jessica Riskin's "sentimental empiricism," a concept curiously applied by Riskin to the physiocrats (this volume).

side, worked out an original reading of the Aristotelian and Scholastic tradition, with the purpose of bringing it into line with the new scientific method. The process results in the idea of *civil economy*.

It emerges as the special character of the Italian tradition in general that the dynamics of the economy in the light of the principles of the new science do not exhibit mechanical features. They rather lead to that kind of civic conception which supposes such a sophisticated blend of institutional interactions as is effectively suggested by Genovesi's term *economia civile*; it is a conception, as hinted above, that would continue to exert influence on the Italian tradition even in later periods and probably provides a clue also to the study of political economy in Italy more generally.

References

Amerio, F. 1947. *Introduzione allo studio di G.B. Vico*. Turin: Società editrice Internazionale.

Baron, H. 1988. *In Search of Florentine Civic Humanism: Essays on the Transitions from the Medieval to Modern Thought*. Princeton, N.J.: Princeton University Press.

Beccaria, C. [1764] 1965. *Dei delitti e delle pene*. Edited by Franco Venturi. Turin: Einaudi.

———. 1993a. Frammento sullo stile. In *Il Caffè* [1764–66] 1993, 277–84.

———. 1993b. Tentativo analitico su i contrabbandi. In *Il Caffè* [1764–66] 1993, 173–75.

Bellamy, R. 1987. "Da metafisico a mercatante": Antonio Genovesi and the Development of a New Language of Commerce in Eighteenth-Century Naples. In Pagden 1987, 277–99.

Bianchini, L. 1845. *Della scienza del ben vivere sociale e della economia degli stati*. Palermo: Stamperia di Francesco Lao.

Boscovich, R. Estratto del Trattato astronomico del sig. de La Lande. In *Il Caffè* [1764–66] 1993, 344–49.

Bruni, L. 2003. The "Technology of Happiness" in the Tradition of Economic Science. *Journal of the History of Economic Thought*, forthcoming.

Bruni, L., and R. Sugden. 2000. Moral Canals: Trust and Social Capital in the Work of Hume, Smith, and Genovesi. *Economics and Philosophy* 16:21–45.

Il Caffè. [1764–66] 1993. Edited by G. Francioni and S. Romagnoli. Torino: Boringhieri.

Capra, C. 2002. *I progressi della ragione: Vita di Pietro Verri*. Bologna: Mulino.

Cohen, I. B. 1980. *The Newtonian Revolution*. Cambridge: Cambridge University Press.

———, ed. 1994. *The Natural Sciences and the Social Sciences: Some Critical and Historical Perspectives*. Boston: Kluwer.

Condillac, É. B. de. [1754] 1803–13. *Traité des sensations*. In *Oeuvres Complètes, revues et corrigées par l'Auteur et imprimées sur des manuscrits autographes*. Paris: Dufart Imprimeur Libraire.

Cremaschi, S. 1984. *Il sistema della ricchezza: Economia politica e problema del metodo in Adam Smith*. Milan: Angeli.

———. 1992. Iluminismo scozzese e newtonianesimo morale. In *Passioni, interessi, convenzioni: Discussioni settecentesche su virtù e civiltà*, edited by M. Geuna and L. Pesante, 41–76. Milan: Angeli.

Custodi, P., ed. 1803–16. *Scrittori classici italiani di economia politica*. 50 vols. Milan: Stamperia e fonderia G. Destefanis.

De Mas, E. 1971. *Montesquieu, Genovesi e le edizioni italiane dello Spirito delle leggi*. Florence: Olschki.

Ferrone, V. 1982. *Scienza, natura, religione: Metodo newtoniano e cultura italiana nel primo settecento*. Naples: Jovene.

Frisi, P. 1993a. Degl'influssi lunari. In *Il Caffè* [1764–66] 1993, 291–95.

———. 1993b. Saggio sul Galileo. In *Il Caffè* [1764–66] 1993, 431–42.

Galiani, F. [1751] 1803. *Della moneta*. In vols. 3 and 4 of Custodi 1803–16.

Garin, E. [1947] 1994. *L'umanesimo italiano*. Bari: Laterza.

Genovesi, A. 1748. *Elementorum Metaphysicae*. Naples: Bettinelli.

———. 1749. *Elementorum Artis Logico-Criticae*. Naples: Gessari.

———. [1765–67] 1824. *Lezioni di commercio o sia di economia civile*. Milan: Società Tipografica dei Classici Italiani.

———. 1963. *Autobiografia e lettere*. Milan: Feltrinelli.

———. [1766] 1973. *Della diceosina o sia della filosofia del giusto e dell'onesto*. Milan: Marzorati.

———. 1979. *Scritti*. Milan: Feltrinelli.

Giannetti da Fonseca, E. 1991. *Beliefs in Action: Economic Philosophy and Social Change*. Cambridge: Cambridge University Press.

Hirschman, A. O. 1982. Rival Interpretations of Market Society: Civilizing, Destructive, or Feeble? *Journal of Economic Literature* 20.4:1463–84.

Hume, D. [1777] 1975. *Enquiries concerning the Principles of Morals*. Oxford: Clarendon Press.

———. [1739–40] 1978. *A Treatise of Human Nature*. 2d ed. Edited by L. A. Selby-Bigge. Oxford: Clarendon Press.

———. [1778] 1983. *The History of England*. With a foreword by W. B. Todd. 6 vols. Indianapolis, Ind.: Liberty Fund.

Hutchison, T. W. 1988. *Before Adam Smith: The Emergence of Political Economy 1662–1776*. Oxford: Blackwell.

Intieri, B. 1733. *Notizie e considerazioni sulla nuova invenzione di stufare i grani esposte agli eccellentissimi signori. . . .* Naples.

Loria, A. [1893] 1904. *Verso la giustizia sociale*. Milan: Società Editrice Libraria.

Luini, L. 1996. Scienze naturali e scienze sociali: Le chiose matematiche di Frisi a Verri e Lloyd. In *Alle origini del pensiero economico in Italia*, edited by A. Quadrio Curzio, 127–46. Bologna: Il Mulino.

Musschenbroeck, P. van. 1745. *Elementa physicae conscripta in usus academicos*. Edited by A. Genovesi and G. Orlandi. Naples.

Pagden, Antony, ed. 1987. *The Language of Political Theory in Early Modern Europe*. Cambridge: Cambridge University Press.

Pantaleoni, M. [1889] 1898. *Pure Economics*. London: Macmillan.

Parisi, D. 1984. *Il pensiero economico classico in Italia, 1750–1860*. Milan: Vita & Pensiero.

Pii, E. 1984. *Antonio Genovesi: Dalla politica economica alla "politica civile."* Florence: Olschki.

Porta, P. L. 1990. Le lezioni di economia di Cesare Beccaria. In *Cesare Beccaria tra Milano e l'Europa*, 356–70. Rome: Cariplo-Laterza.

Porta, P. L., and R. Scazzieri. 1999. Il contributo di Pietro Verri alla teoria economica: Società commerciale, società civile e governo dell'economia. In vol. 2 of *Pietro Verri e il suo tempo*, edited by C. Capra, 813–52. 2 vols. Milan: Cisalpino.

———. 2002. Pietro Verri's Political Economy: Commercial Society, Civil Society, and the Science of the Legislator. *HOPE* 34.1:83–110.

Schumpeter, J. A. 1954. *History of Economic Analysis*. Edited by E. B. Schumpeter. New York: Oxford University Press.

Silver, A. 1990. Friendship in Commercial Society: Eighteenth-Century Social Theory and Modern Sociology. *American Journal of Sociology* 95:1474–1504.

Smith, A. 1976–95. *The Glasgow Edition of the Works and Correspondence of Adam Smith*. 8 vols. Oxford: Oxford University Press.

Theocharis, R. D. 1961. *Early Developments in Mathematical Economics*. London: Macmillan.

Venturi, F. 1962. Riformatori napoletani, vol. 5 of *Illuministi Italiani*. In *La Letteratura Italiana: Storia e Testi*, edited by R. Mattioli, P. Pancrazi, and A. Schiaffini. Milan: Riccardo Ricciardi.

———. 1969. *Settecento riformatore*. Vol. 1. Turin: Einaudi.

———. 1983. Scottish Echoes in Eighteenth-Century Italy. In *Wealth and Virtue: The Shaping of Political Economy in the Scottish Enlightenment*, edited by I. Hont and M. Ignatieff, 345–62. Cambridge: Cambridge University Press.

Verri, P. 1763. *Meditazioni sulla felicità*. Leghorn.

———. [1773] 1781. *Discorsi sull'indole del piacere e del dolore, sulla felicità e sulla economia politica*. Milan: Giuseppe Marelli. Also in Verri 1964, 1–260.

———. [1771] 1964. *Meditazioni sulla economia politica*. In Verri 1964, 125–260.

———. [1796] 1964. *Riflessioni sulle leggi vincolanti principalmente nel commercio de' grani, scritte l'anno 1769 con applicazione allo Stato di Milano*. In Verri 1964, 261–408.

———. 1964. *Del piacere e del dolore ed altri scritti*. Edited by R. De Felice. Milan: Feltrinelli.

———. 1986. *Reflections on Political Economy*. Edited by P. D. Groenewegen. Sydney: University of Sydney.

———. 1993a. Gli studi utili. In *Il Caffè* [1764–66] 1993, 1:311–18.

———. 1993b. Pensieri sullo spirito della letteratura d'Italia. In *Il Caffè* [1764–66] 1993, 211–22.

———. 1993c. Sulla spensieratezza nella privata economia. In *Il Caffè* [1764–66] 1993, 322–30.

———. [1763] 1997. *Meditazioni sulla felicità*. Milan: Fondazione Feltrinelli.

Contributors

Luigino Bruni is a lecturer of economics at the University of Milano–Bicocca.

C. George Caffentzis is a professor of philosophy at the University of Southern Maine. He is the author of *Clipped Coins, Abused Words, and Civil Government: John Locke's Philosophy of Money* (Autonomedia, 1989) and *Exciting the Industry of Mankind: George Berkeley's Philosophy of Money* (Kluwer, 2000).

Paul P. Christensen is an associate professor of economics at Hofstra University, where he teaches European and U.S. economic history and the history of economic thought. He is finishing a book on the influence of natural science on the evolution of preclassical and classical theories of production.

Alix Cooper teaches early modern European history, environmental history, and the history of science at the State University of New York at Stony Brook. At the moment, she is completing a book on ideas of the "indigenous" and the "exotic" in early modern Europe.

Neil De Marchi is at Duke University. He is currently at work on Adam Smith and pleasure, on visualization in twentieth-century trade theory, and on models of art-market behavior in early modern Europe.

Evelyn L. Forget is a professor of economics in the Faculty of Medicine at the University of Manitoba. She publishes work on the history of economics and on health policy.

S. Todd Lowry is an emeritus professor of economics at Washington and Lee University. He served as book review editor of *HOPE* from 1974–95 and as president of the HES in 1990–91, and was named a Distinguished Fellow of the society in 2001. He has published in forest economics, law and economics, and the history of economic thought. His major works are *The Archaeology of Economic Ideas: The Classical Greek Tradition* (Duke University Press, 1987) and an edited collection with Barry Gordon, *Ancient and Medieval Economic Ideas and Concepts of Social Justice* (Brill, 1998). His focus is on the administrative and efficiency tradition in economics. His latest publication on that topic is "The Training of the Economist in Antiquity: The 'Mirror for Princes' Tradition in Alcibiades Major and Aquinas on Kingship," which appears in *Economics Broadly Considered* (Routledge, 2001).

Harro Maas lectures on the history and methodology of economics at the University of Amsterdam. His research focuses on the role of mechanical images in the shaping of the social sciences, especially of nineteenth-century economics. He is currently working on a book on William Stanley Jevons that will be published by Cambridge University Press.

Staffan Müller-Wille is a researcher at the Max-Planck-Institute for the History of Science, in Berlin. He received his Ph.D. in philosophy from the University of Bielefeld for his dissertation on Linnaeus and his natural system of plant classification. He is the author of the book *Botanik und weltweiter Handel* (Verlag für Wissenschaft und Bildung, 1999) and is currently working on the history of classical genetics and structuralist anthropology.

Pier Luigi Porta is a professor of economics and chair of the Department of Political Economy at the University of Milano–Bicocca. He is the author of over a hundred essays and books on the classical school of economics, rationality and the economics of interpersonal relations, and the different traditions of economic thought, among other topics. He was one of the founding members of the European Society for the History of Economic Thought (ESHET), of which he is currently the general secretary. He is also a member of the Presidential Council of the Italian Economic Society.

Lisbet Rausing is a senior research fellow at Imperial College and a former assistant professor at the Department of the History of Science, Harvard University. Under the name of Lisbet Koerner, she has published widely on Linnaeus and in the history of science.

Jessica Riskin is an assistant professor of history at Stanford University. She is the author of *Science in the Age of Sensibility: The Sentimental Empiricists of the French Enlightenment* (University of Chicago Press, 2002) and is currently writing a history of artificial life and intelligence circa 1730–1950.

Margaret Schabas is a professor of philosophy at the University of British Columbia. Her current work is on David Hume's political economy. In addition to *A World*

Ruled by Number (Princeton University Press, 1990), she has written *Nature in Classical Economics*, which will be published in 2004 by the University of Chicago Press.

E. C. Spary is an independent scholar. She has jointly edited *Cultures of Natural History* with N. Jardine and J. A. Secord (Cambridge University Press, 1996) and has published *Utopia's Garden: French Natural History from Old Regime to Revolution* (University of Chicago Press, 2000). She is currently working on a book-length history of food and the sciences in eighteenth-century France, *Eating the Enlightenment*. Among her interests are the history of natural history, agriculture, chemistry, medicine, and eighteenth-century Europe.

Edith Dudley Sylla is a professor of history at North Carolina State University. She specializes in the history of late medieval and early modern science and has recently been working on an English translation of Jacob Bernoulli's *Ars Conjectandi*.

Carl Wennerlind is an assistant professor at Barnard College, Columbia University, where he teaches economics and the history of economic thought. His research interests include David Hume's political economy and the conceptual origins of the financial revolution. Among his publications are "The Death Penalty as Monetary Policy: The Practice and Punishment of Monetary Crime, 1690–1830" (in the spring 2004 issue of *HOPE*) and "David Hume's Political Philosophy: A Theory of Commercial Modernization" (forthcoming in *Hume Studies*).

Index